Emotions in Indian Thought-Systems

The stereotypical image of the Indian holy man, or the Buddha, detached from the world and unencumbered by emotional states, encourages the impression that Indian spirituality has no place for emotion. While acknowledging the disparagement of emotion in certain schools of thought, the book draws attention to the range of Indian traditions — from philosophy to aesthetics to tantra — that value it profoundly and look upon emotions as offering pragmatic processes for moral, aesthetic and spiritual development. The subtle understandings of emotional life outlined in these essays will be useful not only to those interested in Indian thought as such, but to those concerned with emotional intelligence in cross-cultural thinking.

— **Kathleen Higgins**, University of Texas

The book presents an excellent array of scholarly essays to be read by South Asian specialists. Indeed, they offer Western (and Indian) researchers and laypersons myriad pointers within dharma traditions that enrich the much-popularised concept of 'enlightenment-as-sheer-presence' with an emotional (rasa) infusion of auspicious longings, conative-affective truths, transformable feeling-states, spiritually matured erotic passion and ranges of personal 'intensity'. Thus, the volume continues the Foucaldian critique of the current scientia sexualis *psychologies with their terminal maturity of the 'well-adjusted, desiring-ego', while also presenting glimpses of alternative 'paths of emotional profundity'.*

— **Stuart Sovatsky**, California Institute of Integral Studies

Emotions in Indian Thought-Systems

EDITORS

Purushottama Bilimoria
Aleksandra Wenta

INDIAN INSTITUTE OF ADVANCED STUDY

Routledge
Taylor & Francis Group
LONDON NEW YORK NEW DELHI

First published 2015 in India
by Routledge
912 Tolstoy House, 15–17 Tolstoy Marg, Connaught Place, New Delhi 110 001

Simultaneously published in the UK
by Routledge
2 Park Square, Milton Park, Abingdon, Oxon OX14 4RN

Routledge is an imprint of the Taylor & Francis Group, an informa business

Typeset by
Glyph Graphics Private Limited
23 Khosla Complex
Vasundhara Enclave
Delhi 110 096

Printed and bound in India by
Avantika Printers Private Limited
194/2 Ramesh Market, Garhi, East of Kailash
New Delhi 110 065

British Library Cataloguing-in-Publication Data
A catalogue record of this book is available from the British Library

ISBN 978-1-138-85935-7

For Professor Peter Ronald deSouza

Contents

Preface | ix

Emotions in Indian Thought-Systems: An Introduction | 1
Purushottama Bilimoria and *Aleksandra Wenta*

Part I: Tantrism

1. Passions and Emotions in the Indian Philosophical–Religious Traditions | 57
   Raffaele Torella
2. Intensity of Emotions: A Way to Liberation in the Advaita Śaiva *Āgama*s and Their Exegetes | 102
   Bettina Sharada Bäumer
3. Between Fear and Heroism: The Tantric Path to Liberation | 114
   Aleksandra Wenta

Part II: The Bhakti Movement

4. Principal Emotions Contributing to the Supreme Love of Śiva: A Study of Early Śaiva Hymnal Corpus | 137
   T. Ganesan
5. Love Never Tasted Quite Like This Before: *Śṛṅgāra-rasa* in the Light of Two Texts from a Sahajiyā Vaiṣṇava Notebook | 156
   Neal Delmonico and *Aditi Nath Sarkar*

Part III: Buddhism, Pātañjala Yoga and Śaiva Siddhānta

6. The Buddhist Psychology of Emotions | 185
Varun Kumar Tripathi
7. Between Impetus, Fear and Disgust: 'Desire for Emancipation' (Saṃvega) from Early Buddhism to Pātañjala Yoga and Śaiva Siddhānta | 199
Andrea Acri

Part IV: Aesthetics

8. Moha Kāla: Aporias of Emotion in Indian Reflective Traditions | 231
D. Venkat Rao
9. Aesthetics of Despair | 266
Sharad Deshpande

About the Editors | 281

Notes on Contributors | 282

Index | 285

Preface

This volume consists in a selection of essays stemming from papers originally presented at the seminar, 'Reflection on Emotions in Indian Thought-Systems', held at the Indian Institute of Advanced Study (IIAS) in Shimla on 4–6 September 2012. The seminar provided a forum where eminent scholars from India and the West could present stimulating papers covering a wide range of approaches to conceptualising emotions in pre-modern Indian traditions of knowledge. For both intellectual and practical reasons, the editors have included essays from authors who were unable to attend the seminar, but whose presence was, in a way, still felt — their long-standing engagement in our chosen field of enquiry informed our debate on several occasions. As it turns out, the topics and approaches of their essays nicely complement those of our initial pool of participants.

The essays in this volume are based on either textual or theoretical research (or both) on a variety of classical Indian traditions, such as Jainism, Buddhism, Classical Yoga, Bhakti, Śaiva and Vaiṣṇava Tantrism, and Aesthetics. Most essays deal with Sanskrit texts and some with vernacular (i.e., Tamil, Bengali, Pāli, and Old Javanese) texts; as such, they include a large body of quotations from primary sources in those languages.

Special thanks go to Professor Peter Ronald deSouza, former Director of IIAS, for kindly agreeing to host and sponsor this event, as well as for encouraging me to carry out this kind of intellectual inquiry; and to Dr Debarishi Sen, Academic Officer, IIAS, for successfully handling the organisational matters. I express my gratitude to Professor T. R. S. Sharma, a senior fellow at IIAS, who selflessly dedicated much of his personal time and skills to making this event happen. My special thanks go also to Dr Andrea Acri, who, in a true spirit of *sevā*, helped us tremendously with the editorial process. Many thanks go also to the Editorial team at Routledge, New Delhi, for their enthusiasm and commitment to publishing this book, and to the anonymous reviewer whose suggestions helped us to improve the contents of this volume.

Aleksandra Wenta

Emotions in Indian Thought-Systems

An Introduction

PURUSHOTTAMA BILIMORIA AND
ALEKSANDRA WENTA

It would be hard to deny the important role played by emotions in the religious and philosophical landscape of India, from the most remote past to the present. The emotional attitude pervades most – if not all – intellectual and religious discourses of Indian culture. In a variety of knowledge traditions, emotions often provide a basis for the affective unfolding of conscious thought, thereby revealing its depth and intensity; emotions also constitute the most tangible and fundamental attitude in humankind's quest for the sacred and self-discovery.

The development of appropriate conceptual models for emotions in India has been discussed in recent years by scholars interested in various empirical domains and theoretical approaches. Studies have dealt with the social construction of emotions in India (Lynch 1990), historical-cultural anthropology (Michaels and Wulf 2012), analysis of emotional complex, such as *bhāva* in the Bengali Vaiṣṇava tradition (McDaniel 1989), the holistic nature of emotions in early Buddhist thought (de Silva 1995), or the ethics of emotions (Bilimoria 1995). The most comprehensive account on emotions in India still remains the pioneering three-volume work, *Indian Psychology* (2008), by Jadunath Sinha. Much more work, however, needs to be done to improve our understanding of emotions in India, especially with regard to historical development of emotional experience and the methods of its conceptualisation. This book constitutes a modest step in this direction, as it wishes to address the complex, and at times paradoxical, character of emotions in Indian thought-systems, with an emphasis on the role of emotions in the construction of religious identity. It poses a question about the definition and validity of emotions in classical India (3rd BCE–13th CE) by engaging more fully with the argumentative context proposed by Corrigan (2008: 7) that 'human emotionality is a constituent element of religious life'. Grounded in an analysis of the great textual cultures of India, among which the Sanskritic one stands out, the essays in this volume provide, as a whole, a theoretical evaluation of 'Indian' emotions by viewing them not merely as universal facts but also as culture-specific and historically determined phenomena. In so doing, the book makes an attempt to venture into the multi-faceted reality of emotions, unravelling its apparent equivocality and seeming inconceivability. It provides a glimpse of and tries to systematise historical and textual data on emotions in order to arrive at a conceptual schema that would be instrumental in defining the phenomenon of 'human feeling' in its various and multi-dimensional embodiments. An effort is made to provide an ingenious account of the mechanism of spontaneous activation of feelings in religious experience, and to elaborate emendations to the theoretical maze confounding the emotional and cognitive domains. Through the intellectual fusion and fruitful mingling of many theoretical perspectives, the book intends to broaden our understanding of the differences in the conceptualisation of emotions as they occur in the learned traditions of both India and 'the West'. Some essays provide an opportunity for looking with a fresh perspective at the so-called 'negative emotions', such as fear, despair or disgust, by showing the distinctive ways in which they become conceptualised in the Indian context.

Before entering our discussion, something must be said first about the etymology of the word 'emotion' and its Indian equivalent. The English term 'emotion' comes from the Latin *emovere* or *exmovere* ('to move out', 'move away', 'remove', 'stir up', 'agitate'); hence Old French *emouvoir* ('stir up'); Middle French *ésmovoir* ('something moves inside when an emotion arises'); and French *emotion* (Freud used to speak of 'flows of energy', from the unconscious to the conscious and vice versa). Robert C. Solomon, following David Hume (but with markedly different emphasis), preferred to call 'emotion' by the term 'passion/passions' (from Greek *pathos* and Latin *pati* ['to suffer', '*be* pathetic']). But what exactly is 'emotion' or 'emotions'? Both Western and Indian theories often speak of three mental states involved in the arousal of emotions: cognitive, conative (i.e., desire) and affective. Volition or will straddles the first two. In the classical Sanskritic and Pāli tradition, there is no single term that is a direct equivalent of the Western term 'emotion'. In fact, there are several and they appear to be intermingled: some settle for *bhāva* or *vedanā* that are used in reference to the 'emotive state', which includes both the internal feeling and expressed emotion; others prefer *vikāra*, 'mental excitement', or *rasa* — though mostly in the context of drama, theatre (i.e., mime and *nāṭya*, or dance) and religious experience, expressed through *bhakti* in devotional traditions.

Theorising Emotions in the West

In the West, theorising on emotions begins with Aristotle (actually with Plato in *Phaedo*, who was, however, narrowly concerned with grieving for the suicidal ingestion of hemlock by his teacher, Socrates). Where he took emotions seriously, Aristotle — along with Plato in *Phaedo* (sections 246a–254e, in Plato 2002: 96) — saw them as 'bondage', i.e., as the unruly horses which have to be restrained by reason, the charioteer; this judgment, as well as the very metaphor through which it is expressed, finds a parallel in mainstream Sanskrit literature from the Upaniṣads onwards, which provides the image of the chariot (the human body) driven by horses (*indriyas*, the sense organs) controlled (or rather not) by a charioteer (*buddhi*, the intellect). For the one who is not in control of his intellect, the sense organs become unmanageable, like the wicked horses of the charioteer. On the contrary, for the one who has a disciplined intellect, the sense organs are obedient horses subordinate to the charioteer (cf. *Kaṭha Upaniṣad* 3.11). The worldview presented in this early metaphor — that seems to belong to a common Indo-European ancestry — delineates a sharp distinction between 'reason' and 'emotions'; the 'emotions-senses' are considered to be wild and disordered beasts that must be properly tamed by reason, otherwise they can only drive one astray. For Aristotle, emotions served an important function within his prime interest in ethics, i.e., the good life that involved cultivation of virtues for the 'political zoon' — man of excellence. The Greek philosopher concerned himself with a limited range of emotions, such as *eros*, a desirable emotion; *akrasia*, moral weakness; desire; pleasure (undesirable emotions); and the culmination of moral training (self-control and cultivation of the worthy emotions) in the ultimate good of *eudaimonia* that is the fulfilment or happiness by which one's lived life is judged.

Then, there were the Stoics who vied for a theory of complete dispassion — what we may call 'asceticism' in English — wherein emotions are curbed as they stand in the way of reasoned life; in some ways, perhaps also due to historical links, the Stoics' view paralleled the view of Jainas, or in any event the broadly Śrāmaṇic concept of emotions (intended as sense-organs, or *indriyas* and their domains, the *viṣayas*) and desire considered to be the chief obstructions to the good life. The Stoics were opposed by the Epicureans who, much like the materialistic and atheistic Cārvākas known in Sanskrit sources, believed in gratifying the senses and living-up passions to the fullest.

The mediaeval period of Western philosophical development witnessed a remarkable interest in emotions, intended as 'higher passions', i.e., 'pure' love and faith, as well as 'lower passions', *alias* 'sin', which included unmitigated appetite, desire for intoxicants and sexual urge (Solomon 2004: 3). Renaissance, marked by obsession with Humanism, revived the neo-Platonic understanding of emotions. The most popular Renaissance thinkers, viz., Marsilio Ficino and Giovanni Pico della Mirandola, offered a unique approach to the discourse on 'Platonic love' (Allen 2002: 923). Interesting contribution to the study of emotions came also from a politician and philosopher, Machiavelli, whose understanding of emotions was close to the *realpolitik* of public psychology. Machiavelli's concept of 'glory' (*gloria*), which was recognised as 'ambition' or the emotion for honour, 'was to become an important element in the list of emotions acknowledged by figures from Montaigne to Hobbes' (Zalta 2012). Closer to the Enlightenment period, Baruch Spinoza was fascinated by the idea of developing a geometry of passions, i.e., a ratio-centric model of emotions, to be achieved through meticulously individuating the thought components of each passion/emotion (de Silva 2011: 261). This model was later undone, or reversed by David Hume in defence of passion.[1] Immanuel Kant (1996), for his part, excluded passions from the concerns of metaphysics, except for aesthetic judgments, and the 'sublime' in particular. Kant's original view privileged the cognitive over the affective and placed action within volition, which stood at the helm; this entailed a 'deontological', i.e., an impersonal life devoted to duty without regard for the fruits of action. According to this view, reason, rather than emotion, determines — in cohort with will — how one ought to act. Kant was not concerned with how and why one *feels*, or even why one acts, but rather with why would one act in such and such a way; thus, our base actions and such emotions as desire or anger that propel us are irrational and have no real place in the language of morality or ethics.

Following the Enlightenment, there was no real philosophical space left for interest in, and debate over, emotions; emotions were regarded as mere subjective, passive and passing events, at best 'irrational' states, i.e., non-cognitive aspects of human and animal life. Life, whether intelligent or not, was conceived of as nothing more than physiology and sensorial stimuli; no conceptual mileage could ever be gained by dwelling on emotions. The early psychologists, however, showed slightly more interest in emotions. William James and James Lange developed theories of the physiological origin of emotions as *feelings* that happen primarily in the body and, although lacking in cognitive content (though they can move to become such), represent the other extreme from the rationalist dismissal of emotions. With all its limitations, James' theories are being passionately revived in our times, especially with the rise of neurophysiology and somatic studies (see Prinz 2003). Freud, the father of psychoanalysis, following Hume, explored the etiology of emotions and concluded that emotions are constituted by both affects and ideas. Freud dedicated much of his time to the understanding of 'unconscious emotions' caused by repression, which 'results not only in withholding things from consciousness, but also in preventing the development of affect' (see Green 1992: 58). The concept of repressed emotions, buried in a disguised form in the unconscious and popping up from time to time in dreams, was Freud's most important contribution to the study of emotions. His psychoanalytic therapy focused on examining dreams as a way to reveal buried feelings resulting from childhood traumas.

Closer to our times, it was Solomon who opened new doors to philosophical thinking on emotions. For him, a passionate life 'must be understood in terms of the desirability of strong passions in a rather particular sense, a sense that may well include romantic love, religious ecstasy, strong aversions, even hatred and the desire for vengeance and a highly charged sense of the drama of life' (Solomon 1995: 290). Emotions, Solomon (2004: 117) contends, are orientated toward maximising self-esteem. For him, this is the form of spirituality, albeit *secular spirituality*, which human beings should aspire to, one which is 'through and through an emotional spirituality'; a 'spiritual life' is 'a life lived in accordance with the grand and thoughtful passions of life' (Higgins 2011: 240). Solomon's account of 'naturalized spirituality' prominently involves some of the — to use an oxymoron — calm passions (though not ending in the dispassionate detachment or 'indifference', as he saw it in Jainism, Buddhism or Sāṃkhya–Yoga, and much less the dispassionate life of pure reason); his view also combines reflective orientation with emotion, to be fully attuned to attractions, gratitude, humour, grief (where this is needed), care for other human beings, and trust and authenticity in our relationship with other human beings and the world at large. Absurdity, dialectical tensions, challenges, confusions, etc., should also be acknowledged with embrace, for they contribute to the unfolding evolution of human consciousness and provide a basis for the conviction that one's life is worth living to reach the full potential of being human (and, hence, part of the shared ecological–animal habitat). One might even 'live dangerously'. Along with Jean-Paul Sartre, Solomon argued that 'our emotions structure the world we encounter, and no account of relationship to the world can dispense with acknowledging their constitutive role' (Higgins 2011: 242–43).

Cognitive Theory versus Conative-Affective Theory

Besides the oppositional division of reason and emotion into the respective categories of rational and irrational that is popular in Western mainstream culture — and which some Western philosophers still hold on to — a 'cognitive' versus 'non-cognitive' divide has been elaborated in recent studies which are very differentially marked to the former divide, in that no judgment as such is made on whether passions are rational or irrational dispositions. Nevertheless, there is still much at stake in the latter theorising inasmuch as emotions are aligned much closer to the cognitive processes than to the conative, volitional, or purely affected, i.e., processes that are desire-based in a primitive or crude sense. The role of the body, the embodied presence, and feelings, are accorded scant attention in this theory. The cognitive theory, 'the dominant ideology among emotions theory today' (Solomon 1995: 290) focuses on 'thought' and appraisal, with a teleology or purpose and meaning undergirding the process, while the non-cognitive or anti-cognitive theories (or, roughly, the so-called 'conative-affective theories'), focus on physiological arousal centred in the body and feelings, as well as on neurophysiological processes, sometimes also with a strong desire-component. So, the cognitive theory is tantamount to a mind–body dualism — a legacy of the Cartesian turn — or, in modern terms, the *ideogenic* view (attributed to Freud) and the *somatogenic* view (attributed to James) (de Silva 2011: 224).

The former view, which we may call 'cognitivism', looks for the cognitive content of emotions in terms of potentially rational (i.e., rationally accessible) content of emotions, perceptions, or perspectives. In short, it regards 'thought' and, more importantly, 'evaluative judgment' or beliefs, as the category of propositional attitudes that philosophers have been most at home with, though not necessary excluding desires. According to cognitivist theories of emotion, 'emotions logically or quasi-logically presuppose beliefs that both define the emotion and, if true, justify it. Love involves thinking highly of the beloved; embarrassment presupposes the belief that one has committed a faux pas; jealousy requires a belief in one's entitlement to attention from another, and so on' (Calhoun 2004: 116; cf. Calhoun 1990) and grief underscores the belief that someone valuably dear and close to one has been lost (Bilimoria 2012a, 2013a).

Against the inadequacy of the view of emotions as mere 'feelings', cognitivism holds that emotions themselves are (or involve) varieties of cognitive states (Marks 1995: 3). These relevant states have been variously argued to be a belief, a judgment, a thought, a construal (or 'seeing as'), an evaluation, etc. Solomon — once an ardent defender of this theory — believed that judgments, unlike beliefs, do not imply or suggest impersonality, value neutrality, or, to get to the point, lack of desire. He suggests that most of the judgments that constitute emotion do not clearly involve desires. Grief, for example, involves a judgment of severe loss. One might suggest that this reduces to belief, *that* someone has died, for example, and a desire (or rather counterfactual wish), namely, that they would not have died. But even if such an analysis is necessary, does it clarify or rather confuse the nature of the emotion? Solomon argues 'that such belief-desire analyses . . . are misleading and often quite beside the point' (Bilimoria 1995: 191).

Solomon here is attacking two different theories about the significant components of emotions. One is that emotions are beliefs without desires. The second is that emotions are beliefs with desire. One may argue that beliefs without desires are an essential ingredient of emotion, or vice versa. Yet, this view muddies the analysis by taking both desires and emotions in tandem — which is precisely what the adversary whom he is attacking, Joel Marks, tends to do. Belief retains a necessary place within cognitive theories of emotions as the evaluative judgment component, whereas desires are reduced counterfactually to the 'wish' — or, indeed, the counter-belief that the given event that triggered an emotion, such as grief, could or might have been otherwise. Alternatively, desires are sometimes relegated to a secondary status, as necessary yet not sufficient conditions for an analysis of emotions. In grief, for example, the intense evaluative judgment or 'appraisal' element would include increasing references to an agent's desires and goals, or the frustration of them. Since Solomon's discussion with Marks, philosophers, such as William Lycan, William Alston, Roland Alan Nash, and to an extent Martha Nussbaum, among others, have insisted on the bodily disturbances — 'unthinking energies' — and perturbations of non-intellectual mentation processes (Nussbaum's 'thought') in the agent, thereby including experiences, such as trembling, blushing, perspiring, pangs, throbs, tingles, burning and other sensations, adrenalin secretions, increase in heart and respiratory rates, alterations of blood flow, changes in blood pressure, digestive processes, and other neurological symptoms. Indeed, these bodily reactions are considered fundamental structural markers of emotional response. And this is evidenced not just in human beings with their quaint sentimentality, but also in animals (Bilimoria 2012a).

These non-cognitive features of emotions, however, are not their essential ingredients, for they themselves as such are not the necessary and sufficient conditions for the emotional encounter. Necessary and sufficient conditions for emotion are relevant beliefs (of which there are three types, as indicated later) and perceptions. The rest of the features, viz., the non-belief, the 'non-thinking features', as Nussbaum calls them, or the objectless wandering feelings of pain and/or pleasure, are relegated to the *constitutive* parts — even while she wonders aloud: 'What are they like if they are not about anything?'. The three beliefs are: (*a*) that the suffering is serious; (*b*) that the person does not deserve the suffering; and (*c*) that the possibilities of the person who experiences the emotion are similar to those of the sufferer (Nussbaum 2001: 62). And so the jab in the stomach and sensations of being ripped by slivers of glass at the news of her mother's impending death — like Arjuna's inner tears at the death of his relatives in the *Mahābhārata* — are recastable in plain-language propositional terms, i.e., resembling the structure of belief, or better, value judgments. The massive ramblings of her to me apart, what Nussbaum has ended up with is rather closer to the Hybrid Cognitive Theory that has been around since the late 1980s, in which perception and belief-state still maintain a hegemony, or are called the 'paradigm case', but in which non-propositional contents are not excluded, though these are viewed as the 'messier' side of emotion, linked to its own specific evaluative continuum and affective contents — see, for example, the works of Don Gustafson (1989), Ronald Alan Nash (1989) and Dan Moller (2007). The only exception is the perspicuous underscoring of resilience and caring by Moller. Nussbaum's adversaries maintain that the unthinking markers are, indeed, the sufficient elements of grief, and that the belief-propositional ingredients are constitutive or rather supplementary. This adversarial view, first used against the Stoics, is that emotions are 'unreasoning movements', unthinking energies that simply push the person around and do not relate to conscious perceptions. Emotions are 'bodily' rather than 'mental', and it is sufficient to make them unintelligent rather than intelligent.

Yet, one may ask if emotions could not be (a combination of) both 'bodily' and 'mental'? Perhaps, as Marks (1995) remarks, the most intriguing implication of the cognitive view is that emotions are subject to the same amount of criticism and control as cognitions are. While useful for the therapeutic encounter, the cognitive view has been challenged severally by evolutionary (survival) approach to emotion influenced by Charles Darwin, and more vehemently by Continental and Feminist philosophers. Some from these camps do not believe that either beliefs, judgment, evaluation, or cognition are essential *components* of emotion; these elements may be there in various phases of the arising, manifestation, impact, and effect of the emotion, and introspective or reflective after-thought, but are otherwise peripheral, or at best supplementary to the feeling component, or whatever it is that makes an emotion what it is.

Solomon, towards the later years of his life, revised his earlier heavily cognitive account. He asked the question, which, we believe, needs to be asked of the cognitivist: 'Can you make all of the evaluative judgments that supposedly constitute the emotion and nevertheless not have that emotion?' And his verdict was:

> I have come to the conclusion after many years that the Adversary (now reinforced with some powerful studies in neurobiology) must be reckoned with, and that my old, rather ruthless line between those cognitive features of emotion that are essential and those non-cognitive features of emotion that are not essential was (in the context of the time) heuristic and is no longer so (Solomon 2002b: 900).[2]

Elsewhere, Solomon (2004: 85) elaborated on his retraction:

> But what led me to an increasing concern about the role of the body and the nature and role of bodily feelings in emotion was the suspicion that my judgment theory had been cut too thin, that in pursuit of an alternative to the feeling theory I had veered too far in the other direction. I am now coming to appreciate that accounting for bodily feelings (not just sensations) in emotion is not a secondary concern and not independent of appreciating the essential role of the body in emotional experience.

By the same token, there are those who would concur with Solomon's revisions to the dominant theory, but lay stress on other factors they consider essential in emotion, such as *intellectualisation*, not in a cognitive, belief-propositional sense, but rather akin to what the *Bhagavadgītā* 2.42 terms as *vyavasāyātmikā buddhir eka eva* ('intellect is the only [sense organ] fixed in determination'). The claim is that there are 'deep and systematic connections between emotional, evaluative, and intellectual strengths and abilities'; just as there are important emotional 'aspects' of the intellect, such as intellectual interest and excitement, an excellence celebrated, there are also intellectual 'aspects' to emotions (Stocker 2004: 144). Post-Freudian psychoanalytical thinking has been attempting to close the chasm between intellect and emotion, or perhaps better put, between the 'life of the mind' and the 'stirrings of the heart', without rendering one dysfunctional at the expense of the other.

Theorising Emotions in India

The starting point of our inquiry into emotions in India is a thesis about the Brāhmaṇical ideal of emotionlessness that became the paradigm of classical Indian systems of knowledge and practice. On the basis of this premise, we construct our model of theorising emotions in India that rests on three basic presuppositions. We define these presuppositions in the following manner. First, there is an alleged dualism between the mind–body complex and the Self variously termed as *ātman*, *puruṣa*, *brahman*, etc., that led to the devaluation of the body in relation to the Self. Second, emotions are the 'foes' that exist on the account of their association with the body; therefore, they should be rejected. Third, the body with its cognitive, emotional and sensorial apparatus is controlled through purity mechanism that involves, among other things, renunciation of desire and *yoga* techniques. These general presuppositions informing the tradition of Brāhmaṇical emotionlessness are formulated differently in distinct theoretical frameworks of Indian thought-systems, and the specific structures in which they are implicated will become clearer once we embark on the systematic exposition of these systems.

In the modern and contemporary Western (and perhaps 'Indian' as well) imaginary, India, as opposed to the West, never elaborated a clear-cut dichotomy between mind, body, and soul or Self, but rather propounded a 'holistic' approach. That such allegations, by no means confined to the popular dimension but widespread in academic circles, find little if no support in the primary sources of the Sanskrit philosophical tradition is revealed in this introduction. This basic premise provides an appropriate starting point in theorising emotions in India insofar as it conspicuously acknowledges the strict distinction between materiality of the 'body' and immateriality of the 'spirit' or 'Self' elaborated in Brāhmaṇical tradition. This way of conceiving the absolute distinction between the mind–body complex and the Self had its philosophical basis in the Upaniṣads, of which the earliest texts were composed between 700 and 300 BCE (Olivelle 1998) and in the school of Sāṃkhya represented by the *Sāṃkhyakārikā* of Īśvarakṛṣṇa dated to *c.* 4th century CE. These two thought-systems were directly responsible for the development of the Brāhmaṇical ideal of emotionlessness.

The Upaniṣads with their distinctive 'attitude of renunciation' (see Padoux 1990: 38), firmly rooted in the contemplative stasis that barred the doors to the realm of the embodied existence experienced through the psychophysical aggregate of the body, are, perhaps, the first to blame, for they provided conceptual insights that were appropriated into more explicit theoretical frameworks of later philosophies and theological systems of India (Olivelle 1998: 10). For example, the philosophical system of Advaita Vedānta, promulgated by Gauḍapāda (7th century CE) and Śaṅkara (8th century CE), is typically regarded as the most direct continuation of Upaniṣadic thought. The most striking innovation of the Upaniṣads for its time was the one that arose in direct response to Vedic ritualism. Questioning the dogmatic thrust of Vedic sacrifices, the Upaniṣads offered an opportunity for the deepest and most reflective debate on the nature and meaning of the Self, life, death, and immortality (see Black 2007). Upaniṣadic attention was being irresistibly drawn to the philosophical concept of the Self (*ātman*) 'that could be associated with a wide range of meanings including body and soul, and could sometimes refer to the ontological principle underlying all reality' (ibid.: 7). Most of the Upaniṣads drew on Sāṃkhya metaphysics in accepting dualism between the consciousness-self (*puruṣa*) and the matter-body (*prakṛti*). According to the Sāṃkhya, the body, the psychosomatic apparatus, is the effect of *prakṛti* and, therefore, is considered to be the non-self that stands in opposition to the true Self (*puruṣa*). In the Upaniṣads, however, this alleged distinction between the spirit and matter is problematic and should be handled with care, as it has been challenged by many authors. The Upaniṣadic *ātman* can be said to both transcend the body and inhabit it as the agent of both sensing and cognising, but, nevertheless, it remains outside the body as the immortal soul. On this account, it is asserted that *ātman* has a capability of standing behind the various psychophysical operations of the body as their inner controller. The *Chāndogya Upaniṣad* (8.12.5, in Olivelle 1998: 285) refers to it in the following words:

> He sees but he can't be seen; he hears, but he can't be heard; he thinks, but he can't be thought of; he perceives, but he can't be perceived. Besides

> him, there is no one who sees, no one who hears, no one who thinks, and no one who perceives. It is the self of yours who is the inner controller, the immortal. All besides this is grief.

This passage explicitly distinguishes between the subject and the object, posing, thus, a split at the heart of the Upaniṣadic epistemology and ontology. The immortal, non-empirical Self is conceived of as a perceiving subject that can never be an object of perception, even if it exists as the unitary ontological foundation responsible for the respective functions of the mind–body complex. Even more important in this regard is the notion that the mind–body apparatus is controlled by a single, self-regulating and immaterial principle of *ātman*. The concept of bodily, mental and emotional control that implied 'overcoming one's attachment to the body-mind complex' (Holdrege 1998: 361) by cultivating the ascetic body witnessed a dramatic resurgence in the later Upaniṣads, particularly in the so-called *Saṃnyāsa Upaniṣads* promulgating a life of a world-renouncer (*saṃnyāsin, parivrājaka, bhikṣu*). Nevertheless, this 'ambiguous' language of the Upaniṣads has invited divergent and mutually exclusive interpretations from some scholars that systematically invalidate the Self–body dualism. An example of such divergent interpretations of a fundamental Upaniṣadic doctrine is illustrated in the following passage:

> In the Upanishads there is no indication of this antagonistic relation of the body and spirit. On the other hand bodily existence was regarded as an opportunity for spiritual realisation. The body is not the prison of the soul but a habitat for it, or a temple in which the soul can work out its salvation by worship and meditation (Tiwari 1985: 178).

Obviously, this position demonstrates the pitfalls and possibilities of the hybrid interpretations of the Upaniṣadic thought from a wide array of vantage points.[3] In our view, however, the Self–body dualism is inherently presupposed in the Upaniṣadic discourse, for, it is declared in the *Chāndogya Upaniṣad* (8.12.5, in Olivelle 1998: 285):

> This body, Maghavan, is mortal; it is in the grip of death. So, it is the abode of this immortal and nonbodily self. One who has a body is in the grip of joy and sorrow, and there is no freedom from joy and sorrow for one who has a body. Joy and sorrow, however, do not affect one who has no body.

Not only is body effectively contrasted with non-bodily Self as its negative counterpart, as if its sole purpose was to expose the inevitability of death attached to the body, it is also posited as the source of both positive and negative emotions, which are regarded as bondages. All the emotional states experienced by an individual are being closely connected with the functioning of the body. The release from the body is congruent with freedom from emotional processes. The desirability of liberation presupposes turning away from the imperfect body, which is additionally assigned with the moral attribute of evilness:[4] 'Shaking off evil, like a horse its hair, and freeing myself, like the moon from Rāhu's jaws, I, the perfected self (*ātman*), cast off the body, the imperfect, and attain the world of *brahman*' (*Chāndogya Upaniṣad*, 8.15.1, in Olivelle 1998: 287). Here, the inevitable drama of life that inheres in the darkness of embodiment may be overcome through the relinquishment of the evil body. Casting off the body includes implicitly the attainment of a metaphysical principle of identity in which the perfected self (*ātman*) and the Absolute (*brahman*) are harmonised. Similar dialectical devices employed in making the duality between the Self and the body explicit are found in the *Muktika Upaniṣad*, *adhyāya* 2: 'This body is very impure while the one (*ātman*) that dwells in it is very pure' (Khanna and Aiyar 2011: 11). Here, a criterion of division between the body and the Self (*ātman*) is laid down along the lines that establish the duality of pure and impure. From the aforementioned premises that systematically rejected the notion of the body, it is generally accepted that the Upaniṣads are the first texts to be credited with conceiving of the figure of world-renouncer[5] in a manner that became paradigmatic to the entire Brāhmaṇical model of emotionless spirituality.[6] Now, in order to delineate the soteriological principles inherently present in the ascetic way of life promulgated by Upaniṣadic thought, we take a closer look at the later Upaniṣads, of which the *Nāradaparivrājaka Upaniṣad*, the text classified as belonging to the genre of the *Saṃnyāsa Upaniṣad*s, stands out. The first two passages quoted from different texts formulate their concept of the body as being essentially impure. Interestingly, in the first passage this impurity of the body is articulated in terms of a caste-structured Brāhmaṇical society, in which an outcast is traditionally regarded impure:[7] 'Shun like an outcast (*cāṇḍāla*) [the thought of] the body, which is generated out of the impurities of parents and is composed of excreta and flesh. Then you will become Brahman and be in a blessed [state]' (*Adhyātma Upaniṣad*, ibid.: 54). In the second passage, the impurity of the body is directly connected with its given attribute of being the seat of emotions:

> This body is subject to birth and death. It is of the nature of secretion of the father and mother. It is impure, being the seat of happiness and misery. [Therefore] bathing is prescribed for touching it. It is bound by the *dhātus* (skin, blood, etc.), is liable to severe disease, is a house of sins, is impermanent and is of changing appearance and size. [Therefore] bathing is prescribed for touching it. Foul matter is naturally oozing out always from the nine holes. It [the body] contains bad odour and foul excrement. [Therefore] bathing is prescribed for touching it . . . The release from [the body] is spoken of as the perfect purification. (*Maitreya Upaniṣad*, Khanna and Aiyar 2011: 24).

Apart from the emotional drives through which the human body becomes submerged in dirt, the Upaniṣads saw this impurity in relation to body's natural physiological processes, as well as in the very act of conception resulting in the embryo. To provide some sense of the scope of the Upaniṣadic notion of spiritual perfection, a few of the many themes which reverberated down through Indian intellectual history are outlined in the following sections.

'Purification' and 'Control'

The Upaniṣads argue that central to salvation, understood in terms of release from the impure body, is a set of practices which they identified as 'purification' and 'control'. These can be regarded as two complementary aspects of the Brāhmaṇical model of spirituality. The body and emotional apparatus that belongs to the body are considered to be essentially impure and evil, and so is the sensory experience, 'sound, touch, and others which seem to be wealth (*artha*) are in fact evil' (*Maitreya Upaniṣad*, ibid.: 24). Thus, subjugation or control of the sensory experience is thought of as purification (*śauca*).[8] On the contrary, the lack of control means being dragged down to the weakness of the flesh. The conquest of the senses leads to the destruction of emotional fluctuations that impel *saṃsāra*:

> Through attraction of the senses, he becomes subject to fault, there is no doubt: through their control, he gains perfection . . . It should be known that that man who does not rejoice or grieve through hearing, touching, eating, seeing, or smelling is a conqueror of the organs (*Nāradaparivrājaka Upaniṣad*, *upadeśa* 3, ibid.: 132).

Therefore, '[h]e becomes fit for salvation through the control of the organs, the destruction of love and hate and non-injury to beings. He should abandon all identification with this feeble, perishable and impure body' (*Nāradaparivrājaka Upaniṣad*, *upadeśa* 3, ibid.: 133). Indeed, the highest spiritual state of perfect isolation (*kevala*) is achieved when one is freed from emotions-*cum*-sins, namely the stains of passion, anger, fear, delusion, greed, pride, lust, birth, death, miserliness, swoon, giddiness, hunger, thirst, ambition, shame, fright, heart-burning, grief, and gladness (*Yogatattva Upaniṣad*, ibid.: 181).

As Gavin Flood (2006: 40) has observed, the restraint of the senses and the body that is aimed at controlling the senses and avoiding the impurity seems to have been an underlying message of the *Manusmṛti* or the 'Laws of Manu' (*c.* 200 BCE–200 CE), arguably the principal *Dharmaśāstra*. Similar disclaimers of the sensory and emotional experiences in favour of a higher knowledge are found in the *Arthaśāstra* (*c.* 4th century BCE–1st century CE), an ancient Indian treatise on statecraft devoted to the subject of a 'social body' (ibid.: 43) and to the description of king's duties formulated in the concept of the kingly sage (*rājarṣi*). Thus, according to the exposition given in the *Arthaśāstra*, the kingly sage who wishes for a long and prosperous rule should follow the rules of conduct that include the control of his senses 'by eliminating vices of lust, anger, greed, pride, arrogance and excitability' (ibid.). The control of the senses later became the crux of the Sāṃkhya–Yoga practice.

'Removal of the Pains of Agency'

The Upaniṣads claim that a person is an agent (*kartṛ*) on account of his association with a psychophysical mind–body apparatus. A characteristic feature of an agent is his capability to experience 'pleasure' and 'pain'. These experiences are immediately processed by the mind resulting in emotional reactions characterised by feelings of 'love' and 'hate'. Thus, an individual is called an agent because he is capable of experiencing emotional effects fraught with the feelings of 'love' and 'hate' that are procured by his engagement in the sensory experience. These types of experiences pertaining to the agent are, according to the Upaniṣads, the source of *saṃsāra* or bondage. In addition, they are also qualified as constituting the primordial ignorance (*avidyā*). On this account, 'the attainment of eternal bliss takes place through the removal of the pains of agency' (*Muktika Upaniṣad*, in Khanna and Aiyar 2011: 6) that belongs to the agent. The *Sarvasāra Upaniṣad* (ibid.: 14) elucidates on this topic in the following words:

> The actor (or agent) is the one who possesses the body and the internal organs through their respective desires proceeding from the idea of

> pleasure and pain. The idea of pleasure is that modification of the mind known as love. The idea of pain is that modification of the mind known as hate. The cause of pleasure and pain are sound, touch, form, taste and odour. The original ignorance has the characteristics of the above five groups.

At least two issues regarding the etiology of emotions are outlined here. First, all types of emotions, whether 'positive' or 'negative', seem to be triggered by fivefold sensory perception, comprised of sound, touch, form, taste, and odour. Second, emotions, such as 'love' or 'hate', are considered to be modifications of the mind in a sense in which they are a result of mental processing of sensory data experienced as 'pleasure' or 'pain'. The concept of emotions outlined in the aforecited passage resembles that of the Sāṃkhya system which believes that intellect (*buddhi*) is the primary organ for experiencing feelings or emotions, evaluated as 'pleasure' or 'pain'. According to the Sāṃkhya, the realm of affects composed of positive (i.e., 'pleasure') and negative (i.e., 'pain') feelings is considered to be an unconscious mode of *prakṛti.*

In the Upaniṣadic thought, therefore, the notion of 'agency' is confined to the manner in which a person engages himself in the sensory experience, thereby prompting the arousal of emotions and identifying them as being coordinated by mind. Sensing, thinking and feeling exist in conformity with the primarily axiom of 'agency'. Moreover, sensing, thinking and feeling have an important bearing on the ontological and epistemological underpinnings of the Upaniṣadic doctrine insofar as they undermine the value of a person who, on account of being an agent, is held in bondage and ignorance. It then appears that the liberating movement away from bondage and ignorance indicates the 'removal of the pains of agency' and, hence, the elimination of any kind of sensory and cognitive activity. It is stated in the *upadeśa* 3 of *Nāradaparivrājaka Upaniṣad* (Khanna and Aiyar 2011: 135): 'He who, having withdrawn the organs within, like a turtle its limbs [within its shell], is with the actions of the organs and the mind annihilated, without desire . . . he alone is emancipated'. Hence, liberation, understood in terms of suspension of all activities, results in the attainment of the state of 'witness-consciousness' (*sākṣin-caitanya*): 'Having subdued the sensual organs and having given up the conception of "mine" in all objects, you should place your consciousness of "I" in me who am the witness-consciousness' (*Varāha Upaniṣad*, ibid.: 206). This state of witness-consciousness is characterised as wisdom and absolute Self because 'it is the seat of the eternal and emancipated *brahman* which is far superior to breaths, the organs of sense and action, the internal organs of thought, the *guṇas* and others, which is of the nature of *saccidānanda* and the witness to all' (*Nirālamba Upaniṣad*, ibid.: 22). The idea of liberation promoted here, in fact, replaces the agency pertaining to the embodied individual with the non-agency of the Self assuming the form of a static witness. This particular model of disembodied and non-agential spirituality is most fully developed in the philosophical system of Advaita Vedānta, 'the most widely accepted system of thought among philosophies of India' (Gupta 1998: 1) and promulgated primarily by Śaṅkara (8th century CE). For Śaṅkara, the Self is without action, and the realisation of the non-agency of the Self is a goal of an ascetic practice. Śaṅkara's position has been summarised by Flood (2004: 68–69) in the following words:

> As action pertains only to the body and senses, it is really non-existent in the self (*ātmani karmābhāva*), as has been taught in primary and secondary revelation and in logic (*śruti, smṛti* and *nyāya*). Action is falsely attributed to the self, and should anyone think 'I am the agent' (*ahaṃ kartā*) or 'I act' (*ahaṃ karomi*), he or she would be mistaken in attributing qualities to the immutable self that do not belong to it. The person who understands this is a controlled yogi (*yukto yogī*), wise, free, and whose purpose has been achieved. For Śaṇkara, self-knowledge is the wisdom that the self is without agency and that agency is illusory within the realm of nature (*prakṛti*) . . . Liberating knowledge means the realisation that the self is passive. The true self for Śaṅkara is the immutable, passive witness (*sākṣin*)[9] who in reality is untouched by action and ignorance or by the coverings (*upādhi*) that appear to separate the self from true, reflexive knowledge. This undifferentiated self is not individual, but universal consciousness or spirit (*brahman*).

The second strand of thought that influenced the Brāhmaṇical ideal of emotionlessness was the Sāṃkhya–Yoga. These two systems, featuring among the six orthodox schools of Indian philosophy (*darśanas*),[10] are usually treated as equally justified aspects of a unitary thought-system. On this account, Sāṃkhya is understood to provide the metaphysical framework or the theory of the system, while Yoga furnishes this theory with practice. The most representative text of the Sāṃkhya system is the *Sāṃkhyakārikā* of Īśvarakṛṣṇa (*c.* 4th century CE). Among the commentaries on the *Sāṃkhyakārikā*, the most frequently studied is the *Tattvakaumudī* (*c.* 940 CE), composed by Vācaspati Miśra. A few independent works were also composed over the centuries. The most popular among them is the anonymously authored *Yuktidīpīka* of *c.* 680–720 CE (Potter 2005: 626). The classical Yoga system is represented by the *Yoga Sūtra* of Patañjali (*c.* 200 CE). The most important commentary on the *Yoga Sūtra* is the *Vyāsabhāṣya* attributed to Vyāsa (*c.* 650–850 CE).

The fundamental metaphysical premise of the Sāṃkhya–Yoga doctrines is the absolute distinction between the consciousness-self (*puruṣa*) and matter or nature (*prakṛti*). *Puruṣa* is the seat of pure consciousness (*cetanā*) without content, the inactive spectator, dissociated from any empirical experience, while *prakṛti* is the real cause of real effects responsible for bringing forth the psychophysical organism of macrocosmic (nature) and microcosmic (mind–body complex) type consisting of a different modes of awareness, emotions, sensations, physicality, and the senses; *prakṛti*, therefore, accounts for everything that constitutes the world of our empirical existence. According to the precepts of the *Sāṃkhyakārikā* (*SK* 1, in Burley 2007: 6) and *Yoga Sūtra* (*YS* 2.16, ibid.), the empirical experience given to us is a result of our embodiment. It is negatively evaluated as the source of distress or suffering (*duḥkha*) and, thus, 'the utter relinquishment of experience and of the embodied personality' is said to be the precondition (*SK* 68, ibid.: 20) of liberation (*kaivalya*). The ultimate soteriological goal of the Sāṃkhya–Yoga is the attainment of the state of *puruṣa* who is additionally characterised as the seer (*draṣṭṛ*) and witness (*sākṣin*) (*SK* 19; *YS* 2.20, ibid.: 77). The movement in the direction of *puruṣa* implies, on the metaphysical level, the return of the manifest *prakṛti* into its un-manifest source (*prakṛtilaya*)[11] which, in turn, on the individual level, implies 'forsaking everything that marks one out as a person in the first place including body, mind, memory, etc.' (Burley 2007: 133). In effect, as Georg Feuerstein (1989: 74) points out, 'emancipation . . . abolishes man's false organismic identity and relocates him into the Self', the *puruṣa*. In the Sāṃkhya–Yoga, the fact of embodiment lies at the centre of something antithetical to all knowledge and truth. Vociferous insistence on the embodiment's essential worth lessness is followed by an insistence on its being the cause of distress. Since *duḥkha*, understood as an unfortunate consequence of embodiment, acquires such a prominent place in these systems, it is important to look at the wider metaphysical context in which it is formulated.

The negative conclusion regarding the existential pain of embodiment is derived entirely from *prakṛti*. *Prakṛti* is said to be endowed with three qualities (*triguṇa*): *sattva*, *rajas* and *tamas*. The entire psychophysical conception of the world of experience is built up and supported by this threefold constitution (*triguṇa*) inherently present in *prakṛti*. In other words, each object of perception given in empirical experience is a result of the transformation or the creative co-mingling of these three *guṇas*. Interestingly, the *guṇas* are defined in accordance with the emotional attitudes that operate in them. Therefore, each object of experience has the capability to give rise to the divergent and mutually disparate emotions of joy, pain, or sorrow. The *Sāṃkhyakārikā* gives a systematic classification of the *triguṇa* and the emotional attitude specific to each of them. On this account, *sattva-guṇa* governs the pleasurable (*SK* 12, in Jacobsen 2002: 245), the joyful (*prīti*) and the satisfactory experience (*sukha*). Thus, according to the *Sāṃkhyakārikā* (*SK* 54, ibid.), the divine world is rich in the emotional dimension of *sattva*. *Rajas* gives rise to distress (*duḥkha*), unhappiness (*aprīti*), hatred (*dveṣa*), malice (*droha*), envy (*matsara*), blame (*nindā*), pride (*stambha*), sexual desire (*utkaṇṭhā*), dishonesty (*nikṛti*). *Rajas* is the determining factor which causes excitement, misery, anger, and anxiety; as such, it is said to dominate the emotional distraught of the human world (ibid.: 245–46). *Tamas* governs the experience of stupefaction and bewilderment. It is responsible for grief (*viṣāda*), confusion (*moha*), fear (*bhaya*), depression (*dainya*), intoxication (*mada*), and insanity (*unmāda*). It dominates animal and plant life (ibid.: 246). This classification is helpful in understanding the division into the three divergent tendencies that operate in the world. Nevertheless, one has to remember that every phenomenon is a specific combination of these three distinct emotional tendencies. In addition, *triguṇa* exists in a state of constant transformation that gives rise to different juxtapositions between the *guṇas*. Because of its mutable structure innately constituted by the fluctuating character of *triguṇa*, the same phenomenon may cause pleasure to some and pain to others. This position is summarised by S. N. Dasgupta (1979: 85) in the following words:

> [A]ll the mental states as well as all kinds of things are characterised as pleasurable (*sukha*), painful (*duḥkha*), and blinding (*moha*); it is therefore that these [three] *guṇas* being also transformed as the external objects as the jug, etc., produce by mutual correlations the feelings of pleasure, pain and blindness. If the objects were not modified in that way, there should be no reason why with the merest connection with the objects there should rise painful or pleasurable states of mind. It is for this reason that we hold that the modifications in the objects, which serve to determine the mental states in a painful or pleasurable way, are nothing but themselves the transformations of the elementary feeling entities (*guṇas*) of pleasure, pain, etc.

The *Yoga Sūtra* 2.15 (Jacobsen 2002: 245) associates this constant transformation of the three *guṇas* in the objects of perception with the source of suffering: 'The discriminating person sees all objects as painful because they cause suffering as a consequence, as affliction (*kleśa*) and as *saṃskāra*, and because of the mutual opposition of the transformations of the *guṇas*'.[12]

The Sāṃkhya–Yoga continues to refine our understanding of the threefold constitution (*triguṇa*) that is structurally present in every phenomenon or object of the empirical world and the emotional distress (*duḥkha*) that underlines all existence in the sophisticated setting of interrelatedness based on the philosophical dictum that 'everything is of a nature of everything else' (*sarvaṃ sarvātmakam*). As Knut A. Jacobsen (ibid.: 250) demonstrates:

> It is in fact because of the interdependency of all the products of *prakṛti* that freedom from *duḥkha* cannot be attained without total separation from *prakṛti*. The fact that everything is connected to everything else is the cause of misery and disharmony, according to Sāṃkhya and Yoga. Connected things act both harmoniously and disharmoniously because they act according to their own nature.

According to the commentary of *Vyāsabhaṣya* on *YS* 2.15, because of the interconnectedness of all things, 'no enjoyment is possible without hurting others (*nānupahatya bhūtāni upabhogaḥ saṃbhavati*), so every enjoyment produces demerit' (ibid.: 246). The author refers here to the threefold suffering (*duḥkhatraya*) mentioned in the first verse of the *Sāṃkhyakārikā*. One type of *duḥkhatraya* is the suffering caused by other beings (*ādhibhautika*) which is the specific manifestation of a mutual interdependency discussed earlier. Liberation involves freeing oneself from this interdependency that must necessarily lead to the destruction of embodiment, for, according to the precepts of the *Sāṃkhyakārikā* (*SK* 55, in Larson 2001: 155), 'as long as there is embodiment, there will be suffering'.

The central aim of Sāṃkhya–Yoga is a negative utility, namely freeing oneself from the entanglement of embodiment caused by *prakṛti* that naturally leads to the eradication of future suffering (*YS* 2.16, in Burley 2007: 6). The Yoga suggests methods for its elimination from the human scene which are missing in the theory-oriented Sāṃkhya. These methods, comprised of a closely connected set of disciplines that include 'practice' (*abhyāsa*) and 'detachment' (*vairāgya*), developed out of the

Brāhmaṇical 'obsession' with control and purification. The word *yoga* is derived from the verbal root *yuj*, meaning 'to control', or 'to yoke'. The proper sense of *yoga*, thus, predicates 'mastery' and 'subjugation' (Tola and Dragonetti 1987: 1). Employment of the word *yoga* to denote 'restraint' or 'control' was already known in the Upaniṣads, where its linguistic usage was applied to the control of the senses. In the *Kaṭha Upaniṣad* (2.6.11), 'the firm holding back of the senses is called Yoga' (Dasgupta 1979: 44). Such a controlling predicate of the term *yoga* was certainly retained in the restraining disciplines of *abhyāsa* and *vairāgya* that aimed at 'immobilising the continual fluctuation of the individual body-emotions-mind complex' (*citta-vṛtti-nirodha*) through suppression of bodily and mental instability (Torella 2011: 92–94). Before turning to the description of these disciplines in more depth, however, it is worth pausing to make a few remarks about the specific place occupied by emotions in India, the place in between 'mind' and 'heart'. Theorising emotions in India poses some difficulties, for unlike emotions in the West, 'Indian' emotions cannot be reduced either to the affective-conative theory, nor to the cognitive theory. On the contrary, 'Indian' emotions seem to oscillate freely between the two, that is to say they are not entirely cognitive on the one hand, nor entirely reducible to feelings as sensations, but rather something mid-way between reason's thought and an inspirational 'heart-felt feeling', on the other. As June McDaniel (2008: 54) observes: 'In the Bengali and Sanskrit languages, terms for emotion and thought, mind and heart, are not opposed. Indeed, most frequently the same terms are used for both'. This implies that emotion and cognition do not seem to be opposite to each other, forming two exclusive classes. In accordance with the classical Indian philosophy, emotions are cognitions (*jñāna*, *vijñāna*), the justified mental phenomena not less rational than complex thought-processes. In this regard, the term *citta*, as it has been used in the Yoga system, is generally translated as the 'mind' and consists of a creative mingling of cognitive, conative and affective aspects. The *citta* is not only mind, it is precisely the body–emotions–mind complex which is considered to be the oppressive burden that needs to be purged. This can be accomplished through the restraining disciplines of *abhyāsa* and *vairāgya* (*YS* 1.12–16, in Jacobsen 2002: 284). Practice (*abhyāsa*) is defined as a continuous effort to acquire stability (*sthiti*) of *citta* (*YS* 1.13, ibid.), which is characterised by its peaceful flow (*praśāntavāhitā*) (*YS* 3.10, ibid.). Detachment (*vairāgya*) involves forsaking the thirst (*tṛṣṇā*) for worldly objects (*YS* 1.15, ibid.). *Vairāgya*, which is translated by Monier-Williams as the 'freedom from worldly desires' and whose semantics includes also the meaning of 'dispassion', puts emphasis on the renunciation of the objects of desire, and as such it can be said to be the main spiritual attitude of an adept aspiring for liberation in the Brāhmaṇical context.

In terms of the precise meaning of this term given in the *Yoga Sūtra*, *yoga* as a technique of spiritual discipline involves the cessation of the activity of body–emotions–mind complex (*yogaś-citta-vṛtti-nirodhaḥ*) by engaging oneself in the practices that aim at reversing the tendency for the outward flow of the mind and the senses directed towards the objects of perception. By 'turning within', a *yogin* induces the reversal process that attempts, in the Sāṃkhya terms, to free *puruṣa* from the shackles of *prakṛti*. That is achieved by *puruṣa*'s 'split with the body' (*śārīra-bheda*) and by *prakṛti*'s withdrawal to the dormant state (*SK* 65, Burley 2007: 134). As Mikel Burley says: 'Not only, then, does the mind (*citta*) cease to operate, but the entire world of ostensibly physical objects dissolves, leaving only an unmanifest and dormant *prakṛti*, plus, of course the now solitary *puruṣa*, who abides in purely its own nature (*svarūpa*)' (ibid.). The salvific goal of Sāṃkhya–Yoga is the same state of perfect isolation (*kaivalya*) of *puruṣa* that entails a termination of *puruṣa*'s false identification with that which is not self (*anātman*) (*YS* 2.5, ibid.: 131), namely *prakṛti*. As Burley (2007: 140–41) has demonstrated, from the aforestated premises, it, then, appears that liberation (*kaivalya*) in Sāṃkhya–Yoga is considered to be a disembodied and mindless state in a sense in which the *yogin*'s body and mind, as a part of a wider psychophysical nature (*prakṛti*), get dissolved into the unmanifest state upon *prakṛti*'s return to inactivity. Thus, upon the total cessation of *citta* that is the body–emotions–mind complex, only the solitary *puruṣa* remains who is pure consciousness beyond empirical experience. This is the condition of liberation which Gerald Larson (2001: 205) calls 'emptiness': '"Emptiness" or "nothingness" appears to be appropriate terms, for the condition of salvation in classical Sāṃkhya is the condition of the *puruṣa* in itself. It is the reversal of the dialectical relationship of *prakṛti* and *puruṣa*'.

An idea, attended to clearly in the Sāṃkhya–Yoga system, purposefully holds human body–emotions–mind complex as the domain of bondage and suffering and presents a framework for its suppression, control, or its realisation of being the form of ignorance (*avidyā*) that stands in opposition to pure consciousness of *puruṣa*, the solitary witness and the seer. The practical devices for this realisation comprise different forms of meditative techniques of concentration based on the principle of reversal (*pratiprasava*) of the mind–body–senses from the objects given in the empirical existence. This practice has at its aim the return to the pristine state of utter disembodiment, where only 'emptiness' shines forth.

The Upaniṣads and the Sāṃkhya–Yoga were fundamental in building up the theoretical framework of the Brāhmaṇical thought that, in effect, paved the way for an all-encompassing spiritual ideal of emotionlessness that promoted the value of renunciation and disembodied purity achieved through the control of mind, emotions, body, and senses. As Alexis Sanderson (1985) has demonstrated, the Brāhmaṇical orthopraxy was constructed from the notion of 'identity–through–purity' that operated on two levels, the physical and the social. The ideal Brāhmaṇa was required to avoid any contact with substances, places, persons, foods, drinks, and dresses that were marked impure in the orthodox scriptures. Brāhmaṇical 'identity–through–purity' was, therefore, necessarily subject to the implicit norms of beliefs and conduct imposed by scriptural injunctions and prohibitions. In conformity with Brāhmaṇical orthopraxy, the greatest enemy of the ideal Brahman was 'the spontaneity of the senses and his highest virtue immunity to emotion in unwavering self-control' (ibid.: 193). It is important to remember that Brāhmaṇical discourse, formulated along the lines of emotional immunity and self-control, heavily influenced the soteriological concepts of Buddhism,[13] Jainism and Śaiva Siddhānta, and that it was itself influenced by their discourses. At least three distinctive Indian traditions took a very different stand on emotions, i.e., one that systematically rejected, or at least challenged, the Brāhmaṇical view. Among them, we find Tantrism, the Bhakti movement and Aesthetics. These three unique thought-systems of India arose in response to the Brāhmaṇical orthopraxy. It was through participation in this Brāhmaṇical emotionless worldview that all of these new discourses were created to present new vistas for spiritual perfection, positively engaging the realm of emotions. In examining what often seem to be competing and opposing discourses, this book makes an attempt to reconstruct, in a way, the discussion on emotions expounded in different religious and philosophical traditions of India that clashed with the Brāhmaṇical emotionlessness. Building on the theory of socio-cultural evolution, understood in terms of a historical development of ideas that are actively shaped by mainstream categories of understanding, this book tries to anchor the process of theorising emotions in India within a wider framework of the Brāhmaṇical orthopraxy. In this way, the commonly accepted canon of the Brāhmaṇical emotionlessness is regarded as a shared basis on which all these new discourses yield their revelation of emotional richness. In addition, this book also allows discussion with those thought-systems of India that are typically regarded as continuing the Brāhmaṇical legacy of emotionlessness: Buddhism, Jainism, Pātañjala Yoga, and Śaiva Siddhānta, by showing how surprisingly far these systems go toward explaining the seemingly dysfunctional character of emotions, regarding them as a necessary aid to spiritual development. The collection of essays constituting the present volume is divided into four parts reflecting four streams of Indian thought-systems: (*a*) Tantrism; (*b*) the Bhakti movement; (*c*) Buddhism, Jainism, Pātañjala Yoga, and Śaiva Siddhānta; and (*d*) Aesthetics. Each part includes two or three essays offering different approaches in conceptualising emotions in India. Before turning to the respective essays, a reader is advised to read an introduction to each part first. The purpose of the introduction is, primarily, to provide a reader with a theoretical foundation for the discussion on emotions that is followed in the essays.

Tantrism

Tantrism was a socio-religious movement that represented a concentrated effort to counteract the prevailing Brāhmaṇical orthodoxy by rejecting its purity-bound system of belief and practice. Interestingly, this rejection of orthopraxy was not achieved by a simple elimination of its dogmatic injunctions but rather by its implicit inclusion in a typology of graded revelation of the *śāstra*s, where the orthodox scriptures, i.e., the Vedas, occupied a lower position. Tantric scriptures wanted to distance themselves from the scriptural canon of Brāhmaṇism, maintaining that their stance was not to condemn the Brāhmaṇical practice but to demonstrate that the tantric revelation was superior to it. Central to this assertion was the establishment of a division between the particularity of revelation (*viśeṣa-śāstra*) attributed to the tantric scriptures (*Āgama*s) and the generality of revelation (*sāmānya-śāstra*) attributed to the Vedas and orthodox scriptures (Flood 2006: 63). According to this view, the more esoteric and, therefore, particular is the revelation transmitted only to the initiates, the higher it is on the scale of a graded hierarchy and, thus, closer to the truth. On the other hand, the more general and easily accessible is the revelation, the lower it is on the scale and further removed from the truth (ibid.). There existed, thus, a hierarchy of different levels of discourse within which tantric revelation took the highest place. This hierarchy, based on the principle of inclusion, was projected onto the tantric conduct sanctioning a multi-layered personality of a tantric adept. Abhinavagupta (10th–11th century CE), Kashmiri philosopher and tantric master, makes an oft-quoted remark 'that externally one follows vedic practice, in the domestic sphere one is an orthodox Śaiva, but in one's secret life one is follower of the extreme, antinomian cult of the Kula which involves disruption of the Vedas through ritual transgression of Vedic norms and practices' (ibid.: 21). The tantric adept acts out different lives, which can be classified as the public life, the domestic life and the secret life, and in doing so he literally embodies different levels of discourse arranged in a graded array, from the most exoteric to the most esoteric. Again, Abhinavagupta conclusively justifies the superiority of tantric scriptures (*Āgamas*) over the 'lower' types of orthodox scriptures in his monumental *Tāntrāloka* (*Tā* 37.1–14, ibid.: 58–59):

> [T]he scripture (*āgama*) should be followed in order to reach perfection. This perfection is achieved quickly through pursuing the teachings in the scriptures of the left stream (*vāmaśāsana*) and transcending the Vedic scriptures, which rest in the "womb of illusion" (*māyodarasthitam*). These scriptures lead to the highest perfection of consciousness, a perfection to be realised in one's own experience (*svānubhavasiddham*) beyond the mere ritual action declared in the Veda that should be forsaken. Relying on Śaiva scriptures allows us to go beyond apprehension or fear (*śaṅkā*) characteristic of the Veda and orthodox Brāhmaṇical teachings, for the Śaiva teachings are their reversal (*viparyaya*).

What becomes evidentially clear here is that Tantrism sought to graft its secret, transgressive practices onto the Brāhmaṇical principles of purity and control, thereby using them as an ideological background to establish its own legitimacy and authority. What we have here, then, is an attempt to, first, absorb the teachings of the opponent only to reject them in an act of transgression. The validation for this transgression comes from ascribing a lower status to the teachings contained in the scriptural canon of the orthodoxy than to the teachings exposed in the tantric revelation. Among these absorptions-transgressions, one of the most significant was tantric rediscovery of desire (*kāma*) to which Raffaele Torella takes recourse in his essay, 'Passions and Emotions in the Indian Philosophical–Religious Traditions' (Chapter 1, this volume), placing it at the centre of his discussion on emotions in India. In making such declarations, Torella follows the lead of previous scholars, such as Madeleine Biardeau, who claims that Tantrism is 'an attempt to place *kāma*, desire, in every meaning of the word, in the service of liberation . . . not to sacrifice this world for liberation's sake, but to reinstate it, in varying ways, within the perspective of salvation' (1989: 4). Torella's main assertion is that the entire Indian culture has been always aware of the significance of *kāma* as the storehouse of human and divine energy, characterised by drive dimension. The primary trigger for arousal of emotions has always been *kāma.*

In the *Bhagavadgītā* 3.37, Arjuna asks Lord Kṛṣṇa about the trigger that prompts man's engagement in a wrong activity. Kṛṣṇa replies: 'It is desire indeed, which, being obstructed, becomes anger that prompts man thus'. The main point of Kṛṣṇa's reply is that desire is closely related to the emotional structure of human beings. All emotions are perpetuated by desire to prolong pleasure and escape pain. The desire to be united with the object of pleasure results in attachment (*rāga*); on the contrary, the desire to avoid an object of pain results in repulsion (*dveṣa*). The frustration of the object of desire leads to anger, longing, etc. In this context, the *Bhagavadgītā* and *Manusmṛti* declare *kāma* to be the insatiable consumer (*mahāśana*). In the *Manusmṛti*, it is said that '*kāma* is recurrent even after its fulfillment, just as ghee poured as oblation in fire makes the flame rise higher and higher' (*Manusmṛti* 2.94, in Rao 2011: 418–20). The very nature of desire is wanting something, longing for something, being anxious for something. This thirst (*tṛṣṇā*) for the objects of perception is inherently present in desire. In the *Bṛhadāraṇyaka Upaniṣad* (4.4.7, in Witz 1998: 74), it is said that the human person (*puruṣa*) consists only of desire; this desire determines one's conduct through life prompting good and evil actions (*karma*) that are based on attachment, greed, etc., that ultimately result in *saṃsāra.* The way out of *saṃsāra* is an attainment of a 'desireless state'. The *Bṛhadāraṇyaka Upaniṣad* (4.4.9, ibid.: 75) further says: 'When all desires are expelled, which lurk within his heart, then a mortal becomes immortal; he attains the Brahman here (in this world)'. The transcendence of desire that consequently led to emotional deprivation has become a crucial aspect of spiritual perfection in the Brāhmaṇical tradition, but the precise way in which it was actually accomplished needs to noted here. As Flood (2006: 47) points out, pleasure (*kāma*) shaped social values and meanings within the dhārmic system of human goals of life (*puruṣārthas*) and, in a way, constituted a normative rule to which every Brāhmaṇa found himself committed. In accordance with the implicit norms of belief and conduct imposed by the Brāhmaṇical purity-bound mentality, founded on the renunciation of desire and the denial of body–emotions–mind–senses complex, liberation (*mokṣa*) was antithetical to pleasure (*kāma*).

This tension between the conflicting values within the tradition 'was resolved through the institution of the stages of life (*āśrama*), where *mokṣa* was left to the renouncer' and itself relegated to the last stage of human life. Another example of a skilful resolution of this conflict within the Brāhmaṇical tradition is the *Bhagavadgītā*. The *Bhagavadgītā* with its spiritual ideal of a *karmayogin* incorporated the troubled notion of 'desire' into the field of action (*karma*), promoting unattached, selfless activity of the 'desireless action' (*niṣkāma karma*). The desire-motivated actions (*sakāma karma*) were depreciated; on the other hand, those actions that were unmotivated by desire (*niṣkāma karma*) became dignified. The ideal of the *Bhagavadgītā* effectively destroyed the primal motivating force that stood behind all human activities in the world and gave rise to the 'detached performance of an act' (Krishnan 1989: 177). Torella incorporates this idea as the starting point of his argument claiming that Tantrism replaced the 'desireless action' of the *Bhagavadgītā* with a spiritual ideal of a pure 'desiring condition' without any object or action (*niṣkarma kāma*). In Tantrism, the pure 'desiring condition' is both a goal and a path leading towards liberation. Rather than escaping 'desire' that arouses emotions and passions, Tantrism encourages the fullest engagement in the emotional states and passions that act as a direct link connecting with the infinite potential energy that lies behind them. In this way, Tantrism reacted against what it regarded as a lower and limited revelation of the dhārmic renunciation of desire. While reinstating the strictly avoided notion of desire into its system of practice, Tantrism sanctioned the transgression of conventional norms of the Brāhmaṇical *dharma*. According to Torella, this reinstatement of desire enabled Tantrism to assign value to the body, senses and, thus, to emotions that became equally appropriated as the means of liberation (*mokṣa*). The major contribution of Tantrism, relatively unknown to earlier philosophies and religious systems, was actually constituted by a great importance attached in this system to the human body blooming with a dazzling array of emotions and passions. The intensity of emotional experience became incorporated into tantric *yoga* practice.

This theme is explored by Bettina Bäumer in her essay, 'Intensity of Emotions: A Way of Liberation in the Advaita Śaiva *Āgama*s and Their Exegetes' (Chapter 2, this volume). She starts her argument from the premise that the standard paradigm of Indian spirituality was formulated upon the suppression of *citta* (the body–mind–emotions complex). In making this claim, she refers to the Pātañjala Yoga's famous statement: 'Yoga is the suppression of psychosomatic states' (*yogaś-citta-vṛtti-nirodhaḥ*). The tantric *yoga*, better known as the means of realisation (*upāya*), apparently developed against the self-control of a classical Pātañjala Yoga as its exact opposition. Surveying textual examples from the tantric *yoga* manuals, such as the *Vijñānabhairava* and the *Spandakārikā*, Bäumer shows to what extent emotions have been appropriated into yogic practice of Tantrism. The most fascinating issue she brings out in her exposition is the tantric absorption of the yogic notion of one-pointedness (*ekāgratā*) that becomes positively reformulated in the tantric practice. According to Vyāsa's commentary on the *Yoga Sūtra* (*YK* 1.1, in Āraṇya 1963: 2–5), *citta* habitually abides in five states. Of these, the first is 'distraught' (*kṣipta*), in which neither patience nor concentration of *citta* is possible; the second is 'stupefaction' (*muḍha*), in which *citta* is obsessed with one thought, i.e., the thought of family or wealth; the third is 'restlessness' (*vikṣipta*), in which *citta* is sometimes calm and sometimes disturbed; the fourth is 'one-pointedness', in which *citta* holds to one thought, whether in dream or in the awakened state; the fifth is 'suppression' (*niruddha*), in which different psychosomatic states of *citta* are shut out. The Pātañjala Yoga distinguishes between two types of *samādhi* that correspond to the fourth and the fifth condition of *citta* respectively: (*a*) *samprajñāta-samādhi*, which is attained by the mastery of one-pointedness; and (*b*) *asamprajñāta-samādhi*, which is the state of total cessation of *citta*, ensuring liberation (*kaivalya*). According to the precepts of the *Yoga Sūtra*, restless *citta* can never develop concentration leading to liberation. Only *citta* that develops a lasting one-pointedness (*ekāgratā*) is secure in reaching the state of liberation. In the state of one-pointedness, the restlessness of *citta* that sets in when one is happy, unhappy or stupefied is diminished. In the one-pointed state of concentration, the feelings and emotions are gradually eliminated, and, therefore, this state directly leads to the suppression of *citta*, and, thus, to liberation (ibid.). In tantric *yoga*, on the other hand, the state of one-pointed concentration does not entail the removal of emotions, but, on the contrary, the fullest engagement in their power. The tantric texts, referred to by Bäumer in her essay, describe yogic practices that advocate one-pointed concentration on the various intense emotional states of anger, desire, greed, delusion, intoxication, and envy, in which the bliss of consciousness alone arises. She rightly points out that the tantric incorporation of emotions into its system of yogic practice depends mainly on the emotion's inherent intensity. Only in the states of extreme anger, great fear, or intense joy, all other mental movements come to stop, and the *yogins* become one-pointed in the experience of *spanda* (the experience of the Absolute).

Particularly noteworthy in this connection is the tantric critique of Pātañjala Yoga, directed against the suppression of emotions belonging to *citta.* In tantric understanding, emotions are direct means for *citta*'s transformation. When *citta* becomes one-pointed through its engagement in the powerful emotional states, she gives up the limited tendency of extroversion and becomes introverted, then the aspect of limitation that normally contracts her, becomes dissolved and she becomes transformed into *cit* (universal consciousness) (*Pratyabhijñāhṛdayam* 13, in Singh 1977: 86). In Tantrism, *citta* is not to be suppressed, but transformed into highest consciousness. This transformation is enacted through yogic practice that advocates total immersion in the emotional states. Another important point Bäumer brings out in her discussion on emotions in India is the notion of *kṣobha* in the sense of 'restlessness', 'agitation', or 'excitement'. What sets the tantric *kṣobha* apart from its earlier forms developed in the Sāṃkhya–Yoga is its tangible association with yogic, aesthetic and emotional levels of experience. The Sāṃkhya–Yoga's attitude to 'restlessness' is entirely negative. The restlessness of *citta* should be suppressed in a yogic concentration, for she is a negative result of creation brought about by disturbance (*kṣobha*).[14] For the Buddhists, who enumerate 10 stages that obstruct the peace of mind along the way to final emancipation (*nirvāṇa*), 'excitement' or 'agitation' occupies the ninth place and, therefore, requires elimination. In Tantrism, however, *kṣobha,* like desire (*kāma*), acts as a stimulus for the activation of emotions that arise in connection with agitation caused by vital energy present in the body. For an experienced tantric *yogin*, the agitation of the vital energy (*vīryakṣobha*) that occurs in the middle channel of *suṣumnā*[15] is fully responsible for aesthetic-*cum*-spiritual experience of *camatkāra* (wonder, astonishment). All the sensory experiences and emotional states, whether negative or positive, which are also the form of agitation (*kṣobhātmakam*), can become the source of *camatkāra* when they are recognised in harmony with the creative excitement taking place within the Absolute. This excitement caused by the sensory experiences or emotional states should not be suppressed but cultivated, for it acts as a trigger for the arousal of the vital energy in the yogic body culminating in the aesthetic-*cum*-spiritual experience of *camatkāra.*

The portrayal of Tantrism as a primarily transgressive movement going against the Brāhmaṇical norms of purity and control is best represented in the essay by Aleksandra Wenta, 'Between Fear and Heroism:

The Tantric Path to Liberation' (Chapter 3, this volume). Basing her main argument on Alexis Sanderson's famous dialectics of purity and power in which the division is established between those who seek depersonalised purity (Brāhmaṇas) and those who seek omnipotence through the transgression of powerless orthopraxy (Tāntrikas), she shows how the logic of this dialectics can be extended even to include the sphere of emotions. Her assumption is that the Brāhmaṇical obsession with purity logically entailed such psychological predicates as fear of contamination. On the basis of this premise, she claims that the tantric path is characterised by a direct face-to-face confrontation with this very fear that was radically avoided in the Brāhmaṇical orthodoxy. It turns out that Tantrism consciously and overtly modelled itself upon those ideas that were intolerable to the orthodoxy. The transgressive character of the tantric movement can be seen, once again, in the absorption of the orthodox ideas that are deliberately being subverted by stressing its limited degree of truth. Wenta's argument is consistent with claims regarding 'Brāhmaṇical fear' expounded by tantric authors, such as Abhinavagupta or his commentator Jayaratha. In his *Tantrāloka*, Abhinavagupta says that 'relying on Śaiva scriptures allows us to go beyond apprehension or fear (*śaṅkā*) characteristic of the Veda and orthodox Brāhmaṇical teachings, for the Śaiva teachings are their reversal (*viparyaya*)' (*Tā* 37.1–14, in Flood 2006: 58–59). In a similar manner, Jayaratha conspicuously declares that 'those practitioners who do not do what is forbidden due to fear experience a thousand torments in hell' (*Tā* 29.99–100a and Jayaratha's commentary, ibid.: 112). The declaration that tantric practice is justified by appeal to do anything that is forbidden and feared in the orthopraxy is, without doubt, a powerful statement of Tantrism. Wenta's essay takes us on a journey to this 'forbidden land', comprised of fear-eliciting places, substances and deities wherein tantric confrontation with the deep-rooted 'Brāhmaṇical fear' takes place. In Tantrism, this fear is personalised and sacralised, becoming a deity, Bhairava. It was in confrontation with the 'Brāhmaṇical fear' that the tantric path of heroism (*vīra-sādhanā*) emerged, trespassing the boundaries of impure and pure imposed by the Brāhmaṇical worldview. The path of heroism was conceptually grounded in the wider practice of non-duality (*advaitācāra*), according to which the dualistic perception that causes fear (characteristic to the orthodoxy) is considered to be the enemy which must be destroyed and supplanted with the vision of non-duality of the Self, wherein all opposites merge in oneness.

The Bhakti Movement

In the beginning of his exposition on *bhakti*, R. C. Zaehner (1962: 164) recalls the famous episode from the *Mahābhārata*, in which the righteous king Yudhiṣṭhira is refused entry into heaven with his beloved dog by the gods of the Brāhmaṇical pantheon. The dog, says Zaehner, is an exemplar of a true *bhakta*, 'devoted, loyal creature', and Indra is forced to reprove Yudhiṣṭhira 'for still being subject to human love, for in *mokṣa*, there is no love'. Yudhiṣṭhira protests and refuses to enter the gates of heaven without his beloved pet. This single image is enough to capture the central feature of the Bhakti movement that opposed the Brāhmaṇical ideal of emotionlessness, an ideal that Brāhmaṇism shared with Buddhism and Jainism. The Bhakti movement had its origins in the works espoused by the Vaiṣṇava Āḷvārs ('those immersed in God')[16] (6th–9th century CE) and the Śaiva Nāyaṉārs (5th–10th century CE) and rose into importance in mediaeval Tamil Nadu, wherefrom it began to spread quickly to the north, especially in the late mediaeval period when India was struggling under Turkish invasions. Bhakti protagonists, who were traditionally called 'saints', 'elaborated [an] egalitarian doctrine that transcended the Brāhmaṇical caste system and encouraged individuals to seek personal union with the divine' (Bentley 1993: 120). The most appealing aspect of Bhakti movement was that it assisted the development of a religiously motivated affective life, in which emotions came to be seen not as unwelcome obstructions for spiritual growth but as the very medium through which this growth and transformation were ensured. In its emphasis on intense emotionalism, the Bhakti movement reacted against 'cold' traditions of Brāhmaṇism, Buddhism and Jainism that propagated the ascetic ideal of world-renouncer. In the words of Kamil Zvelebil (1973: 199):

> [I]n comparison with the decayed, deteriorated Southern Buddhism and Jainism we see in the Tamil Hindu revival [of *bhakti*] the triumph of emotion over intellect, of the concrete over the abstract, of the acceptance of life over its ascetic denial, of something near and homely against something alien and distant, and, above all, the acceptance of positive love against cold morality or intellectually coloured compassion.

Even though, it is certainly true that the richness of emotional life played a very important role in *bhakti*, one should not understand from it that the emotionalism of *bhakti* was all about uncritical emotions. As Karen Pechilis Prentiss (1999: 20) declares in her excellent study on

Tamil Śiva-*bhakti* tradition, *bhakti* is 'committed engagement' that, on the one hand, involves emotional dedication, but, on the other, also makes a space for a critical reflection directed against the ascetic ideal promulgated by 'cold' traditions; such criticism usually belongs to the sphere of intellect. From this premise, she constructs her argument that defines *bhakti* as a 'theology of embodiment' (Prentiss 1999: 6), which implies participation in God (*bhakti*, derived from Sanskrit verbal root *bhaj*, meaning 'to participate'). Such participation in God is meant to include all aspects of human activity in the world, in a sense in which a *bhakta* is expected to devote his whole being to God, reflecting upon Him with his mind and heart (interestingly, 'mind' and 'heart' are linguistically expressed by the same Sanskrit-derived word in Tamil, *ma<u>n</u>am*) (ibid.: 53). It appears, then, that the emotionalism of *bhakti* should not be reduced to the sphere of feelings, to the exclusion of everything else, for the active participation in God, redefined as a 'theology of embodiment', seems to have cognitive overtones as well. In this context, it must be emphasised that emotional involvement of a *bhakta* inheres in a certain cognitive dynamism, in which his 'mind' and his 'heart' are equally approximating the presence of God.

The Bhakti movement's disagreement with the ascetic traditions of Buddhism and Jainism was on two grounds. First, the metaphysical attitude towards reality, which was no longer to be denied but rather appreciated as the manifestation of a theistic God, enshrined in a concrete temple. Second, the worship of God had an ecstatic character that clearly contrasted with the 'cold' practices of self-denial embedded in the spiritual ideal of world-renouncer. To a great extent, the ecstatic type of *bhakti* worship relied upon a total psychophysical engagement of a *bhakta* expressed in his singing, dancing and weeping which Indira Peterson (1991: 42–43) has called 'spontaneous, unstructured ways of worship'. Scholars specialising in Tamil Śiva-bhakti (Zvelebil 1973: 197; Yocum 1973: 4–11) point out that the motifs of ecstatic dancing, singing and weeping recur in *bhakti* poems in the context of a *bhakta*'s 'emotional outpouring of love to God' (Yocum 1973: 4). The emotional response signified by the feeling of love towards God became the central motif of *bhakti* poetry. The worship inspired by this intense love drove affective expressions, i.e., shedding tears, dancing and singing. This type of worship was effectively comingled with religious experience that the Tamil saints called 'melting of one's own heart and mind in love for God (*u<u>ll</u>am uruku*)' (ibid.).

The essay by T. Ganesan, 'Principal Emotions Contributing to the Supreme Love of Śiva: A Study of Early Śaiva Hymnal Corpus' (Chapter 4, this volume), explores the emotionalism of *bhakti* primarily in the context of Tamil Śiva-bhakti tradition extending back to the earliest saints (*nāyaṉār*), known as 'the three' (*mūvar*), viz., Tiruñāṉacampantar (Campantar), Tirunāvukkaracar (Appar), and Cuntaramūrti (Nampi Ārūrar), who lived between 7th and 9th centuries CE. Their works, collectively called the *Tēvāram* (Tamil *teva* 'god', *aram* 'garland'), is a collection of first seven volumes of the *Tirumurai*, the 12-volume anthology of the Tamil Śaiva devotional songs which were defined as a canon during the reign of Cōla king Rājarāja I. Among the other authors of *Tirumurai* anthology, Ganesan takes recourse to Mānikkavācakar's 9th-century-CE works, which constitute the eighth volume of the *Tirumurai*; saint-poetess Kāraikkāl Ammaiyar's 6th-century-CE poems, which constitute the eleventh volume of the *Tirumurai*; and Cēkkiḻār's 12th-century-CE hagiography of Tamil Śaiva saints, the *Periyapurāṇam*, which constitutes the twelfth volume of the *Tirumurai.* In the devotional hymns of the Tamil Śaiva saints, subjectivity, visibly foregrounded in the first-person narrator, takes on increasing importance. Prentiss (1999: 44) claims: '[T]he Tamil hymns appear to be the first in Hindu literature to use the first person singular voice, conveying that the author is speaking from experience'. The first person narrations are very personal reports, firmly grounded in the experiential and emotional hardships of daily life. Since the poems were written from the standpoint of existential troubles of a *bhakta*, they could be more instructive and accessible to the wider Tamil Śaiva community because they taught about human condition, providing stories and images from daily life. Often, the tone of these poems is bitter, as it arises from an emphasis on the 'human inadequacy' (ibid.: 50). In addition to such reports of existential trials and inner struggle, the poems provide accessibility to a whole spectrum of emotions carrying with themselves an explosive mixture of impulsiveness, love, joy, sorrow, heroism, frustration, self-repentance, intense longing, anger, awe, and disgust. In some instances, God is overtly criticised by a *bhakta* through harsh speech; this estrangement from God is a sign of his intimacy with Him (ibid.: 67). In his essay, Ganesan tracks a great variety of emotional meanings that have enormous devotional power. It is definitely this emotional dramatisation itself that provides the experience of participation in the praise of Śiva that, in a significant part, predicates God's total accessibility. Access to God, arising from emotional involvement, is not exclusively limited to the poets; the audience, too, could participate in their emotions. In his adaption of the classical *rasa* theory of aesthetics, Norman Cutler (1987) argues that the Tamil Śaiva hymns could provide the audience with *rasa*-like experience if the poem is 'reincarnated' in the psyche of the audience. Anthony G. Harris (2008: 37) summarises Cutler's 'reincarnation theory' in the following words:

> In a ritual context, the audience must be receptive to the emotion in the poem. In this way, the audience (in a ritual context) can "reincarnate" the original context of the hymn because, by nature, the hymn is not bound to a historical context, in the sense that, say, a classical Tamil poem on kingship is. But the *bhakti* poem has the ability to migrate through space and time if the audience is willing to serve as a psychological vessel for its reincarnation; and this also happens with a total identification with the poet.

The most pervasive human emotion that shapes an intimate relationship between the devotee and his personal God is love, which assumes myriad aspects, among which 'filial love' and 'erotic love' become the most prominent. Defining Cuntaramūrti's poetry, Zvelebil (1973: 203) points out that it is 'close to erotic lyrics intimately connected with his innermost emotions . . . with the body of the Beloved'. On Mānikkavācakar's poems, he says: '[T]he love of the devotee which is central . . . is responded to by the object of worship with divine grace (*aṛuḻ*)' (ibid.: 204). Stylistically, the Tamil Śaiva hymns were projected onto the landscape of the *akam* genre of the ancient Tamil Caṅkam poetry communicating different types of love relationship. In some poems, the aspect of physical separation between the lovers that adds to their suffering becomes visibly pronounced. In other instances, the poet-saint takes on the form of a young maiden emotionally overwhelmed by the unconditional love for her hero. The impact of this emotion is undeniable when, against all conventions, she leaves her parental home in search for her lover. Ganesan illustrates in his essay that this intense love for God is often 'blind' insomuch as it involves extreme and harsh behaviour, including self-infliction and injury — something that can be seen as voicing approval of religious extremism. Another interesting trend of the Tamil Śiva-bhakti poems is the one in which the *bhakta* is portrayed as a slave or a servant (*toṇṭar*) of God. Some scholars opine that it was, in fact, the lord–servant relationship existing at the nucleus of the feudal society that became reduplicated into the deity–devotee relationship in *bhakti* tradition. The devotee very often addresses the deity as the lord or the master, placing himself in a relation of affective subordination to the lord-deity, in the position of a slave. The recurrent theme of *bhakti* poetry is 'bondage', understood as the highest objective in life, more desirable than wealth or liberation. Thus, viewed through the prism of *bhakti* ideology, the feudalistic hierarchy of the mediaeval period became idealised and romanticised. The slavery and servitude became sublimated through the emotional appeal of *bhakti* (Narayanan and Veluthat 1978: 51–54).

The Bhakti movement that originated in Tamil Nadu and spread to north India in the late mediaeval period. While the southern movement proclaimed its devotion to Śiva or Viṣṇu, the northern movement favoured Rāma or Kṛṣṇa, the incarnations of Viṣṇu. During the 14th–17th centuries CE, the northern stream of the Bhakti movement gathered around various saint-teachers, among whom Caitanya Mahāprabhu (1486–1533 CE), a saint from eastern India, initiated the Bengali Caitanya Vaiṣṇava tradition. Caitanya was regarded as the embodiment of a sublime erotic love (*śṛṅgāra*) between Lord Kṛṣṇa and his lover Rādhā, and his arrival on the earth was already prophesied in the *Bhāgavata Purāṇa*, the main scriptural authority of the Caitanya Vaiṣṇavism. He left no writings; therefore, the task of systematising the tradition was left to his disciples who came to be known as the Six Gosvāmins. Of these, Rūpa Gosvāmin (early 16th century CE) is considered to be the one who established the theoretical foundations of the Bengali Vaiṣṇavism. Rūpa Gosvāmin's contribution to the aestheticisation of *bhakti* is of enormous importance. He is the one who appropriated the entire structure and terminology of Bharata's *rasa* theory into his 'aesthetics of *bhakti*' or *bhakti-rasa* – a relatively new phenomenon in mediaeval India. As Donna M. Wulff (1986: 683) summarises: 'His [Rūpa Gosvāmin's] conception of devotion is a fundamentally aesthetic one, in which the development of *bhakti* toward the Lord involves a gradual refining and intensifying of emotion through repeated encounters with the eternal drama of Krishna and his close associates in Vraja'. Rūpa Gosvāmin's 'aesthetics of *bhakti*' was undoubtedly influenced by Abhinavagupta's theory of aesthetics expounded in the *Abhinavabhāratī*, a commentary on Bharata's *Nāṭyaśāstra*. Nevertheless, Rūpa introduced a number of important changes to both Abhinavagupta's and Bharata's theories of aesthetics. For this reason, it is plausible to claim that his conception of *bhakti-rasa* was a truly innovative contribution to the aesthetic transfiguration of the Bhakti movement.[17] The Sahajiyā Vaiṣṇava tradition that flourished in Bengal from 16th to 19th centuries CE is regarded as the tantric offshoot of the Bengali Caitanya Vaiṣṇavism.

The essay by Neal Delmonico and Aditi Nath Sarkar, 'Love Never Tasted Quite Like This Before: *Śṛṅgāra-rasa* in the Light of Two Texts from a Sahajiyā Vaiṣṇava Notebook' (Chapter 5, this volume), is dedicated to the Sahajiyā Vaiṣṇava tradition, which asserted itself more clearly against the institution of Brāhmaṇas as the ritual specialists and the 'corruption' of Buddhism. The Sahajiyā Vaiṣṇavism rejected the Brāhmaṇical caste system and intrinsic rigidity of the Brāhmaṇical forms of worship in favour of innate spontaneity (*sahaja*) which 'applied to a system of worship and belief in which the natural qualities of the senses should be used, not denied or suppressed' (Dimock 1991: 20–22). Cultivation of spontaneity was propagated through forms of worship that gave rise to the expansion of senses, expressed in dancing and singing. This performative type of worship was, in itself, a part of immediate communion with the divine 'which they [the Sahajiyās] have also conceptualised as the very essence (*rasa*) of devotion or love (*bhakti*)' (Feuerstein 1998: 234). The notion of *rasa* as the essence of religious devotion, in which the senses and the mind–body complex are totally immersed in Kṛṣṇa, constitutes the crux of Sahajiyā Vaiṣṇava tradition (Dimock 1991: 20–22). The essay by Delmonico and Sarkar shows to what extent the emotions experienced in *bhakti* contribute to the praxial modes of religious being-in-the-world. *Becoming emotion*, or in this context *becoming śṛṅgāra rasa*, carries with itself onto-behavioural signature directed towards the construction of the embodied and enacted mode of religious identity. In the Sahajiyā Vaiṣṇava tradition, a dynamic construction of religious identity is highlighted in the context of achieving a sublime, erotically charged emotion, personified by Rādhikā, Kṛṣṇa's lover. Sharing in Rādhikā's emotional experience of sublime erotic love for Kṛṣṇa plays a pioneering role in the development of a religious persona or identity, expressed metaphorically as the 'flowering bud identity' (*mañjarī-svarūpa*). Moreover, such an emotional involvement is a medium of psychophysical transfiguration, engendering a complete transformation of both body and consciousness resulting in the divinisation of the body–mind–emotions complex. This complete transfiguration is additionally enacted through tantric-*cum*-alchemical practices in which *rasa*, the immortal nectar, is produced and sustained.

Buddhism, Jainism, Pātañjala Yoga, and Śaiva Siddhānta

Buddhism[18] and Jainism[19] were the two almost contemporary Śrāmaṇic movements that originated in the Greater Magadha, the north-eastern region of India in around 5th–6th century BCE. Both systems' philosophical views had grown out of a reaction against the Brāhmaṇical forms of ritualism (especially against the animal sacrifices which they regarded as an example of cruelty) and against caste system.[20] Scholars generally agree that these two socio-religious movements were aware of each other's existence, a fact that can be attested by Buddha's polemics directed against Jainism (Bronkhorst 1993; Gombrich 1994). Although divergent from one another in their ontologies and epistemologies, they generally shared the same negative valuation of human existence, which they regarded as being exclusively the source of suffering (Pāli: *dukkha*, Sanskrit: *duḥkha*). In both systems, this 'suffering' constituted a negative affective dimension of human existence and, therefore, gave them a more pressing reason to pursue ascetic practice, thanks to which one could alleviate it. In Jainism, the suffering was a result of an activity (Pāli: *kamma*, Skt: *karma*), hence its strong emphasis on the practice of becoming motionless as the means to eradicate it. One of the earliest Jaina texts, the *Āyāraṃga* (Skt: *Ācārāṅga Sūtra* 1.3.1.3–4, in Bronkhorst 2007: 17–18) says: '[K]nowing that all this suffering is born from activity'; 'no action is found in him who has abandoned activity, the condition [for rebirth] originates on account of activity'. The Jainas visualised *karma* as a kind material substance, a moist dirt that 'flows in' (Pāli: *avassava*, Skt: *āsava*) on the soul and sticks to it. The path to liberation lay in expunging (Pāli: *nijjarā*, Skt: *nirjarā*) *karma* through asceticism that involved the total restraint of the body–mind–emotions complex. The Jaina stress on the ideal of inactivity had at its aim the wearing out of the old *karma* and the freedom from future *karma* which was accomplished by the suspension of all activities. As a result, says the *Cūla Dukkha-kkhandha Sutta*, '[this] wearing out of their *karma* [led] in turn to the wearing out of their suffering, that to the wearing out of sensation (*vedanā*), and that to the expunging of all suffering' (Gombrich 1994: 1089–90). This manner of coming to terms with the painful agony of human existence led the Jaina monks to undertake extreme ascetic practices, such as a ritual of death by fasting (*sallekhanā*), in which 'the monk abstains from food and prepares for death in a position which is as motionless as possible' (Bronkhorst 2007: 18). It seems, then, that in the Jaina rigorous practice, there was no place left for emotions, except maybe for the misery of suffering that one was told to expunge through practices that rested on the principle of inactivity. Upon investigating the ideological framework of early Buddhism, one comes to the conclusion that the inclination towards the pessimistic outlook of the 'Four Noble Truths' — (*a*) 'there is suffering'; (*b*) its 'cause'; (*c*) its 'cessation'; and (*d*) the 'path leading to cessation' — revealed by the Buddha emerged from the surrounding cultural milieu of ascetic denial. The first Noble Truth, 'there is suffering', constituted a powerful statement of the Buddha's teachings, especially when coupled with the view that the entire realm of becoming which is additionally conceived as impermanent (Pāli: *anicca*, Skt: *anitya*) and not the self (Pāli: *anatta*, Skt: *anātmā*) is situated within a dynamic philosophical framework of dependent origination (Pāli: *paṭccasamuppāda*, Skt: *pratītya-samutpāda*). Thus, as Richard F. Gombrich (1996: 33) remarks: '[W]hat gives the first noble truth its emotional force is its application to human life and the remainder that that always ends in death'. In accordance with the second Noble Truth, it was 'craving', 'thirst' (Pāli: *taṇhā*, Skt: *tṛṣṇā*) that was a necessarily affirmed primary cause of suffering. In the etiology of emotions expounded by the Buddha, 'thirst' was a primarily drive that stood behind all the passions, desires and emotional reactions caused by the sensory experience. The path to Enlightenment, thus, entailed the elimination of 'thirst'. However, unlike the case in Jainism, in Buddhism this elimination was not dependent on the total immobilisation of the body–mind–emotions complex, but rather on a set of psychological practices closely related to the 'virtue ethics'.

In his essay, 'The Buddhist Psychology of Emotions' (Chapter 6, this volume), Varun Kumar Tripathi makes a penetrating analysis of the concepts that contribute to our understanding of emotions in the Buddhist system of thought and practice. His analysis begins with the exposition of the three constituent roots of emotional disorders originating from 'thirst' or 'craving': (*a*) 'passion' or 'attachment' (*rāga*); (*b*) 'hatred' or 'repulsion' (*dveṣa*); and (*c*) 'delusion' (*moha*). These three are known as the 'three roots of evil' or 'the three fires' that have to be blown out (Pāli: *nibbāna*, Skt: *nirvāṇa*) like a flame. According to Gombrich (1996: 65; cf. Gombrich 2006), the Buddha introduced the metaphor of 'the three fires' of passion, hatred and delusion in the third sermon, the *Āditta-pariyāya* ('The way of putting things as being on fire'), as an open critique of the Brāhmaṇical orthopraxy of sacrifice. In discussing 'the three fires' metaphor, the Buddha claimed that everything, including the five sense faculties, the sense objects and the feelings, are aflame with passion, hatred and delusion (Gombrich 1996: 66). While the first two, 'passion' and 'hatred', belong to the affective dimension of human being, the third one, 'delusion' is a form of ignorance (Pāli: *avijjā*, Skt: *avidyā*) that belongs to the cognitive dimension. In the psychology rendered by early Buddhism, then, cognitions are collocated with emotions: 'you cannot see things straight because you are blinded by passion, and you allow your emotions to run you, because you do not see things as they are. The false view that feeds the emotions is that there is an eternal self' (Gombrich 2006: 67). As a result, says Gombrich (ibid.: 65), '*nibbāna* [concomitant with Enlightenment] is not a "thing" but the experience of being without greed, hatred and delusion'. Among the most important delusions enumerated in the Buddha's teachings are the following: (*a*) taking 'permanent as impermanent'; (*b*) taking 'impure as pure'; (*c*) taking 'suffering as pleasure'; and (*d*) taking 'non-self as self'. These delusions give rise to attachment, desire, repugnance, hatred, etc. The path leading to *nibbāna* is purely psychological insofar as it involves the cultivation of mindfulness on the essential impermanence of all things: 'by being aware of his own physique, feelings, states of mind and thoughts the Buddhist will cease to identify with them as his self, to introject a sense of ego into what are but transient phenomena, constantly coming into being and passing away' (ibid.). Through mindfulness arise non-attachment, non-repugnance, tolerance, patience, etc. Another interesting way of analysing emotions in the Buddhist context, as expounded by Tripathi, comes from 'virtue ethics' (mostly derived from the 5th-century-CE Buddhist scholar Buddhaghoṣa), which, indeed, is identical with a continued effort at self-development and annihilation of negative 'inflows' of emotional traits (*āsava*). The term *āsava* was taken by the Buddhists from Jainism to refer to the emotional predispositions of a person that were effectively cultivated or nourished by ignorance-*cum*-delusion. According to the logic of *paṭccasamuppāda*, the emotions were not fixed states but rather cultivated transitory moments derived from ignorance, and as such they could be de-cultivated through the process of nourishment of suitable counter-virtues. Therefore, certain emotional traits that were believed to have a cognitive component as well could be pragmatically utilised to develop suitable counter-virtues. For example, a person in whom passion (*rāga*) was predominant could begin to practise virtues, such as service or right faith. It was ascertained that these negative emotional traits could be removed through their replacement by positive emotional traits. The nourishment of suitable counter-virtues acted as a medicine which cured the 'illness' in a sense in which the negative emotional traits became completely dissolved. The culmination of this replacement resulted in the attainment of the highest ethical virtue which was compassion (*karuṇā*) and the highest intellectual virtue, i.e., wisdom (*prajñā*) for the Buddhists. In this view, the Buddhist practice can be thought of as representing the specific technique of spiritual psychotherapy, built upon working *with* emotions.

Emotions are utilised as practical tools for self-development. As Flood (2004: 130) remarks: 'For Buddhaghoṣa the development of asceticism is fundamentally linked to the development of Buddhist virtue as a means for controlling desire and the senses. Not only are the higher stages of the path built upon virtue, they can also be strengthened by the ascetic practices'. An enlightened one (*buddha*) is emotionally unperturbed. He still has emotions and feelings; however, unlike the ordinary person, he does not act upon them, but merely observes them with a calm, detached distance. He is the embodiment of ethical virtues of compassion and wisdom.

The essay by Andrea Acri, 'Between Impetus, Fear, and Disgust: Desire for Emancipation (*saṃvega*) from Early Buddhism to Pātañjala Yoga and Śaiva Siddhānta' (Chapter 7, this volume), shows yet a different way in which the dysfunctional character of emotions is practically employed in the spiritual practice. Acri collected evidence for the continuity of conceptual development of *saṃvega* from early non-Brāhmaṇical Buddhist and Jaina ascetic milieu to the Brāhmaṇical tradition of Pātañjala Yoga and early Śaiva Saiddhāntika tradition. In discussing this development, he points out that *saṃvega* was most probably borrowed by the Brāhmaṇical tradition of the Pātañjala Yoga and early Śaiva Siddhānta (the Śaiva tradition adhering to the key tenets of Vedic teachings and Brāhmaṇical orthodoxy) from Buddhist and Jaina sources. The conceptual development of *saṃvega* is intimately tied to the assignment of variant meanings expressed by it. Thus, in early Buddhism and Jainism, *saṃvega* appears to be the emotional stimulus that presupposes emotional perturbation, experienced as fear of or disgust for *saṃsāra* that ultimately results in a religious motivation that impels the desire for emancipation. The Pātañjala Yoga's semantic field of *saṃvega* was, to the great extent, formulated upon the earlier Buddhist and Jaina counterpart. While retaining the 'original' meaning of the term to denote a fear of or disgust for *saṃsāra*, the Pātañjala Yoga also ascribed to it different denotations, such as, 'intensity', employed in reference to the yogic practice. In conformity with this 'new' meaning, the *yogins* were arranged hierarchically according to the *saṃvega* or intensity of their yogic practice. Vācaspati Miśra (9th century CE), commentator on the *Yoga Sūtra*, goes much further in equating *saṃvega* with *vairāgya* in a sense of 'detachment' or 'passionlessness'. Thus, it, then, appears that *saṃvega*, coupled with the semantic field of *vairāgya*, contained a hint of qualified perfection as something exclusive or proper to an excellent *yogin*. From the premises thus investigated, Acri comes to the conclusion that the semantic field of *saṃvega* in the Pātañjala Yoga was considerably extended to include the inner quality of a *yogin* as well. In this connection, an assumed meaning attached to *saṃvega* was not exclusively limited to 'disgust' as a motivational impulse for spiritual emancipation, a meaning characteristic to early Buddhism and Jainism. The Śaiva Saiddhāntika tradition is yet another example in support of a conceptual development of *saṃvega* in which the construction of meaning is tied up with the principal Śaiva Saiddhāntika's presuppositions, such as the depletion of soul's impurities (*mala*) and the descent of Lord's grace. In this view, *saṃvega*, which implies a feeling of disgust for and fear of *saṃsāra* is concomitant with the Lord's grace and love directed toward a Śaiva adept. As Acri points out, the Śaiva Saiddhāntika tradition furnishes *saṃvega* with a theistic dimension that is absent in the early Buddhist and Jaina understanding of this specific term.

Aesthetics

The third tradition that facilitated emotional experience was Aesthetics (generally treated within a framework of the *rasa* theory), represented by the works of aesthetic theoreticians, such as Rājaśekhara (the 9th–10th-century-CE author of *Kāvyamīmāṃsā*), Bharata (the legendary author of *Nāṭyaśāstra*), Ānandavardhana (the 9th-century-CE author of *Dhvanyāloka*), Bhaṭṭa Lollaṭa (9th century CE), Śaṅkuka (9th century CE), and Bhaṭṭa Nāyaka (9th–10th century CE), to name a few. The most important among them was Abhinavagupta (10th–11th century CE), who consolidated and systematised the insights of his predecessors into the fully-fledged *rasa* theory, which is the best-known part of his philosophy. The *rasa* aesthetics developed partly under the influence of Sanskrit *kāvya*, 'poetic drama', which, in turn, constituted a vital centre of mediaeval courtly life in India (Ali 2006). In the context of theoretical background, the *rasa* aesthetics was an immediate successor of the 'cold' Brāhmaṇical legacy, characterised by emotional restraint that was driven by ascetic denial and renunciation of desire[21] (*vairāgya*). This mainstream spiritual ideal clearly influenced aestheticians in shaping their own particular form of 'aesthetic emotionalism' that allowed for the experience of 'refined' emotions (*rasa*s) that were clearly distinguished from the ordinary emotions (*bhāva*s) condemned by the Brāhmaṇical orthodoxy. Taking as their point of departure a troubled notion of 'desire', aesthetic theoreticians built on its basis the entire framework of 'aesthetic emotionalism'. Thus, even though 'desire' was vehemently denounced and declared as the source of 'evil' emotions in virtually all spiritual traditions of India rooted in the cultural milieu of asceticism, in the *rasa* aesthetics, on the contrary, 'desire' was made the basis of an argument for satisfactory aesthetic experience. Needless to say, the *rasa* aesthetics was not concerned with a real everyday world, in which the emotional factors often determined conative responses, but with a virtual, fictional world, set exclusively for the spectator's aesthetic 'savour' (*rasa*) or 'relish' (*āsvāda*). The spectator was partaking in fictional reality, a mere product of creative imagination which he was encouraged to embrace in his sympathetic emotional response (*sahṛdaya*). The consonance of the heart (*sahṛdaya*) was a primary quality of an ideal spectator (*prekṣaka, rasika*).[22] *Sahṛdaya* was characterised by inner openness that resulted in a sympathetic response (*hṛdayasaṃvāda*) to the work of art. This aesthetic sensibility required an acute, receptive observer, whose heart and mind were pure, resembling a mirror and, therefore, capable of receiving all the images reflected in them (*Abhinavabhāratī*, p. 37, in Gnoli 1968: xliv). Since its inception, however, the consonance of the heart was being closely related with an attitude of passionate-*cum*-emotional engagement in the world of art. An earliest example of a passionate spectator (*anurāgin*) is given in Bharata's *Nāṭyaśāstra* (27.53–55, in Goodwin 1998: xi) when he says: '[O]ne who feels happiness at the portrayal of happiness, grief at the portrayal of grief, misery at the portrayal of misery: such is the spectator of drama'. This passage shows that the possession of an 'emotional temperament' (ibid.) was the most necessary quality of an ideal spectator.[23] Similar emphasis on passionate character as an intrinsic feature of a good poet is given by Ānandavardhana in the *Dhvanyāloka* (3.42, ibid.: 11): 'If the poet is a man of passion (*śṛṅgārin*), the world of poetry is full of *rasa*. But if he is passionless (*vītarāga*), that world is devoid of *rasa* altogether'. Here again, 'passion' in the sense of emotional sensibility of a poet is a determining factor responsible for endowing the poetry or drama with an aesthetic delight (*rasa*). Moreover, the aestheticised passion (*śṛṅgāra rasa*) figured prominently among the eight *rasas* listed in the *Nāṭyaśāstra* (Gerow 1984). The *śṛṅgāra rasa* became a dominant theme of every court drama or literary work[24] from the 4th to 13th century CE. In the words of Daud Ali: 'By the eleventh century, the sentiment of *śṛṅgāra* had become so important that the king Bhoja (r. 1011–55) in his *summa poetica*, the *Śṛṅgāraprakāśa* or "Light on Passion", made it the basis of a superordinate experiential "sense of the self' which encompassed not only erotic love, but all the emotions and sentiments of an exalted life' (2006: 209; cf. Pollock 1998: 117–92). In this way, we can see how 'desire', avoided in the Brāhmaṇical orthopraxy, was relegated to the aesthetic domain where it assumed a prominent place.

The 'aesthetic emotionalism' promoted by the *rasa* aesthetics gave people — who were brought up in the emotionally 'cold' Brāhmaṇical environment, obsessed with taboos of purity and detachment — the possibility for emotional engagement in the aesthetic world, which, in turn, effected the 'transcendence of affective limitations' imposed by Brāhmaṇism, and allowed them to finally make a 'breakthrough into freedom-in-feeling' (Goodwin 1998: 8). The incorporation of 'passion' into the aesthetic framework of *rasa* aesthetics was not the only example of Brāhmaṇical influence on the development of the theory of aesthetics. On the other side of the spectrum, we see in the theories of aesthetics of the mediaeval period an attempt to reconcile with the Brāhmaṇical ideal of ascetic denial. As Robert E. Goodwin (1998) points out, *kāvya* (and also the theories of aesthetics that emerged from the Sanskrit *kāvya* milieu) was a reflection of the conflicting tendencies of the paradigmatic worldview of Indian culture, eternally torn between a desire for sensual pleasure that led to emotional fulfilment and an ascetic ideal of complete detachment from emotions (*vairāgya*).[25] He elaborates on it in the following words:

> [T]he *rasika* (the poet or spectator of the *kāvya*) was genuinely aware of a fundamental powerlessness vis-à-vis the transcendental authority figurally represented by the ascetic sage but diffusely present throughout Indian culture in *guru*-reverence, the *vairāgya* ideal, etc. There is a deep-rooted conviction in the Indian worldview that power and insight come only through self-restraint, i.e., through the denial of the emotional life (ibid.: 154).

Perhaps the best example of an attempt to reconcile this conflict between emotionalism and ascetic denial within the theory of aesthetics is the concept of *śānta rasa*. The *śānta rasa*, 'the state of tranquility or calmness' as the source of all other *rasa*s, was introduced by Abhinavagupta as the ninth *rasa* to a classical list of the eight *rasa*s. In holding that the culmination of aesthetic experience results in tranquility, Abhinavagupta, a tantric master *par excellence*, surprisingly echoes the views of the mainstream ascetic and Brāhmaṇical milieu of emotionlessness. However, his explanation shows greater originality, even if it still exhibits the same dialectical struggle for the reconciliation of opposites that takes place between affirmation of the emotional life and the *vairāgya* ideal. In his exposition of the *śānta rasa* (given in Chapter 7 of the *Abhinavabhāratī*), Abhinavagupta is very conscious of the *pūrvapakṣa* position held by Ānandavardhana: *śānti* that has *śama* (the absence of passion) as its *sthāyibhāva* (stable emotion) is an attitude of disgust (*nirveda*) towards worldly enjoyment; in the absence of passion which is the meaning of *tṛṣṇā-kṣaya-sukha* ('pleasure is [derived from] destruction of desire'), *śānti* is a state of complete emotional detachment (*vairāgya*) that leads to *mokṣa*. Abhinavagupta refutes the *pūrvapakṣa* position by showing that 'since the state *śānti*, as a goal of the *varāgin*, involves renunciation of emotional attachment, the *rasaśānta* would appear to be capable of being focused on any *bhāva* whatsoever, but a purely negative content, and would in effect become the emotional awareness of the absence of emotion!' (Gerow and Aklujkar 1972: 82). The only way to avoid the pitfalls of depriving *śānta rasa* of its emotional component was to relegate its *sthāyibhāva* to another ontological dimension. In this view, the *sthāyibhāva* of *śānta rasa* became *ātman* itself or, in other words, the aesthetic experience of the pure Self (Gerow 1994).

The essay by D. Venkat Rao, '*Moha Kāla*: Aporias of Emotion in Indian Reflective Traditions' (Chapter 8, this volume), shows the paradoxical nature of Indian traditions, eternally torn between the passions of the body and the invisible Self (*para*). Basing his exposition in a deconstructionist interpretation of the theories of aesthetics by Rājaśekhara, Ānandavardhana and Abhinavagupta, he argues that this paradox was the result of a close affiliation that existed between the *śāstra*- and the *kāvya-vāṅmaya* in a sense in which the two set the same goal — the release of the Self from the prison of embodiment — but they argued for different strategies to obtain it. His main argument rests on the premise that the *śāstra-vāṅmaya* was mostly concerned with the teaching about the 'double bind of existence': the pure Self (*para*) imprisoned in the body that constituted the aporia of cognitive–affective motifs in existence; nevertheless, it refrained from experiencing it, at least not to the extent that the *kāvya-vāṅmaya* did. If the *śāstra-vāṅmaya* taught us about the paradox of living in the double bind of existence, the *kāvya-vāṅmaya* induced the experiential flavour (*rasa*) of living in the chiasmatic antimonies of existence. Rao elaborates his argument by saying that the main innovation of Bharata's *rasa* theory lay in introducing the experiential flavour of *rasa* into the aporia of cognitive–affective motifs of existence derived from the *śāstra-vāṅmaya*. If it is said that the two strains of the individual body–emotions–feelings complex and the absolute Self met in the *kāvya-vāṅmaya*, it can be added that the theories of aesthetics formalised much of the tension that already existed in the *śāstra-vāṅmaya*. In this view, the poetic drama (*kāvya*), unlike the *śāstra*, was itself analogised to the body complex inhabited by the Self (*ātman*). In the latter part of his essay, Rao concentrates on showing that the emphasis on repletion of desire in the construction of *śānta rasa*, detected in the works of Ānandavardhana and Abhinavagupta, was a legacy of the Brāhmaṇical emotionlessness. Rao's argument, however, is framed in such a way as to formulate broad generalisations and simplifications that could be avoided by introducing, for example, the relation between the 'desire' and the 'ascetic denial' as forming an aporetic basis of the theories of aesthetics, to which we have referred briefly earlier. Still keeping in mind the bulk of the largely repetitive literature written on Indian aesthetics in the last few years, Rao's essay makes an original contribution to this topic.

The essay by Sharad Deshpande, 'Aesthetics of Despair' (Chapter 9, this volume), is primarily a critique of the ancient *rasa* theory. He argues that the ancient *rasa* aesthetics promoted specific emotions that are no longer adequate measures to structure contemporary aesthetic sensibilities, since they do not recognise what is peculiarly modern, namely the emotions of despair, banality and absurdity. Despair, argues Deshpande, is a dominant emotion in our contemporary times, and as such, it is a result of industrialism impelled by the pending forces of technology and globalisation. In this scattered reality of existential dislocation and fragmented self, despair becomes the existential position of the postmodern world. Despair is no longer a part of a cosmic understanding of our existence (an understanding available to ancient people of pre-modern times, i.e., Arjuna in the *Bhagavadgītā*),[26] but it is rather a sign of existential alienation fuelled by materialism and spiritual ignorance. In this view, Deshpande argues, that the critique of the ancient *rasa* aesthetics makes us recognise that the aesthetic emotions are structurally related to the socio-economic constituencies that appear to be mandatory in shaping the general psychology of historical communities.

Jadunath Sinha's Indian Psychology

Though it is true that psychology, unlike other branches of knowledge, did not reach the privileged status of an independent discipline in ancient India, it is also true that psychology, understood as an inquiry into the functioning of mind, occupied a central place in the Indian intellectual traditions. In the words of Swami Veda Bharati (2009):

> [I]f one were to ask: on which science the Indian sages have done the most thinking, short of meditation itself, the answer would be 'psychology', understanding mind. It has been done not by objective observations alone. The sages have used themselves as guinea pigs. They led their own mind through various states of sentiments, concentrations, visualisations, silent recitations and other interior devices and observed their effects on the mind.

Bharati makes an important point in asserting that the ancient sages of India derived their self-knowledge from introspection, from the shrewd observation of mental and emotional states. Moreover, this quest for self-knowledge was often deeply embedded in the quest for the 'given' elements in experience, i.e., 'there is suffering' and, consequently, in the pursuit of happiness that involved transformation of a person. The plethora of topics, such as consciousness, cognition, emotions, perceptions, feelings, affect, will, intention, desires, etc., which are understood by a prevailing scientific attitude of our times as necessary constituencies of 'psychology', were a part of a philosophical and religious inquiry in virtually all Indian systems of knowledge and practice. Jadunath Sinha's three volumes on *Indian Psychology* — volume 1: *Cognition* (1933), volume 2: *Emotion and Will* (1961), and volume 3: *Epistemology of Perception* (1969) — is the best example to illustrate the great extent to which the so-called psychological topics are present in the religious and philosophical systems of India. Sinha recognises the fact that Indian psychology is based on metaphysics that locates the potentialities of human existence in a broader, more universal scheme of things. In his monumental study, Sinha makes a survey of a vast plethora of Indian traditions, showing their keen engagement with various psychological themes that range from the 'dualism of the body and the Self' to the 'different degrees of consciousness and unconsciousness'; the exposition of the so-called 'three faults': desire, aversion and emotion; the 'distinction of the desire as conation'; and the 'pleasure and pain as feelings'; and ending with a comprehensive and explanatory list of the emotional states, such as: (*a*) depression (*viṣāda, avasāda, glāni, dainya*); (*b*) fear (*bhaya*) as the apprehension of fear or loss of a desired object; (*c*) anxiety (*udvega*) as a mental agitation governed by fear; and (*d*) non-egoism (*anahaṃkāra*) as the absence of longing (*spṛhā*) for the object of enjoyment, to name a few. Sinha's *Indian Psychology* is a fascinating account of the richness of psychological themes present in the Indian intellectual traditions. Its far-reaching scope is such that it is impossible to give a summary of its contents. The author does not concentrate on the historical development of psychological ideas that cannot be isolated from their metaphysical and philosophical content. This task remains a desideratum for future generations of scholars interested in the nature of emotions in India.

Notes

1. Hume was suspicious of the excessive resort to reason in philosophy, and in life generally; he made a strenuous defence of passion, leaving us the famous adage: 'Reason is and ought to be the slave of passion'. What, however, Hume meant by 'passion' were simply the feelings, sensations and base affects, in which 'thought' played an accidental role. Even though he reversed the Spinozian model of 'reason over emotion', he failed to provide any deeper insights into the nature of emotions. For these reasons, Hume's theory has been criticised by de Silva (2011) as 'shallow'.
2. Nussbaum insists on necessary and sufficient conditions in her study (2001: 62).
3. Especially in the early Upaniṣads, the connection between the cosmos and the human body is predominant. As has been demonstrated by Patrick Olivelle (1998: 24–27), the Vedic concept of connection (*bandhu*) employed in relation to the cosmic ritual spheres is relegated in the Upaniṣads to demonstrating the connection between the cosmic parts and the parts of the human body.
4. According to the *Nāradaparivrājaka Upaniṣad, upadeśa* 3, 'The ignorant man that is fond of this body, which is but a compound of flesh, blood, ill-smelling urine and offal, nerve, fat and bone, will be fond of hell too' (Khanna and Aiyar 2011: 133).
5. That such allegations may not be entirely justified have been demonstrated by Brian Black (2007: 95). According to him, 'Yājñavalkya is the first and the only Brahmin in the early Upaniṣads who advocates a life of mendicancy' (ibid.).
6. According to the *Vajrasūci Upaniṣad* (Khanna and Aiyar 2011: 105), freedom from emotion, malice, thirst for worldly objects, desire, delusion, pride, and egoism is a qualifying feature of the Brāhmaṇa.
7. Louis Dumont (1988) demonstrates how the caste-structured Brāhmaṇical society was organised in accordance with the legitimising principle of 'relative purity', founded on the distinction between the pure (represented by the Brāhmaṇas) and the impure (represented by the untouchables). In *upadeśa* 3 of the *Nāradaparivrājaka Upaniṣad*, an analogy between the impure body and the lowest strata of Brāhmaṇical society is even more dramatic:

'An idea of the body being the self should be strenuously abandoned, though all should perish. That love of the body is not fit to be felt by one intent upon his welfare, just as a low-caste woman eating dog's flesh is unfit to be touched' (Khanna and Aiyar 2011: 133).

8. According to the *Skanda Upaniṣad*, '[t]o free the mind from sensual objects is meditation. The subjugation of the senses is cleanings (*śauca*)' (Khanna and Aiyar 2011: 41).
9. For a discussion of the concept of 'disinterested witness' (*sākṣin*) in the Advaita Vedānta, see two excellent studies by Bina Gupta (1995, 1998).
10. The other four are Nyāya, Pūrva-Mīmāṃsā, Advaita Vedānta, and Vaiśeṣika.
11. For a detailed description of the *prakṛtilaya*, see Jacobsen (2002: 273–308).
12. *pariṇāma-tāpa-saṃskāra-duḥkhair guṇa-vṛtti-virodhāś ca duḥkham eva sarvaṃ vivekinaḥ.*
13. For the possible Brāhmaṇical influences on Buddhism, see Bronkhorst (2011).
14. In Sāṃkhya cosmology, *kṣobha* is the 'disturbance' caused by the proximity of *puruṣa* and *prakṛti* which disrupts the balance of *triguṇa* (*sattva*, *rajas* and *tamas*) in *prakṛti*. When this happens, the unmanifest *prakṛti* gives rise to the manifestation of the entire phenomenal existence, which is negatively evaluated as the source of suffering.
15. *Suṣumnā* is a subtle canal located along the spinal cord in the yogic body through which *kuṇḍalinī* rises.
16. For an exposition of the emotional dimension in the poetry of the Vaiṣṇava Āḷvārs, see Hardy (2001).
17. For a discussion on Rūpa Gosvāmin's 'aesthetics of *bhakti*', see Haberman (2001); Wulff (1986).
18. Buddhism was founded by Gautama Buddha who lived between 563 and 483 BCE.
19. The most famous representative of Jainism was Mahāvīra who lived probably between 540 and 468 BCE.
20. As Richard F. Gombrich (2006: 68–70) suggests, the greatest innovation of early Buddhism was the implementation of the 'ethic of intention', in which the moral valuation of an act was dependent solely on the intention behind the act; 'this single move overturns Brāhmaṇical, caste-bound ethics. For the intention of a Brahmin cannot be claimed to be ethically of quite a different kind from the intention of an outcaste . . . The true Brahmin, said the Buddha, was the man of universalistic values as gentleness and compassion. An outcast, man with the corresponding vices'. As a matter of fact, says Buddha, 'Not by birth is one a Brahmin or an outcaste, but by deeds (Pāli: *kamma*, Skt: *karma*)' (ibid.).
21. 'Desire' is, in this context, a generic category that includes closely related terms, such as *kāma*, *rāga* and *tṛṣṇā*. A future study is needed to examine the distinctions and similarities between these distinct concepts.

22. Among other characteristics of an ideal spectator delineated by Abhinavagupta was the spectator's capacity to experience the 'universalised' emotions (*sādhāraṇīkaraṇa*), unaffected by the constraints of individuality. The spectator experiencing the 'universalised' emotions remained unaffected, as it were, by the limiting agents of time, space and the knowing subject. To illustrate this argument, we might turn to the following example. In the ordinary reality, a potentially dangerous situation, such as an approaching tiger, causes fear and anxiety in the subject that shape intervention-decisions, in this case 'running away'. However, in the fictional reality created by art, the arousal of emotions, such as fear, would not urge an impulse to run away, even though the emotions experienced at that time might affect bodily reactions (sweat, horripilation). It happens so because the emotion of fear arising in the spectator viewing a play is not delimited by the restriction of time, space and subjectivity. This disengagement from the bounds of spatio-temporal limitations and the confines of individuality that results in the 'universalisation' of emotions directly leads to the aesthetic experience. Another factor that played a crucial role in 'aesthetic emotionalism' was 'identification' (*tanmayībhāva*) with the emotional situation depicted by the *dramatis personae* that was so strong that the distinction between the experiencing subject and the experienced object became blurred. Such a complete emotional involvement on the part of the spectator facilitated aesthetic experience *sui generis* that culminated in the savouring of aesthetic delight (*rasāsvāda*). See also Gerow (1984, 1994); Bilimoria (2013a).
23. In contrast, a passage from the *Nāradaparivrājaka Upaniṣad, upadeśa* 4, is the apotheosis of emotional detachment: '[E]ven should he witness or hear of the happiness or grief of his wife, brother, son and other relatives, he should not be affected thereby. He should abandon all joy and sorrow' (Khanna and Aiyar 2011: 138).
24. *Kāvya* refers to the court poetry dominated by one particular theme, that of erotic love conveyed by the aesthetic term, *śṛṅgāra* (Goodwin 1998: 9).
25. Goodwin (1998: xvi–vii) says that the hero of the *kāvya* myth, which 'functions as a narrative paradigm of a worldview, depicting essential areas of conflict', is, above all, 'the portrait of the sentimental hero in his struggle with cultural norms that attach a low value to emotion and individual autonomy'.
26. In the ancient times, negative emotions, such as despair (*viṣāda*), gave rise to ethical virtues. In a famous passage of the *Bhagavadgītā* (1.29), Arjuna experiences grief (*śoka*) and laments over the death of his relatives. Enveloped in despair (*viṣāda*), he drops his arrow and bow. The experience of despair makes his mind torpid and drains up all his senses. Arjuna's pitiable emotional state is a classic example of the psychology of affect. The intrinsic complexity of *viṣāda* carries within itself the meanings of grief, sorrow, distress, suffering, and despair. This negative emotional

state is successfully overcome by a quasi-*ethical virtue* of courage when Kṛṣṇa instructs Arjuna about the universality of *dharma*. In this process, a deeply subjective emotional state of grief and despair is replaced by the quasi-*ethical virtue* of courage. In this way, courage, which is precisely the responsibility for 'living the life according to the universal law of *dharma*', assumes a greater moral importance than the grief and despair of an agent coping with intolerable loss.

References

Primary Sources

Pratyabhijñāhṛdayam of Kṣemarāja: Singh, Jaideva (trans.). 1977. *Pratyabhijñāhṛdayam*. Delhi: Motilal Banarsidass.

Śrīmadbhagavadgītā:

Rao Shastri, Shakuntala (trans.). 1959. *The Bhagavadgita*. New York: East West Institute.

Upaniṣads:

Khanna, Madhu (ed.) and K. Narayanasvami Aiyar (trans.). 2011. *Thirty Minor Upaniṣads*. Delhi: Tantra Foundation.

Olivelle, Patrick (trans.). 1998. *The Early Upaniṣads: Annotated Text and Translation*. New York: Oxford University Press.

Secondary Works

Ali, Daud. 2006. *Courtly Culture and Political Life in Early Medieval India*. Cambridge: Cambridge University Press.

Allen, Prudence. 2002. *The Concept of Woman: The Early Humanistic Reformation, 1250–1500*, vol. 2. Grand Rapids, MI, and Cambridge: William B. Eerdmans Publishing Co.

Āraṇya, Swami Hariharānanda. 1963. *Yoga Philosophy of Patañjali*, trans. P. N. Mukerji. Calcutta: University of Calcutta.

Bentley, Jerry H. 1993. *Old World Encounters: Cross-cultural Contacts and Exchanges in Pre-Modern Times*. New York: Oxford University Press.

Biardeau, Madeleine. 1989. *Hinduism: The Anthropology of Civilization*. Delhi: Oxford University Press.

Bilimoria, Purushottama. 1995. 'Ethics of Emotions: Some Indian Reflections', in Joel Marks and Ames T. Roger (eds), *Emotions in Asian Thought: A Dialogue in Comparative Philosophy, With a Discussion by Robert C. Solomon*, pp. 65–91. Albany: State University of New York Press.

———. 2004. 'Perturbations of Desire: Emotions Disarming Morality in the "Great Song" of the Mahābhārata', in Robert C. Solomon (ed.), *Thinking About Feeling: Contemporary Philosophers on Emotions*, pp. 214–32. New York: Oxford University Press.

Bilimoria, Purushottama. 2012a. 'Of Grief and Mourning: Thinking a Feeling, Back to Robert Solomon', in Kathleen Marie Higgins and David Sherman (eds), *Passion, Death and Spirituality: The Philosophy of Robert C. Solomon*, Sophia Studies in Cross-cultural Philosophy of Traditions and Cultures, pp. 149–74. Dordrecht: Springer.

——. 2012b. 'Why is there Nothing rather than Something? An Essay in the Comparative Metaphysics of Nonbeing', *Sophia: International Journal of Philosophy and Traditions*, 51(4): 509–30.

——. 2013a. 'Grief and Dharma: Suffering, Empathy and Moral Imagination', *Studies in Humanities and Social Sciences*, Inter University Centre for Humanities and Social Sciences, Indian Institute of Advanced Study, Shimla, 20(1): 33–54.

——. 2013b. 'Virtue and Emotions in Classical Indian Thinking', in Stan van Hooft, Nafsika Athanassoulis, Jason Kawall, Justin Oakley, Nicole Saunders, and Liezl Van Zyl (eds), *The Handbook on Virtue Ethics*, pp. 294–305. Durham: Acumen Press.

Black, Brian. 2007. *The Character of the Self in Ancient India*. New York: State University of New York Press.

Bronkhorst, Johannes. 1993. *The Two Traditions of Meditation in Ancient India*. Delhi: Motilal Banarsidass.

——. 2007. *Greater Magadha: Studies in the Culture of Early India*. Leiden and Boston: E. J. Brill.

——. 2011. *Buddhism in the Shadow of Brahmanism*. Leiden and Boston: E.J. Brill.

Burley, Mikel. 2007. *Classical Sāṃkhya and Yoga: An Indian Metaphysics of Experience*. London and New York: Routledge.

Calhoun, Cheshire. 1990. 'Cognitive Emotions?' in Robert C. Solomon and Cheshire Calhoun (eds), *What is an Emotion: Classic Readings in Philosophical Psychology*, pp. 327–42. New York: Oxford University Press.

——. 2004. 'Subjectivity and Emotion', in Robert C. Solomon (ed.), *Thinking about Feeling: Contemporary Philosophers on Emotions*, pp. 107–24. New York: Oxford University Press.

Corrigan, John (ed.). 2008. *The Oxford Handbook of Religion and Emotion*. Oxford: Oxford University Press.

Cutler, Norman. 1987. *Songs of Experience: The Poetics of Tamil Devotion*. Bloomington, IN: Indiana University Press.

Dasgupta, S. N. 1979. *Yoga Philosophy in Relation to Other Systems of Indian Thought*. Delhi: Motilal Banarsidass.

de Silva, Padmasiri. 1995. 'Theoretical Perspectives on Emotions in Early Buddhism', in Joel Marks and Ames T. Roger (eds), *Emotions in Asian Thought: A Dialogue in Comparative Philosophy, With a Discussion by Robert C. Solomon*, pp. 109-20. Albany: State University of New York Press.

——. 2011. 'Thinking and Feeling: A Buddhist Perspective', *Sophia*, 50(2): 253–63.

Dimock, C. Edward.1991. *The Place of the Hidden Moon: Erotic Mysticism in the Vaiṣṇava-Sahajīya Cult of Bengal*. Delhi: Motilal Banarsidass.

Dumont, Louis. 1988. *Homo Hierarchicus*. Delhi: Vikas Publishing House Pvt. Ltd.
Feuerstein, Georg. 1989. *Yoga: The Technology of Ecstasy*. Los Angeles: Tarcher.
Feuerstein, Georg. 1998. *Tantra: The Path of Ecstasy*. Boston and London: Shambala.
Flood, Gavin. 2004. *The Ascetic Self: Subjectivity, Memory and Tradition*. Cambridge: Cambridge University Press.
——. 2006. *The Tantric Body: The Secret Tradition of Hindu Religion*. London and New York: I. B. Tauris.
Gerow, Edwin. 1984. 'Sanskrit Dramatic Theories and Kālidāsa's Plays', in Barbara Stoler Miller (ed.), *Theater of Memory: The Plays of Kālidasa*, trans. Edwin Gerow, David Gitomer and Barbara Stoler Miller, pp. 42–62. New York: Columbia University Press.
——. 1994. 'Abhinavagupta's Aesthetics as a Speculative Paradigm', *Journal of the American Oriental Society*, 114(2): 186–208.
Gerow, Edwin and Ashok Aklujkar. 1972. 'On Śānta Rasa in Sanskrit Poetics', review of *Śāntarasa and Abhinavagupta's Philosophy of Aesthetics* by J. L. Masson and M. V. Pathwardhan, *Journal of the American Oriental Society*, 92(1): 80–87.
Gnoli, Raniero. 1968. *An Aesthetic Experience According to Abhinavagupta*. Varanasi: Chowkhamba Publications.
Gombrich, Richard F. 1994. 'The Buddha and the Jains: A Reply to Professor Bronkhorst', *Asiatische Studien Etudes Asiatiques*, 48(4): 1069–96.
——. 1996. *How Buddhism Begun: The Conditioned Genesis of the Early Teachings*. London and Atlantic Highlands, NJ: Athlone.
——. 2006. *Theravāda Buddhism: A Social History from Ancient Benares to Modern Colombo*. London and New York: Routledge.
Goodwin, E. Robert. 1998. *The Playworld of Sanskrit Drama*. Delhi: Motilal Banarsidass.
Green, O. H. 1992. *The Emotions*. Dordrecht: Kluwer Academic Publishers.
Gupta, Bina. 1995. *Perceiving in Advaita Vedānta: Epistemological Analysis and Interpretation*. Delhi: Motilal Banarasidass.
——. 1998. *The Disinterested Witness: A Fragment of Advaita Vedānta Phenomenology*. Evanston, IL: Northwestern University Press.
Gustafson, Donald. 1989. 'Grief', *Noûs*, 23(4): 457–79.
Haberman, L. David. 2001. *Acting as a Way of Salvation: A Study of Rāgāṇugā Bhakti Sādhana*. Delhi: Motilal Banarsidass.
Hardy, Friedhelm. 2001. *Viraha-Bhakti: The Early History of Kṛṣṇa Devotion in South India*. Delhi: Oxford University Press.
Harris, G. Anthony. 2008. 'Obtaining Grace: Locating the Origins of a Tamil Śaiva Precept'. PhD Dissertation, University of Texas at Austin.
Higgins, Kathleen Marie. 2011. 'Introduction: Robert C. Solomon and the Spiritual Passions', *Sophia*, 50(2): 239–45.
Holdrege, Barbara A. 1998. 'Body Connections: Hindu Discourses of the Body and the Study of Religion', *International Journal of Hindu Studies*, 2(3): 341–86.
Jacobsen, Knut A. 2002. *Prakṛti in Sāṃkhya-Yoga: Material Principle, Religious Experience, Ethical Implications*. Delhi: Motilal Banarsidass.

Kant, Immanuel. 1996. *The Metaphysics of Morals.* Cambridge: Cambridge University Press.

Krishnan, Y. 1989. 'Doctrines of Karma, of Mokṣa, of Niṣkāma-karma and the Ideal of Bodhisatva', *Annals of Bhandarkar Oriental Research Institute*, 70(1/4): 163–80.

Larson, Gerald James. 2001. *Classical Sāṃkhya: An Interpretation of Its History and Meaning.* Delhi: Motilal Banarsidass.

Lynch, Owen M. (ed.). 1990. *Divine Passions: The Social Construction of Emotions in India.* Delhi: Oxford University Press.

Marks, Joel. 1995. 'Emotions in Western Thought: Some Background for a Comparative Dialogue', in Joel Marks and Ames T. Roger (eds), *Emotions in Asian Thought: A Dialogue in Comparative Philosophy, With a Discussion by Robert C. Solomon*, pp. 1–38. Albany: State University of New York Press.

McDaniel, June. 1989. *The Madness of the Saints: Ecstatic Religion in Bengal.* Chicago: Chicago University Press.

——. 2008. 'Hinduism', in John Corrigan (ed.), *The Oxford Handbook of Religion and Emotion*, pp. 51–72. Oxford: Oxford University Press.

Michaels, Axel and Christoph Wulf (eds). 2012. *Emotions in Rituals and Performances.* Delhi: Routledge.

Moller, Dan. 2007. 'Love and Death', *Journal of Philosophy*, 104: 301–16.

Narayanan, M. G. S. and Kesavan Veluthat. 1978. 'Bhakti Movement in South India', in S. C. Malik (ed.), *Indian Movements: Some Aspects of Dissent Protests and Reform*, pp. 33–66. Simla: Indian Institute of Advanced Study.

Nash, Ronald Alan. 1989. 'Cognitive Theories of Emotion', *Noûs* 23(4): 481–504.

Nussbaum, Martha. 2001. *Upheavals of Thought: The Intelligence of Emotions.* Cambridge: Cambridge University Press.

Padoux, Andre. 1990. *Vāc: The Concept of the Word in Selected Hindu Tantras.* Delhi: Sat Guru Publications.

Pechilis Prentiss, Karen. 1999. *The Embodiment of Bhakti.* New York: Oxford University Press.

Peterson, V. Indira. 1991. *Poems to Śiva: The Hymns of the Tamil Saints.* Delhi: Motilal Banarsidass.

Plato, 2002. *The Five Dialogues: Euthypro, Apology, Citro, Meno, Phaedo*, trans. G. M. A. Grube, Indianapolis: Hacket Publishing Company Inc.

Pollock, Sheldon. 1998. 'Bhoja's *Śṛṅgāraprakāśa* and the Problem of *Rasa*: A Historical Introduction and Annotated Translation', *Asiatische Studien*, 52(1): 117–92.

Potter, Karl. 2005. 'Indian Philosophy', in Donald M. Borchert (ed.), *Encyclopedia of Philosophy*, vol. 4, pp. 623–34. Detroit and New York: Thomson Gale.

Prinz, Jeese. 2003. 'Emotion, Psychosemantics, and Embodied Appraisals', *Royal Institute of Philosophy Supplement*, 52(1): 69–86.

Rao, K. L. Seshagiri (ed.). 2011. *Encyclopedia of Hinduism.* Delhi: India Heritage Research Foundation and Rupa & Co.

Sanderson, Alexis. 1985. 'Purity and Power among the Brahmans of Kashmir', in Michael Carritthers, Steven Collins and Steven Lukes (eds), *The Category of the Person: Anthropology, Philosophy, History*, pp. 190–216. Cambridge: Cambridge University Press.
Solomon, Robert C. 1995. 'The Cross-cultural Comparison of Emotion', in Joel Marks and Roger T. Ames (eds), *Emotions in Asian Thought: A Dialogue in Comparative Philosophy, With a Discussion by Robert C. Solomon*, pp. 253–94. Albany: State University of New York Press.
——. 2002a. 'Reasons for Love', *Journal for the Theory of Social Behaviour*, 32(1): 1–28.
——. 2002b. Review of *Upheavals of Thought: The Intelligence of Emotion* by Martha Nussbaum, *Mind*, 111(444): 897–901.
——. (ed). 2004. *Thinking about Feeling: Contemporary Philosophers on Emotions*. New York: Oxford University Press.
Sinha, Jadunath. 2008. *Indian Psychology*, 3 vols. Delhi: Motilal Banarsidass.
Sovatsky, Stuart. 2014. *Advanced Spiritual Intimacy: The Yoga of Deep Tantric Sensuality*. Rochester, Vermont: Inner Traditions & Destiny Books.
Stocker, Michael. 2004. 'Some Considerations about Intellectual Desire and Emotion', in Robert C. Solomon (ed.), *Thinking About Feeling: Contemporary Philosophers on Emotions*, pp. 135–48. New York: Oxford University Press.
Stocker, Michael and Elizabeth Hegeman. 1996. *Valuing Emotions*, Cambridge Studies in Philosophy. Cambridge, MA: Cambridge University Press.
Tiwari, Ramanand. 1985. *Secular, Social and Ethical Values in the Upanishads*. Delhi: Agam Kala Prakashan.
Tola, Fernando and Carmen Dragonetti. 1987. *The Yogasūtras of Patañjali: On Concentration of Mind*. Delhi: Motilal Banarsidass.
Torella, Raffaele. 2011. *The Philosophical Traditions of India: An Appraisal*. Varanasi: Indica Books.
Witz, Klaus. 1998. *The Supreme Wisdom of the Upaniṣads*. Delhi: Motilal Banarsidass.
Wulff, M. Donna.1986. 'Religion in a New Mode: The Convergence of the Aesthetic and the Religious in Medieval India', *Journal of the American Academy of Religion*, 54(2): 673–88.
Veda Bharati, Swami. 2009. 'Mind-field: The Playground of Gods', http://ahymsin.org/main/swami-veda-bharati/mind-field.html (accessed 20 January 2014).
Yocum, E. Glenn. 1973. 'Shrines, Shamanism, and Love Poetry: Elements in the Emergence of Popular Tamil Bhakti', *Journal of the American Academy of Religion*, 41(1): 3–17.
Zaehner, R. C. 1962. *Hinduism*. London: Oxford University Press.
Zalta, Edward N. (ed.). 2012. *The Stanford Encyclopedia of Philosophy*,
http://plato.stanford.edu/entries/emotions-17th18th (accessed 19 May 2013).
Zvelebil, Kamil. 1973. *The Smile of Murugan: On Tamil Literature of South India*. Leiden: E. J. Brill.

PART I

Tantrism

1

Passions and Emotions in the Indian Philosophical–Religious Traditions

RAFFAELE TORELLA*

Anyone enquiring into the status of passions and emotions in traditional India is surprised to find that the subcontinent, so avid for analysis in every field of knowledge, has never produced any science similar to Western psychology. As a first response, what comes to mind is the gymnosophist's answer to Socrates who was questioning him about man's nature: 'But how can we deal with the human before knowing about the divine?' Too busy contemplating the fearful symmetries of the supernatural, were the Indians consequently not particularly interested in untangling the developments of human behaviour? The absence of psychology, as an independent discipline at least, appears all the more surprising if one considers that the Indians have never lacked a capacity either for introspection or for cataloguing. With the former, they have achieved results never surpassed in research on the two realities which, since they naturally coincide with the observer–subject, lend themselves the more readily to eluding observation. I refer to breathing, the breath of life, literally dissected by yoga, and language, the subject of the most discerning analysis that humankind has ever devoted to this fundamental and pervasive reality. The Indians have never been in short supply with regard to their cataloguing ability and, on the contrary, have raised it to even maniacal levels, so that it is rampant in all scientific, aesthetic, philosophical, and religious literature, and is often one of the prime reasons for making its reading so arduous. The first great philosophical system to develop from Upaniṣadic and epic speculation was given the name Sāṃkhya, meaning (related to) 'enumeration', 'listing'.

It is in fact in philosophical texts, starting precisely from those of the Sāṃkhya school, that we should look for a *thesaurus* of human passions and emotions, analysed and classified with obstinate accuracy and an absolutely neutral and scientific grasp, as in the classical texts of Vaiśeṣika, or else with a mixture of coldness and preoccupation, as often occurs in Buddhist and Jaina texts that describe them, keeping their gaze fixed on the meditating devotee who might be threatened by them. But the researcher into Indian passions and emotions will soon discover with equal surprise that he must delve into treatises on aesthetics and rhetoric perhaps even more than into philosophical and religious texts. Risking here, moreover, to lose both the reader and himself in labyrinthine systematics, in his investigation of the essence of poetry and the theatre, the Indian rhetorician must first tackle the basic human passions/emotions (*bhāva*), which the poet or actor must portray so that the reader or spectator can savour their essence, finally liberated from the restrictions of the individual ego.

If, now satiated by descriptions — albeit often of great precision — the researcher of passions wishes to discover how they are assessed in the Indian world, things become even more complicated. Passions are differently assessed according to the subject's social position — his belonging to one or another of the four basic stages of life (*āśrama*) — and according to caste. While anger and disdain (*manyu*), as Minoru Hara (2001) has demonstrated in one of his seminal lexical analyses, are generally reprehensible in the man of the street, they are even obligatory for those belonging to the *kṣatriya* class of sovereigns and warriors.

In examining the philosophical–religious texts of Hinduism on such themes, we must first be aware that the greater part of them comes from the Brāhmaṇical elite, which thus seeks to envelop the entire Indian reality in its coils. Our first impression after observing the central stream of Brāhmaṇical thought is of a considerable integration — mostly absent in the West[1] — of the individual's physical, psychic–emotive and intellectual dimensions. A single nature runs through them uninterruptedly: it passes fluidly from one level to another, gradually including the animal and vegetal worlds. In the words of Louis Dumont:

> *Il n'y a pas de coupure entre l'homme et la nature. La chose est sensible dans le vêtement — le corps s'enroule dans une pièce d'étoffe — dans la simplicité de la*

vie matérielle et la forme des objets d'usage courant. En musique, l'heure de la journée prescrit le ton sentimental de la mélodie: impossible d'être nostalgique le matin et gai le soir.

There is no hiatus between man and nature. This is appreciable in clothing — the body wraps itself in a piece of cloth — or in the simplicity of material life and the form of objects we use every day. In music, the time of day prescribes the sentimental mode of the melody: impossible to be nostalgic in the morning and gay in the evening (1975: 30, in Bouiller and Tarabout 2002: 18).

Albeit deeply rooted in common opinion, such a view is, however, substantially a blunder: far from being absent, dualism is merely radicalised to the extreme. In Sāṃkhya, for example — and Sāṃkhya with its cosmogenesis remains the model for much of the later Brāhmaṇical speculation (cf. Torella 1999) — an apparently unbridgeable abyss separates the world of nature (*prakṛti*), which comprises the body, senses, passions, and mental functions that form an integrated whole, from the world of the spirit, which alone is responsible for striking the spark of consciousness, without which the continual gross activity of the sensorial faculties, of the inner sense, of the I-notion, and the intellect could never finally shine as 'knowledge'. An integrated monism of body, senses, emotions, and intellectual faculties consequently exists, but leaves out that very principle that alone can give meaning to the whole. The goal is not the final achievement of greater unity, but the recognition of an irremediable otherness, having reached which, the psyche–body–nature complex progressively withdraws from the scene, 'like a dancer', recounts a famous stanza of the *Sāṃkhyakārikā* (59), 'having presented her performance to her audience', leaving the spirit to shine in undisturbed solitude. The material, emotional and psychic universe thus comes into existence solely so that the soul can recognise itself as being foreign to it and isolate itself in its own self-identity. Even this recognition is made possible by the action of *prakṛti* itself, which thus finds in its own negation its ultimate reason for existence.

Based on such a premise, two alternatives are possible: to accentuate the integrated and unitary aspect of the body–senses–psyche–intellect complex, or to concentrate on the otherness of the knower principle, the 'spirit'. Brāhmaṇical philosophy — and, *mutatis mutandis*, Jaina and even Buddhist philosophy, despite a programmatic rejection of any substantiality of the subject — decidedly takes the second alternative, the option that we might, somewhat roughly, term 'ascetic'. The whole fermenting energy potential of human drives, including the intellectual, which the West would place on the other side, is seen as troublesome ballast from which man must free himself. Solely over the desert of body and passions can the moon of the spirit rise. An incurable ontological weakness undermines the roots of whatever is tinted with pleasure or sorrow, or arouses desire or aversion. The whole human adventure may thus take on a fainter outline — or sometimes a more sombre one, as in the scenario depicted by the Vedāntin Sureśvara in his sub-commentary on the *Taittirīya Upaniṣad*, which explores man's wretchedness right from his mother's uterus, a place of ineffable delights for the West:

> *anubhūtāḥ purāsahyā mayā marmacchido 'sakṛt* |
> *karambhavālukās taptā yā dahanty aśubhāśayān* ||
> *jāṭharānalasaṃtaptāḥ pittākhyarasavipluṣaḥ* |
> *garbhāśaye nimagnaṃ tā dahanty atibhṛśaṃ tu mām* ||
> *audaryakṛmivaktrāṇi kūṭaśālmalikaṇṭakaiḥ* |
> *tulyāni vitudanty ārtaṃ pārśvāsthikrakacārditam* ||
> *garbhe durgandhabhūyiṣṭhe jāṭharāgnipradīpite* |
> *duḥkhaṃ mayāptaṃ yat tasmāt kanīyaḥ kumbhipākajam* ||

> Having entered this uterus [the foetus is speaking], I am suffering unbearable, devastating pain. Several times in past existences I have fallen into the scorching sands of hell that burn wicked souls, but these drops of bile superheated by the fires of digestion make my tender body suffer much more. Stomach worms with mouths as sharp as thorns torture me, already tortured enough by the bones of my mother's body that cut into me on all sides. The miseries of the Kumbhipāka hell are nothing compared to the tortures I experience in the uterus, full of the most disgusting miasmas that burn owing to the stomach's digestive fire (*Taittirīyopaniṣadbhāṣyavārttikam, Brahmavallī, prathamaḥ khaṇḍaḥ*, 191–94, in *Taittirīyopaniṣadbhāṣyavārttika* 1911: 86).[2]

Conception was achieved during a rude nocturnal encounter, all heaviness and no grace:

> *nijāvidyāmahājālasaṃvītadhiṣaṇaḥ pumān* |
> *mohotthānalakāmākhyavaḍiśāpahṛtāśayaḥ* ||
> *tamasā kāmaśārṅgeṇa saṃkalpākarṣaṇena saḥ* |
> *rāgākhyaviṣalepena tāḍito viṣayeṣunā* ||
> *grahāviṣṭa ivānīśaś codito janyakarmaṇā* |
> *yoṣidagniṃ pataty āśu jyotirlobhāt pataṅgavat* ||

> The mind enveloped in the suffocating coils of innate ignorance, the heart dragged away by the hook of insatiable lust born of obnubilation, the father of the yet unborn is assailed by darkness, pierced by the arrows of the objects of the senses poisoned by passion and shot by the bow of desire drawn by his resolution. Deprived of all control as though a demon possessed him, driven by the karma of the creature yet unborn, [the father to be] plunges rapidly into the woman's fire, like a moth avid for the flame (*Taittirīyopaniṣadbhāṣyavārttikam, Brahmavallī, prathamaḥ khaṇḍaḥ*, 166–68, ibid.: 81).

In a manner no less atrocious than life in the uterus is presented the moment of birth and infancy and youth as they come along — tormented by sexual desire, blinded alternately by one passion or another, by love and anger — up to the rabid impotence of old age. The epilogue that follows is not exactly an apotheosis:

> *hā kānte hā dhane putra krandamānaḥ sudāruṇam |*
> *maṇḍūka iva sarpeṇa gīryate mṛtyunā naraḥ || . . .*
> *viśrāmavṛkṣasadṛśaḥ khalu jīvalokaḥ ||*
> *sāyaṃ sāyaṃ vāsavṛkṣaṃ sametāḥ*
> *prataḥ pratas tena tena prayānti |*
> *tyaktvānyonyaṃ taṃ ca vṛkṣaṃ vihaṅgāḥ*
> *yadvat tadvaj jñātayo 'jñātayaś ca ||*
> *mṛtibījaṃ bhavej janma janmabījaṃ tathā mṛtiḥ |*
> *ghaṭiyantravad aśrānto bambhramīty aniśaṃ naraḥ ||*

> While weeping bitterly over his beloved, his wealth and the son he has to leave, the man is swallowed up by death, like a toad by a serpent . . . This world of mortals is indeed like a tree used for shelter. One evening birds perch on it in search of a haven for the night and next morning leave it and fly away each wherever he will. Similarly, men encounter, for a brief time, friends or strangers in this world and then disperse. Birth leads to death and death to birth: thus, men ceaselessly circle forever, like the wheel that draws water from the well (*Taittirīyopaniṣadbhāṣyavārttikam, Brahmavallī, prathamaḥ khaṇḍaḥ*, 212–21, ibid.: 89–90).

Niṣkāma-karma ('Action without Desire') of the *Bhagavadgītā* versus *Niṣkarma-kāma* ('Desire without Action'[3]) of Non-Dualist Śaivism

The element around which the whole body-senses-emotions constellation seems to turn is attachment or desire. In any final analysis, it is from its grip that man must free himself in order to rise toward the *ātman* or *nirvāṇa*. Even a text certainly not focused on asceticism, like the *Bhagavadgītā*, does not fail to launch a lengthy, venomous attack against desire:

> *Arjuna uvāca:*
>
> *atha kena prayukto 'yaṃ pāpaṃ carati puruṣaḥ |*
> *anicchann api vārṣṇeya balād iva niyojitaḥ ||*
> *śrībhagavān uvāca:*
> *kāma eṣa krodha eṣa rajoguṇasamudbhavaḥ |*
> *mahāśāno mahāpāpmā viddhy enam iha vairiṇam ||*
> *dhūmenāvriyate vahnir yathādarśo malena ca |*
> *yatholbenāvṛto garbhas tathā tenedam āvṛtam ||*
> *āvṛtaṃ jñānam etena jñānino nityavairiṇā |*
> *kāmarūpeṇa kaunteya duṣpūreṇānalena ca ||*
> *indriyāṇi mano buddhir asyādhiṣṭhānam ucyate |*
> *etair vimohayaty eṣa jñānam āvṛtya dehinām ||*
> *tasmāt tvam indriyāṇy ādau niyamya bharatarṣabha |*
> *pāpmānaṃ prajahihy enaṃ jñānavijñānanāśanam ||*
>
> Arjuna said: Moved by what does man do evil? By what is he driven almost by force, O Kṛṣṇa? The Blessed One replied: It is desire (*kāma*) that drives him, it is anger, arising from the *rajas*[4] component. This is the great devourer, the great Evil One. Recognise in it your enemy. As fire is covered by smoke, as the mirror is covered by a spot and the embryo by the womb, so is our knowledge covered by it [desire]. By this reality that takes the shape of desire, a fire that nothing satiates, eternal enemy of the knower subject, knowledge is covered. Of desire, the senses, the mind and the intellect are the substrate. Through them desire, covering knowledge, beclouds the incarnate soul. Therefore, O Bull among the Bharatas, curb first of all the senses and then abandon this Evil One who destroys knowledge and spiritual science (3.36–41, in Krishna Warrier 1983: 127–31).

The Kashmiri recension of the *Bhagavadgītā* lays it on thicker, inserting, after the first verses of Kṛṣṇa's reply, five further verses:

> *Arjuna uvāca:*
>
> *bhavaty eṣa kathaṃ kṛṣṇa kathaṃ caiva vivardhate |*
> *kimātmakaḥ kimācāraḥ tan mamācakṣva pṛcchataḥ ||*
> *śrībhagavān uvāca:*
> *eṣa sūkṣmaḥ paraḥ kṣatruḥ dehinām indriyeṣu ha |*

sukhatantra ivāsīno mohayan pārtha tiṣṭhati ||
kāmakrodhamayo ghoraḥ stambhaharṣasamudbhavaḥ |
ahaṃkāro 'bhimānātmā dustaraḥ pāpakarmabhiḥ ||
harṣam asya nivartyaiṣa śokam asya dadāti ca |
bhayaṃ cāsya karoty eṣa mohayaṃś tu muhur muhuḥ ||
sa eṣa kaluṣaḥ kṣudraś cchidraprekṣī dhanañjaya |
rajaḥpravṛtto mohātmā manuṣyāṇām upadravaḥ ||

Arjuna said: But how is it born, O Kṛṣṇa, and how does it grow? What is its essence, what its operation? Answer, I pray you, this my question. The Blessed One replied: It is the subtle enemy, supreme, of bodily beings and the senses. It appears as an instrument of pleasure, O Arjuna, but in reality it obfuscates. Cruel, its essence being desire and rage, source of the evil pleasure of pride, cause of the ego, by nature presumptuous, only with difficulty can it be overcome by the wicked. First it takes pleasure from man and gives him sorrow and, that done, fills him with terror, obfuscating him increasingly. It is dark, vile, it spies on the weak points, O Arjuna; it is born of rubedo [*rajas*] and its essence is obfuscation: it is the plague of mankind (3.38–42, in Sankaranarayanan 1985: 55–56).

One of the five major vows absolutely required by the highest Jaina ideal (the other four being non-violence, truthfulness, honesty, and absence of greed) is continence itself. It is defined in the following manner by Hemacandra's *Yoga Śāstra*:

divyaudārikakāmānāṃ kṛtānumatakāritaiḥ |
manovākkāyatas tyāgo brahmāṣṭādaśadhā matam ||

The eighteen kinds of continence, in our tradition, consist of abandoning desires (*kāma*) with regard to heavenly, human and animal beings, in mind, word and body, whether one experiences them oneself, or approves their enjoyment, or ensures that others enjoy them (1.23, in Jambūvijaya and Dharmacandravijaya 1977: 200).

Equipped with such readings, the first to filter through systematically in the West and to be firmly fixed in *communis opinio*, how often must the Western traveller, landing in India in the expectancy of an ascetic and disincarnate world, have been stunned by the untiring proliferation of colours, odours and sounds of life in all its most splendid and ephemeral forms! Consequently, it seems that something is not right, or that there is at least a hiatus between the theories and prescriptions of traditional philosophical-religious texts and what then occurs in real life. This, however, is only a part of the truth. Indeed, there exists a highly significant sector of Indian thought and religious experience — Tantrism — that became increasingly important until it imbued the whole spiritual life of India starting from the Middle Ages and literally turned the tables. With regard to Hemacandra's passage on desire, what the greatest master of Tantrism, the Śaiva Abhinavagupta, says in one of his most difficult works, the *Mālinīvijaya-vārttika*, is in total opposition:

> *kāmaḥ* [*kāmaḥ*, in Hanneder 1998: 104; *kāmaṃ*, in Śāstrī 1921: 28] *svīkartum icchaiva tadācchādanayogataḥ* |
> *viśvaṃ sādhayet kāmī kāmatattvam idaṃ yataḥ* ||
>
> Desire (*kāma*) is the will to take possession [of the other] (to make the other oneself). Veiling everything with his desire, the desirer can accomplish everything, since everything has as its ultimate principle desire itself[5] (1.281, in Hanneder 1998: 104).

And again:

> *kiṃ nākarṣati kiṃ naiṣa ca* (*ca* em. Hanneder 1998: 104; *na* Sāstrī 1921: 27) *bhāvayati yogavit* |
> *tata evocyate śāstre nārakto rañjayed iti* ||
>
> Whoever knows this path, what may he not draw to himself or realise mentally? For this very reason, traditional texts say, 'He who is not impassioned cannot arouse passion [in others]' (1.279, in Hanneder 1998: 104).

The energy of desire, according to non-dualist Śaiva Tantrism, is what is manifested in the fruition and enjoyment of the senses, that which gives life to the ferment of the emotions, which has one of its peaks in the passion of love. The whole universe is pervaded by this energy, the sole matrix of any form of dynamism and life, whose single thread crosses both the most extreme abstractions of thought and our modest daily round. The first worship that the devotee is bound to render is to the goddesses of his own consciousness (*svasaṃvid-devīs*), who are none other than the *karaṇeśvarīs*, the mistresses of his sensorial faculties.[6] The sacrificial offering is, thus, made of everything within the bounds of ordinary life which, when all is said and done, is not all that ordinary. Neither clarified butter nor flowers are offered to the goddess' icon, but increasingly penetrating and intense enjoyments to those unbridled goddesses that 'are' our senses. As stated in a verse of the *Mālinīvijayottara Tantra* or *Mālinīvijaya Tantra*:

> *bandhamokṣāv ubhāv etāv indriyāṇāṃ jagur budhāḥ |*
> *nigṛhītāni*[7] *bandhāya vimuktāni vimuktaye ||*
>
> The cause of both bonds and liberation are the senses: this is what the wise said. Fettered they lead to bonds, freed they lead to liberation (15.44, in Śāstrī 1922: 102; Vasudeva 2004: 112).

This is echoed by Abhinavagupta in the *Tantrāloka*:

> *antarindhanasaṃbhāram anapekṣyaiva nityaśaḥ |*
> *jājvalīty akhilākṣaughaprasṛtograśikhaḥ śikhī ||*
> *bodhāgnau tādṛśe bhāvā viśantas tasya sanmahaḥ |*
> *udrecayanto gacchanti homakarmanimittatām ||*
>
> Perennially, whatever the fuel provided, burns within us the blazing fire of all our senses. The various knowable things, entering this consciential fire and increasing its radiance, thereby become the cause of oblation (4.201–02, in Śāstrī and Śāstrī 1918–38, vol. 3: 232).

To yoga, which requires, firstly, detachment (*vairāgya*) and repetitious and gradual practice (*abhyāsa*),[8] non-dualist Śaiva Tantrism responds by opposing to the former attachment and passion (*rāga*), and to the latter the silent vortex of the instant (*kṣaṇa*). But why attachment and passion and, first and foremost, what is in this word *rāga* whose semantic area is so evasive? *Rāga*, meaning 'attachment, affection or desire', as also 'colour' or 'the fact of being coloured by emotions' in Śaiva theology and psychology, constitutes one of the individual's three innermost 'cuirasses', the complex and many-faceted concept of 'cuirass' irresistibly recalling Wilhelm Reich's similar motif (Reich 1973).[9] It is a fact accepted by all, say the Śaiva masters, that there is no action in ordinary life that does not proceed from an idea or expectation of pleasure. Furthermore, the most disparate philosophical schools and prescriptive texts coincide in considering *rāga* as the root of all feelings, emotions and mental activities. The Buddhists would object that this holds only for individuals in the grip of *saṃsāra*, while the Buddha is exempt from *rāga*. Thus, a debate, destined to continue for centuries (see Dunne 1996; Franco 2004; Pecchia 2008; Taber 2011), started in the Buddhist community about a dilemma which might not sound that dramatic to us: did the Buddha have desires (*rāga*)? Or, is it possible to act compassionately, as the Buddha did, without some kind of inner emotional thrust, in other words, without some kind of *rāga*? In the main, Dharmakīrti's solution will prevail: compassion may be the outcome of a purified form of *rāga*, quite different from ordinary *rāga*, which is imbued with misjudgments (*viparyāsa*), making it into *abhiṣvaṅga* 'craving'.[10] The desire without misjudgment (the belief in the self, the mine, etc.), and not turned to a corrupted object,[11] of the Buddhists may in some way be likened to *niṣkāma-karma* of the *Bhagavadgītā*, in which the action obtains its dignification from the very absence of desire, or of desire for its result. By contrast, the need for such anesthetisation of *rāga* is by no means felt by the Śaiva Advaita. On the contrary, the metaphysical ancestor of human *rāga* is placed at the very heart of supreme Consciousness, just as *kāma* is by the Ṛgvedic hymn cited in the next section. While the most widespread Śaiva doctrine conceives of three main *śakti*s of Śiva: *icchā-*, *jñāna-* and *kriyāśakti*, a distinction into five *śakti*s is also well known. According to the seminal text of the Pratyabhijñā, the *Śivadṛṣṭi* by Somānanda, there are two more *śakti*s above or 'behind' the three aforementioned *śakti*s. *Icchā* is considered a higher *śakti* than *jñāna* and *kriyā*, for both knowing and acting rest on an act of volition. In its turn, *icchāśakti* has two parts, a previous and a subsequent one (*tasyāḥ pūrvāparau bhāgau kalpanīyau*, *Śivadṛṣṭi* 1.1.19cd, in Śāstrī 1934: 17). While the subsequent part is the full-fledged will (*icchāśakti* proper), the previous part is the first outline of a dynamic wave stirring the surface of the quiescent bliss of Śiva consciousness (the first *śakti*), named after a concept that also has a strong aesthetic connotation: *nirvṛti* 'lysis, contentment', the deep sense of inner satisfaction that is associated with an intense aesthetic enjoyment; this dynamic wave represents the very first opening of a disposition to create, still in the form of undifferentiated striving towards creation of the universe (*bodhasya svarūpaniṣṭhasya viśvaracanaṃ praty abhilāṣamātraracanāyogyatāyā yaḥ prathamo vikāsaḥ*, Utpaladeva's *vṛtti* on *Śivadṛṣṭi* 1.15, in Śāstrī 1934: 16). Such desiring state, still without a definite object (the second *śakti*), technically called *aunmukhya* 'tension towards . . .', will only later condense into *icchāśakti* (ibid.: *tasyaunmukhyasyecchā kāryā*). This divine desire is in its essence the same as the desire in individual soul. Just like *aunmukhya* is the first expansion or blossoming of supreme Consciousness (*tadāsthāpravikāsaḥ*, *Śivadṛṣṭi* 1.15c, in Śāstrī 1934: 15; *tadvikāsitā*, *Śivadṛṣṭi* 1.20b, ibid.: 17), its energetic dimension, so is the indefinite desiring state emerging from the very root of individual soul: a subtle frenzy having neither outline nor horizon, a 'desiring condition' without any object or any action (Jayaratha on *Tantrāloka* 9.62: *niṣkarmā . . . icchāmātrasvabhāvābhilāṣitā*, in Śāstrī and Śāstrī 1918–38, vol. 6: 56), from which all activities — both mundane and ultramundane — will spring.

Under the banners of *niṣkāma-karma* of the *Bhagavadgītā* and *niṣkarma-kāma* of the non-dualist Śaivism we can see two different worldviews confronting each other.

In order to act on these profound structures, the traditional yoga seems to Tantrism like a blunted weapon:

> *vastuto 'sti na kasyāpi yogāṅgasyābhyupāyatā |*
> *svarūpaṃ hy asya nīrūpam avacchedavivarjanāt ||*
> *upāyo 'py anupāyo 'syāyāgavṛttinirodhataḥ |*
> *recanāpūraṇair eṣā rahitā tanuvātanauḥ ||*
> *tārayaty evam ātmānaṃ bhedasāgaragocarāt |*
> *nimañjamānam apy etan mano vaiṣayike rase || . . .*
> *tathāhi gurur ādikṣad bahudhā svakaśāsane ||*
> *anādaraviraktyaiva galantīndriyavṛttayaḥ |*
> *yāvat tu viniyamyante tāvat tāvad vikurvate ||*
>
> In actual fact, no member of yoga can really serve as a means of achieving [the condition of *anuttara* or 'that which nothing transcends'].[12] The means to it is, in fact, a non-means,[13] since it comprises neither ritual practices nor the blocking of mental functions. It is a boat designed for a light breeze, without exhalation or inhalation,[14] which thereby carries itself beyond the ocean of duality, albeit in the meantime the mind is immersed in the fluid of the objective world . . . This is what the master demonstrates in various forms in his treatise:[15] the impulses of the senses can only be thrown off thanks to a highly special kind of detachment, a detachment practiced in elegant *souplesse* (*anādaravirakti*). On the contrary, if we try to subdue them, they end up becoming ungovernable (*Mālinīvijaya-vārttika* 2.106–12, in Śāstrī 1921).

Passions and emotions are consequently allowed to flow freely without attempting to safeguard the mind from their impact. Not only: 'Passion should not be extinguished by reason, but reason converted into passion' (except that here it is not a Tantric master speaking, but the early-19th-century Italian poet and philosopher Giacomo Leopardi in his *Zibaldone*).[16]

Indeed, Tantrism, especially in its most extreme forms, goes far beyond any instrumental acceptance of the emotive dimension (for the purpose of neutralising it). If the divine is, first and foremost, the energy that unites and overwhelms all provisional levels of being, it is in the tumult of the passions that we best meet it face to face. Emotional states, whether sexual excitement or fright, joy or terror, not only should not be obliterated, any more than they should be merely accepted, but they should also be cultivated, skilfully intensified, and then exploded and spread in order to create subtle rents in the veil of ordinary existence, through which we can contact the magma of universal consciousness/energy. Liberation does not occur, therefore, in spite of human passions, but precisely by virtue of them. By way of a provisional conclusion, we may cite a passage from the *Kiraṇa Tantra* (4.29a, in Goodall 1998: 109), which ventures, if possible, even farther: 'Without the body, there can be no liberation (*na dehena vinā muktiḥ*)'.[17]

Desire (*kāma*)

> Death consists of two syllables; the Eternal Brahman consists of three. Death's two syllables are *mama* 'mine'; the three syllables of the Eternal are *na mama* 'not mine'. The Brahman and Death, O King, dwell unseen in the bosom of all creatures and stir them ceaselessly . . . If a man should conquer the entire Earth and all that moving and unmoving dwells within it, but within himself develops no idea of appropriation "this Earth is 'mine'", what will the Earth that he has conquered be for him? If, on the other hand, O Son of Pṛthu, a man living as a hermit in the forest, feeding on wild herbs, should develop a feeling of belonging toward his poor possessions, this man is living in the jaws of death . . . Men blame one who is penetrated by desire, yet no action is born from the absence of desire, neither generous giving, nor study of the Vedas, nor asceticism: the vedic rites are nourished by desire . . . Indeed, whatever a man desires for himself is dharma; dharma does not have restriction as its foundation.[18] To this purpose the wise men of old quoted a few strophes that were sung by Kāma himself. Hear me, O Yudhiṣṭhira, while I now recite all those strophes to you.
>
> 'No being may think of killing me without recourse to some means. If one seeks to kill me knowing the effectiveness of reciting mantras, in his very recitation I once more show myself. If one seeks to kill me with sacrifices and many offerings to the officiant, I reappear in him as action, as in the beings that move; if one seeks to kill me with the Vedas and the Upaniṣads that bring them to fulfilment, then I reappear in him in a quiescent form,

as in motionless things. If one seeks to kill me with fearless perseverance, I show myself in him in his state of noble heroism, and he is not aware of me. If one seeks to kill me through asceticism, then in his ascesis I am reborn in the form of unshakable perseverance. If one, a sage, seeks to kill me by devoting himself wholeheartedly to liberation, I dance and laugh in him, in his passion for liberation. Of all beings, eternal am I alone and I cannot be killed' (*Mahābhārata* 14.13.3–18, in Sukthankar and Karmakar 1960).

The passage quoted does not come from just any text, but from the very source of Brāhmaṇical culture, the *Mahābhārata*. Traditionally, it is known as the *Kāmagītā* or 'Song of Desire', the umpteenth variation of an illustrious model, the *Bhagavadgītā*. To give a new vigour to the sovereign Yudhiṣṭhira, now weary and demotivated, Vāsudeva resorts to an injection of desire and who better than Kāma, the divine personification of desire, could accomplish this task?[19] He, therefore, recites to the king the verses that Kāma once composed in his self-exaltation. Swarms of similar passages spring to mind from literature throughout the world. One of the many, at the opening of the brilliant libretto of Monteverdi's *Incoronazione di Poppea*, the work of Giovanni Francesco Busenello, is where Amore turns to Fortuna and Virtù, each convinced of being the power that drives the world:

Che vi credete o Dee / divider fra di voi del mondo tutto / la signoria e 'l governo, escludendone Amore, / *Nume ch'è d'ambe voi tanto maggiore? / Io le virtudi insegno, / io le fortune domo, / questa bambina età / vince d'antichità / il tempo e ogni altro Dio: / gemelli siam l'eternitade ed io. / Riveritemi, adoratemi, / e di vostro sovrano il nome datemi.*

Who do you think you are, Goddesses, / to divide between yourselves / the sovereignty and governance of the world / to the exclusion of love, / a divinity so much greater than the two of you? / I tell the virtues what to do, / I govern the fortunes of men. This childlike form of mine / surpasses in antiquity / time itself and every other God. / We are twins, eternity and I. / Revere me, / worship me / and acknowledge me as your sovereign.[20]

The *Kāmagītā* shows us the god of Desire (*kāma*, which originally meant just 'desire', progressively came to mean desire *par excellence*, i.e., erotic desire) boasting of lying concealed even in the bosom of what would appear to be his opposite: ascesis. At the same time, however, the opposite is also true, as revealed by the mythology of Śiva, the sovereign creator/destroyer god, at the centre of the spiritual experience of Tantrism, supremely ascetic and simultaneously supremely erotic, whose sexual embraces may last thousands of years. When we seek the source of his sexual energy, we unfailingly come up against *tapas*, ascesis. The terrible austerities that Śiva can bear — here too, for thousands of years — often include among their results, and sometimes even as their purpose, the regeneration of sexual energy: the contrary is also possible, i.e., that sexual activity produces *tapas* as its fruit. In iconography, Śiva is usually represented with the attributes of the ascetic: he wears the skin of a black antelope, his head is strewn with ash, he wears a garland of skulls, ornaments made of human bones, and is substantially described as an ascetic by the most ancient texts. He — the *yogin par excellence* (*yogīśvara*) — withdraws to the most inaccessible solitudes and drives his *tapas* to such extreme levels that the force generated thereby yet again, as with sexual power, risks overturning the universe. Only after enormous difficulties does Pārvatī, the daughter of the Himālaya, falling in love with the god, manage to lead him to marriage, i.e., only after she, too, has practiced *tapas*. Ordinary life and sensual pleasures seem to Śiva irreconcilable with his nature: his *tapas* would be hindered by them. Whenever this occurs, his wrath, always primed, explodes. The one who pays for it, in a famous myth cycle with abundant variations, is, of course, Kāma, the main antagonist of the ascetic Śiva. He attempts to disturb his concentration with one of his amorous darts, now exploiting the inexhaustible desires of Pārvatī, now causing fascinating nymphs to appear. Śiva's reaction is lethal: the fire from his vertical third eye that opens immediately in his forehead reduces Kāma to cinders. The result is that the whole universe enters upon a spiral of death: colours fade, plants start to languish, all begins to fade away as in a long twilight, to the point that Śiva is obliged to bring Kāma back to life.

The total negation of the desire-polarity is unexpected and seems to reduce Śiva to much more circumscribed dimensions. It suffices to consider the sequel of the tale to see that Śiva, to please Pārvatī or Rati (Kāma's consort), resurrects the god; or that the fire of the third eye destroys only Kāma's body, and even bodiless he still exists, becoming even more fearsome owing to his invisibility. Significant too is the gist of the gods' protests to Śiva against his action: they accuse him of killing one of his creatures and, in so doing, of inexplicably depriving of desire a universe that he himself had created as pervaded by desire. The circle then closes with the consideration that, in Indian mythology — where the phoenix theme is very much alive — death by fire never means a final end, but is always a prelude to resurrection.

The Kāma of the *Mahābhārata* and the Purāṇas has, however, a very long history behind him, both as an abstract principle and as a divine incarnation. The cosmogonic hymn of Canto 129 of the 10th *maṇḍala* of the *Ṛgveda*, as celebrated as it is mysterious, constitutes Kāma's first archaic apotheosis:

> Then Non-Being did not exist, and not even Being. Aerial space did not exist, nor the firmament beyond it. What is it that moved so powerfully? And where? And controlled by whom? Was it the waters, unfathomably deep? At that time neither death, nor non-death existed: there was no distinguishing sign for night and day. The One breathed with its own vital force, without there being breath. Beside this, nothing else existed. Originally the darkness was hidden by the darkness. This universe was nothing but an indistinct wave. Then, through the power of *tapas*, the One came into being, empty, covered with vacuity. Desire (*kāma*) was its primordial development, [Desire] that constituted the original seed of Consciousness. Inquiring within themselves, Poets knew through their reflection how to find the link of Being in Non-Being. Their cord was stretched between. What was there beneath: what was above? There were the procreators; there were powers. Inherent Power (*svadhā*) was beneath; Exertion (*prayati*) was uppermost. In truth, who knows, who could proclaim whence this secondary creation was born, whence it comes? The gods were born later, through the secondary creation of our world. But who knows whence this creation arose, whether it was He who brought it into being or not, He who watches over this world in the highest firmament, He alone knows. Or perhaps even He knows it not.[21]

So, long before the birth of the gods, when neither being nor non-being existed, but only darkness and chaos, there began to issue forth a 'heat' or *tapas*, i.e., the same heat that is born of and coincides with ascesis. The form that then first takes shape is that of Desire (whose heat is, moreover, the same as that of ascesis). Whereas the later Brāhmaṇical culture sought to maintain an unbridgeable opposition between desire and consciousness, in the aforequoted passage from the *Ṛgveda* not only are they *not* presented as antithetical, but desire is identified as the very matrix of consciousness and ontologically ranked before it.[22]

Amongst the many other instances of praise of Kāma, at least another passage of the Vedic literature deserves to be quoted, the so-called Hymn to Desire, in the *Atharvaveda*.

> Kāma was born first, him neither the gods, nor the Fathers, nor men have equalled. To these art thou superior, and ever great; to thee, O Kāma, do I

verily offer reverence. As great as are the heavens and earth in extent, as far as the waters have swept, as far as fire; to these art thou superior . . . Not, surely, does the wind equal Kāma, not the fire, not the sun, and not the moon. To these art thou superior. With those auspicious and gracious forms of thine, O Kāma, through which what thou willst becometh real, with these do you enter into us, and elsewhere send the evil thoughts! (9.2.19–25, trans. Bloomfield 1987: 93).

The same thread is conspicuously present, some centuries later, in a famous passage of the *Manusmṛti*:

> Being governed by desire is not recommended, yet there is nothing devoid of desire in this world. For even for the study of Veda and for the performing of vedic rituals desire is necessary . . . There is no action whatsoever in one who is without desire, for whatever may be done is accomplished due to desire (2.2–4, in Jolly 1887: 14).

These and many other quotations demonstrate that the force and value of desire are deeply rooted in the Indian culture from its very origins. Under the banner of 'desire', we place — with risky but necessary simplification — the entire human energy and drive dimension, as manifest, first and foremost, in sensory activities, in the emotions and passions.[23] The mainstream of Brāhmaṇical thought, as well as most of the texts aimed at regulating the socio-religious dimension of the ideal Hindu man, tend to draw an absolute line of demarcation between desire–senses–passions and the intellectual–spiritual element. Consciousness must be 'pure' (*śuddha*), transparent and weightless, and any activation of the 'desire' pole can only muddy its necessary clarity, preventing it from being itself, from 'functioning'.[24] Statements of this kind, in the Brāhmaṇical as also in the Buddhist and Jaina literature, are innumerable. For its exemplary nature, as well as the consequences that derive from some of its assertions, we will examine at least one other text, belonging to the set of so-called Middle Upaniṣads (certainly prior to the Common Era), the *Kaṭha Upaniṣad*. The setting is a sublime and tormented dialogue between the young Naciketas and Death, to which he is driven by an imprudent statement of his father's, the Brāhmaṇa Vājaśravasa. Naciketas descends to the realm of Yama, the God of Death, and goes straight to his dwelling. Yama is not at home (Death, as we know, is always extremely busy here and there). The young man stays waiting for him on the threshold for three nights, neither eating nor drinking. On his return, Yama, admiring the young man's constancy and austerity, grants him three wishes. For his first wish, Naciketas asks for permission to return to earth and find his father calm after his anger and well-disposed toward him; for his second, he requests that Yama teach him the ritual way of reaching heaven. While Yama benignly grants his first two wishes, he does everything possible, without success, to escape from the third: Naciketas asked him to reveal man's destiny after death. Yama's teaching essentially concerns man's true nature as coinciding with the Universal Being, the Brahman — the path to realise it necessitates the death of desire.

> When all desires harboured in man's heart have been expelled, only then can the mortal become immortal and experience the Brahman here (*Kaṭha Upaniṣad* 2.3.14, in *Īśādidaśopaniṣadaḥ śaṅkarabhāṣyasametāḥ* 1978, vol. 1: 103).

Since the senses embody the subject's projection toward the world, it is necessary to block their course and force them inward. The *Kaṭha Upaniṣad* goes on:

> The Self-Begotten Lord has pierced the cavity of the senses toward the outside, so that the individual looks outward and not within himself. But the sage, aspiring to non-death, will turn his eye inward and see his inner self (2.1.1, ibid.: 85).

According to the commentator Śaṅkara, 'pierced' does not simply mean 'opened', but contains a punitive implication, an act of aggression against the senses, so as to castigate them for their impudent vitality (ibid.). And the *Kaṭha* goes on: 'Fools follow their desires; they fall into the snares of vast Death'. (2.1.2ab, ibid.: 86). In order to outline the taxonomy of man's faculties, Yama uses an ancient simile, that of the chariot, also well-known in the West:[25]

> Know that the self is the master of the chariot, whereas the body is the chariot itself. Know that the intellect is the charioteer and the mind the reins. It is said that the senses are the steeds and the objects of the senses the tracks (1.3.3–4ab, ibid.: 79–80).

At first sight, the *Kaṭha* seems to set out an integrated view of the human character but, in the verses that follow the aforecited ones, a further motif emerges: the elements identified are not placed on the same level, but are subject to a rigorous hierarchy in ontological terms:

> Superior (*parāḥ*)[26] to the senses are the objects of the senses; superior to the objects of the senses is the mind; superior to the mind is the intellect; superior to the intellect is the Great Self[27] (1.3.10, *Īśādidaśopaniṣadaḥ śaṅkarabhāṣyasametāḥ* 1978: 81).

The senses have a value only to the extent to which they are dominated by the intellect and the mind:

> If one is not united with his intellect and his mind is not always properly subjugated, his uncontrolled senses will be for him like skittish horses for the charioteer (1.3.5, ibid.: 80).

Such a categorical message from the very heart of the Brāhmaṇical world leads us back antiphrastically to the Tantric text *Mālinīvijaya-vārttika* partly quoted in the previous section:

> *nāntarārdratvam abhyeti niścchidraḥ tumbakaḥ yathā* |
> *svaṃ panthānaṃ hayasyeva manaso ye nirundhate* ||
> *teṣāṃ tatkhaṇḍanāyogād dhāvaty unmārgakoṭibhiḥ* |
> *kiṃsvid etad iti prāyo duḥkhe 'py utkaṇṭhate manaḥ* ||
> *sukhād api virājyeta jñānād etad idaṃ [tv iti]* |
> *tathāhi gurur ādikṣad bahudhā svakaśāsane* ||
> *anādaraviraktyaiva galantīndriyavṛttayaḥ* |
> *yāvat tu viniyamyante tāvat tāvad vikurvate* |
>
> Consider what is involved when one decides to put the natural course of the mind under control, i.e., when one wishes to put a bit on a wild horse. Owing to the violence of the procedures, the mind — like the horse — will start running here and there, taking many wrong directions. Why does this occur? We all know that the mind can even delight in pain and, conversely, retreat disgusted from pleasure and knowledge. This is what the master demonstrates in various forms in his treatise: the impulses of the senses can be made to cease thanks to a highly special kind of detachment, a detachment practiced in elegant *souplesse*. If, on the contrary, one attempts to subjugate them, they end up becoming ungovernable (2.109–12, in Śāstrī 1921: 114).

In the background a world view is outlined, marked, as it were, by healthy realism. Instead of issuing precepts (often, as in the Brāhmaṇical *śāstras*, with a fair dose of wishful thinking), it prefers to accept the evidence, at least as a starting point. Significant in this connection is what we find in a 10th–11th-century-CE treatise, the *Mahānayaprakāśa* or the 'Light of the Great Method', belonging to one of the more extreme Tantric schools, the Krama:

> *prāyo hi maithune madye māṃse ca paridṛśyate |*
> *āsaktiḥ sarvajantūnāṃ viśeṣāt kasyacit kvacit ||*
> *yadi tattyāgasaṃrambhaḥ pūrvaḥ teṣāṃ vidhīyate |*
> *upadeśo na sa manāg api citte prarohati ||*
> *janmāntaraśatābhyastā viśayeṣu matir nṛṇām |*
> *jaradgaur iva sasyebhyaḥ sā hi duḥkhena vāryate ||*
> *iti saṃvādatas teṣāṃ parityāgo hi duṣkaraḥ |*
> *abhyasūyanti te yasmād upadeśakarāya ca ||*
> *yathāsthitopabhogātma pūrvaṃ yat tūpadiśyate |*
> *tatrādhirarūḍhir lokasya śraddhāpūrvaḥ prajāyate.*

> Common experience shows us that all creatures, broadly speaking, are addicted to sex, meat and alcoholic drinking; some are more addicted to one of them, some to another. If, from the very beginning, they are asked immediately to proceed to the abandonment of all this, the teaching will not in the least take root in them. Human mind is turned towards these objects since hundreds of previous existences, and it is hardly possible to turn it away from them, just like to turn an old cow away from the fields. There is a general agreement on this: the abandoning of such things is hard to obtain, also because men would end up by hating those who put forward such a teaching. If, on the contrary, a teaching is such as preliminarily to leave their enjoyments intact, common men will adhere to it with faith (9.4–8, in Śāstrī 1937: 48–49).

Passion (*rāga*) as One of the 'Cuirasses'

The novelty of the worldview proposed by Tantrism is not, however, condensed in this pragmatic attitude, as articulated by the *Mahānayaprakāśa*. Behind it, there is a profound and articulated analysis of the human character in all its complexity, accompanied by an equally penetrating and original development of the spiritual tools that can lead to its emancipation, to 'liberation' (*mokṣa*).

Of the many cues that the Tantric literature provides, I have chosen one that seems to have central importance. Once more, we find ourselves within the world of the Tantric Śaiva schools, which developed in Kashmir starting from the 8th–9th century CE: here, philosophical and aesthetic speculation and spiritual wisdom reach the highest peaks — simultaneously elegant and extreme — of Indian culture as a whole.

Among the basic principles (*tattva*) that form the structure of the universe according to the Śaiva Tantric tradition, the group named *kañcuka*s certainly do not constitute a mere doctrinal detail among many others, but the theorisation, also translated into ritual, of a central point of Tantric thought, which may tell us very much about its concept of man and his life.

The word *kañcuka* is taken for granted in all sources and, no doubt, belongs to a common layer of teachings. On the contrary, the same cannot be said of its meaning, the number of the *kañcuka*s and their genesis. The two principal meanings of *kañcuka*, 'cuirass, armour' and 'a kind of dress, bodice' both fit the main function of these principles, which is that of 'covering, sheltering' the individual soul, destitute of its full powers because of maculation (a kind of innate and primordial 'contraction' of the spiritual substance of the soul), but the texts constantly also refer to their 'hardness' or 'force' and 'strengthening power' (*udbalana*). Therefore, let us take the meaning 'cuirass', which, perhaps, may be better assumed in an 'organic' sense, as the thick skin of an animal, i.e., as something able to protect and strengthen, not being superimposed from without but being an integral part of the individual it protects. This would fit well the very tight, almost inextricable, connection with the individual soul which the texts assign to the *kañcuka*s, and particularly to some of them. The only one to state it explicitly is the dualist Śaiva philosopher Rāmakaṇṭha (10th–11th century CE) when he compares the *kañcuka*s to the snake's skin (*Vṛtti* on *Mataṅgapārameśvarāgama*, Vidyāpāda, in Bhatt 1977: 334). Their number varies (six, five, four, or three), but according to the most common conception they are five: Energy, Knowledge, Passion, Time, and Necessity. However, among them there is a group of three that enjoy a privileged status, so that sometimes the appellation *kañcuka* applies to them only.[28] They are *kalā*, *vidyā* and *rāga*, or 'Energy, Knowledge, and Passion'. Our considerations will be mainly devoted to them.

Among the *kañcukas* proper, *kalā* (commonly translated as 'energy', '[limited] power to act') is the one which is unanimously considered the most closely linked to, or rather intertwined with, the subject — a 'second consciousness' as it were, as Bṛhaspati says.[29] The individual soul, whose powers of knowledge and action have been blurred by an innate 'maculation' (*mala*), finds its deepest support in *kalā*, a kind of injection of basic energy (indeed, the very 'inciting power' of the Lord is acting in it), which, at least partially, revives the powers of the soul. An objection comes spontaneously to one's mind: why does the Lord's power not intervene directly but resorts, in order to release the soul, to something which is in itself a bond? This objection indirectly reveals the paradoxical nature of *kalā*, and of human dimension as a whole. The scriptures reply that the intervention of the Lord's power would entail the immediate manifestation of the soul's powers in their fullest glory, viz., liberation, whilst the question here is to fit out the soul for its worldly adventure, to which the ripeness of *mala* and the karmic impulses direct it (*Mataṅgapārameśvarāgama*, Vidyāpāda, 9.25cd–26ab, in Bhatt 1977: 302; *Tantrāloka* 9.182, in Śāstrī and Śāstrī 1918–38, vol. 6: 141). As in the nice simile found in a Śaiva Siddhānta text *Śivajñāna-siddhiyār*, *kalā* is like the club Śiva (or the *guru*) makes use of in order to awaken the adept, who would not be able to stand his direct touch (Devasenapathi 1960: 47).[30] *Kalā* and individual soul (*aṇu*) can never be seen as separate from one another, they seem to be one single entity. 'Just as a clay pot, once heated by fire, can absorb shellac, so the *aṇu*, permeated by *kalā*, can receive the fruitions obtained by him with great joy'. And again: '*Kalā* brings about fruition and is the abode of the individual soul. Resting on *kalā*, imbued with karma, the individual soul cannot leave it anymore and becomes attached more and more' (*Mataṅgapārameśvarāgama*, Vidyāpāda, 9.28–29a, 9.31cd–32, in Bhatt 1977: 303).

But if *kalā* is the most internal and important factor leading the soul towards the world of experience, it is not the only one, however.

> Just as, by virtue of its swelling, due to union with substances such as water or the sun's heat, fire becomes the cause of the sprout's birth, so *kalā* is the cause of the union with Knowledge and of the awakening brought about by Passion with a view to promoting the fruition in the soul.[31]

In the soul made active by *kalā*, the process of knowledge cannot take place yet, owing to the lack of a specific instrument. The latter cannot be represented by the senses or the mind (*buddhi*), since they do not figure in all kinds of knowledge; the mind itself, though having a role of its own in all forms of everyday life, is not able to cognise itself. Since it fully belongs to the material world, it is not enabled to be anything more than a mirror in which equally material things are reflected. *Vidyā* or 'Knowledge' is the necessary link between the knowing subject — exclusively represented by the individual soul (*aṇu*) — and object images (and the respective organs of cognition).

Everything is now ready for the subject to begin having experiences, but for a factor, subtly noted by the Śaiva scriptures, the absence of which would make the entire process actually motionless or merely virtual: the *desire* to have experiences, the longing for them. Or, as the *Mṛgendra Tantra*, Vidyāpāda, 10.11 (Śāstrī 1930: 210) puts it, now the soul can cognise objects thanks to the manifestation of the power of consciousness, but he does not turn to seize them; for this reason, the Lord creates *rāga*. *Rāga*, i.e., 'attachment, passion, affection, the fact of being coloured by emotions' is the last of the three cuirasses proper. In fact, it is difficult, if not impossible, to establish an absolute priority of order between *rāga* and *vidyā* (Passion and Knowledge), i.e., to say whether he who knows then desires or vice-versa, so intimately do they refer to each other. As Abhinavagupta says in his long commentary on the most important philosophical text of Śaiva Tantrism, Utpaladeva's *Īśvarapratyabhijñākārikā*, referring to the *kañcukas* as a whole: 'These cuirasses mingle with each other, in the sense that they support each other in their functions. They are like the various flavours and ingredients in a sweet' (*Īśvarapratyabhijñā-vivṛtivimarśinī*, in Śāstrī 1938–43, vol. 3: 92).

It is a given fact that there is no action in ordinary life that does not proceed from an idea or expectation of pleasure. Moreover, the various philosophical schools and authoritative texts agree on considering *rāga* as the root of all feelings, emotions and activities of the mind.[32] As in the case of *vidyā*, the *rāga*-principle should not be mistaken for what is only a particular epiphenomenon of it. To begin with, *rāga* is not the craving for objects but what lies behind it (cf. *Vṛtti* on *Mṛgendra Tantra*, Vidyāpāda, 11.16ab, in Śāstrī 1930: 236). Nor is it to be mistaken for a 'disposition' to attachment, such as *avairāgya* ('the absence of renunciation'), which is a quality of the mind and, therefore, essentially belongs to the sphere of objects. Indeed, in everyday life, man continuously experiences disaffection after fruition is accomplished, but *rāga* rises again immediately afterwards, with a different object. This *rāga* that never ceases in ordinary life — in the sense that it is continuously actualising itself in the various specific *rāgas* as actual experiences and feelings (*pratyayas*) — is precisely the *rāga* made of latent impregnations (*vāsanārūpa*).[33]

At the root of both kinds of *rāgas* lies, finally, the *rāga* 'pertaining to the knowing subject' (*vedakagata*) — the *rāga* as an ontological principle.[34] If the single episodes of passion in the individual can drive him towards particular experiences, this is only due to their being supported by the inner energy of such a root-*rāga*, i.e., *rāga* as cuirass. It is not pleasure that directly moves *rāga*, as *Mataṅgapārameśvarāgama* 11.13ab (Bhatt 1977: 328) states shrewdly, but it is *rāga* that creates pleasure with respect to the particular object it turns to.[35] In this way, we can account for attachment to their own status that even those which belong to the lowest strata of being (dogs, worms, etc.) show. This does not mean that the adept who has overcome this individual *rāga* is cut off from pleasure. Instead, he enjoys a particular form of pleasure in all actions. The very existence of the *vītarāga* or 'the one who has transcended passions' is one of the recurring arguments in all the texts to prove that *rāga* rests in the depths of the subject, not in objects, for in the latter case the mere existence of objects would suffice to keep *rāga* alive.

Therefore, like *vidyā* 'science, knowledge', *rāga* or 'emotion–passion–attachment', too, is both a complex and an elementary reality, which is all the more difficult to define the more internally it abides in the structure of the 'I'. Let us take into account, again, the insightful considerations made by Abhinavagupta in his *magnum opus*, *Tantrāloka* (9.61–64, in Śāstrī and Śāstrī 1918–38, vol. 6: 55–58).[36] The universe has been created in order to satisfy the souls in which a frenzy, a feverish craving for fruition, has been aroused. This frenzy (*lolikā*) leads to no definite action. It is, so to speak, just a 'desiring state' (*abhilāṣitā*, 9.62b), free from limitations as it has no specific object (Jayaratha thereon: *pratiniyataviṣayābhāvād avacchidojjhitā*); a state of indefinite, passionate expectation. Hence the thinking of oneself as imperfect, a kind of nescience, in a word: the basic impurity, *mala*. This is only the readiness to assume future limitations, which is why it does not constitute a *tattva*, as on the contrary *rāga* does. *Rāga* is essentially this same frenzy once it has been limited by a still indistinct object. The individual *avairāgya* or 'absence of renunciation' is only a qualification of the mind, and consists of its being continuously modified and 'coloured' by the various objects.

The cuirasses constitute the most internal and concealed structure of individual personality. In establishing their existence, the Tantric traditions in general, including even those grounded on dualistic presuppositions, seem to have been driven by a twofold need: to overcome the dualism and basic incommunicability of the purely spiritual and the purely material components — *puruṣa–prakṛti* or *puruṣa–buddhi* in the Sāṃkhya outlook — and to single out a boundary within the human being where the two components touch one another, as it were. What the Tāntrikas' thought and action seem most interested in are precisely borderlines, rather than the definite states of being. In particular, the nondualistic schools of Kashmir end up seeing borderlines everywhere or, in other words, infinite potential openings, which make the spiritual/material dichotomy more and more problematic, and finally overthrow it altogether. Attention is obviously focused primarily on the human being, no doubt the most paradoxical being in the universe. Of all possible subjectivity levels, the most crucial is, after all, the lowest one, the level of human beings, since it is the only one — as the *Mataṅgapārameśvarāgama* and its commentator state (10.23a–c, in Bhatt 1977: 318) — that has the privilege of containing in itself the whole path of the universe, from Śiva down to the earth. And, in the human being, paradoxical *par excellence* are the cuirasses, which, on the one hand, partially restore the power of the spiritual principle and, on the other, embrace it so tightly that they may prevent it from expanding in all its potential glory. Thus, the individual gains weight and a definite structure from the cuirasses, but at the same time he also sacrifices his fluidity or, in other words, his free pervasiveness and sovereignty. In presenting sometimes one aspect, sometimes the other, the texts do nothing but refer to the two sides of the same coin. This also has a probably involuntary correspondence at a lexical level, in the recurrence of two almost identical terms (that look totally identical in most Indian scripts) having an opposite meaning: ([*ud*]*balita-valita* 'reinforced-surrounded/encircled/limited).

The essentially ambiguous nature of the cuirasses is indirectly highlighted by the hint at their also having a 'pure' form. For example, pure *kalā* brings about a series of actions which, though still limited in themselves (adoration of Śiva, meditation, etc.), enable the individual soul to rid itself of *saṃsāra*. There is a pure form of *rāga*, too, which arises in those who are detached from bonds; by virtue of it, the limited soul experiences a drive to the *summum bonum*, the search for a *guru* and passionate devotion to Śiva.

This structure supporting the 'I' has one more characteristic, which is not explicitly mentioned but occasionally hinted at in the texts. This characteristic is directly connected with the deep level where the cuirasses are located and act, always behind any visible manifestation: the fact that they are subliminal and escape perception. The secrecy of the cuirasses is precisely that peculiar to any real borderline, in which one may find oneself without knowing it in advance, as it were. In fact, as it seems, the moment when the cuirass is fully cognised is also the moment when it becomes incapable of performing its task, thus opening the way to going beyond it.

This overall conception of the cuirasses is basically shared by the dualist and non-dualist Śaiva tradition, too. For its part, the latter seems particularly interested in developing two aspects, viz., the direct correspondence of cuirasses with the highest powers of Śiva, on the one hand; and their being 'intermediate' (or, in a sense, also 'mediating') realities and 'supports', on the other. As to the first point, we can limit ourselves to pointing out that the cuirasses of Energy, Knowledge, Passion, Time, and Necessity are considered to be the contracted forms of the divine powers of Consciousness, Bliss, Will, Knowledge, and Action, respectively; or, in different contexts, Māyā (also a cuirass), Energy–Knowledge (taken together), Time–Necessity, and Passion are taken as the contracted forms of the Pure Principles, viz., Anāśrita-Śiva, Sadāśiva, Īśvara, and Sadvidyā; or, yet again, a homology is established between *sarvakartṛtva* ('absolute power of action') and *kalā*; *sarvajñatva* ('absolute power of knowledge') and *vidyā*; *pūrṇatva* ('fullness, perfection') and *rāga*; *nityatva* ('eternity') and *kāla*; and *vyāpakatva* ('pervasion') and *niyati*.

But it is the second point which deserves closer examination. Among the Śaiva scriptures that have come down to us, the *Parātrīśikā* presents a different designation for this group of principles, i.e., *dhāraṇā* or 'support'. Thus says Abhinavagupta in his short commentary, the *Parātrīśikā-laghuvṛtti*:[37]

> *yad vedyarāśer eva atyaktavedyabhāvasya bhinnavedyavedakaikīkaraṇaṃ tadvyāpṛtāni* [em.: °*vyāvṛttāni*, in Śāstrī 1947] *tattvāni . . . tā etāś catasraḥ śaktayaḥ puruṣaṃ dhārayanti madhye triśaṅkuvad viśramayanti.*
>
> Though the specific nature of these principles does not cease to belong to the realm of the object, their function is to bring about the unification of the knower and the knowable, differentiated as they are in the sphere of *māyā* . . . These powers "hold up" (*dhārayanti*), that is, make the soul stand midway (*madhye*), like Triśaṅku[38] (Śāstrī 1947: 6–7).

If these principles did not exist, Abhinavagupta goes on, either the individual soul would become insentient, like a stone, or it would directly enter the sky of supreme Consciousness, like Parameśvara: in both cases, however, the knowable would equally cease to be, since it presupposes the existence of a māyic knowing subject.[39]

From this short immersion into the metaphysics and psychology of Śaiva Tantrism, we emerge with a few 'strong', highly peculiar ideas (of course, necessitating more extensive and in-depth research), which can be summarised as follows:

(*a*) Identification, deep within the individual subject, of a sustaining/limiting structure acting as a link between the material sphere and the spiritual sphere.

(*b*) This structure consists mainly of three 'cuirasses' — *kalā*, *vidyā* and *rāga* — apparently very different from each other, responsible for the energetic, intellectual and passional/emotional dimensions respectively.
(*c*) These three dimensions are not viewed as watertight compartments, but as strictly intertwined realities, communicating with and feeding each other.
(*d*) They are the very playground where human adventure is played out, and can act as a means of bondage, as well as of liberation.

Again, the Senses

In one of the early chapters of the *Bhagavadgītā*, we read:

> After creating the creatures and also the sacrificial offering, of old Prajāpati said, 'Increase yourselves through the sacrifice; may it be for you the cow that fulfils all your desires. Through the sacrifice, you feed the gods and the gods in turn feed you. Feeding each other, you will achieve the supreme good. The gods, fed by the sacrifice, will provide you with all the enjoyments you seek. Who so enjoys such experiences without offering them back to the gods that have provided them, that man is none other than a thief' (3.10–12, in Sankaranarayanan 1985: 45–46).[40]

For us, the interest of these verses is rather indirect, lying wholly in the way in which they were commented on by Abhinavagupta, totally revolutionising their meaning. Thus speaks the *Bhagavadgītārthasaṃgraha* ('Compendium of the Meanings of the Song of the Blessed One'):

> The gods, i.e. 'those used to taking pleasure',[41] are the sensorial functions, the Goddesses of the Senses, deities well-known to the secret traditions [i.e., the Krama]; those you must satisfy with the [sacrificial] act; in other words, you must devour the objects of the senses as much as possible. Once satisfied, in your self these goddesses will bring about supreme bliss in accordance with what is their own nature, they being naturally inclined to resting in the self. In such a way, incessantly, that is, by the alternating of moments of ordinary consciousness and of perfect absorption, reciprocal nourishment is achieved, characterised by the [joint] satisfaction of the senses and identification with the self, by virtue of which you will rapidly obtain the supreme good, the *brahman* in whom all reciprocal differentiations dissolve. Satisfied by this sacrificial act, the senses take up their abode in any object of meditation, etc. . . . The general meaning of the sentence is thus as follows: 'Whoever aspires to achieve

supernatural powers and liberation with slight effort must devote himself with abandonment to enjoyments as they occur, aiming, as his only goal, to make the febrile restlessness of the senses cease' (Sankaranarayanan 1985: 46).[42]

It is not a question for the senses to be pure or impure — as is, i.e., from the Buddhist standpoint — which may accept *rāga* or desire only on condition that it is not imbued with misjudgements and not addressed to defiled objects, which would make it into *abhiṣvaṅga* or 'craving'. In the Śaiva outlook, merely their 'neutral' dynamic power is emphasised. The *Mālinīvijayottara Tantra* even adds that they can become a means of liberation if they do not restrain their activity but, on the contrary, if they expand it towards more and more 'pervasive' objects:

etāni vyāpake bhāve yadā syur manasā saha |
vimuktanīti vidvadbhir jñātavyāni tadā priye ||
yadā tu viṣaye kvāpi pradeśāntaravartini |
saṃsthitāni tadā tāni baddhānīti pracakṣate ||

When these senses, along with the mind, focus on a pervasive reality, then, O Dear, they are called 'liberated' by the sages. When, on the contrary, they exercise their activity on any localised object, then they are called 'fettered' (15.45–46, in Vasudeva 2004: 112).

Thus, when the *Siddhayogeśvarīmata* (*Mālinīvijayottara Tantra* 15.47, ibid.: 112–13) divides the senses into pure and impure, it does so only having in mind their power: the more powerful they are and to a wider horizon they open the more 'pure' they are.

In order not to remain with the suspicion that the aforecited passage is merely the result of a capricious and momentary virtuosity of Abhinavagupta — an attitude, moreover, that would be anything but alien to the Kashmiri masters of supreme non-duality, who call themselves 'upholders of freedom' (*svātantrya-vādin*) — we should extend our research to other texts of Tantric Śivaism. We find the same concept also outlined in one of the *sūtras* (1.11) of the *Śiva Sūtra*, enigmatic but, fortunately for us, aptly clarified by Kṣemarāja: *tritayabhoktā vireśaḥ* ('Enjoyer of the triad, lord of the heroes'). Kṣemarāja's commentary *Śivasūtravimarśinī* on is as follows:

Mixing the three states of wakefulness, sleep and deep sleep with the bliss of the fourth by virtue of meditation on the Wheel of Powers, he who, thoroughly pervaded by such cogitation, manages to see every karmic impression of duality dissolved in them, now reduced to the continual flow of the essence of bliss, that man is the enjoyer of the triad, the one who tastes it with wonder (*camatkartā*).[43] Consequently, according to the principle expressed in the verse that says, 'There is in the three states what is called the enjoyer and what is called the enjoyable; but he who knows them both, he, albeit enjoying, is not stained [by the enjoyment]', such a yogin is, in the Great Traditions [the Krama], described as the uncontested dominator of himself, full of supreme bliss, the *lord of the heroes* (*vīra*)[44] intent on devouring the differentiation of beings — the lord, that is, of the senses — imbued by the being of Manthāna Bhairava. He who does not manage to achieve such a condition is none other than the common herd, the *enjoyed by* [and not the *enjoyer of*] the three states of wakefulness, etc. He who has not raised himself to this peak — even if he is a yogin — does not deserve the name of *lord of the heroes*: he is in actual fact nothing but befuddled. This is said. This is demonstrated in detail in various texts, such as for example the *Svacchanda*,[45] where we read: 'Thanks to free (*svatantra*) yoga which moves on the free path, the yogin united with the plane of the Free [Bhairava] achieves identification with the Free' (Torella 2013: 123–24, emphasis mine).[46]

Once the adept identifies with what is his true centre, sensorial experience will cease to be a tie and can be used as an instrument of liberation. Suitably saturated by extreme intensification, accompanied by release from all individual yearning, the senses are restored to their nature as an expression of the Power.

Again, in commenting on *Śiva Sūtra* 1.12: 'The stages of yoga are amazement', Kṣemarāja, states:

> Just as one who sees something out of the ordinary experiences a feeling of amazement, so the feeling of amazement in enjoying contact with the various manifestations of knowable reality is continually produced in this great yogin with the whole wheel of the senses increasingly expanded, motionless, fully disclosed, by virtue of penetrating into its most intimate nature, the compact union of consciousness and ever-renewed wonder, extreme, extraordinary (Torella 2013: 126–27).[47]

Powers themselves (we should not forget that the most common term for 'sense' is *indriya*, whose original meaning is '[power] of Indra') are nourished and increased — as Abhinavagupta states in the passage from the *Bhagavadgītārthasaṃgraha* quoted earlier[48] — by the objects of the senses themselves in a context of 'purified' enjoyment, in turn sustaining and strengthening the individual on the path toward liberation.

A hymn by Abhinavagupta is entirely devoted to this theme, the *Dehasthadevatācakrastotra* ('Hymn to the Wheel of the Deities Residing in the Body', Pandey 1963 [1935]: 952–53). The supreme god in the form of Ānanda-Bhairava ('Bhairava-Bliss'),[49] embracing his consort Ānanda-Bhairavī who represents his energy aspect (if Bhairava is consciousness in his form as pure light, Bhairavī is the projective–cognitive drive inherent in consciousness), is visualised at the centre of an ideal eight-petalled lotus flower. On each petal is seated a deity, portrayed in the act of rendering cult to the god (or the divine couple) who is in the middle. The deities are the eight Mātṛs (or Mātṛkās), a group of powerful and dangerous goddesses who, despite their apotropaic name of 'Mothers' or 'Little Mothers', are unhappily known to the nocturnal frequenters of the cremation grounds, and are considered as a sort of emanation or double of the Supreme Goddess. The procedures and ingredients of this imagined *pūjā* are rather unusual: Vaiṣṇavī as the sense of hearing offers, instead of the prescribed flowers, sounds; Vārāhī as the sense of touch offers tactile sensations; Indrāṇī as the sense of sight offers the most beautiful forms and colours; Cāmuṇḍā as the sense of taste offers delicious tastes; and Mahālakṣmī as the sense of smell offers rare scents. And that is not all. The remaining three Mothers are linked to the intellectual functions: the haughty Śāmbhavī as the sense of the 'individual ego' offers Bhairava, instead of flowers, acts of 'presumption';[50] Kaumārī, the capricious adolescent goddess, as mind (*manas*), offers fantasies and mental constructs (*vikalpa*); and the solemn Brāhmaṇī, as intellect (*buddhi*), offers Bhairava acts of final ascertainment (ascertainment or *niścaya* constitutes the final phase of the cognitive process). It should be said, by the way, that these eight elements often constitute the so-called *puryaṣṭaka*, the 'eightfold body' or, according to another interpretation, the 'ogdoad that lies in the body', a kind of bearing structure within the human being that sums up the cognitive and emotional aspects; it is the eightfold body that constitutes the transmigratory nucleus of the individual at death. Yet again, we see that Tantrism responds to the Brāhmaṇical separation into 'high' intellectual functions and 'low' sensorial functions not only in terms of integration and affirmation of equal dignity, but even deification. The energy that makes them function is none other than the energy that coincides with supreme Consciousness or, in religious terms, with Śiva himself.

In truth, the Śaiva masters thrust much further. The intrinsically unbridled and only superficially trainable nature of the senses actually places them in a privileged position as compared to the mind which, on the other hand, is for its own part more at risk of becoming a sort of blanket that every day smothers the fire of the individual's deepest identity that, in any final analysis, coincides with God himself. The same is true of the emotions, the more so the stronger and more uncontrollable they are. Within Śaiva non-dualistic traditions, there thus arises a school of teachings aimed at enrolling the senses, passions and emotions *against* the mind. The duration–continuity of the mind is maliciously contrasted with the instant of the emotion. As an antecedent and also theoretical presupposition of such a position, a laconic *sūtra* (3.23) of the *Śiva Sūtra* may be invoked, a text to whose programmed obscurity we are by now habituated: 'In the middle the lower birth is produced' (*madye 'varaprasavaḥ*). To try to unravel this statement, we once more have recourse to the commentator Kṣemarāja:

> For him who only at the initial and final extremes tastes the essence of the fourth, 'in the middle', in the intermediate area, 'the lower birth is produced', wretched, the lowest creation, the ordinary way of living (Torella 2013: 234).[51]

What is certain is that here our commentator risks being even more obscure than the *sūtra* he wishes to elucidate. What the Kashmiri master has in mind is the well-known distinction of human experience into four conditions (*avasthās*), already encountered in the Upaniṣads. The first three (wakefulness, sleep with dreams and dreamless deep sleep) together constitute the modality of ordinary experience, whereas the fourth corresponds to the status of the liberated. According to the spiritual tradition from which Kṣemarāja draws his inspiration, experience of the fourth state in actual fact also occurs within the other three, but solely at two special moments of each act: the initial instant, in which the very first vibration of the still wholly undifferentiated will comes directly into contact with the energy of consciousness; and the final instant, in which the initial impulse, having completed its outer curve (in which it has become other than itself), fades away once more in the vibrating light of consciousness. The whole intermediate zone is the māyic sphere of differentiation. The median zone is, thus, the canonical locus of the ordinary mind, in which the instant falls asleep into duration. The author of the other major commentary on the *Śiva Sūtra*,

Bhāskara, in two passages of his *Vārttika*, further elaborates on this theme: the privileged moments represented by the 'extremities', both initial and final, also concern human passions and emotions, and the sounds of language. At the very first and last moment of a feeling of joy, anger, love, greed, etc., the *ātman* manifests itself (*Śivasūtra-vārttika*, in Chatterji 1916: 49). In our ordinary speech, each phoneme is composed of three parts: the first and the last have the nature of Śiva, while in the middle the phoneme is debased to ordinary sound, losing its divine nature (ibid.: 64).

The instant is 'wakened' by the teachings — experiential rather than theoretical — that we find in particular in three texts: the first, the *Vijñānabhairava Tantra* ('Bhairava-as-consciousness'), is of a scriptural nature and is attributed to Śiva himself, who is portrayed, in his terrifying and absolute form as Bhairava, in dialogue with his divine consort; the second is the *Spandakārikā* by Vasugupta or Bhaṭṭa Kallaṭa; and the third is the *Svabodhodayamañjarī* ('The Little Bunch of Flowers of the Rising of One's Intimate Awareness'), a brief 10th-century-CE work (45 *ślokas*) by the Kashmiri Vāmanadatta (Torella 2000a). It is worth our while to focus our attention at least on the latter, the teachings of the *Vijñānabhairava Tantra* and the *Spandakārikā* being comparatively more well-known.

The central teaching of the *Svabodhodayamañjarī*, thus, concerns how to dissolve the mind 'effortlessly'. The method proposed is extremely subtle: the mind (for which the terms *manas* and *citta* are used indifferently) is never attacked frontally, but is, so to speak, outflanked, taken from behind, exploiting its normal functioning in order to block it. For example, the adept is instructed to let his mind focus with special intensity on an object presented by the senses until it is totally occupied by that object. Then, when its object vanishes naturally, the mind is still too closely linked to it to be able to withdraw once again within itself and ends up dissolving itself after the object. This occurs in the case of an adept who focuses his attention fixedly on the noise of thunder, a pleasant sound or music; or else on the beauty of an object seen. In other cases, the same result is obtained without the object vanishing, but hinging on the natural, progressive fading away of the sensation itself. Here, Vāmanadatta refers to the enjoyment that comes from tasting choice food, smelling the scent of jasmine or reaching orgasm. As we see, to dissolve the mind even the 'minor' sensorial faculties can be used, such as touch, taste or smell, largely overlooked by the *Vijñānabhairava* and *Spandakārikā*. Following Vāmanadatta's discerning examination, we face a third situation: when the mind is totally and suddenly invaded by a sensation or emotion, creating as it were a vacuum around itself, for example, when a person remembers something he thought he had forgotten; when a person finally manages to identify with certainty something that he has seen only vaguely from a distance; or when a person gives himself over to any sensual pleasure. Or again, when it is not the fullness of presence, but on the contrary an absence, an empty space — whether caused deliberately, or occurring on its own — that takes over the mind and finally brings about its dissolution.

Let us, however, take up, at least, a few of these verses, as terse as they are astonishing, of the *Svabodhodayamañjarī*.

> In the past, the Masters have taught the means to dissolve it [the mind]. Being afraid that this authoritative teaching should decay, I will illustrate it. (4).
>
> The ancient masters have shown how to block it through detachment and repeated practice.[52] [Instead], we will teach how to obtain the blocking [of the mind] with no effort. (12).
>
> This is just like what happens when a rumbling thunder gradually vanishes: once the thunder has completely vanished, the mind too, due to its resting on it, becomes extinguished. (14)
>
> The adept should fix his exclusive attention on any pleasant sound coming to his ears, till the moment in which the sound, having disappeared, becomes the cause of the blocking [of the mind]. (15).
>
> In this practice, the sensorial faculties, which are the instruments of perception, are to be brought to a state of 'equality'. Equality comes from the escaping from attachment, as well as from the extinction of aversion. (18)
>
> One should escape from all attachment, and from all aversion as well. Attached to all, just like the fettered man, is Bhairava, and averse to all.[53] (19).
>
> Sensorial faculties, when bereft of perceptible objects and void, are dissolved into the Self. The happiness of isolation arises in him, who attains the dissolution of the sensorial faculties. (20).
>
> If one is running without being determinately aware of his own efforts in making steps, and, consequently, has his mental activity free from intentions and constructs, the supreme Self shines in him. (24).
>
> Whatever longing he may experience for any object, like food and so on, he should satisfy it as far as possible. Thus, he will become full and without support. (28).

> At the end of coitus, the adept should project his mind into the place between the navel and the sexual organ. When the love bliss dissolves, he becomes waveless in one instant. (38).
>
> If, in the manners outlined so far, instant by instant he brings about the dissolution of the mind into the Self, he attains the essence of consciousness. He is called 'liberated-while-living'. (24)[54] (Torella 2000a: 402–06).

Desire: A Tantric Invention?

At the end of this excursion into the lesser known folds of Hindu Tantrism — a journey that does not follow straight paths, but is necessarily winding and uncertain — we have at least managed to understand the title of the last section correctly, itself not a little ambiguous. Does India really owe to Tantrism the invention (understood in its etymological meaning of *inventio*) of desire? As we have seen, the reply is certainly negative: neither its invention, nor even its re-invention after a period of eclipse. India has always been fully aware of the centrality of the body[55] and the drives of the psyche, in a single word, of the 'desiring' dimension of man. The fact that this is not clear externally is due to the work of containment erected by the Brāhmaṇical elite over the almost 2000 years of its grandiose attempt at dominating the Indian world as a whole. Lacking any direct power, it has replaced it by successfully imposing, as an alternative, an opposition between purity and impurity that has marked every aspect of Indian culture: purity of spirit, purity of philosophy, purity of rites, purity of language, purity of social and religious conduct, etc. On the impure side, all 'power' (excluding its own) is tacitly placed, any reality that, owing to its intrinsic nature, tends to escape control and standardisation: most of all, the tumult of the body, and of the sensorial–emotional–passional sphere. In the latter, special importance is given to eros. Although eros has only been dealt with fleetingly in this essay, it has been so done not in order to undervalue it, but, on the contrary, to react against its overvaluation (the congeries of studies on Tantric eros, for the most part generally of inferior quality, end up leaving in the shade the rest of the emotional sphere, much less documented and perhaps even much more hair-splitting to investigate) on the one hand, and not to over-burden what is intended to be only a preliminary study, on the other.

A last blunder would be to see in Tantric teachings the sophisticated result of a protest by subtle theologians inclined to private transgressions. On the contrary, Tantrism represents an open response to the

Brāhmaṇical world, just as grandiose as the challenge that triggered it and with goals just as vast. The counter-attack occurs precisely at the central point, i.e., questioning the legitimacy and the very basis for the division between pure and impure, destined to crumble progressively beneath the thrust of a deliberate 'non-dual' behaviour (*advaitācāra*), in which the more authentic meaning of Tantric transgression can be sought.[56] But who and what takes responsibility for this 'response'? To speak, as has commonly been done, of popular incitement that includes the re-emergence of ancestral doctrines and non-Aryan, or even pre-Aryan, motifs, means, first and foremost, an unawareness of the profound cultural unity of the Indian subcontinent, albeit with its thousands of variations. It means, furthermore, not being aware that many of the Tantric 'rebels' are themselves Brāhmaṇas, neither more nor less than their antagonists. In Tantrism, it is not another India coming to the foreground, but the *only* India feeling, within a part of its own Brāhmaṇical elite, that the moment has come to reformulate itself in order to guarantee its own future survival in a historically changed world.

Notes

*All translations of excerpts from Sanskrit texts cited in this chapter are by the author.

1. Among the most conspicuous exceptions is Aristotle.
2. Similar passages can be found in *Garuḍa Purāṇa*, *Pretakalpa*, *Adhyāya* 6 (Abegg 1956 [1921]: 91–99), as well as in several other Purāṇas (ibid.: 93n6). I thank K. Preisendanz for this reference.
3. Or: 'without object'. Of the two possible meanings of *karma* in this context, the latter is certainly the one meant by Abhinavagupta (*niṣkarmā yābhilāṣitā*, *Tantrāloka* 9.62b, in Śāstrī and Śāstrī 1918–38, vol. 6: 56). However, the parallel between *niṣkāma-karma* and *niṣkarma-kāma* can be maintained, since, as Jayaratha explicitly says in commenting on this passage, the absence of an object in this desiring condition is linked to the absence of any definite action in it (*niṣkarmā kriyārūpatvābhāvāt*).
4. Desire and anger are deemed strictly as a pair, or rather as two aspects of the same reality. As Śaṅkara says in his commentary on this passage, it is frustrated desire that is transformed into anger. *Rajas*, along with *sattva* and *tamas* (a doctrine belonging to Sāṃkhya, significantly present in the *Bhagavadgītā*) are at the same time psychic states and cosmic forces — an ambiguity that is unresolved in classical Sāṃkhya, which inherits and unites highly differentiated ancient doctrines. *Sattva* is characterised by joy and light: it is gentle and illuminating. *Rajas* is characterised by an absence of joy and by dynamism: it is unstable and stimulating. *Tamas* is characterised

by inertia and restriction: it is heavy and obstructive. Passions and emotions are, of course, expressions of the *rajas* component.

5. My translation of the phrase *kāmatattvam idaṃ yataḥ* significantly differs from Hanneder's ('for this [world] is the reality of desire', in 1998: 105).
6. See particularly the *Dehasthadevatācakrastotra* ('Hymn to the Wheel of Deities Residing in the Body') in Pandey (1963[1935]: 952–53; cf. p. 85, this volume).
7. I read *nigṛhītāni* instead of *vigṛhītāni*, as found in both editions of the text by Śāstrī (1922) and Vasudeva (2004). The reading *nigṛhītāni*, strictly required by the context, can be found in the quotation of this passage in *Tantrāloka* 17.112c.
8. *Yoga Sūtra* 1.12: *abhyāsavairāgyābhyāṃ tannirodhaḥ* ('The blocking of the mental functions is caused by repeated practice and detachment').
9. On the doctrine of the 'cuirasses' in Tantrism, see Torella (1998). Also, see the section titled 'Passion (*rāga*) as One of the 'Cuirasses' in this essay.
10. See particularly *Pramāṇavārttika* 1.12 and *svavṛtti* p. 9.3–18 (Gnoli 1960: 9), examined and variously translated in the aforementioned articles (Dunne 1996; Franco 2004; Pecchia 2008; Taber 2011).
11. *sāsravadharmaviṣayam* (*Pramāṇavārttika-svavṛtti*, in Gnoli 1960: 9.5–6); *sāsravaviṣayam* (*Sarvajñasiddhi*, in Thakur 1975: 23.25).
12. On *anuttara*, see Bäumer (2011: 67–90).
13. On the 'non-means' (*anupāya*), see Torella (2000b: 121–22).
14. This is a clear allusion to yoga practices focused on breathing.
15. Here, Abhinavagupta is possibly referring to Vāmanadatta's *Svabodhodaya-mañjarī*. On this interesting, and very peculiar, text see Torella (2000a). See also p. 87, this volume.
16. It is worth presenting the full passage (Leopardi 1937: 173–74) in which the sentence quoted above is contained:

    Ma la ragione non è mai efficace come la passione. Sentite i filosofi. Bisogna fare che l'uomo si muova per la ragione come, anzi più assai che per la passione, anzi si muova per la sola ragione e dovere. Bubbole. La natura degli uomini e delle cose, può ben esser corrotta, ma non corretta. E se lasciassimo fare alla natura, le cose andrebbero benissimo, non ostante la detta superiorità della passione sulla ragione. Non bisogna estinguer la passione colla ragione, ma convertir la ragione in passione; fare che il dovere la virtù l'eroismo ec. diventino passioni. Tali sono per natura. Tali erano presso gli antichi, e le cose andavano molto meglio. Ma quando la sola passione del mondo è l'egoismo, allora si ha ben ragione di gridar contro la passione. Ma come spegner l'egoismo colla ragione che n'è la nutrice, dissipando le illusioni? E senza ciò, l'uomo privo di passioni, non si muoverebbe per loro, ma neanche per la ragione, perchè le cose son fatte così, e non si possono cambiare, chè la ragione non è forza viva nè motrice, e l'uomo non farà altro che divenirne indolente, inattivo, immobile, indifferente, infingardo, com'è divenuto in grandissima parte (22 ottobre 1820)'.

    The translation of the passage is as follows:

'But reason is never as effective as passion. Listen to the philosophers. Men should be led to act in accordance with reason as much as, indeed much more than, out of passion; in fact their actions should be determined solely by reason and duty. Nonsense. The nature of human beings and other things can easily be corrupted but not corrected. And if we let nature take its course, things would run very smoothly, despite the said dominance of passion over reason. Rather than extinguish passion with reason, it would be better to turn reason into passion: to make duty, virtue, heroism etc. become passions. So they are in nature. So they were among the ancients, and things were much better. But when the only passion in the world is egoism then it is right to cry out against passion. But how can selfishness be eliminated by reason, which fosters it by destroying illusions? And without it, a man deprived of passions would not be motivated by them, or by reason, either, because things being like that, and unable to change, reason is neither a living nor a motive force, and man will do nothing but become lazy, inactive, immobile, indifferent, uncaring, as in large parte he has (22 Oct. 1820)' (Caesar and D'Intino 2013: 191).

17. It is also worth noting what Kṣemarāja says in his *Vimarśinī* on *Śiva-sūtra* 3.26 (Chatterji 1911: 54; Torella 2013: 239): 'Living in the body: this is the religious observance' (*śarīravṛttir vratam*); '[t]he compenetration with Śiva is achieved *only* by the yogin who resides in the body, the *prāṇa*, etc.' (*dehaprāṇādyavasthitasyaiva śivasamāviṣṭatvam uktam*).
18. My interpretation is diametrically opposed (see note 19, this chapter) to that given by the principal commentator of the *Mahābhārata*, Nīlakaṇṭha (16th century CE).
19. I must admit that my interpretation of the meaning of the entire passage (the textual transmission of which is, however, uncertain at several points, with various differences between the vulgata and the Pune critical edition) is not at all in line with the current Brāhmaṇical interpretation, which tends to consider it as a warning against the subtle snares of desire. Whatever be the case, even if one admits the 'ascetic' intent of its original composer, the entire passage resounds as a paradoxical celebration of the ineludible presence and power of desire.
20. English translation of the libretto by Avril Bardoni, 1989, included with the 1990 Virgin Classics recording VCT 7 90775-2-4.
21. Translation partly based on Renou (1956: 125–26).
22. Interestingly, the idea of the centrality of desire survives precisely in the Mīmāṃsā, the school of Vedic exegesis that later developed into a *darśana* (philosophical system) proper. The self as the ritual agent hinges on desire (*kāma*): without the desire for a certain fruit no individual would engage in sacrificial activity, or more in general, in any kind of activity, the disappearing of desire only occurring on the way to liberation (Freschi 2007). This may be likened to the Śaiva concept of the self as *kartṛ* (doer) as opposed to the *akriya* (inactive) self of Vedānta.

23. Here we are supported by the authority of the *Bhagavadgītā* which, in the verse 3.40ab, states: 'Of desire, the senses, the mind and the intellect are the substrate'.
24. By way of an antidote, I quote the strong words of Remo Bodei (2003: 8–9):

    'Nothing prevents us, however, from thinking of the "passions" (emotions, feelings, desires) as states that are not added from the outside at a zero level of indifferent consciousness, to excite and confuse it, but are ingredients of the tone of any psychic state of being and even of any cognitive orientation . . . Despite everything, the passions cannot be reduced just to conflict and mere passivity. They tint the world with lively subjective colours, accompany the unravelling of events, shake experience from inertia and monotony, and make existence flavoursome, discomfort and pain notwithstanding. Would it be worthwhile living if we felt no passion, if tenacious, invisible threads did not bind us to what — in various ways — we are "fond of", whose loss we fear?' ('*Nulla impedisce tuttavia di pensare le "passioni"* [*emozioni, sentimenti, desideri*] *quali stati che non si aggiungono dall'esterno a un grado zero della coscienza indifferente, per intorbidarla e confonderla, ma che sono costitutivi della tonalità di qualsiasi modo di essere psichico e persino di ogni orientamento cognitivo . . . Malgrado tutto, le passioni non si riducono però soltanto a conflitto e a mera passività. Esse tingono il mondo di vivaci colori soggettivi, accompagnano il dipanarsi degli eventi, scuotono l'esperienza dall'inerzia e dalla monotonia, rendono sapida l'esistenza nonostante disagi e dolori. Varrebbe la pena vivere se non provassimo alcuna passione, se tenaci, invisibili fili non ci avvincessero a quanto — a diverso titolo — ci sta "a cuore", e di cui temiamo la perdita?*').

    Yet again, referring to Spinoza, Bodei (2003: 58) states:

    'Conditionings of all kinds mould him [man] indeed like "clay in the potter's hands": to escape them, without prejudice to the laws of this world, appears just as absurd and undesirable as living under an eternally serene sky' ('*Condizionamenti di ogni genere lo* [*l'uomo*] *plasmano infatti al pari della "creta nelle mani del vasaio"; immaginare di sfuggirvi, ferme restando le leggi di questo mondo, appare altrettanto assurdo e indesiderabile quanto vivere sotto un cielo eternamente sereno*').
25. In analogous terms, this motif recurs, e.g., in the Platonic dialogue *Phaedrus* (Yunis 2011, sections 246a–247c).
26. The Sanskrit term *para* may mean 'superior, supreme' and 'other' as well. All the ancient commentators of the *Kaṭha* agree in taking it in the sense of 'superior' in ontological terms (*Īśādidaśopaniṣadaḥ śaṅkarabhāṣyasametāḥ* 1978: 81–82), glosses it by *sūkṣmatara* — or 'more subtle', meaning that it possesses a higher ontological rank. The verse of the *Kaṭha Upaniṣad* is taken up again in *Bhagavadgītā* 3.42 (Krishna Warrier 1983: 133) almost literally, and even in that case all the commentators take it in the same way (Śaṅkara, if possible, is even more explicit: *para* means *prakṛṣṭa* — 'more elevated'

[in the hierarchy of being]). There is only one exception: the Tantric Abhinavagupta, who in his *Bhagavadgītārthasaṃgraha* (Sankaranarayanan 1985: 59) impassibly glosses *para* by *anya*: 'The mind is not "superior" to the senses and the objects of the senses, it is only "different" from them'.

27. Immediately after the verse 1.3.10, things get complicated and one realises that the Upaniṣad is moving into an unequivocally Sāṃkhya scenario, albeit far from the form of classical Sāṃkhya. The Great Self of the previous verse is yet another intermediate dimension: 'Superior to the Great Self is the Unmanifest; superior to the Unmanifest is the Spirit (*puruṣa*). Superior to the Spirit there is nothing. It is the deadline, the supreme goal' (1.3.11, *Īśādidaśopaniṣadaḥ śaṅkarabhāṣyasametāḥ* 1978, vol. 1: 82).
28. See, for instance, *Mataṅgapārameśvarāgama*, Vidyāpāda, 14.2 (Bhatt 1977: 362): 'Permeated by the triad of the cuirasses, softly pushed by Time, enveloped by Necessity, this principle proceeds with the quality of 'individual soul', pertaining to the Self'.
29. No work of Bṛhaspati, one of the oldest Śaiva masters (certainly earlier than the 10th century CE), has come down to us. The sentence attributed to him is quoted by Abhinavagupta in *Tantrāloka* 9.208c (Śāstrī and Śāstrī 1918–38, vol. 6: 168) and by Nārāyaṇakaṇṭha in his commentary on *Mṛgendra Tantra* (Śāstrī 1930: 208).
30. The simile is likely to be from Śivāgrayogin's commentary on the *Śivajñāna-siddhiyār.*
31. Rāmakaṇṭha's commentary on *Mataṅgapārameśvarāgama*, Vidyāpāda, 9.11cd et seq. (Bhatt 1977: 298).
32. *abhidharmādau bhāratādau ca darśitaś cittavṛttigaṇo rāgamūla eva* (*Īśvarapratyabhijñā-vivṛtivimarśinī* , in Śāstrī 1938–43, vol. 3: 291).
33. Here, the Śaiva philosophers refer to the Sāṃkhya doctrine of the eight *bhāvas* and 50 *pratyayas*. The *bhāvas* are the basic predispositions of the human mind: righteousness, knowledge, detachment, and sovereignty, along with their opposites; and the *pratyayas* represent the totality of the psychical processes of human life (cf. Torella 1999: 557–60).
34. Cf. Rāmakaṇṭha's commentary on *Mataṅgapārameśvarāgama*, Vidyāpāda, 11.4cd–5ab (Bhatt 1977: 326).
35. A passage by Spinoza comes to mind: 'Toward nothing do we strive, nothing do we want, we crave and desire because we judge it good; but, on the contrary, we judge something good because we strive toward it, we want it, we crave it and we desire it' (*Etica*, III, prop. 9, scolio, in Bodei 2003: 61).
36. See p. 67, this volume.
37. Abhinavagupta's authorship of the *Parātrīśikā-laghuvṛtti* has recently been questioned (Sanderson 2005: 142).
38. King Triśaṅku, who wanted to ascend to the heaven with his physical body, was hurled down from the heaven by the gods and then arrested midway by Viśvāmitra, thus remaining suspended in the sky; he was then transformed

into a constellation. The story of Triśaṅku, so popular in India, is narrated in many texts (and with many variants); see, for instance, *Rāmāyaṇa*, Bālakāṇḍa, Chapters 57–60; *Skanda Purāṇa*, Nāgarakāṇḍa, Chapters 2–6, etc. This story also reached the West, and we can even find it condensed in a lovely poem *Viswamitra the Magician* by Henri Wadsworth Longfellow (1878: 63):

'By his spells and incantations, / Up to Indra's realms elysian / Raised Trisanku, king of nations. Indra and the gods offended / Hurled him downward, and descending / In the air he hung suspended, / With these equal powers contending. / Thus by aspirations lifted, / By misgivings downward driven, / Human hearts are tossed and drifted / Midway between earth and heaven'.

39. *anyathā pāṣāṇādivat jaḍabhūmim evāpatet parameśvaravad vā saṃvidgaganam evāpapet / ubhayathāpi māyāpramātṛtābhāve vedyam api na kiṃcid iti* (*Parātrīśikā-laghuvṛtti*, in Śāstrī 1947: 7). It is worth noting that in the many descriptions of the emanation of the universe in the form of the gradual emanation of Sanskrit phonemes found in the Śaiva scriptures, it is always the semi-vowels that are related to the cuirasses! These very subtle arguments elaborated by the Śaiva doctors are explained in Torella (1998: 55–86).
40. *sahayajñāḥ prajāḥ sṛṣṭvā purovāca prajāpatiḥ | anena prasaviṣyadhvam eṣa vo 'astv iṣṭakāmadhuk || devān bhāvayatānena te devā bhāvayantu vaḥ | parasparaṃ bhāvayantaḥ śreyaḥ param avāpsyatha || iṣṭān bhogān hi vo devā dāsyante yajña-bhāvitāḥ | tair dattān apradāyaibhyo yo bhuṅkte stena eva saḥ ||.*
41. One of the traditional ancient etymologies for the word *deva* ('god') makes it derive from the root *div-* in the sense of 'to take pleasure, to play, to act freely and gratuitously'. Here, Abhinavagupta is, of course, utilising this etymological artifice to introduce his daring metaphorical interpretation (gods = senses).
42. *devāḥ krīḍāśīlāḥ indriyavṛttayaḥ karaṇeśvaryo devatā rahasyaśāstraprasiddhāḥ, tāḥ anena karmaṇā tarpayata, yathāsaṃbhavaṃ viṣayān bhakṣayatety arthaḥ / tṛptāś ca satyas tā vo yuṣmān ātmana eva svarūpamātrocitāpavargān bhāvayantu svātmasthitiyogyatvāt | evam anavaratam vyutthānasamādhisamayaparamparā-yām indriyatarpaṇatadātmasādbhāvalakṣaṇe parasparabhāvane sati śīghram eva paramaṃ śreyaḥ parasparabhedavigalanalakṣaṇaṃ brahma prāpsyatha . . . yajñatarpitāni hīndriyāṇi sthitiṃ badhnanti yatra kvāpi dhyeyādāv iti . . . ato 'yaṃ vākyārthaḥ yaḥ sukhopāyaṃ siddhim apavargaṃ vā prepsati tena indriyakautuha-nivṛttimātraphalatayaiva bhogā yathopanatam āsevyā iti ||.*
43. The theme of wonder, which appeared earlier in the *Śiva-sūtra* as *vismaya* or 'amazement', was destined to undergo major developments in subsequent philosophical and aesthetic speculation with the synonymous term *camatkāra*, used, perhaps, for the first time in a pregnant sense by Utpaladeva. 'Wonder' is the condition of the enlightened subject, his becoming aware of the Self and of everything under the sign of a perpetual

and infinite 'wondering enjoyment', as opposed to the restricted nature and automatism of ordinary consciousness. The essence of *camatkāra* may be identified in the act of opening oneself to experience of the all in the most intense and penetrating manner, while firmly maintaining the centre of gravity on the subject that perceives rather than on the object perceived.

44. It should be noted that the term *vīra* ('hero') is commonly adopted to designate the most famous type of Tantric adept, inclined to practices centred on energy, often consisting in tackling reality (sex, inebriating beverages, meat, etc.), whose 'negative' nature has to be dominated and overturned.
45. *Svacchanda Tantra* 7.260, in Dvivedi (1985, vol. 2: 57).
46. *etajjāgarāditrayaṃ śakticakrānusaṃdhānayuktyā turyānandācchuritam yaḥ tatparāmarśānupraveśaprakarṣād vigalitabhedasaṃskāram ānandarasapravāhamayam eva paśyati, sa tritayasyāsya bhoktā camatkartā | tata eva triṣu dhāmasu yad bhogyaṃ bhoktā yaś ca prakīrtitaḥ | vedaitad ubhayam yas tu sa buñjāno na lipyate || iti nītyā niḥsapatnasvātmasāṃrājyo 'yaṃ paramānandaparipūrṇo bhavabhedagrasanapravaṇānāṃ vīrāṇām indriyāṇām īśvaraḥ svāmī, śrīmanthānabhairavasattānupraviṣṭo mahāmnāyeṣūcyate | yas tu evaṃvidho na bhavati, sa jāgarādyavasthābhir bhujyamāno laukikaḥ paśur eva | yogy api imāṃ dhārām anadhirūḍho na vīreśvaraḥ, api tu mūḍha evety uktaṃ bhavati | etac ca "yogī svacchandayogena svacchanda-gaticāriṇā | sa svacchandapade yuktaḥ svacchandasamatāṃ vrajet" ityādinā śrīsvacchandādiśāstreṣu vitatya darśitam* (Chatterji 1911: 27–28).
47. *yathā sātiśayavastudarśane kasyacit vismayo bhavati tathā asya mahāyogino nityaṃ tattadvedyāvabhāsāmarśābhogeṣu niḥsāmānyātiśayanavanavacamatkāracidghanasvātmāveśavaśāt smerasmerastimitavikāsitasamastakaraṇacak-rasya yo vismayo 'navacchinānande svātmani aparitṛptatvena muhur muhur āścaryamāṇatā* (ibid.: 29).
48. See also p. 82, this volume, where other relevant passages are quoted.
49. The God Bhairava embodies the terrifying form of Śiva and represents the upsetting of all individually limited forms.
50. A strange offering in a world apparently so depersonalised as the Indian one. In actual fact, *abhimāna*, although meaning 'presumption, pride' in everyday language, is used in the philosophical lexicon to designate, within the cognitive process, the moment at which the cognition taking shape connects with a given individual ego ('I' perceive this vase).
51. *pūrvāparakoṭyos turyasamāsvādayato madhye madhyadaśāyām avaraḥ aśreṣṭaḥ prasavo vyutthānātmā kutsitaḥ sargo jāyate* (Chatterji 1911: 107–08).
52. See p. 65, this volume.
53. Regarding the text of this verse there is a notable fluctuation in the manuscripts and old quotations (Torella 2000a: 398, 405).
54. *tasyaiva vilayopāyaḥ pradiṣṭo gurubhiḥ purā | tadāgamaparibhraṃśabhayāt spaṣṭīkṛto mayā || 4 || pūrvair nirodhaḥ kathito vairāgyābhyāsayogataḥ | ayatnena nirodho 'yam asmābhir upadiśyate || 12 || yad yan manoharaṃ kiṃcic*

chrutigocaram āgatam / ekāgraṃ bhāvayet tāvad yāval līnaṃ nirodhakṛt || 15 || grahaṇānīndriyāṇīha samānīti prabodhayet / samatvaṃ rāgahāneḥ syād dveṣasyopakṣayāt tathā || 18 || sarvarāgāt sahāniḥ syāt sarvadveṣāt tathaiva ca | baddhavat sarvarāgī syāt sarvadveṣṭā ca bhairavaḥ || 19 || agrāhyam indriyaṃ śūnyaṃ svātmany eva pralīyate / pralīnendriyavṛttes tu kaivalyābhyudayodayaḥ || 20 || dhāvataḥ padavikṣepaprayatnānavadhāraṇāt / niḥsaṃkalpamanovṛtteḥ paramātmā prakāśate || 24 || yatra yatra bhaved vāñchā bhojanādiṣu vastuṣu | pūrayet tāṃ yathāśakti bhavet pūrṇo nirāśrayaḥ || 28 || nābhimedhrāntare cittaṃ suratānte vinikṣipet / līyamāne ratānande nistaraṅgaḥ kṣaṇaṃ bhavet || 38 || itthaṃ pratikṣaṇaṃ yasya cittam ātmani līyate || sa labdhabodhasadbhāvo / jīvanmukto 'bhidhīyate || 44 ||.

55. In this connection, I would like to recall a personal experience. In the summer of 2004, I was at Helsinki for the World Sanskrit Conference. I was listening to a paper by Rama Nath Sharma, the illustrious scholar of Sanskrit grammar and the language sciences, when I was struck by a quotation, apparently taken from the Dharmaśāstras, the vast corpus of texts that have always governed the socio-religious behaviour of the orthodox Hindu. In this quotation, the body is mentioned as the prime tool in achieving *dharma*. Inquisitive, at the end of the conference, I approached my Indian colleague to ask him the specific source. Sharma replied (accompanying his answer with a vague smile of understanding): 'But everybody knows'.
56. Another major challenge is represented by the universalistic approach to revelation as preached by non-dualistic Śaivism against the strict control performed by Brāhmaṇical élite (Torella 2013).

References

Primary Sources

Atharvaveda:

Bloomfield, Maurice (trans.). 1987 [1897]. *Hymns of the Atharva-Veda: Together with Extracts from the Ritual Books and the Commentaries.* Delhi: Motilal Banarsidass.

Īśvarapratyabhijñāvivṛtivimarśinī of Abhinavagupta:

Śāstrī, Madhusūdan Kaul (ed.). 1938–43. *Īśvarapratyabhijñāvivṛtivimarśinī*, 3 vols. Kashmir Series of Texts and Studies (KSTS) 60, 62 and 65. Bombay: Research Department, Srinagar, Jammu and Kashmir State.

Kiraṇa Tantra:

Goodall, Dominic (ed. and trans.). 1998. *Bhaṭṭarāmakaṇṭhaviracitā kiraṇavṛttiḥ: Bhaṭṭa Rāmakaṇṭha's Commentary on the Kiraṇatantra*, vol. 1, chapters 1–6. Pondicherry: Institut Français de Pondichéry and École française d'Extrême-Orient.

Mahābhārata (Āśvamedhikaparvan)

Sukthankar, V. S. and R. D. Karmakar (eds). 1960. *The Mahābhārata for the First Time Critically Edited*, vol. 18: *Āśvamedhikaparvan.* Pune: Bhandarkar Oriental Research Institute.

Mahānayaprakāśa:
Śāstrī, K. Sāmbaśiva (ed.). 1937. *Mahānayaprakāśa*. Trivandrum Sanskrit Series 130. Trivandrum: Government Press.
Mālinīvijaya-vārttika of Abhinavagupta:
Hanneder, Jürgen (ed. and trans.). 1998. *Abhinavagupta's Philosophy of Revelation: An Edition and Annotated Translation of Mālinīślokavārttika I, 1–399*. Groningen Oriental Studies 14. Groningen: Forsten.
Śāstrī, Madhusūdan Kaul (ed.). 1921. *Mālinīvijayavārttikam*. KSTS 31. Srinagar: Research Department, Jammu and Kashmir State.
Mālinīvijayottara Tantra or *Mālinīvijaya Tantra*:
Śāstrī, Madhusūdan Kaul (ed.). 1922. *Mālinīvijayottaratantram*. KSTS 37. Bombay.
Vasudeva, Somadeva (ed. and trans.). 2004. *The Yoga of the Mālinīvijayottaratantra*, chapters 1–4, 7, 11–17. Collection indologie 97. Pondicherry: Institut Français de Pondichéry and École Française d'Extrême Orient.
Manusmṛti:
Jolly, J. (ed.). 1887. *Mānava-dharma-śāstra: The Code of Manu*. London: Trubner & Co.
Mataṅgapārameśvarāgama:
Bhatt, N. R. (ed.). 1977. *Mataṅgapārameśvarāgama (Vidyāpāda), avec le commentaire de Bhaṭṭa Rāmakaṇṭha*. Publications de l'Institut Français d'Indologie 56. Pondicherry: Institut Français d'Indologie.
Mṛgendra Tantra:
Śāstrī, Madhusūdan Kaul (ed.). 1930. *Mṛgendratantra (Vidyāpāda and Yogapāda) with Commentary of Nārāyaṇakaṇṭha*. KSTS 50. Bombay: Nirnaya Sagar Press.
Parātrīśikā-laghuvṛtti of Abhinavagupta:
Śāstrī, Pandit Jagaddhara Zādoo (ed.). 1947. *Parātrīśikālaghuvṛtti*. KSTS 68. Srinagar: Research Department, Jammu and Kashmir State.
Pramāṇavārttika of Dharmakīrti:
Gnoli, R. (ed.). 1960. *Pramāṇavārttika* I: *Pramāṇavārttikam. The First Chapter with the Autocommentary*. Serie Orientale Roma 23. Roma: Ist.italiano per il medio ed estremo oriente (IsMEO).
Sāṃkhyakārikā:
Venkaṭanāthācārya, N. S. (ed.). 1982. *Sāṇkhyadarśanam with Śrīdhara's Sāṇkhyadīpikā vṛtti and Īśvarakṛṣṇa's Sāṇkhyakārikā with Bhāvaprakāśa*. Oriental Research Institute Series 134. Mysore: University of Mysore.
Sarvajñasiddhi of Ratnakīrti:
Thakur, A. (ed.). 1975. *Ratnakīrti-nibandhāvaliḥ* (Buddhist Nyaya works of Ratnakirti). Patna: K. P. Jayaswal Research Institute.
Śivadṛṣṭi of Somānanda:
Śāstrī, Madhusūdan Kaul (ed.). 1934. *Śivadṛṣṭi of Śrī Somānandanātha with the Vṛtti by Utpaladeva*. KSTS 54. Srinagar: Research Department, Jammu and Kashmir State.

Śiva Sūtra of Vasugupta with Commentary *Śivasūtra-vimarśinī* of Kṣemarāja:
Chatterji, J. C. (ed.). 1911. *Shiva Sūtra Vimarshinī; Being the Sutras of Vasu Gupta, with the Commentary called Vimarshini*. KSTS 1. Srinagar: Research Department, Jammu and Kashmir State.
Torella, Raffaele (trans.). 2013. *Gli Aforismi di Śiva con il commento di Kṣemarāja (Śivasūtravimarśinī)*. Piccola biblioteca Adelphi 641. Milano: Adelphi.
Śiva Sūtra of Vasugupta with Commentary *Śivasūtra-vārttika* of Bhāskara:
Chatterji, J. C. (ed.). 1916 *Shiva Sūtra Vārttika by Bhāskara*. KSTS 4–5. Srinagar: Research Department, Jammu and Kashmir State.
Śrīmadbhagavadgītābhāṣya of Śaṅkara:
Krishna Warrier, A. G. (ed. and trans.). 1983. *Śrīmad Bhagavad Gītā Bhāṣya of Śrī Śaṃkarācārya*. Madras: Sri Ramakrishna Math.
Śrīmadbhagavadgītārthasaṃgraha of Abhinavagupta:
Sankaranarayanan, S. (ed.). 1985. *Bhagavadgītārthasaṃgraha: Śrīmadbhagavadgītā with Gītārthasaṃgraha of Abhinavagupta*, part 1. Tirupati: Oriental Research Institute.
Svabodhodayamañjarī of Vāmanadatta:
Torella, Raffaele (ed. and trans.). 2000a. 'The *Svabodhodayamañjarī*, or How to Suppress the Mind with No Effort', in Ryutaro Tsuchida and Albrecht Wezler (eds), *Harānandalaharī: Studies in Honour of Prof. Minoru Hara on His Seventieth Birthday*, pp. 387–410. Reinbek: Verlag für Orientalistische Fachpublicationen.
Svacchanda Tantra:
Dvivedi, Vrajavallabha (ed.). 1985. *Svacchandatantra, with Commentary 'Uddyota' by Kṣemarājācārya*, 2 vols. Parimal Sanskrit Series 16. Delhi: Parimal Publications.
Taittirīyopaniṣadbhāṣyavārttika of Sureśvara:
Taittirīyopaniṣadbhāṣyavārttikam with the Commentary of Ānandagiri. 1911. Ānandāśrama Saṃskrita Granthāvalī 13. Pune: Ānandāśrama Press.
Tantrāloka of Abhinavagupta:
Śāstrī, Mukunda Rāma and Madhusūdana Kaul Śāstrī (eds). 1918–38. *Tantrāloka with Commentary by Rājānaka Jayaratha*, 12 vols. KSTS, 23, 28, 29, 30, 35, 36, 41, 47, 52, 57, 58, and 59. Allahabad: India Press; Bombay: Shri Venkateshvar Press; Srinagar: Research Department, Jammu and Kashmir State.
Upaniṣads:
Īśādidaśopaniṣadaḥ śaṅkarabhāṣyasametāḥ. Delhi: Motilal Banarsidass, 1978.
Yoga Śāstra of Hemacandra:
Jambūvijaya, Muni and Muni Dharmacandravijaya (eds). 1977. *Yogaśāstra* Svopajñavṛttivibhūṣitam (*Yogaśāstram with Autocommentary*). Bombay: Jaina Sahitya Vikasa Mandala.
Yoga Sūtra of Patañjali:
Bhaṭṭācārya, R. Ś. (ed.). 1979. *Pātañjalayogasūtram bhojadevakṛta-rājamārtaṇḍavṛtti sametam*, Delhi and Varanasi: Bhāratīya Vidyā Prakāśana.

Secondary Works

Abegg, Emil. 1956 [1921]. *Der Pretakalpa des Garuḍa-Purāṇa (Naunidhirāma's Sāroddhāra): eine Darstellung des hinduistischen Totenkultes und Jenseitsglaubens*. Berlin: W. de Gruyter.

Bäumer, Bettina. 2011. *Abhinavagupta's Hermeneutics of the Absolute (Anuttaraprakriyā): An Interpretation of his Parātrīśikā Vivaraṇa*. Delhi: D. K. Printworld; Shimla: Indian Institute for Advanced Study.

Bodei, Remo. 2003. *Geometria delle passioni: Paura, speranza, felicità: filosofia e uso politico*. Milano: Feltrinelli.

Bouiller, Véronique and Gilles Tarabout (eds). 2002. *Images du corps dans le monde hindou*. Paris: CNRS.

Caesar, Michael and Franco D'Intino (trans.). 2013. *Giacomo Leopardi: Zibaldone*. New York: Farrar Straus and Giroux.

Devasenapathi, V. A. 1960. *Śaiva Siddhānta as Expounded in the Śivajñāna-siddhiyār and Its Commentaries*. Madras: University of Madras.

Dumont, Louis. 1975. *La civilisation indienne et nous*. Paris: Armand Colin.

Dunne, John D. 1996. 'Thoughtless Buddha, Passionate Buddha', *Journal of the American Academy of Religion*, 64: 525–56.

Franco, Eli. 2004. 'Did the Buddha Have Desires?' in Hendrik W. Bodewitz and Minoru Hara (eds), *Gedenschrift J.W. de Jong*, pp. 39–47. Studia Philologica Buddhica 17. Tokyo: International Institute for Buddhist Studies of the International College for Advanced Buddhist Studies.

Freschi, Elisa. 2007. 'Desidero Ergo Sum: The Subject as the Desirous One in Mīmāṃsā', *Rivista degli Studi Orientali*, 80: 51–61.

Gnoli, Raniero. 1968 [1956]. *The Aesthetic Experience according to Abhinavagupta*. Chowkhamba Sanskrit Studies 62. Varanasi: Chowkhamba Sanskrit Series Office. 2nd edn.

Hara, Minoru. 2001. 'Hindu Concepts of Anger: *Manyu* and *Krodha*', in Raffaele Torella et al. (ed.), *Le Parole e i Marmi. Studi in onore di Raniero Gnoli nel suo 70° compleanno*, 2 vols, pp. 419–44. Roma: Serie Orientale Roma, IsIAO.

Leopardi, Giacomo. 1937. *Zibaldone di pensieri*, vol. 1. Tutte le opere di Giacomo Leopardi, a cura di Francesco Flora. Milano: A. Mondadori.

Longfellow, Henri Wadsworth. 1878. *Kéramos and Other Poems*. Boston: Houghton, Osgood & Company.

Pandey, K. C. 1963 [1935]. *Abhinavagupta: An Historical and Philosophical Study*. Chowkhamba Sanskrit Studies 1. Varanasi: Chowkhamba Sanskrit Series Office. 2nd edn.

Pecchia, Cristina. 2008. 'Is the Buddha Like 'A Man in the Street'? Dharmakīrti's Answer', *Wiener Zeitschrift für die Kunde Südasiens*, 51: 163–92.

Reich, Wilhelm. 1973. *Cosmic Superimposition: Man's Orgonotic Roots in Nature*. New York: Farrar Straus & Groux.

Renou, Louis. 1956. *Hymnes spéculatifs du Véda*. Paris: Gallimard.

Sanderson, Alexis. 2005. 'A Commentary on the Opening Verses of the Tantrasāra of Abhinavagupta', in Sadananda Das and Ernst Fürlinger (eds), *Sāmarasya: Studies in Indian Arts, Philosophy, and Interreligious Dialogue in Honour of Bettina Bäumer*, pp. 89–148. Delhi: D. K. Printworld.

Taber, John. 2011. 'Did Dharmakīrti Think the Buddha Had Desires?' in Helmut Krasser et al. (eds), *Religion and Logic in Buddhist Philosophical Analysis: Proceedings of the Fourth International Dharmakīrti Conference. Vienna, August 23–27, 2005*, pp. 437–48. Wien: Verlag der Österreichischen Akademie der Wissenschaften (Austrian Academy of Sciences).

Torella, Raffaele. 1998. 'The Kañcukas in the Śaiva and Vaiṣṇava Tantric Tradition: A Few Considerations between Theology and Grammar', in Gerhard Oberhammer (ed.), *Studies in Hinduism, II, Miscellanea to the Phenomenon of Tantras*, pp. 55–86. Beitrage zur Kultur- und Geistesgeschichte Asiens 28; Philosophisch-Historische Klasse, Sitzungsberichte 662. Band. Wien: Verlag der Österreichischen Akademie der Wissenschaften (Austrian Academy of Sciences).

——. 1999.'Sāṃkhya as *Sāmānyaśāstra*', *Asiatische Studien/Études Asiatiques*, 37: 553–62.

——. 2000b. s.v. *anupāya* in *Tāntrikābhidhānakośa I, Dictionnaire des termes techniques de la littérature hindoue tantrique*, sous la direction de H. Brunner, G. Oberhammer et André Padoux, Österreichische Akademie der Wissenschaften, Philosophisch-Historische Klasse, Sitzungsberichte, 681. Band, Wien.

——. 2013. 'Inherited Cognitions: *Prasiddhi, Āgama, Pratibhā, Śabdana* (Bhartṛhari, Utpaladeva, Abhinavagupta, Kumārila and Dharmakīrti in Dialogue)', in Vincent Eltschinger and Helmut Krasser (eds), *Scriptural Authority, Reason and Action, Proceedings of a Panel at the XIV World Sanskrit Conference, Kyoto, September 1st-5th 2009*, pp. 455–80. Vienna: Verlag der Österreichischen Akademie der Wissenschaften (Austrian Academy of Sciences).

Torella, Raffaele and Giuliano Boccali (eds). 2007. *Passioni d'Oriente. Eros ed emozioni in India e in Tibet*. Torino: Einaudi.

Yunis, Harvey (ed.). 2011. *Plato: Phaedrus*. Cambridge Greek and Latin Classics. Cambridge and New York: Cambridge University Press.

2

Intensity of Emotions

A Way to Liberation in the Advaita Śaiva Āgamas and Their Exegetes

BETTINA SHARADA BÄUMER

In contrast to other systems of Indian spirituality, which consider emotions as an obstacle on the spiritual path, thinking them to be as *cittavṛttis* that are to be suppressed or subdued, the Tāntrikas emphasise the importance of the intensity of any experience. Alexis Sanderson (1996: 79–81) has coined the term 'the prescription of intensity', which he has mostly applied to the transgressive rituals of the so-called Tāntric 'left-path'. These rituals — and their mental substitutes — are an expression of the 'non-dual practice' (*advaitācāra*) of the non-dualist Kashmiri Śaivism, according to which, in the concise formulation by Sanderson (ibid.: 86), 'transgression is translated into transcendence'. According to him, it is not only the transgressive ritual, but also the aesthetic intensity that leads to liberation from bondage. Writing about the 10th–11th-century-CE non-dualist Kashimiri Śaiva polymath Abhinavagupta, Sanderson (1996: 87) notes:

> [T]he shift from the appetitive to the aesthetic mode of awareness is seen . . . as the divinisation of the senses themselves, or rather as the recognition of their divine nature as projections or avenues of the blissful but egoless consciousness which is the underlying identity of all awareness.

The purpose of this essay is to analyse neither specific rituals nor the aesthetic experience ensuing from them, but the underlying theory that regards pure Consciousness (*cit, saṃvit*) as informing every human experience, perception and emotion. The text that immediately comes to mind with regard to teaching of practices leading to such experiences is the *Vijñānabhairava*, one of the most frequently quoted Tantras by the non-dualist Kashmiri Śaiva exegetes, from the early times to this day.

We may first look at some textual references that directly pertain to emotions. A well-known verse (101) of the *Vijñānabhairava* is as follows:

> *kāmakrodhalobhamohamadamātsarya-gocare/*
> *buddhiṃ nistimitāṃ kṛtvā tat tattvaṃ avaśiṣyate//*
>
> If one makes one's mind stable in the various states of desire, anger, greed, delusion, intoxication, or envy, then Reality alone will remain.[1]

The text here enumerates the six core emotions that in all mainstream Brāhmaṇical texts are described as negative, being the greatest obstacles on the spiritual path. Here, these emotions are not merely allowed to arise, but a meditative practice is also implied: 'If one makes one's mind stable in' (*buddhiṃ nistimitāṃ kṛtvā*). In the words of the commentator Śivopādhyāya on *Vijñānabhairava* 101, this would mean 'establishing the one-pointed intellect which is one's own consciousness'. It, thus, appears that the power, intrinsic in these 'negative' emotions, may serve as an entry point into pure Consciousness, provided they are not allowed to flow outwards. Again, in the words of Śivopādhyāya commenting on *Vijñānabhairava* 101: 'Drawing these emotions into one-pointedness and thus removing them from their external objects, the state of the bliss of consciousness (*cidānandamayatvam eva*) alone arises'. According to the last master in the line of non-dualist Kashmiri Śaivism, Swami Lakshmanjoo (1907–91), '[The *yogin*] must transform that excitement not when it has risen, but as it is rising' (2002: 121). The transformation that takes place here leads directly, i.e., without any intermediary stages, to the realisation of the true or ultimate reality. This reality alone remains, in the end, because it is the same Consciousness that is underlying all the states. This is the crucial insight underlying the entire philosophy of Consciousness of the Trika and Pratyabhijñā schools of Śaivism.

Another oft-quoted verse (118) of the *Vijñānabhairava* speaks of intense experiences that are not all, or exclusively, emotions, but where emotions are definitely implied:

> *kṣutādyante bhaye śoke gahvare vā raṇād drute/*
> *kutūhale kṣudhādyante brahmasattā samīpagā//*

> At the beginning and end of sneezing, in a state of fear or sorrow, (standing) on top of an abyss or while fleeing from a battlefield, at the moment of intense curiosity, at the beginning or end of hunger; such a state comes close to the experience of Brahman.[2]

Since here no practices are mentioned in this verse, it would seem that such moments of intensity lead directly to the experience of the Absolute. However, commenting on the aforecited verse, Śivopādhyāya rightly differentiates between the subjects experiencing these moments: 'Wherever such occasions arise, the well-awakened one (*suprabuddha*) becomes absorbed, having reflected (on them), whereas the unenlightened one (*aprabuddha*) remains stupefied'.

What is striking is that both the aforecited (so-called) *dhāraṇās* (concentration practice or praxis), which take their impetus from intense emotions or experiences, are classified under the highest means of liberation (*upāya*), i.e., the *śāmbhava* or the 'Divine Means'. These *upāyas* do not require any activity or even reflection, but allow one to enter directly into the state of divine absorption (*samāveśa*) that is free from thought-constructs.

Let us now take one example of joyful emotions:

> *ānande mahati prāpte dṛṣṭe vā bāndhave cirāt/*
> *ānandaṃ udgataṃ dhyātvā tallayas tanmanā bhavet//*
>
> At the time of experiencing great bliss, or the joy of seeing a friend or relative after a long time, one should meditate on the rising of this bliss and, while merging with it one's mind will become one with it (*Vijñānabhairava* 71).

In place of the immediacy of the aforecited verse 71, here, the experience of great joy has to be carried forward in three steps: first, a meditation on the very arising of the joy, which itself leads to a merging or absorption within it, and finally to a state of union. Since it takes place in stages, this experience is classified in Śivopādhyāya's commentary as belonging to the 'Means of the Power' (*śāktopāya*). Yet, the intensity of such an experience is emphasised by qualifying the joy as 'great bliss' (*mahānanda*), and through the example of meeting a loved one after a long time. As again, the commentator emphasises, it is only the intensity of the first moment of arising that can lead, first, to absorption and, then, to a state of repose (*viśrānti*).

Another, apparently trivial, example of joyful emotion is the pleasure derived from eating and drinking, as illustrated in *Vijñānabhairava* 72:

> *jagadhi pāna kṛtollāsarasānanda vijṛmbhaṇāt/*
> *bhāvayed bharitāvasthām mahānandas tato bhavet//*

> When one is filled with joy arising from the pleasure of eating and drinking, one should meditate on the state of fullness. Then the great bliss will arise.

Here, it is not simply a question of experiencing the state of fulfilment after having enjoyed good food, but a process of meditation (*bhāvanā*) is implied, by means of which one contemplates on the state of fullness (related to, but not coinciding with, the enjoyment of food) that leads to great bliss. What is common to both painful or fearsome and joyful emotions, whether they lead to a state of thought-free awareness (*nirvikalpa*) immediately or through a process of meditation, is that the condition for their becoming means (*upāya, yukti*) to reaching a divine state is primarily their intensity.

In trying to analyse such examples of extreme fear, sorrow or joy, we can see them in the light of two words that are frequently used in the context of both aesthetic and erotic experiences. One is a sense of wonder or surprise: *camatkāra*. Although this term is mostly used for joyful or blissful experiences, such as any pleasant sense-perception, or for the surprise produced by a spiritual experience (called *vismaya* in *Śiva Sūtra* 1.12), it can equally be applied to fearful or painful emotions, in the sense that they produce surprise or even shock, as portrayed in the examples of running for one's life, or peering down into an abyss (*Vijñānabhairava* 118).

Emotions, and in particular the intense or unexpected ones, certainly share a sense of surprise, astonishment, or wonder. A difference can be drawn between general sensorial experience and the aesthetic experience, yet in both cases the question is how far they are capable of leading one to liberation, or, in any event, to a state of pure or divine Consciousness. As Śivopādhyāya in his commentary on *Vijñānabhairava* 118 points out, one important factor is the subject of the experience, i.e., the experiencer itself, whether he is already enlightened, spiritually advanced, or unenlightened. One may have to concede that even an unenlightened person may receive a transformative jolt from any of the emotions or experiences described in the *Vijñānabhairava*. Thus, sorrowful news about the death of a beloved person (*Vijñānabhairava* 118), or great joy caused by an intense aesthetic experience, may give access to contact — be it even momentary — with the divine Consciousness underlying these experiences. Interestingly, in the Trika system, *camatkāra* is related to the divine power of Will or *icchāśakti*. In his *Tantrasāra*, Abhinavagupta states that the absolute Light of Consciousness is one, but possesses five energies. Out of its own freedom, the energy of bliss arises, and its sense of wonder is identified with the energy of Will (Śāstrī 1918: 6).[3] This is significant for understanding the effect of intense emotions as related to the divine *icchāśakti*, since they partake of an innate impulse that is not of the individual will, but rather of the very power of astonishment they produce. The other implication of this connection is the importance of spontaneity, another aspect of the power of freedom (*svātantryaśakti*).

The psychology of emotions in the non-dualist Kashmiri Śaiva texts is related with another concept: *kṣobha*, meaning 'agitation', 'perturbation'. Naturally, it is mental agitation that causes the greatest obstacle to attaining the clarity of pure Consciousness. The most frequently quoted stanza of the *Spandakārikā* (1.9) says it clearly:

> *nijāśuddhyāsamarthasya kartavyeṣv abhilāṣiṇaḥ/*
> *yadā kṣobhaḥ pralīyeta tadā syāt paramaṃ padam//*

> When the perturbation of that empirical individual who is incapacitated by his own impurity and is attached to actions disappears, then the highest state appears.

Agitation is closely related to the impurities of the individual, and to the resulting restless activity promoted by one's desires. The supreme state is simply attained by getting rid of this disturbance and restlessness.

Abhinavagupta depicts a similar situation when praising the Supreme Goddess (*devī*) in one of his benedictory verses to his *Parātrīśikā-Vivaraṇa* (*maṅgala* verse 2, in Singh 1988, part 2, Sk.: 1; Bäumer 2011: 50): *kṣobhe kṣīṇe 'nuttarāyāṃ sthitau tām* ('I praise that [Goddess] who is realised in the state of the Absolute as soon as agitation has ceased'). *Vijñānabhairava* 112 describes a similar experience:

> *ādhāreṣvathavā aśaktyā jñānāc cittalayena vā/*
> *jātaśakti samāveśa kṣobhānte bhairavaṃ vapuḥ//*

> When, owing to the lack of the capacity to know objects, or by the dissolution of the mind, there is cessation of agitation caused by the energy of absorption, then the nature of Bhairava (manifests itself).

The starting point for this *dhāraṇā* is a state of helplessness. The commentator Śivopādhyāya glosses *kṣobhānte* as *cañcalatāvirāme*, 'at the cessation of restlessness'. The divine state attained is filled with the bliss of one's own experience (*svānubhavānandāvasthā*).

This implicitly negative view of disturbances and perturbations in favour of clarity and stillness seems to contradict a verse of the *Spandakārikā* (1.22) describing intense emotions:

> *atikruddhaḥ prahṛṣṭo vā kiṃ karomi iti vā mṛśan/*
> *dhāvan vā yatpadaṃ gacchet tatra spandaḥ pratiṣṭhitaḥ//*
>
> (In states of) extreme anger or great joy, of not knowing what to do, or running for life, one attains the state in which the reality of *spanda* is established.

These emotions may be regarded as the result of *kṣobha*, yet the text attributes them to *spanda*, the original vibration, which could be called the substratum of all agitation. Kṣemarāja, in his commentary on *kārikā* 1.22 (Singh 1980: 101), explains such a state of intensity:

> *samastetaravṛttipraśamapūrvam-ekāgrībhavanti yoginaḥ*
>
> All other mental movements come to a stop and the *yogins* become one-pointed.

Even in the case of extreme anger (*atikruddha*) the *yogin* becomes suddenly introverted (*jhaṭity antarmukhībhavanti*, ibid.). Kṣemarāja goes further into the psychological states connected with such emotions (ibid.: 101–03). As far as they are related to *spanda*, the vibration of consciousness, they do not distract the *yogin* from his interiority — quite the contrary. What is, then, the relation between *spanda* and *kṣobha*? As we have seen, *kṣobha* occurs more in the negative sense of 'disturbance' (Dyczkowski 1994: 344n40). But in his extensive commentary on the *Parātrīśikā Tantra*, the *Vivaraṇa*, Abhinavagupta's comes to the astonishing conclusion that neither the sensory, nor the aesthetic, nor the spiritual experiences are possible without *kṣobha*, an initial agitation. The context in which he develops an entire psychology of emotions is a commentary on the compound *khecarī-samatā* occurring in the first verse of the Tantra (Singh 1988: 38–46). *Khecarī-samatā* may be translated as 'harmony with the power of Consciousness Moving-in-the-Void' (Bäumer 2011: 91ff.). Abhinavagupta goes into a lengthy analysis of the contrast between a state of sameness or harmony with that supreme power, and its contrary, *vaiṣamya* or disharmony, which he regards as the cause of alienation from the pure Consciousness. The examples he provides for *vaiṣamya* are precisely the same emotional states of desire, anger, etc., but when perceived as separated from Consciousness, whereas harmony (*samatā*) is of the nature of the fullness of divinity (*paripūrṇabhairavasvabhāvā*, Singh 1988, part 1, trans.: 14). Abhinavagupta regards *vaiṣamya* or disharmony as caused by even an infinitesimal ignorance of the undivided nature of the Absolute (*aṇumātram api avikalānuttarasvarūpāparijñānam eva . . . vaiṣamyam*, ibid.). However, he immediately concedes:

> When, owing to the cessation of limitation, the disharmony (or aberration) of the mental states caused by the non-recognition of the essential nature ceases, the very states of anger, delusion, and so on, appear as only an expression of the consciousness of the perfect revered Lord Bhairava Himself (Singh 1988, part 1, trans.: 40, translation modified).

In a truly non-dualistic spirit, Abhinavagupta connects the very negative emotions with the manifestation of the senses as aspects of divine consciousness:

> Even the states of anger etc., exist because of their identity with the wondrous play of the (divine) consciousness, otherwise their very existence would be impossible (lit., otherwise the very acquisition of their nature would be impossible). The divine sense-goddesses themselves carrying out the various play (of life) are like the rays of Śiva-sun (ibid.: 40).
>
> When their real nature is known, then these very mental states (such as anger, delusion, etc.) bring about, by the means referred to (viz. *khecarī-samatā*) liberation in life itself (ibid.: 41).

But what is the process of transforming these emotions into liberating factors? Here follows an analysis of the emotional experience:

> This is what is meant by the knowledge of their real nature (i.e. of the states of desire, anger, and so on). These states of anger, and so on, at the time of their arising are of the form of *nirvikalpa*, i.e. they are sheer energy of the divine. So even when an aberrant thought-construct (*vikalpa*) (such as *kāma* or *krodha*) arises (which at the time of arising is non aberrant) and is influenced by the varied words which are the outcome of the multitude of letters, it is not united with the group of the *śakti*s associated with

the multitude of the letters so that it cannot annul the *yogin*'s nature determined by his earlier state of *nirvikalpa* (ibid.).

> Therefore, homogeneousness (or 'harmony', *samatā*) of the *khecarī-śakti* constitutes liberation. This homogeneousness (or 'sameness') of the *khecarī-śakti* is due to the awareness of the essential nature of the *anuttara* (i.e. the unsurpassable Absolute Reality), which is constantly present and which arises from the bliss of the recognition of the completion of the union of the divine Śakti with Śiva, and acquires stability by the realisation of the consciousness of bliss of both (ibid.: 42).

Abhinavagupta goes even further into the psychophysical factors that give rise to emotions:

> Now whatever enters the inner psychic apparatus or the outer senses of all beings, that abides as sentient life-energy (*cetanarūpeṇa prāṇātmanā*) in the middle channel, i.e. *suṣumnā,* whose main characteristic is to enliven all the parts of the body. That life energy is said to be vital lustre (*ojas*), that is then diffused as an enlivening factor in the form of common vital energy (*vīrya*) in all parts of the body. Then when an exciting visual or auditory perception enters the percipient, then on account of its exciting power, it fans the flame of passion in the form of the agitation of the vital energy (ibid.).

> When the vital energy that has been lying within, and that is identical with one's Self in a placid state is agitated (*vikṣobha*), i.e. when it is in an active state, then the source of its pleasure is the Supreme I-consciousness full of creative pulsation, beyond the range of space and time (*adeśa-kālakalitaspandamayamahāvimarśarūpameva*), of the nature of perfect Bhairava-consciousness, the absolute sovereignty, full of the power of bliss (ibid.: 43).

Kṣobha is understood here in the completely neutral sense as the impulse that causes various feelings to arise. The way of connecting to the divine energy of *khecarī* through these feelings is hinted at in two observations: the first is the moment of the arising of any emotion in the mind while it is still in a thought-free state (*nirvikalpa*); the second refers to the arising of the life-energy in the central channel of the subtle body (*suṣumnā*). Now it is only the arousal of the vital energy (*vīryakṣobha*) that makes for the aesthetic and spiritual sensibility or *sahṛdayatā*, which corresponds to the capacity of experiencing a sense of wonder (*camatkāra*).

The very basis and cause of such a state is the unconditional divine Consciousness (*mahāvimarśa*) consisting of vibrative energy. The relation between *kṣobha* and *spanda* is an important key to understanding the very nature of emotional agitation: it is the psychic correspondent to the ontological movement. As Abhinavagupta explains:

> To the extent to which an object cannot bring about full excitement to that extent it can provide only limited delight. If there is complete absence of delight, it only spells insentience. Engrossment in a profuse delight alone excites the vital energy and that alone signifies a taste for beautiful things (*sahṛdayatā*). Excessive delight is possible only to those whose heart is expanded by vital energy which has the boundless capacity to strengthen sensibility and which is established in them by repeated association with objects of enjoyment (Singh 1988, part 1, trans.: 43).

But this expansion does not only occur by the perception of beauty and blissful experiences, as Somānanda had already stated in *Śivadṛṣṭi*. It also occurs in painful experiences. Thus Abhinavagupta analyses the emotion of grief:

> In grief also, there is the same wondrous experience of delight [in those who have *khecarī-sāmya*]. Whatever pleasure is derived from one's wife and son, the pleasure which is animated by vital energy, and which abides in the heart (*antarvyavasthitam*), when contrary to all anticipation (*bhāvanāsadṛśa*) there is an apprehension of the loss of the loved one aroused by tears and shrieks, that very pleasure becomes the cause of grief of the nature of agitation (*kṣobhātmakaṃ*) and when that grief reaches its climax (*vikāsam āpannaṃ*) and one thinks that pleasure will not be experienced any longer, then owing to despair (*nairapekṣyavaśa*) the nature of that grief is suddenly turned into the wonder of joy (*camatkriyātma*) [owing to the expansion of the essential nature or *khecarī-sāmya*], so it has been said (by Somānanda in *Śivadṛṣṭi* 5.9): 'Even in grief, by the expansion of the essential nature etc.' (Singh 1988, part 1, trans.: 43–44).

Ultimately, it is the excitement caused by vital energy that leads through the senses to the non-dual ultimate experience:

> When there is dissolution of *prāṇa* and *apāna* (*marudādi*), in *suṣumnā* which, as the central channel, is full of the storage of the energy of all the senses, then one's consciousness gets entry into that stage of the great central *suṣumnā* channel where it acquires union with the pulsation of

> one's Śakti (*nijaśaktikṣobhatādātmyaṃ*), then all sense of duality dissolves, and there is the perfect I-consciousness generated by the abundance of the perfection of one's own inherent Śakti. Then by one's entry into the union of Śiva and Śakti (*rudrayāmalayogānupraveśena*) which consists in the bliss of their essential nature of manifestation and by one's complete integration with the expansive flow of the energy of the great mantra of perfect I-consciousness, there is the manifestation of the *akula* or *anuttara* (absolute) Bhairava nature which is beyond all agitation (*nistaraṅga*),[4] unalterable and eternal (*dhruvapadātmaka*) (ibid.: 44).

Having analysed the implications of *kṣobha* in the context of emotions, we must now place this concept in its cosmological context. In the Tāntric worldview, psychology and cosmology are closely connected and reflect one another. Without agitation or stimulation there is no creation. The most concise expression of this axiom is found in Amṛtānanda's *Yoginīhṛdaya-dīpikā* (Dvivedī 1988: 77): *sṛṣṭir eva kṣobhaḥ* ('creation/emanation is verily agitation'). The *Āgama*s elaborate upon this theme, and it will suffice to give only a few examples.[5]

For *kṣobha* to be a creative force it needs an agent to incite, and one who is incited. At the divine and cosmological level, it is Śakti who incites Śiva and moves him towards creation from his transcendent state. When describing this Śakti, *Netra Tantra* 7.42 (Śāstrī 1926, vol. 1: 65) states: *tasmāt pravartate sṛṣṭirvikṣobhya paramaṃ śivam* ('from Her creation comes forth, having agitated the supreme Śiva'). On this Kṣemarāja comments:

> The Energy, being thus (i.e. the cause of creation, continuation and dissolution), excites the Supreme Śiva to make Him descend from His state of balance/equilibrium and to turn towards creation (*Netra Tantra* 51, ibid.: 174).

This 'turning towards' creation corresponds to a descent to the level of *samanā*, with both spiritual and cosmological implications. No creation is possible at the Transmental or *unmanā* stage; this incitement and descent on the side of Śakti happens 'playfully, by the play of absolute freedom' (*līlayā svātantryakrīdayā*) (ibid.).

Without going further into the cosmological meaning of *kṣobha* in the Tantras and in Abhinavagupta's *Tantrāloka*, what is important to note in the context of emotion is the creative force of stimulation or agitation. If seen in this light, this term again substantiates the close link between the emotional, aesthetic, spiritual, and cosmological levels in the Trika system. The negative and disturbing aspects of agitation are entirely linked with the level of the Individual (*āṇava*), but become transformed into creativity at the stages of Energy (*śākta*) and of the Divine (*śāmbhava*). Thus, ultimately, there is nothing negative, only — as described in the famous verse of the *Spandakārikā* 22 — the same intensity of an apparently negative emotion that becomes transformed and sublimated into its original nature of thought-free Consciousness.

Notes

1. All translations are mine unless indicated otherwise.
2. The last line has a variant: *brahmasattāmayī daśā* ('the state of the reality of the Absolute'), instead of *brahmasattā samīpagā* ('coming close to the reality of the Absolute').
3. *ekaḥ prakāśaḥ — tasya ca svātantryam ānandaśaktiḥ, taccamatkāra icchāśaktiḥ.*
4. Lit. 'waveless', i.e., a state of stillness of consciousness.
5. For a list of references to *kṣobha*, *kṣobhana*, see Brunner et al. (2004: 158ff.).

References

Primary Sources

Netra Tantra:

Śāstrī, Madhusūdana Kaul (ed.). 1926, 1939. *The Netra Tantram with Commentary by Kshemarāja*, 2 vols, KSTS 46 and 61. Bombay: Tatva Vivechaka Press.

Parātriṃśikā:

Śāstrī, Mukunda Rāma (ed.). 1918. *The Parātrimshikā with Commentary. The Latter by Abhinava Gupta*, KSTS 18. Bombay: Tatva Vivechaka Press.

Parātrīśikā-Vivaraṇa of Abhinavagupta:

Singh, Jaideva (ed. and trans.). 1988. *The Secret of Tantric Mysticism: Parātrīśikā-Vivaraṇa*. Delhi: Motilal Banarsidass.

Śivadṛṣṭi of Somānanda:

Śāstrī, Madhusūdana Kaul (ed.). 1934. *The Śivadṛṣṭi of Śrīsomānandanātha with the Vṛtti by Utpaladeva*. KSTS 54. Srinagar: Research Department, Jammu and Kashmir State.

Śiva Sūtras:

Singh, Jaideva (ed. and trans.). 1991. *Śivasūtras: The Yoga of Supreme Identity, Text of the Sūtras and the Commentary Vimarśinī of Kṣemarāja*. Delhi: Motilal Banarsidass.

Spandakārikā:

Singh, Jaideva (ed. and trans.). 1980. *The Divine Creative Pulsation: Spandakārikās with the Commentary by Kṣemarāja (Spandanirṇaya)*. Delhi: Motilal Banarsidass.

Tantrāloka of Abhinavagupta:
Śāstrī, Mukundarāma and Madhusūdana Kaul Śāstrī (eds). 1918–38. *The Tantrāloka with Commentary by Rājānaka Jayaratha*, 12 vols. Kashmir Series of Texts and Studies (KSTS) 23, 28, 29, 30, 35, 36, 41, 47, 52, 57, 58, and 59. Allahabad: India Press; Bombay: Shri Venkateshvar Press; Srinagar: Research Department, Jammu and Kashmir State.
Tantrasāra of Abhinavagupta:
Shāstrī, Mukundarāma (ed.). 1918. *The Tantrasāra*. KSTS 17. Bombay: Nirnaya Sagar Press.
Vijñānabhairava:
Lakshmanjoo, Swami. 2002. *Vijñānabhairava: The Practice of Centering Awareness*. Varanasi: Indica Books.
Śāstrī, Mukunda Rāma (ed.). 1918. *The Vijñānabhairava with Commentary Partly by Kṣhemarāja and Partly by Shivopādhyāya*, KSTS 8. Bombay.
Singh, Jaideva (ed. and trans.). 1979. *Vijñānabhairava or Divine Consciousness*, Sanskrit text with English translation. Delhi: Motilal Banarsidass.
Yoginīhṛdaya:
Dvivedī, Vrajavallabha (ed.). 1988. *Yoginīhṛdaya with Commentary by Amṛtānandayogin*. Delhi: Motilal Banarsidass.

Secondary Works

Bäumer, Bettina. 2011. *Abhinavagupta's Hermeneutics of the Absolute: Anuttaraprakriyā*. Shimla: Indian Institute of Advanced Study; Delhi: D. K. Printworld.
Brunner, H., G. Oberhammer and A. Padoux (eds). 2004. *Tāntrikābhidhānakośa* II. Wien: Verlag der Österreichischen Akademie der Wissenschaften.
Dyczkowski, Mark. 1994. *The Stanzas on Vibration*. New York: State University of New York Press.
Sanderson, Alexis. 1996. 'Meaning in Tantric Ritual', in A. M. Blondeau and K. Shipper (eds), *Essais sur le Rituel III*, pp. 15–95. Paris: Bibliotheque de l'Ecole des Hautes Etudes.

3

Between Fear and Heroism

The Tantric Path to Liberation

Aleksandra Wenta

The very notion of Tantrism appears to rest on misunderstandings fostered by various explanatory enterprises that enjoy labelling Tantrism as the daring hunt for a widely defined power, a ritualised form of sexual activity or executive competence to perform six acts of magic (*ṣaṭkarmāṇi*). However, in all these different approaches to Tantrism, spinning out semantically broader applications of this vague term, there has hardly been an attempt to look at the aspect of tantric lore that lies deep in a psychological domain of the individual. It was none other than Sri Aurobindo who in his, however brief, remarks on tantric traditions claimed that 'Tantras contain some original psychological intuitions which have a living relevance for the spiritual seekers' (The Mother 1978: 30–33). The most unique and pivotal contribution to the psychological dimension of Tantrism comes from two Jungian theoreticians on religion: Joseph Campbell and Heinrich Zimmer who analysed tantric *sādhanā* in terms of a spiritual quest for self-discovery of one's own true identity. Implicit in this approach is the assumption that confrontation with unconscious part of the psyche, however unpleasant and terrifying, is a necessary preliminary for any spiritual growth. Following this line of reasoning, I argue in this essay that the tantric path, especially in certain aspects of the non-dualistic Kashmiri Śaiva tradition, is a spiritual discipline that found a new way to challenge one of the most powerful experiences in the dynamics of emotions: fear. Fear participates in several conceptual patterns: (*a*) it is sacralised as the god Bhairava; (*b*) it constitutes, through fear of transmigration, a powerful stimulus for undertaking tantric *sādhanā*; and (*c*) ritualistic ingestion of fear-eliciting substances is used to reduce contraction of consciousness (*saṃkoca*), the cause of bondage, consequently leading to the expansion of consciousness (*vikāsa*) and liberation (*mokṣa*). Thus, liberation is approached here through the paradigm of psychological growth that involves a direct, face-to-face confrontation with fear. Fear, so conceived, becomes a principal driving force for undertaking a tantric path of heroism. Fear functions as a central organising feature in a dynamic construction of tantric identity. The tantric practitioner is called a Hero (*vīra*). His heroism, religiously motivated, lies in the conquest of fear. It is fear that he is compelled to face both in the outer realm and in the deepest recess of his soul. Such confrontation endows a Hero with steadfastness (*dhairya*) that becomes a heroic-personhood-defining feature and leads a Hero significantly farther, to the ultimate knowledge of the goddess Kālī.

'Tantrism' is a term used to characterise a corpus of 'heterodox religious teachings' covering a wide range of esoteric practices that enveloped Hindu, Buddhist and Jaina traditions, becoming a widespread 'trend' in South and South-east Asia from the 5th century CE onward. Perhaps, the most prominent feature of Tantrism was its radical break with the traditional Brāhmaṇical caste-structured society that consequently opened up the possibility for spiritual realisation for everyone, equally. In my essay, the word 'Tantrism' is employed in reference to the non-dualistic Kashmiri Śaiva traditions that developed in Kashmir between 9th and 13th centuries CE, and spread to south India and far beyond the Indian subcontinent.

Bhairava and Sacralisation of Fear

Sacralisation of fear has a long history in the phenomenology of religion. It was Rudolf Otto's epochal book *The Idea of the Holy* (1917) that set forth a completely new understanding of the sacred. As Otto pointed out, the experience of the 'wholly other' instigates a powerful psychological mechanism that gives rise to the emotional response of fear and awe. Otto's classic definition of the sacred avers thus: '[T]he sacred is the mystery that causes both threat and fascination' (*mysterium tremendum et fascinosum*). In this definition, the inexplicable encounter with the sacred is highlighted in the perspective of the emotional response *par excellence*, which is, at the same time, overwhelmingly dreadful and wonderful. Otto's position is important because it concentrates on the analysis of religious feeling by showing 'how this feeling becomes manifest in elements given to consciousness' (Corrigan 2008: 466). This approach bears the mark of the non-dualistic Kashmiri Śaiva own methodology, according to which the ultimate status of a religious emotion is acknowledged in the symbol of the Heart, the affective seat of both feeling and consciousness. Yet, the Kashmiri Śaiva Tāntrikas provide us with another far more complex example of sacralisation of fear. In his *Tantrāloka*, Abhinavagupta (10th–11th century CE) appeals to traditional semantic analysis (*nirvacana*) to establish an etymological foundation for the sacralisation of fear. He starts his argument by tracing the etymology of the word *bhairava* to 'sound of terror' (*bhaya*: fear, terror, dread; *rava*: sound, roar). Thus, Bhairava, the fierce form of Śiva and a popular god of the tantric pantheon, becomes a religious representation of the affective experience of fear, expressed in the audible sound of terror. Abhinavagupta's argument is purported to show that the sacralisation of fear, epitomised in the figure of Bhairava, does not belong to the category of otherworldly, transcendent experience that is inaccessible to mortal man; rather it turns out to be just the opposite. Abhinavagupta shows that fear is a sacralised emotion because it results from the most tangible and profane experience given to man entangled in everyday human affairs: fear of transmigration. Here, the distinction between sacred fear (embodied in Bhairava) and ordinary fear (reflected in the emotional response to human misery) is blurred.[1] This is in accordance with the fundamental 'tantric' presupposition that continuously makes an attempt to unify the two apparently contradictory spheres of reality, sacred and secular. Abhinavagupta clarifies it in the following words: 'Bhairava (The Sound of Terror) is so called because He is born in the Heart (of consciousness) by the reflection aroused by the cry of fear of transmigration' (*Tantrāloka* 1.1, in Dyczkowski forthcoming). It is at this crucial moment when the awareness of existential fear of *saṃsāra* comes into being that the sense of the supernatural overwhelming presence of Bhairava's great power is attested. Of special significance is the emphasis put on the 'Heart', the affective centre of conscious life. Moreover, the actual experience of fear that is aroused by the dreadful realisation of transmigratory existence is reflected upon as Bhairava's bestowal of grace.[2] In other words, to be afraid of *saṃsāra* is to be blessed by Bhairava himself. Abhinavagupta avers thus: 'He is called Bhairava, "The Sound of Terror"' because 'he helps those who are frightened by transmigration. It is by virtue of his grace that the awareness of the fear of bonded existence is clearly apparent' (ibid.). It should be noted that fear of transmigration plays important role in stimulating reflective awareness which is in itself just a prelude to the religious experience culminating in the 'encounter' with Bhairava.

For the Kashmiri Śaiva Tāntrikas, intensity of emotional life is valued as the source of spiritual power. In these powerful emotional states, even the most negative ones, the ongoing agitation of thought-constructs is suspended. As a consequence, expansion of consciousness (*vikāsa*), evoked by such terms as *sahaja* (spontaneity), *khecarī* (sky-farer), *samāveśa* (possession), *sāmarasya* (one-sentiment), and *spanda* (vibration), takes place (Eliade 1969: 123). For example, the *Spandakārikā*, a seminal text of the Spanda school of non-dualistic Kashmir Śaivism, provides examples of many of these 'negative' emotional states, in which the sense of fear, identified with the 'Bhairava state', becomes activated. Thus, it is declared that one enters the 'Bhairava state' in the moment of great fear, generated by the sight of a lion or python: when all mental activities come to a dead stop, the vibration of consciousness (*spanda*) is established (Singh 1980: 102–03).[3] This passage illustrates that the emotional meaning of fear has been adopted by Kashmiri Śaiva exegetes as a practical device for reaching the spiritually significant level of experience. The function of fear, thus, is to assert the possibility of achieving identification with the supreme reality, represented by Bhairava.

Fear as an Example of Socially, Morally and Culturally Constructed Emotion

Richard A. Shweder and Jonathan Haidt, exponents of the cultural psychology of emotions, suggested that emotional experience depends on the social and moral context. Moreover, emotions can be understood only with reference to a specific cultural setting to which they belong. Cultures generally follow three types of ethics to varying degrees: (*a*) 'ethics of autonomy', which finds its basis in motivation of the individual; (*b*) 'ethics of community', in which the needs of the individual are suppressed for the sake of collective good; (*c*) 'ethics of divinity', in which the religious aspect becomes prominent. Following this scheme of conceptualisation, I argue that, even though both the Brāhmaṇical orthodox tradition and heterodox tantric tradition are governed by the 'ethics of divinity', their radical disparity still holds in regard to the 'ethics of autonomy' and the 'ethics of community'. Seen from this perspective, the Brāhmaṇical orthodoxy favours the 'ethics of community', where 'ontological priority is given to collective social entities (the family, guild, clan, community)' (Shweder and Haidt 2000: 409). In contrast, the tantric heterodoxy is inextricably linked to the 'ethics of autonomy' that implies freedom from socially binding constraints.

Fear is an example of emotion that is socially and culturally constructed. In other words, 'fear' is woven into a wider social and moral context, in which the impurity mechanism is evoked. On the specific ground of the Brāhmaṇical orthodoxy, purity is a guarantee of individual, social and metaphysical security, while impurity stimulates fear-response. The ideal Brāhmaṇa is required to avoid contact with forbidden and contaminated substances, places, persons, foods, drinks, dresses, etc. In a vast spectrum of rules regarding this what should be followed and what must be abandoned, a demarcating line between the pure and the impure is carefully drawn. The tantric Hero is the exact opposition of the ideal Brāhmaṇa. He goes to the cremation ground, the place of the greatest danger and the epitome of pollution and terror. The Karavīra cremation ground is the most sacred place in the tantric universe because it is believed to represent the material location of Kālī, or more precisely Kālasaṃkarṣaṇī (The Enchantress of Time). The act of interiorisation places the outer site of material cremation ground as a symbol for the inner one (Bharati 1980: 155). In this way, the cremation ground, sanctified and personified as the Goddess, becomes the location of the Hero's heart, the seat of both intense feeling and consciousness. This idea is elucidated in the following quotation from verse 82 of the *Cidgaganacandrikā*:

> You are said to be the cemetery, which free of the fluctuating activity of the mind is the cremation ground within the Hero's heart. Difficult to behold, yet you are the meeting ground, the ever illumined light which consumes everything.[4]

The deadly, terrifying cremation ground, considered by ordinary awareness to be an impure and polluted place, becomes here the seat of emotional power and purity of consciousness. It is a symbolic representation of the lucid light of consciousness, freed from the darkness of mental agitation and thought-constructs feeding upon the condition of contraction that belongs to ignorance and bondage. This is in itself just an example of a conceptual shift presupposed in tantric metaphysics that, through a radical break of fears, hates and traditional notions of good and evil, explicitly challenges the play of opposites to behold the perfect harmony of all contradictions.

Fear-eliciting Question that Leads to Liberation

Tantric texts do not seem to praise psychologically calming experiences, nor do they discuss comforting issues regarding human existence. On the contrary, what they tend to convey in their bone-chilling narratives is often expressed in the language of gruesome visuals. Similarly, the philosophical discussions these texts promote have a fear-stirring capacity. A textual example of this kind is found in the *Kramasadbhāva*, one of the root texts of the Krama tradition of non-dualistic Kashmiri Śaivism. As is often the case with the Krama scriptures, textual authenticity is often tightly bound to the potent mythological realm. Myth and text reflect each other. Moreover, the Krama tantric texts claim to have the position of supreme authority in the elaboration of esoteric teachings *because* they were written in the actual cremation ground. This is certainly the case with the *Kramasadbhāva* that, as we are told, was written in the Karavīra cremation ground. The first *paṭala* of the *Kramasadbhāva*, entitled 'A Question Concerning the Teaching of Vyomeśī (Mistress of Emptiness)', focuses on a dialogue between Bhairava and his female counterpart Bhairavī. The central theme of this dialogue is the importance of asking the right question. Abhinavagupta discusses the metaphysical aspect of the 'question' in the context of revelation of knowledge in the sacred texts.[5] He says that question is the essential part of the revelation, for, without question, the answer could not reach a state of certainty. Here, the question is additionally described as eliciting fear; for this reason, perhaps, it is able to trim the path to liberation. Bhairava asks Bhairavī a question concerning the nature of the ultimate reality. Bhairavī replies by saying that the moment this question is asked it leads to liberation (*tathāpi kālaṃ praśnasya mokṣanāya idaṃ bhavet*). This question which brings fear (*bhayāvahā*) and is the object of the quarreling of people is established in Bhairava's own Heart.[6] The main characteristic feature of this question is that it brings fear; it is profound, terrible, secret, and the most secret.[7] The answer to this question is desired by the Great Perfected Ones (*mahāsiddhas*), gods, sages, *brahmarākṣas*,[8] *gandharvas*, *kinnaras*[9], nymphs (*divyas*), celestial beings (*sādhyas*), the lord of Vasus, Rudra, Viṣṇu, Īśvara, Sadāśiva, Bhairava, serpents (*nāgas*) and the lord of the *nāgas*, tree-spirits (*yakṣas*), ghosts (*bhūtas*), *piśācas*,[10] demons (*asuras*), the lord of *rākṣasas* and humans

(*Kramasadbhāva* 1.46–48). Here, the conceptualisation of linguistic inquiry intimately involves affective sensation. More specifically, the question can be truly powerful and liberating only if it has the capacity to cause fear. Here again, the importance of the Heart is evoked. By continuing in the same 'direction', we move toward fear-stirring places and substances that constitute an important part of tantric *sādhanā*.

Fear-stirring Places and Substances: Uprooting *Saṃskāras*

> There is a peculiar and essential trait of the tantric affirmation which distinguishes it from the earliest philosophies. For the ideal of Tantra is to achieve illumination precisely by means of those very objects which the earlier sages sought to banish from their consciousness . . . The tantric Hero goes directly through the sphere of greatest danger. It is an essential principle of the tantric idea that man, in general must rise through and by means of nature, not by the rejection of nature. As one falls onto the ground, so one must lift oneself by the aid of the ground — says *Kulārṇavatantra* . . . The excluded forces . . . are incorporated in Tantra, what is discovered in due is the intrinsic purity and innocence of the seemingly dark and dangerous sphere. In this way, he breaks within himself the tension of the forbidden and resolves everything in light, recognizing in everything the one śakti (Zimmer 1961: 576–79).

In *The Hero with a Thousand Faces* (1973), Campbell developed the theory of a universal hero myth which he believed was common to all cultures and historical periods. He claimed that stories of the Heroes found in mythological narratives 'shared an underlying archetypal unity of common motifs, symbols and themes' (MacWilliams 2005: 1379). They also held universal meaning 'common psychological and metaphysical reality was at work in these tales' (ibid.). Campbell defines 'Hero' as those persons who are able to transcend or go beyond the personal limitations, prejudices and stereotypes. The one attribute, says Campbell, that distinguishes the Hero from the rest of the world is the courage to face alone the 'other' self (Campbell 1973: 19–20). According to his theory of the mono-myth or the Hero's journey, a brave man who sets on a dangerous expedition to the Self, passes through three states or three rites of passage.[11] The first of these states is 'departure', when he is expected to confront the unconscious part of his psyche. The core emotional component of departure is fear. According to John W. Tigue (1994: 49–50):

> Departure is the call to adventure which beckons the latent heroes or heroines into an unplanned encounter with darkness . . . The intrepids enter the darker places of the world: forest, swamp, caves, storm ridden seas; climb treacherous mountains and trek overall hazardous paths.

In the psychological and metaphysical reality specific to the tantric Hero, the moment of departure is enacted when the tantric adept goes directly to the places of greatest danger that give shape to inchoate fears. The basic practices of Tantra must be performed in dark and dangerous areas. The Tantric texts often give a detailed description of such places. The most suitable spot for tantric worship is the cremation ground of Karavīra. As stated in the introductory verses (1.3–6) of the *Devīpañcaśatikā* (*Kālīkulapañcaśatikā*), a root text of the Krama tradition:

> The cremation ground of the venerable Northern Seat (*Uttarapīṭha*) is Karavīra, worshipped by the supreme Śiva, god of gods. The Karavīra is heated by the fire of a funeral pyre (*mahāciti*) and is attended by great *yoginīs*, great ghosts (*bhūtas*) and great mothers (*mātṛs*). Great yogins gather there, and it is respected by the great *siddhas*. A great monastery is established there and it resounds with great sound of *phet*. That cremation ground (Karavīra) gives great accomplishments (*siddhis*) and contains great terror. It is full of Bhairava who is more terrible than terrible, and filled with great power (*tejas*).[12]

Among other locations worth considering for tantric practice is any isolated place that brings fear, such as a big mountain, a crossroads, a river, the deep, scary forest, the great battlefield, greedy to consume every Hero (*Kramasadbhāva* 4.41–43). Such places come to be regarded as *sādhanā* places. Wandering through such places is part of a Hero's vow. Similarly, the ritualistic usage of forbidden, fear-eliciting 'substances', viz., meat (*māṃsa*), alcoholic drink (*madya*), fish (*matsya*), parched grain (*mudrā*) and intimate intercourse (*mithuna*) (known under the rubric of five Ms), based on the Kaula practices,[13] has a psychological function in helping a tantric Hero to confront fear. The five Ms form a part of practice known as the left-hand path (*vāmācāra*). The left-hand path constitutes a specific mode of tantric worship that requires an adept of a heroic disposition (*vīrabhāva*). It stands in a diametrical opposition to the right-hand path (*dakṣinācāra*) meant for adepts of a divine type (*divyabhāva*).[14] Of particular significance is the fact that these two modes of tantric worship are differentiated in accordance with a psychological disposition of an adept, understood as his or her natural tendency.

In modern psychology, this psychological disposition is usually defined as a generalised neuropsychic structure peculiar to the individual that forms an adaptive or stylistic behaviour.[15] In other words, some people are naturally inclined to be shy and introverted, while others tend to be assertive and extroverted. Tantrism assumes a fundamental dichotomy between the psychological dispositions of divine attitude (*divyabhāva*) and heroic attitude (*vīrabhāva*) that are explained in terms of qualities (*guṇas*) of the Sāṃkhya philosophical system. Thus, the adepts classified as *divyabhāva* are believed to be 'pure' in their essential nature (quality of purity or *sattvaguṇa* is predominant in them). Those who are of heroic disposition are said to be 'energetic' (quality of energy or *rajasguṇa* is prevalent in them). A heroic path (*vīra-sādhanā*) is advocated in virtually all the Kaula-based schools of tantric lore. It is traditionally considered to be the most dangerous and challenging of all spiritual paths that requires a great amount of courage and perseverance. Zimmer (1961: 217–18) summarises the heroic path in the following words:

> The contrast of morally reprehensible, forged by the ethical commands that sets[*sic*] the limits, boundaries in the profane world and shape both his behavior and what is permissible and prohibited are abolished through the rites of 5Ms in order to allow for the experience beyond polarity, and reconcile even the most far-fetched bifurcations. The secret of *kulācāra* practice lies in its prescribing for the rite things shunned in the everyday world, for it is obvious that the undifferentiated, suprapolar state of the purely divine stands in clear contradistinction to human existence, which is in so many ways determined and delimited. There seem to be no integrating links between them; the only possibility is to transcend them.

The practice of heroism that aims at the dissolution of all distinctions is characteristic of the wider practice of non-duality (*advaitācāra*) that had been taught by Śiva himself as the highest method of achieving liberation.[16] In thus asserting the irreducible non-duality of consciousness pervading all states and conditions of being, the tantric adepts try to exclude any notion of duality that results in fear. In such a context, the spiritual practice itself becomes a battlefield upon which the struggle against duality takes place. The dualistic perception that causes fear in the subject is considered to be the enemy which must be destroyed and supplanted with the vision of non-duality grounded in the Self. In this process, the sense of duality or this-ness merges into non-duality of the Self, bringing forth the reconciliation of all opposites. The famous stanza of the *Parāpañcāśīkā* advances this notion in the following words:

'Effecting the dissolution of the enemy, [which is] this-ness, in the I-ness, he who is intent upon power (heroism) enjoys the natural state [which is] the destroyer of all that is inauspicious'.[17] It is this within this theoretical framework of inner battlefield, evoked in the language of military conquest, that the culture of heroism has developed. The tantric Hero fights his own fear as well as dangers associated with undertaking the tantric path of heroism; he wears a protective armour (*kavaca*)[18] and holds a weapon (*astra*). He is a warrior engaged in battle against his own deep-rooted fear.

Interestingly, the powerful theme of warfare and fear recurs also in Bengali Tantrism, but in a totally different context. In a beautiful poem (poem no. 76, in Thompson and Spenser 1923) of the 18th-century-CE Bengali poet Rasikachandra Ray, the very worship of fierce Kālī, the goddess of battlefield *par excellence*, is metaphorised as the arena of battle. The devotee invites the goddess to the 'battlefield of worship' with the following words:

> Come, Mother, join the battle with me as I worship.
> Let us see, Mother, who will be conquered, the Mother or the son . . .
> Today the battle shall decide the issue.
> What fear have I of death?
>
> With beating of drums, I will seize the wealth of salvation. In battle after battle you have overthrown the Daityas. This time, O Goddess, come and fight with me. Rasikachandra your votary says: it is in your strength, Mother, that I shall conquer you in battle.

The sense of inner struggle associated with the worship of Kālī is certainly reflected in the poetic expressions of this poem. This struggle somehow recaptures the intensity and power of the tantric tradition. The fear of death does not any longer hold the Tāntrika in its grip. He marches with faithful courage for the final battle with the goddess, for he knows that his strength lies in her hands and liberation is near.

The Tantric approach to fear, and to emotions in general, does not attempt to eliminate, control or withdraw the human psyche from its emotional component; to the contrary, it enables a more constructive understanding of the emotions' irresistible power. This understanding leads to the praxis that seeks to intensify emotional patterns through the fullest engagement in their power. In the *Mahārthamañjarī* of Maheśvarānanda (12th–13th century CE), a Krama text written in

Chidambaram (Tamil Nadu), the ritualistic usage of the five Ms forms a part of Means of Power (*śāktopāya*). In this text, we are reminded of the fact that engagement in forbidden, terrifying practices requires a great amount of bravery. It is not a coincidence that these ritual substances are often called the 'heroic ingredients' (*vīradravya*). The *Mahārthamañjarī* (stanza 58) refers to those who undertake the secret *kulācāra* practice thus: 'Those who give themselves to the pleasure of a Great Union in a Cup of Totality, which contains the essence of nectar are verily those who savour the courage expelling seeds of mental agitation'.[19] These cryptic verses refer to two tantric practices that constitute the core of *kulācāra*: (*a*) the 'intimate intercourse' (*mithuna*) or 'Great Union'; and (*b*) the ritual ingestion of wine (*madya*) or 'Cup of Totality'. Both these practices belong to the conduct of the Hero (*vīrācāra*), whereas wine is additionally described as the 'heroic drink' (*vīrapāna*). Engagement in these transgressive practices is equated with the 'savouring of courage'. Interestingly, 'courage' stands here for a psychological bravery that involves overcoming habitual tendencies of the unconscious latent impressions (*saṃskāras*). The latent impressions are accumulated in the storehouse of past actions (*karman*) residing there in the potential form, as the germs of transmigration (*saṃsāra*). These germs are about to surface again, during each time of human existence on earth, sprouting into 'new growths of entanglement, yielding the fruits of still another destiny of delusory performances and rewards' (Zimmer 1961: 303). The *saṃskāras* are unconscious complexes responsible for casting the shadow of ignorance forged by the impurity of determined thought-constructs. Since they reside in the unconscious sphere of consciousness, it is difficult to take hold of them. In the analysis of psyche rendered by the Tantras, one is supposed to get rid of the *saṃskāras* through the act of purification of the thought-constructs. It happens so that on the ground of the non-dualistic Kashmiri Śaiva tradition, the impurity is not a material substance, as in the dualistic Śaiva Siddhānta, but, on the contrary, it abides in thought only. Therefore, all rituals are performed to eradicate the impurity residing in the mental sphere. Purification implies cleansing of the impurity of determined thought-constructs that directly leads to the uprooting of the seeds of latent impressions from which the impure thought-constructs spring forth. As Hanneder points out, the tantric idea of liberation rests on the fact that the impure thought-constructs are the cause of contraction (of the consciousness) through fear (*śaṅkā*): '[C]ontraction results from fear experienced by the individual who tries to protect his identity continuously recreating his limited, artificial identity (*kṛtrima-aham*)' (1998: 144–45). The contraction of the consciousness (*saṃkoca*) connotes bondage and is the exact opposition of the expansion of the consciousness (*vikāsa*) and liberation. The *Mahārthamañjarī* follows this paradigm when it enumerates eight bondages cultivated in the Brāhmaṇical orthodox society that stand in a sharp opposition to a true tantric Hero. These are hate, doubt, fear, shame, disregard, family, caste, and the (orthodox) way of life.[20] The ritualistic use of fear-eliciting substances and places were thought to be effective in reaching the state of absence of contraction through fear. This experience culminating in true and pure identity (*akṛtrima-aham*) is liberation. Additionally, the *Mahārthamañjarī* defines the condition of a liberated *yogin* in terms of *naiścintyam* or 'absence of fear', which is additionally described as free from limitation caused by the perception of duality. The state of 'absence of fear' is characterised as a sudden expansion of one's own consciousness that brings forth the realisation of the essential non-duality that pervades all states and conditions.[21]

It is now clear that *vīra-sādhanā*, in its more 'liberal' or even 'fearless' attitude for the ritualistic usage of substances normally shunned in the everyday life, aspires for a new psychological paradigm, reflected in the powerful status of a Hero whose 'absence of fear' is perceived as the final emancipation. The *Śiva Sūtras* (1.11) of Vasugupta, the 9th-century-CE scriptural authority held in high esteem by the Kashmiri non-dualist Śaiva exegetes, conforms to this view when it deliberately equates the Lord of the Heroes (*vīreśa*) with the highest spiritual achievement known as the Fourth State (*turīya*).[22] The Krama tradition of Kashmiri Śaivism is particularly aware of its 'heroic' identity that remains central to its concept of historical lineages. According to the *Kālīkulapañcaśatikā*, the first teachers in the Krama's lineage, Vidyānanda and Niṣkriyānanda, were Heroes (*vīra*); and according to *Ciñcinīmatasārasamuccaya* 7.183 they lived in the cremation ground (*śmaśānavāsī*) and practiced the vigilance at night (*niśāṭana*). Also, Prabodhanātha, the author of *Aṣṭikā* and a disciple of Cakrabhānu, was an ascetic who was given the venerable title 'the Lord of the Heroes' (*vīrendra*) (*Mahānayaprakāśa* 163).[23] What becomes immediately clear here is that heroic virtue was not only a sign of tantric practice, but more importantly, a visible mark of a spiritual achievement. In this process, 'heroism' becomes itself a sectarian label that marks and confirms its legitimate authority in the multi-denominational religious world of mediaeval India.

Tantric Hero: A Psychological Profile

Finally, I would like to turn our attention to the psychological portrait of the tantric Hero focusing on the Hero's two inherent qualities: (*a*) heroic steadfastness (*dhairya*), and (*b*) virility (*vīrya*). My argument intends to demonstrate that *dhairya* and *vīrya* are emergent features that constitute heroic personhood.

Heroic steadfastness (*dhairya*) is considered to be a fundamental 'character' trait of the tantric Hero. Interesting parallels can be drawn between Karṇa, a hero figure from the *Mahābhārata*, and the tantric hero as regards *dhairya*. The word *dhairya*, derived from the verbal root *dhṛ*, is often used to designate 'firmness', 'constancy', 'courage', 'psychological composure', 'calmness', and 'mental equilibrium'; these states are often metaphorised as the tranquility of the ocean that, in spite of minor interruptions on the surface, remains largely untroubled (van Buitenen 1958: 307). Bhoja, in his famous *Śṛṅgāra Prakāśa* (11th century CE), avers: '[W]hat makes us call a Hero is the fact of his possessing continuity or stability of character (*dhairyam*)' (Pollock 2001: 225). Aditya Adarkar, who in his analysis of the hero Karṇa in the *Mahābhārata* translates *dhairya* as 'courageous constancy', suggests that the concept of psychological growth through heroic steadfastness can be seen 'as a powerful alternative to the Freudian model of individual change' (2008: 139). The same word *dhairya* is used in two different Krama scriptures, *Kālīkulapañcaśatikā* and *Kramasadbhāva*, for a description of heroic steadfastness, free of mental fickleness, identified with the knowledge of Kālī (*dhairyatvāt kālikājñānaṃ cañcalatvavivarjitam*). The *Kālīkulapañcaśatikā* avers that by means of *dhairya* one acquires the knowledge of Kālī, which is without instability. This condition is imperishable, unmovable. The whole universe is pervaded by it (*Kālīkulapañcaśatikā* or *Devīpañcaśatikā* 1.53). Here, 'courageous constancy' assumes an important epistemological dimension, as a firm knowledge of Kālī emerges from it. Similarly, the *Kramasadbhāva* equates Kālī with the strength of heroic composure when it explicitly says: 'Lay hold of this strength, the essence of heroic steadfastness (*dhairyasadbhāva*), which is named Kālīka' (*Kramasadbhāva* 2.2). Such examples show that the tantric practitioners, despite their outrageous practices, are instructed to remain mentally stable. Mental stability or psychological composure are, therefore, seen as truly heroic virtues that are internal to the tantric practice. This observation, it should be noted, stands in contrast with the mainstream Brāhmaṇical 'hallucinatory' opinion about the tantric adepts, who are perceived as insane fellows roaming in the cremation grounds in the frenzy of demonic seizure.

The second important 'personality' trait in the psychological portrait of the tantric Hero is virility (*vīrya*). Etymologically, the term *vīrya* stands for 'manliness', 'valour', 'strength', 'power', 'energy', 'heroism', 'heroic deed', 'virility', 'semen virile', 'efficacy', 'splendour', and 'dignity' (Monier-Williams 2002). Undoubtedly, the non-dualist Kashmiri Śaivas were aware of the tremendous conceptual potency yielded by this term, as they gave *vīrya* a prominent place in their 'heroic' scheme. The concept of *vīrya* is intrinsically related to the problem of *mantric* efficacy (*mantravīrya*) and the level of spiritual realisation of the tantric adept. In response to such questions as to why *mantra*s are inefficient and why do they bring only limited results, the Kashmiri Śaivas say: they do not have *vīrya* or potency. *Mantra*s which lack potency are only compilations of sounds and do not differ from the thought-constructs. Therefore, only *mantra*s provided with *vīrya* are effective. In examining this topic, the *Mahārthamañjarī* puts emphasis on the relationship between the efficacy of *mantra*s and the spiritual realisation of the tantric adept, when it explicitly says in stanza 26: 'That is called *vīrya* which belongs as an attribute to the Hero (*vīra*)'.[24] *Mantric* potency can be awakened by those adepts who have mastered the great *mantra* AHAṂ, the perfect and full I-consciousness. Padoux (1990: 174) explains that AHAṂ, 'which is regarded as identical with the Heart (*hṛdaya*) that is, with consciousness as the source of the energy, and notably of the potency of *mantra*s (*mantravīrya*), is the reflective awareness (*vimarśa*)'.[25]

However, the 'awakening' of *mantravīrya* is also connected with the discovery of virile power in the subtle physiology of the body. Abhinavagupta provides us with a detailed analysis of this process in his commentary on the *Parātrīśikā Tantra*, when he speaks of the vital energy (*ojas*) abiding in the middle canal of *suṣumnā* that becomes diffused as an enlivening factor in the form of virility (*vīrya*) to all parts of the body (Singh 2000: 42). He writes thus: '[W]hatever is taken in, whether in the form of food or perception (sound, visual awareness of form, savour, contact), first it is converted in the middle channel into the form of *ojas*; then, this *ojas* is converted into virility (*vīrya*), which permeates the whole body' (ibid.). Abhinavagupta enlarges on these glosses by saying that those adepts in whom *vīrya* has not reached its full potential, the energy acquired from the sense-perceptions builds up only in the sense-organ itself. But those in whom *prāṇa* and *apāna* becomes submerged in the middle channel, i.e., *suṣumnā*, *vīrya* automatically connects with the *śakti* — the spiritual enlivening force that stands behind all physical, mental and emotional activities of the *sādhaka*.

These few illustrations demonstrate a number of characteristic features consistently associated with the tantric Hero. The examples cited show that heroic steadfastness arising from mental stability, the development of potency to make *mantras* effective, or the discovery of inner virility triggered by successful practice of 'rising *kuṇḍalinī*' are all part of a heroic ethos which constitutes Tantrism. Therefore, the psychological profile of the tantric Hero presented here is that of a man of Heart, endowed with a fearless attitude, strong mind, firm character, spiritual potency; he is also one who always finds courage to combat the powers of contraction and bondage by which men are beset.

Conclusion

An important conclusion about fear that emerges from my analysis is its ambiguous nature. On the one hand, we have a 'positive' fear, regarded as an emotional peak experience providing religious and spiritual power that is mostly welcomed. On the other hand, we have a 'negative' fear resulting from the *saṃskāras* that gives rise to the contraction of consciousness and bondage. The task of the tantric Hero lies in the conquest of this 'negative' fear. 'Positive' fear differs in regard to its object: it may be a fear of the inescapable force of man's destiny, fear of the cremation ground or fear of philosophical questioning. Nevertheless, despite the diversity of objective stimuli that cause fear, there is an important common element to be found: 'positive' fear always arises in the Heart. The symbol of the Heart has been adopted by the Kashmiri non-dual Śaivas as the locus of both emotive power and supreme liberated consciousness. It is conceivable that this assumption represents an attempt to elevate emotional life that can be seen as a mode of access to the higher metaphysical reality blooming with full glory and impenetrable depth.

Notes

1. Even the great Abhinavagupta struggles under the weight of the fear of transmigration (*bhavabhaya*). In verse 18 of the *Kramastotra*, a devotional hymn dedicated to Kālī, he expresses his anxiety with emotional intensity: 'Let that great goddess entirely remove for me the fear of becoming' (*mahādevī seyaṃ mama bhavabhayaṃ saṃdalayatām*). Another example of the same rhetoric used to explicate the devotee's moving appeal to the goddess is found in verse 23: 'May she (Kālī) lessen my sense of differentation originated from the fear of worldly existence' (*kṛśatu mama bhedaṃ bhavabhayāt*).

2. For an analogous theme in the Śaiva Siddhānta, see Andrea Acri's essay (Chapter 7) in this volume.
3. Similarly, *spanda* manifests in the moment of intense terror at seeing the horrible pain of endless wars. Likewise, one's mind reaches the state of *spanda* during a deeply moving experience of joy and happiness of looking at the beloved person whom he taught was dead. The principle of *spanda* also manifests in the moment of mental confusion when 'there is a confusion as to what to do', for example, when one's kingdom is violently attacked by another cruel king and a decision has to be taken on what should be done; being in this perplexed state, one thinks on and on: 'what should I do?'. *Spanda* is further experienced in the time of misfortune, when one receives the message of the death of a kin; in this moment, in which the state of consciousness is altered, the sorrow grows and the tears flow manifesting suffering, *spanda* is established. Similarly, in the moment of sudden terror, when one is confronted eye to eye with an angered tiger, one experiences *spanda.* And again, in the state of retraction, seeing something horrifying, one enters *spanda.* Or, in a moment, free of thought-constructs, in a state of full enthusiasm, when, for example, a man suddenly finds inside himself the force to complete a difficult task, *spanda* arises. Or else, in seeing something extraordinary beautiful, never seen before, *spanda* is established.
4. The translation of this verse was given to the author by Mark Dyczkowski.
5. In doing so, Abhinavagupta refers to three stages of knowledge in Nyāya, viz., *uddeśa* ('enunciation'), *lakṣaṇa* ('definition') and *parīkṣā* ('examination') (Bäumer 1994: 13).
6. *anekakāraṇaireva vivadanti bhayāvahāḥ*|
   hṛdistham praśnaṃ ajñātaṃ āsāṃ tu paramārthataḥ ||

   'People quarrel for this which brings fear for many reasons, because they do not know the question established within your heart, which is the supreme truth' (*Kramasadbhāva* 1.43).
7. *bhayāvahaṃ mahāraudraṃ bhīmarūpaṃ mahotkaṭam* |
   atyantagahanaṃ gūḍhaṃ guptaṃ guptataraṃ param ||

   '[This question] brings fear; it is greatly terrible, in the form of the terrific, it is proud, deep, profound, secret and the most secret' (*Kramasadbhāva* 1.45).
8. The *brahmarākṣas* are the class of demons who possess persons who dislike study, asceticism, religion, fasting, celibacy, and the worship of the gods, ascetics and gurus; and are unclean or rather arrogant (Sutherland 1991: 167).
9. The *kinnaras*, also called *kiṃpuruṣas* (literally, 'what sort of men?'), are creatures with human bodies and heads of horses. The females of this class function as sirens and seductress (Sutherland 1991: 61).
10. The *piśācas* are lower on the scale of beings than the *rākṣasas*. Often described as 'flesh eaters', ignorant, impure and false, they do not have any benevolent side to their nature (Sutherland 1991: 59).

11. These three rites of passage are identified as 'Departure', 'Initiation' and 'Return'.
12. *śrīmaduttarapīṭhasya [k: śrīmaduttaraṃ-] śmaśānaṃ karavīrakam |*
pūjitaṃ devadevena śivena paramātmanā [k, kh: paramātmane; g: paramātmano] || 1.3 ||
mahācityagnisaṃtaptaṃ mahāyoginīsevitam [k, kh, g: -evitam] |
mahābhūtasamākīrṇaṃ mahāmātṛbhiḥ [k: -mātṛbhiḥ; kh, g: -mātṛbhi] sevitam || 1.4 ||
mahāyogaiśca nicitaṃ mahāsiddhairnamaskṛtam /
mahāmaṭhakasaṃjuṣṭaṃ [k, kh, g: mahāmaṭaka-] mahāphetkāranāditam || 1.5 ||
mahāsiddhipradātāraṃ mahābhairavasaṃkulam /
mahāghorātighorograṃ mahātejopabṛṃhitam || 1.6 ||
13. The *Sarvācāra-tantra*, quoted in the *Parātrīśikā-tantra*, provides us with a very interesting explanation of the 'impure' five Ms by pointing out to their constitutional origins from the five gross elements (*pañca-mahābhūta*). The text says that drinkable and non-drinkable is simply water; eatable and not eatable is simply earth; beautiful and ugly is simply fire; touchable and untouchable is only a matter of air; the hole of male organ or the female organ is nothing more than space (Singh 2000: 222–23).
14. The right-hand path is so called because of its progressive method of worship (*pravṛtti-mārga*), in which the senses are suppressed. On the contrary, the left-hand path advertises a regressive method of worship (*nivṛtti-mārga*), in which 'the senses are deliberately brought into contact with everything that tempts them in order to experience the relativity of this temptation and to rise above it and, thus, to become the master of it' (Pott 1966: 13).
15. See, for example, the 'personality theory' of American psychologist Willard Gordon Allport (1937).
16. *Jayadrathayāmala* 4 folio 127v2–6 = *Tantrāloka* 29.73c–75b (Sanderson 1996: 17).
17. *Parāpañcāśīkā*, verse 50 quoted in the *Yoginīhṛdaya* with *dīpikā* of Amṛtānanda (Mayer-König 2005: 82). See also Mayer-König 2005: 77–81.
18. *Kavaca* in the specific sense means 'armour'. In the context of tantric ritual called *aṅganyāsa* that includes ritual placement of the *mantras* on six parts of the body, viz., heart, head, top-knot, torso, eyes, and weapon, *kavaca* is a term used for the torso. The worshipper covers these places with the *mantras* by touching them with fingertips and at the same time uttering the sacred formulas. This ritual is part of a procedure to transform the human body into a divine body. *Kavaca* is the part of the body which is protected against danger, and the weapon (*astra*) is the means to avert danger (van Kooij 1983: 118–29).
19. *ye kulakumbhasudhāsavapānamahotsavasukhe pravartante |*
te khalu vikalpāṅkurān rasikā upadaṃṣṭuṃ pragalbhante ||
20. Commentary on stanza 58.

21. Commentary on stanza 65.
22. *tritayabhoktā vīreśaḥ.*
23. *śrīcakrabhānupādaistu paramārthārthapāragaiḥ |*
    kṛtaprasādo vīrendraḥ [-de vīrendra] śrīprabodhastapodhanaḥ [-prabodha-] ||

    'The venerable ascetic and Lord of Heroes, Prabodhanātha, was graced (with the teachings) by venerable Cakrabhānu who had grasped the highest truth' (trans. Mark Dyczkowski).
24. *vīrasaṃbandhī hi dharmo vīryam ity ucyate |*
25. This topic is only signalled here; for a full explanation of this practice, see Padoux (1990) and Bäumer (2011: 141–226).

Select References

Primary Sources

Cidgaganacandrikā of Kālidāsa:

Swamī Trivikrama Tīrtha (ed.). 1937. *Cidgagana-candrikā*, with English Introduction by Arnold Avalon (John Woodroffe), Arthur Avalon Series, Tāntrik Texts, vol. 20. Calcutta: Āgamānusandhāna Samiti.

Ciñcinīmatasārasamuccaya:

Manuscripts, National Archives (NA), Kathmandu, Nepal; photographed by the Nepal German Manuscript Preservation Project (NGMPP).

MS Kh: NA MS no.: 1-245 (Tantra) 411; NGMPP reel no.: A 1177/7; no. of folios: 36; size: 22.6 x 5.6 cm; script (remarks): Devanāgarī; folios: 1–21, 24–26, 30–41.

MS Gh: NA MS no.: 1-199 (Śaivatantra) 410; NGMPP reel no.: B123/5; no. of folios: 69; size: 22.5 x 7 cm; script: Devanāgarī.

Kālīkulapañcaśatikā or *Devīpañcaśatikā*:

Manuscript, NA, Kathmandu. MS no.: 5-358 (Bauddhatantra), NGMPP; reel no.: B 30/26; no. of folios: 88; size: 20.5 x 5cm; material: palm-leaf; script: Nevarī.

Kramasadbhāva:

Manuscript, NA, Kathmandu. MS no.: 1-76 (Śaivatantra) 144; NGMPP reel no.: A 209/23; no. of leaves: 15; size: 30 x 10 cm; material: paper; script: Nevarī.

Kramastotra of Abhinavagupta:

K. C. Pandey. 2000. *Abhinavagupta: An Historical and Philosophical Study*. Varanasi: Chowkhamba Sanskrit Series Office.

Mahānayaprakāśa of Arṇasiṃha:

Manuscript, NA, Kathmandu. MS no.: 5-5183 (called *Kālikākulapañcaśatakam*) (Śaivatantra) 157; NGMPP reel no.: A 150/6, no. of leaves: 35 (of which folios 26–33); size: 32.5 × 12.5 cm, material: paper; script: Devanāgarī.

Mahārthamañjarī of Maheśvarānanda:

Dviveda, Vrajavallabha (ed.). 1992. *Mahārthamañjarī of Śrī Maheśvarānanda, with the Auto-commentary 'Parimala'*, Yogatantra-Granthamālā, vol. 5. Varanasi: Sampurnanand Sanskrit University, 1992.

Parātrīśikā Tantra:

Singh, Jaideva. 2000. *Parātrīśikā-Vivaraṇa: The Secret of Tantric Mysticism*. Delhi: Motilal Banarsidass.

Spandakārikā:

Singh, Jaideva. 1980. *The Divine Creative Pulsation: Spandakārikās with the Commentary by Kṣemarāja (Spandanirṇaya)*, Sanskrit text with English translation. Delhi: Motilal Banarsidass.

Śiva Sūtras of Vasugupta:

Singh, Jaideva. 2000. *Śivasūtras: The Yoga of Supreme Identity: Text of the Sūtras and the Commentary Vimarśinī of Ktras and, Translated into English with Introduction, Notes, Running Exposition, Glossary and Index*. Delhi: Motilal Banarsidass.

Tantrāloka of Abhinavagupta:

R. C. Dwivedi and N. Rastogi (eds). 1987. *The Tantrāloka with the Commentary of Jayaratha*, 12 vols. Delhi: Motilal Banarsidass.

Yoginīhṛdaya:

Vraja Vallabha Dwivedi (ed.). 1988. *Yoginīhṛdaya* with *dīpikā* by Amṛtānanda. Delhi: Motilal Banarsidass.

Secondary Works

Adarkar, Aditya. 2008. 'Psychological Growth and Heroic Steadfastness in the Mahābhārata', in Rita Sherma and Arvind Sharma (eds), *Hermeneutics and Hindu Thought: Toward a Fusion of Horizons*, pp. 121–50. New York: Springer.

Allport, Willard Gordon. 1937. *Personality: A Psychological Interpretation*. New York: Henry Holt & Co.

Bäumer, Bettina. 1994. 'Vāc as Saṃvāda: Dialogue in the Context of Advaita Śaivāgamas', in Francis X. D'Sa and Roque Mesquita (eds), *Hermeneutics of Encounter: Essays in Honour of Gerhard Oberhammer on the Occasion of his 65th Birthday*, pp. 11–19. Vienna: De Nobili.

——. 2011. *Abhinavagupta's Hermeneutics of the Absolute: Anuttaraprakriyā*. Shimla: Indian Institute of Advanced Study and Delhi: D. K. Printworld.

Bharati, Agehananda. 1980. *The Ochre Robe: An Autobiography*. 2nd rev. edn, with new Epilogue. Santa Barbara, CA: Ross-Erikson.

Bruckner, H., H. van Skyhawk and C. P. Zoller (eds). 2007. *The Concept of Hero in Indian Culture*. Delhi: Manohar.

Campbell, Joseph. 1973. *The Hero with a Thousand Faces*. Princeton, NJ: Princeton University Press.

Corrigan, John (ed.). 2008. *The Oxford Handbook of Religion and Emotion*. Oxford: Oxford University Press.

Dyczkowski, Mark. Forthcoming. *The Tantrāloka with the Commentary of Jayaratha*. Delhi: Indira Gandhi National Centre for the Arts (IGNCA).

Eliade, Mircea. 1969. *Yoga: Immortality and Freedom*. Princeton, NJ: Princeton University Press. 2nd edn.

Hanneder, Jürgen. 1998. *Abhinavagupta's Philosophy of Revelation: An Edited and Annotated Translation of Mālinīślokavārttika I, 1–339*. Gronignen: Egbert Forsten.
MacWilliams, Mark W. 2005. 'Joseph Campbell', in Lindsay (ed.), *Encyclopedia of Religion*, vol. 3, pp. 1377–80. Boston and New York: Thomson Gale.
Mayer-Kőnig, Birgit. 2005. 'Some Reflections on the Hero in Tantric Texts', in R. Sharma (ed.) *Encyclopedia of Indian Wisdom: Prof. Satya Vrat Shastri Felicitation Volume*, pp. 77–81. Delhi: Bharatiya Vidya Prakashan.
Monier-Williams, M. 2002. *A Sanskrit-English Dictionary*. Delhi: Motilal Banarsidass.
Otto, Rudolf. 1958. *The Idea of the Holy*, trans. John W. Harvey. Oxford: Oxford University Press.
Padoux, Andre. 1990. *Vāc: The Concept of the Word in Selected Hindu Tantras*. Albany, NY: State University of New York Press.
Pollock, Sheldon. 2001. 'The Social Aesthetic and Sanskrit Literary Theory', *Journal of Indian Philosophy*, 29(1–2): 197–229.
Pott, P. H. 1966. *Yoga and Yantra*. Hague: Martinus Nijhoff.
Sanderson, Alexis. 1996. 'Meaning in Tantric Ritual', in A.-M. Blondeau and K. Shipper (eds), *Essais sur le rituel III*, pp. 15–95. Paris: Bibliothéque de l'Ecole des hautes études.
Shweder Richard A. and Jonathan Haidt. 2000. 'The Cultural Psychology of Emotions: Ancient and New', in Michael Lewis and J. M. Haviland-Jones (eds), *Handbook of Emotions*, pp. 379–414. New York and London: The Guilford Press.
Sutherland, Gail, Hinich. 1991. *The Disguises of the Demon: The Development of the Yakca in Hinduism and Buddhism*. Albany, NY: State University of New York Press.
The Mother. 1978. *The Collected Works*, vol. 13. Pondicherry: Shri Aurobindo Ashram.
Thompson, E. J. and A. M. Spenser. 1923. *Bengali Religious Lyrics: Śākta*. Calcutta: Association Press.
Tigue, John W. 1994. *The Transformation of Consciousness in Myth*. Oxford: Peter Lang Publishing.
van Kooij, Karel, R. 1983. 'Kavaca: Protective Covering', in Ria Kloppenborg (ed.), *Selected Studies on Ritual in Indian Religions: Essays to D. J. Hoens*, pp. 118–29. Leiden: E. J. Brill.
van Buitenen, J. A. B. 1958. 'The Indian Hero as Vidyadhāra', *Journal of American Folklore*, 71(281): 305–11.
Zimmer, Heinrich. 1961. *Philosophies of India*. Princeton, NJ: Princeton University Press.

PART II

The Bhakti Movement

4

Principal Emotions Contributing to the Supreme Love of Śiva

A Study of Early Śaiva Hymnal Corpus

T. GANESAN*

One emotion that reigns supreme in the entire gamut of devotional literary corpus is love towards the supreme Being. This love, transcending all physical attributes, is expressed in many ways and in many words. Beginning with a sense of awe (*bhayānaka*) initially, the same devotion (*bhakti*) of the individual self towards the supreme Being tends to become a sweet flow of lovable feelings of the highest order in its development. Naturally, in the mature and highly evolved state, *bhakti* enjoys the supreme status of a sentiment; it becomes a *rasa* in itself, which the connoisseur, i.e., the possessor of that emotion, experiences as inseparable from himself. This sentiment occupies the entire self of the devotee *par excellence*. At the same time, being endowed with a life in the material world and with a psychophysical body, the devotee encounters a number of other emotional outbursts; but intensely permeated with the love of his supreme God, he does not get distracted by these — other than God — feelings or encounters. He directs those emotions towards his beloved supreme Being, thereby giving vent to his various feelings and becoming free from their conflicting influences. These other sentiments, sometimes very intense, also enhance the devotee's *bhakti* and sustain it.[1] This actually makes the *bhaktas* (devotees) choose different emotional ways to direct their sentiments towards God.

Defining *Bhakti* and *Bhaktas*

In one of the ancient Sanskrit lexicons, the *Nānārthaśabdakośa*, *bhakti* is defined as *bhaktiḥ syād bhāgasevayoḥ* ('*bhakti* is used both in 'division' [*bhāga*] as well as in frequent worship or service'). The verbal root of *bhakti* is *bhaja*, meaning 'service' and 'worship'. Historically, the *Śvetāśvatara Upaniṣad* is one of the first texts that speaks about *bhakti* in the context of Rudra devotionalism. It accords to *Śiva-bhakti* the highest place in the scheme of spiritual disciplines. A well-known passage (6.23) of the *Śvetāśvatara Upaniṣad* also stresses *bhakti* towards God (*deva*), namely Śiva and one's own teacher (*guru*):

> *yasya deve parābhaktir yathā deve tathā gurau |*
> *tasyaite kathitā hyarthāḥ prakāśante manīṣiṇaḥ ||*
>
> He who has supreme devotion towards the Deva [Śiva] and as much the same devotion towards his teacher [guru], to such a great soul these meanings [explained above] become clear.

Again, *Śvetāśvatara Upaniṣad* 6.20 throws a challenge to all spiritual seekers:

> *yadā carmavad ākāśaṃ veṣṭayiṣyanti mānavāḥ |*
> *tadā śivam avijñāya duḥkhasyānto bhaviṣyati ||*
>
> When man will be able to roll up the entire sky as an animal hide then he will be able to put an end to all his miseries without knowing (= realising) Śiva!

Just as the first proposition is an impossibility, so is also the second one.

The ancient text of *Śivadharma* (1.27–29) eloquently accords the highest place accorded to *Śiva-bhakti* and to the one who has it in abundance:

> *madbhaktajanavātsalyaṃ pūjāyām anumodanam |*
> *svayam abhyarcanaṃ bhaktyā mamārthe cāṅgaceṣṭitam ||*
> *matkathāśravaṇe bhaktiḥ svaranetrāṅgavikriyāḥ |*
> *mamānusmaraṇaṃ nityaṃ yaś ca māṃ copajīvati ||*
> *bhaktir aṣṭavidhā hyeṣā yasmin mlecche 'pi vartate |*
> *sa viprendro muniḥ śrīmān sa yatiḥ sa ca paṇḍitaḥ ||*

> Śiva says, *bhakti* is eightfold: Love towards my *bhaktas*, to feel happy in my worship, performing my worship with devotion, to be physically busy for my sake, to experience modifications in one's voice, in eyes (as shedding tears of joy) and in other limbs as effects of intense devotion, to hear holy legends related to me, to remember me always and to lead the life taking me as the only support. Even a *mleccha*[2] who possesses this eightfold *bhakti* is equal to a learned Brahmin; he is a sage and is a prosperous man and he is learned.

In the words of the immortal hagiographer, Cēkkiḻār, these devotees *par excellence* are:

> *pūtam aintum nilaiyiṟ kalaṅkiṉum*
> *mātōr pākar malarttā maṟappilār*
> *ōtukātal uṟaippiṉ neṟi niṉṟār*
> *kōtilāta kuṇap peruṅ kuṉṟaṉār.*
> *kēṭum ākkamum keṭṭa tiruviṉār*
> *ōṭuñ cempoṉum okkavē nōkkuvār*
> *kūṭum aṉpiṉil kumpiṭalē aṉṟi*
> *vīṭum vēṇṭā viṟaliṉ viaṅkiṉār.*
>
> Even if the elements five should quake,
> They swerve not from their adoration
> Of the flower-feet of Ammai-Appar (Mother-Father, i.e., Śiva-Pārvatī);
> They stand rooted in *bhakti* hailed by the holy ones;
> They are flawless hills of piety.
> They are the ever-blest who have beyonded
> Both prosperity and adversity;
> Ruddy gold and potsherds, they view alike;
> Adoration of the Lord in love is their sole goal;
> They seek not even Moksha;
> Such is their firmness of purpose (*Periyapurāṇam* 1.4.7–8, in Ramachandran 1990: 40).

Even if the five components of the world (*pañca-mahābhūta*) derail in their state, (devotees) do not forget a flower-like feet of the Lord composed of male and female aspects. They stand by the principle of praising of the Lord with love, which is metaphorically compared to 'the hill of flawless pity', indicating their strength. They have wealth which cannot be destroyed or created. They do not discriminate between tile and gold. Other than folding their hands out of rising love, they do not even want to attain liberation (*mokṣa*) (*Periyapurāṇam*, 1.4.9, ibid.). Cēkkiḻār, having thus described the depth and vastness of devotion of these great devotees of Śiva, concludes by wondering: 'Can I ever describe their peerless valour in words?' (*Periyapurāṇam* 1.4.9, in Ramachandran 1990: 40). The devotion of these *bhaktas* is heroic, a valour-infused devotion. This is an instance of heroism in devotion, heroism in supreme love.

Love

The earliest available literature on the theme of *Śiva-bhakti* in a language other than Sanskrit is in Tamil. The devotional Tamil Śaiva poems, sung by 'the three' (*mūvar*) among the earliest Śaiva saints (*nāyaṉār*) namely, Tiruñāṉacampantar (also called Campantar), Tirunāvukkaracar (also called Appar) and Cuntaramūrti (also called Nampi Ārūrar) who lived from 7th to 9th century CE in the Tamil country, is collectively called the *Tēvāram*.

The *Śṛṅgāra rasa* is a well-known emotive theme in the Sanskrit *kāvya* literature. It is regarded as the most appealing when *śṛṅgāra* is experienced by lovers in separation (*vipralambhaśṛṅgāra*). The same theme is also found in the case of devotion where it is described as the *viraha bhakti*, the pangs of separation and longing experienced by the *bhakta* when he longs for the presence of his most beloved God. This *bhakti rasa*, tinged with *viraha* or separation, is a very interesting theme depicted eloquently in the ancient Śaiva devotional hymns of the Tamil country. The Tamil Śaiva saints, such as Tirunāvukkaracar and Māṇikkavācakar, very often use this theme of *viraha bhakti* in their devotional outpourings to express their supreme *bhakti*, characterised by an intense longing to be fully united with Śiva. They take on themselves the role of a *nāyikā* or a young maiden, fully immersed in the divine *rasa* of *Śiva-bhakti*, and express their pangs of separation from Śiva, their supreme lover. This type of *bhakti* has been studied to some extent in the Vaiṣṇava context, but a study in the domain of Śaiva devotion remains a desideratum. In these poems, *bhakti* is the highest experience and all other emotions and feelings are oriented towards it and, therefore, they are being conceived as contributing to the attainment of *bhakti*. As D. David Shulman (1990: xxiii) observes, the Śiva-bhakti poems are characterised by 'a pervasive emotionalism in both tone and substance, [they represent] an emotional address to the personal domain of struggle and complex feeling which is always permeated by immediate, intensely sensual perception and experience'.

In another hymn (*Tēvāram* 6512), we find that the devotee fully considers himself a young maiden, completely overpowered by love towards her lover; unable to bear the pangs of separation, she finally leaves her parents once for all (transgressing, in this way, the social restrictions that forbid her to leave the parental house) and, then, proceeds single-mindedly towards her lover. The poet Tirunāvukkaracar imagines himself in her place and vividly delineates the development of emotions in his mind, all of them contributing to the full manifestation of the supreme love which is the *parābhakti* towards Śiva, the supreme Hero (*nāyaka*). First, she hears her Hero's name, then his whereabouts and attributes. Unable to bear separation from him, she steps out of her home, leaving behind her loving parents, and directly proceeds towards the holy feet of her supreme Hero, Śiva, completely effacing her individuality. Here, we notice that in the highest state of devotion, the individual self fully merges with the supreme Self — its most beloved — without any trace of its separate name and form, just as a river fully mingles with the ocean without any trace of its earlier identity. For the simple relish of the mellifluous flow of words and the portrayal of the development of love in the mind of a young maiden, we may read the following hymn:

muṉṉam avaṉumaiya nāmam kēṭṭāḷ
mūrtti avaṉirukkum vaṇṇam kēṭṭāḷ
piṉṉai avaṉumaiya ārūr kēṭṭāḷ
peyarttum avaṉukkē picci āṉāḷ
aṉṉaiyaiyum attaṉaiyum aṉṟē nīttāḷ
akaṉṟāḷ akaliṭattār ācārattai
taṉṉai maṟantāḷ; taṉnāmam keṭṭāḷ;
talaippaṭṭāḷ naṅkai talaivaṉ tāḷē.

To begin with, she heard of His name;
She heard of Moorti's way of life;
Then she heard of His Aaroor;[3]
Yet she became mad after Him;
She quit her mother and father that very day;
She forsook the mores of the worldly;
She became oblivious of herself; she became nameless;
The woman was one with the feet of her Lover (*Tēvāram* 6.25.7, in Ramachandran 1995: 181).

The devotee, in his ecstasy arising from seeing his most beloved Śiva, censures himself for neglecting his most loved one all these days. He repents intensely for his failure to show *bhakti* towards Śiva all these years. We see such an emotion of complete repentance in many hymns of Tirunāvukkaracar. In this instance we see the emotion of self-repentance contributing to an outpouring of devotion. As an instance we may cite the entire decads (*Tēvāram* 6795–6804, 7039–48), sung by Tirunāvukkaracar at the holy places of Puḷḷirukkuvēḷūr and Talaiyālaṅkāṭu respectively, where, after singing about the greatness of Śiva with supreme love in various aspects, the poet repents that he had wasted most part of his life without ever taking refuge in the holy feet of Śiva. In each verse, the unlimited love of Śiva towards His devotees and His various acts of grace bestowed upon many devotees of yore, are all recounted by Tirunāvukkaracar in such sweet way that enhances the *bhakti*. One such verse is as follows:

> He is a tapaswi true; He is the Vedas; He is the Seed of the Vedas;
> He is the Vikirtan who wears the bright and great crescent;
> He retrieved me — the poor, fatigued one that roamed about
> Witlessly —, from falling into the sea of troubles;
> And made me pursue the path unknown to pseudo-tapaswis;
> He is the Tattvan who conceals Ganga and is concorporate
> With Uma; He is of Thalaiyaalangkaadu; alas, alas,
> I wasted many many days not seeking Him (*Tēvāram* 6.786, in Ramachandran 1995: 514).

And another one:

> Alas, alas, I have wasted many, many days, not hailing
> Him of Pullirukkuvelur! He is the Lord whom Devas
> Hail with a thousand names; unto the servitors who part not
> From Him, He secures the wealth of salvation; becoming
> Mantra, Tantra and medicine too. He cured the malady —
> Well-nigh impossible to cure; He is the martial One who held
> The strong bow with which He gutted with fire
> The triple, hostile towns (*Tēvāram* 6.548, ibid.: 366).

The external manifestations of the supreme love towards Śiva on the part of the devotee that take place when the God appears before him unexpectedly and blesses him, are narrated in the following verses 213–14 of the *Tiruttoṇṭarpurāṇam* (popularly known as *Periyapurāṇam*) by Cekkiḻār:

You were Our servitor formerly; as on women you set
Your mind, you came to be born on earth
By Our fiat;
That life full of misery may not become your lot
We followed you, interceded and claimed you
In the presence of pious Brahmins.

When Aroorar heard these redemptive words
He cried like a calf that heard its mother's lowing;
In every pore of the limbs in his body, he felt thrilled.
He folded his hands above his head in adoration
And burst out thus: 'O the grace! The grace
Of the divine Dancer of compulsive redemption'! (Ramachandran 1990: 50).[4]

Here, the poet compares the love manifested by the devotee (Cuntaramūrti) on hearing the divine words of Śiva with the love expressed by the calf's cry on hearing the lowing of its mother cow.

The emotional outbursts and the physical manifestations of the boundless joy that the *bhakti*-possessed Cuntaramūrti experiences when beholding Lord Naṭarāja for the first time is expressed in the following stanza:

Great senses five merged in the eyes;
Measureless *antaḥ-karaṇa*s four merged in the *cinta*;
The three *guṇa*s were now but pure *sattva*;
Thus bloomed Sundarar in peerless joy,
Poised in the bliss of the non-pareil dance divine
Enacted in the blissful and sempiternal Ether —
Of Him whose matted hair sports the crescent (*Periyapurāṇam* 1.5.106, ibid.: 57).

The five senses become only the eye, the other four senses do not function. In other words, overpowered by the divine ecstasy, all the other senses of the devotee are overwhelmed and with his entire self he beholds the divine form. The three other modes of inner sense (*antaḥ-karaṇa*) — the intellect (*buddhi*), mind (*manas*) and the I-consciousness (*ahaṃkāra*) — cease to function and become the reflective faculty (*cinta*), completely focused on the form of the God. One rarely comes across such a display of supreme love towards Śiva expressed by a devotee.

The feeling of love towards one's parents is expressed many times in the *Tēvāram* hymns. Among all other emotions, this one is strong and the devotee feels a complete mental satisfaction by directing his love to the Universal Parents — Śiva and Pārvatī. The hymns of Tiruñāṉacampantar, who was blessed by the Goddess through the act of being fed by Her own divine milk when he was a child, bear witness to this emotion of filial love as an expression of supreme devotion towards Śiva and His divine consort Umā-Pārvatī (*Tēvāram* 543). Throughout the *Tēvāram* hymns, sung by Tiruñāṉacampatar, we notice this filial love of a child-devotee towards the Universal Parents (*jagataḥ pitarau*, as the poet Kālidāsa says in his invocatory verse of the *Kumārasambhava*).[5]

Awe

The sense of awe (without the fear element) that arises in the mind of the *bhakta* at understanding the unfathomable greatness and the unlimited beauty of Śiva is another emotional element that inspires the flow of devotional fervour of the *bhakta* to great heights. The immortal verses 1–2 of the *Śivamahimnastava* are the case just in point:

mahimnaḥ pāraṃ te paramaviduṣo yadyasadṛśī
stutir brahmādīnām api tadavasannās tvayi giraḥ |
athā 'vācyaḥ sarvaḥ svamatipariṇāmāvadhi gṛṇan
mamāpy eṣa stotre hara nirapavādaḥ parikaraḥ ||

atītaḥ panthānaṃ tava ca mahimā vāṅmanasayoḥ
atadvyāvṛttyā yaṃ cakitam abhidhatte śrutir api |
sa kasya stotavyaḥ katividhaguṇaḥ kasya viṣayaḥ
pade tv arvācīne patati na manaḥ kasya na vacaḥ ||

O, Lord Śiva, remover of all types of miseries, what wonder is there, if the prayer to you, chanted by one who is ignorant about your greatness, is worthless! Because, even the utterances of Brahmā and other gods is not able to fathom your greatness.

Hence, if persons with very limited intellect (and I am one of them) try to offer you a prayer, their attempt deserve your special favour. If it is so, I should not be an exception. Hence, (thinking like this) I begin this prayer.

Śiva is absolutely different from everything in the manifested material world which He has created and in which He exists as its inner controller. The only ever-imperishable supreme Self, as He is, naturally evokes unstinted devotion and love in the minds of His devotees. Many *Tēvāram* decads are witness to this theme of awe and appreciation of Śiva's beauty. A nine-verse poem (*Tēvāram* 8117–8125) succinctly puts this emotion of divine joy that arises in the *bhakta*'s mind while experiencing the supremely divine Beauty of Śiva. The divine poet Cuntaramūrti runs into raptures by observing the natural beauty of the holy town Tiruppaṉaiyūr and exclaims that the supreme Śiva who resides there is the only Beautiful person in the entire universe. Cuntaramūrti's ecstatic *bhakti* is given for relish in the following piece:

> Drums smeared with earth
> Rumble from high on the palaces and gates
> And the music of the *yāḻ* (lute)
> Echoes through the fields of Tiruppaṉaiyūr
> Where He lives
> As Lord
> Praised by all in heaven and on earth
> Who fixed the white crescent
> In His long, matted hair
> He ho is surely
> The most beautiful God (*Tēvāram* 8117–8125, in Shulman 1990: 552).

Frustration and Anger

The feelings of frustration and even anger are directed to Śiva by his great devotees. Getting oneself entangled in the world of misery is difficult, so the devotee directs to Śiva his anger and frustration, which, as a consequence, express much more vividly the deep faith and love towards Śiva. Saint Cuntaramūrti, in one of his many decads sung at the ancient holy town of Tiruvārūr, approaches Śiva because he was made blind by Him without any reason. Cuntaramūrti says that even though he (the servant of the Lord), whose servitude to Śiva is irrevocable, has been praying to Him continuously for remittance of his many sorrows, Śiva remains impassive. Finally, Cuntaramūrti states in anger, 'We wish you luck; go away!':

> I did nothing wrong
> Yet you blinded me.
> Why, lord,
> Did you take my eye?
> The disgrace is wholly yours
> If you won't restore my other eye-
> Then I wish you luck;
> Go away (*Tēvāram* 7.95.2, ibid.: 594).

Even in these emotional outpourings, we observe a strong and unflinching devotion of the *bhakta.* Just as a child taken to task by his mother comes back only to her call, so also the staunch *bhakta* at the height of his misery finds no one else than his beloved Lord to approach, and even dares to show his displeasure with some of the Lord's acts.

In another instance, the same *bhakta* issues to the people a clarion call that only this great bounteous donor, Śiva, can grant all desires to the earnest devotee. To drive home this point Cuntaramūrti brings out the contrast between a miser in the world who, even after being praised, does not dole out pity, and the almighty Śiva who grants all the boons to His earnest devotees, and concludes saying that one can very well be sure of attaining the highest worlds by His grace. In this context, it is worth quoting a verse (*Tēvāram* 7.34.2) belonging to a decad, sung at the holy town of Tiruppukalūr:

> Even if you call some weakling
> 'Bhīma' ('formidable')
> Or 'a mighty Vijaya with his bow,'
> Or praise a miser as a latter-day Pāri,
> They will still give you nothing !
> Sing, you poets,
> About Pukalūr
> Of our auspicious lord,
> His body covered in ash:
> Without doubt
> You will rule the kingdom of the gods
> Which towers over other worlds
> Piled upon worlds (Shulman 1990: 205).

Awe, Love and Disgust

The sense of complete surrender that the mind experiences when it does not think of any other God, let alone of any other thing in the world, is expressed in the *bhakti*-saturated poems of the great woman devotee of Śiva, Kāraikkāl Ammaiyār:[6]

> *pir̲antu mol̲i payin̲r̲a pin̲n̲ellām kātal*
> *cir̲antu nin̲ cēvaṭiyē cērntē̲n̲ — nir̲antikal̲um*
> *maiññān̲r̲a kaṇṭattu vānōr perumān̲ē*
> *eññān̲r̲u tīrppatiṭar* (*Ar̲puta-t-tiruvantāti* 4.1, in Filliozet 1982).

> After I was born and learned to speak
> With overflowing love I reached

Your sacred red feet;
Oh, Lord of the Gods
whose neck shimmers black,
when will you end my afflictions? (Pechilis Prentiss 2012: 147).

She says that since the very first day of her childhood when she started speaking, she has been completely possessed by love towards the holy feet of Śiva. At the height of her love towards Śiva, she, in another verse of the same poem, sings about covering Śiva from the sight of others by her devotion, and about hiding Him in her own heart:

Who can see?
We have cloaked the Lord called 'Hara'
With our love,
Hiding him within our own hearts
as entitled by our abundant praise
and our devotion (ibid.: 177).

The frightening state of the cremation ground where Śiva dances at midnight is brought out in a picturesque manner in one of the Kāraikkāl Ammaiyār's poems when the emotions of awe (*bhayānaka*) and disgust (*bībhatsa*) enhance the *bhakti*:

Jackals snap at putrid skulls
Picked over by birds
The piercing cry from one owl
Widens the eyes of a small one nearby
While a still larger one menaces
And foxes dart everywhere.
This is the great cremation ground
Where the lord prefers to live and dance (ibid.: 194).

In another verse of the same poem, the images of death and desolation are strikingly contrasted with the abundant vegetation that surrounds the place:

The bushes are scorched
The thicket is blackened
The skulls ooze liquid
And the chaparral have withered
Amidst the tall trees.

In this smoldering burning ground,
Clothed with the hide of the spotted deer
And caped with the pelt of the tiger,
The lord makes his home and performs his dance (Pechilis Prentiss 2012: 195).

The sense of wonder and awe at the various heroic deeds of Śiva enhances the *bhakti* to a great level. These emotions serve as the undercurrent of almost all the poems composed out of love towards Śiva. Reading the poetry of Kāraikkāl Ammaiyār, one can admire the sense of wonder and awe associated with the supreme love:

He is the one whose grandeur
cannot be known by anyone,
yet he is the one whose great consciousness
can be known to us,
for he is our lord adorned with the skulls of others
who joyfully dances on the fire
accompanied by harsh *pey* (ghost)
at night (*Aṟputa-t-tiruvantāti* 30, ibid.: 156).

For ordinary mortals, who cannot comprehend the inner meaning of his actions, Śiva's nature is inscrutable. This is brought out in the following verse of the same poem:

He well-adorned with
One cobra ornamenting his body,
another as a belt across the wild skin
and still another atop his golden locks;
but what is its significance
to me the unfortunate? (Ibid.).

The aforecited verse echoes a passage of the *Kumārasambhava* (5.78):

vibhūṣaṇodbhāsi pinaddhabhogi vā gajājinālambi dukūladhāri vā/
kapāli vā syād atha venduśekharaṃ na viśvamūrter avadhāryate vapuḥ//[7]

The shape of one whose form is the universe cannot be determined: it may be resplendent with ornaments or entwined with serpents, dressed in the elephant-hide or again in silken garments, or it may have a vessel of skull or the moon on the crest (Kale 1917: 37).

Love of a Slave

The extreme love of the *bhakta* towards Śiva openly bursts forth in every pore of the body and every nerve of the *bhakta* when he single-mindedly yearns for Śiva's supreme presence; this is expressed by Māṇikkavācakar — another *śiva-bhakta par excellence* — in the following passage 74–90 from the *Tiruvācakam*:

kaṟṟā maṉam eṉak kataṟiyum pataṟiyum
maṟṟu ōr teyvam kaṉavilum niṉaiyātu
aruparattu oruvaṉ avaṉiyil vantu
kuruparaṉāki aruḷiya perumaiyaic
ciṟumai eṉṟu ikaḻātē tiruvaṭi iṇaiyaip
piṟiviṉai aṟiyā niḻalatupōla
muṉpiṉṉāki muṉiyātu atticai
eṉpu naiṉtu uruki nekku nekku ēṅki
aṉpu eṉum āṟu karaiyatu puraḷa
naṉpulaṉ oṉṟi nāta eṉṟu araṟṟi
urai taṭumāṟi urōmam cilirppa
karamalar moṭṭittu irutayam malarak
kaṇ kaḷikūra nuṇtuḷi arumpa
cāyā aṉpiṉai nāḷ torum taḻaippavar
tāyē āki vaḷarttaṉai pōṟṟi.

As cow yearns for its calf, I moaning, hurried to and fro.
Not even in dreams thought I of other gods.
The One most precious Infinite to earth came down;
Nor did I greatness of the Sage supreme condemn
Who came in grace. Thus from the pair of sacred feet
Like shadow from its substance parting not,
Before, behind, at every point, to it I clung.
My inmost self in strong desire dissolved, I yearned;
Love's river overflowed its banks;
My senses all in Him were centered; 'Lord !' I cried.
With stammering speech, and quivering frame
I clasped adoring hands; my heart expanding like a flower.
Eyes gleamed with joy and tears distilled.
His love that fails not day by day still burgeons forth !
Like mother, Thou hast brought me up, I praise ! (Pope 1900: 34).

In another place, Māṇikkavācakar expresses his supreme joy at the way in which Śiva has graced him, by recounting that He has presented him with a head to bend before Him in veneration, He has endowed him with a mouth to sing His praises and, above all, He has made him move around in the company of great *śiva-bhakta*s, thanks to whom the devotion is enhanced and becomes constant. Thus, everything that the *bhakta* experiences and enjoys in the world is the fruit of the supreme grace of Śiva. The *bhakta* is always conscious of this very grace of Śiva throughout his earthly existence (*Tiruvācakam* 281). The *bhakta*, the most lowly of the slaves, fervently asks the Lord to bestow his grace on him. The Lord exists beyond all feelings and emotions, but at the same time he is present in each one of them insofar as he has entered each and every pore of the devotee's body and self. He is the supreme commander, controlling every movement of the slave. In this emotional outburst, the slave–devotee beseeches the Lord to bestow upon him the highest *bhakti*:

> Inspire me to feel and utter the very truth regarding Thee.
> O King! the slave of Thine own loving ones am I.
> Father! not soul alone but body too,
> Thou enterest melting, and with sweetness fill'st each pore.
> Thou dost disperse false darkness, O true Light!
> Ambrosial Sea, whose clearness knows no ruffling wave!
> Civan, Who dwell'st in Perun-turrai's shrine! Thou Thought unique, thinking what passes word and thought!
> teach me to know the way to speak of Thee! (*Tiruvācakam* 390, in Pope 1900: 220).

As a sign of his utterly low position in the rank of the *bhakta*s, Māṇikkavācakar finally wallows that due to Śiva's unstinted and natural love towards him, the God has fully given Himself to the *bhakta* and has taken his mind as His abode. Exclaiming at His grace, he confesses that he is so meek and that he has nothing to pay back to the Supreme Benefactor as a token of gratitude for his act. Initially, the *bhakta* even taunts the Lord saying, 'I am such a lowly creature but you have given your very Self, the most supreme Being, to me while you have taken me, the worthless, as your slave! O Śaṅkara! Who is clever in this deal?!' (*Tiruvācakam* 397).

This is expressed beautifully by the following verse 22.10 of the *Tiruvācakam*:

> What Thou hast given is Thee; and what hast gained is Me:
> O Cankara, who is the knowing one?
> I have obtained the rapturous bliss that knows no end;
> yet now, what one thing hast Thou gained from me?
> Our Peruman, Who for Thy shrine hast ta'en my thought!

Civan, . . .
My Father, and my Master! Thou hast made this frame
Thine home; for this I know no meet return! (Pope 1900: 224).

In another decad of verses, the *bhakta* earnestly longs for the mystic union with his only beloved Lord Śiva and wallows that the pangs of separation from His supreme Master torments him so much. Each verse ends with the fervent longing, 'When shall I dwell in mystic union joined with Him, my flawless gem?' (*Tiruvācakam* 27.1, in Pope 1900: 243). This is the acme of devotion and every other emotion is turned towards that supreme Beloved, which enhances and contributes to the full development of *bhakti* — that single most important *bhāva* of the *bhakta par excellence*.

Love by All Means

The *Sūta Saṃhitā*, one of the important Sanskrit texts, discusses devotion towards Śiva in the following words (4.3.16): 'Even sins committed for the sake of Śiva become pure acts; this is true without doubt'.[8] Some of the great *bhaktas* even performed seemingly cruel acts out of complete devotion towards Śiva and out of scrupulous care to safeguard the interests of Śiva. We may refer to the examples of Ceruttuṇaināyaṉār who cut the nose of the queen when she smelt a flower meant for Śiva; another devotee, Cattināyaṉār, whose heart was full of love towards Śiva, used to cut the tongues of those who maligned the devotees of Śiva. These acts were prompted only by the highest *bhakti* and the consequent attitude that could not accept or tolerate any blasphemy; there was no malevolence either in their thoughts or in their deeds.

In one of the earliest and widespread Śaiva sects known as the Pāśupata, the hallmark of the highest devotion is considered to be the one that is directed towards one's own spiritual teacher, or to Śiva. This is believed to be of the highest types of devotion, wherein the disciple has a firm conviction that 'his Guru is the only saviour' from the misery of transmigration; and the depth of such an unflinching devotion to one's guru is even defined as 'daring to perform even those acts pleasing to him [to *guru*] even though they are prohibited in the scriptures'.[9]

The supreme manifestation of love on the part of the greatest *śiva-bhakta*, Kaṇṇappar, is when he, on seeing the bleeding eye of the *Śivaliṅga* immediately removes one of his own eyes and puts it in its place. Even though the other one also starts bleeding he does not hesitate to take out his other eye; then Śiva appears before him and blesses him by granting him a constant place on His right side.[10]

Bhakti as Renunciation

Another great *bhakta* of Śiva called Śrīdhara Veṅkaṭeśa, who lived in the 17th–18th century CE in Tamil Nadu, says that by chanting the name of Śiva with fervent love His highest *bhaktas* completely attach themselves to His holy feet forgetting their body, etc., which are transient and prone to disease and death:

> *kāyasya heyanidhitāṃ mṛtirugjarārtyā-*
> *dyānantyam apyalam avetya vimuktasarvāḥ* |
> *śambho caranti virujas tvayi baddhabhāvāḥ*
> *ye sādarās tava hi nāmni mahānubhāvāḥ* || (*Śivabhaktilakṣaṇam* 3).

> O Śambhu! Those great selves after knowing that the physical body is the seat of afflictions such as diseases, old age and death and hence to be discarded, renounce everything and move about happily by fixing their mind firmly on you and on your holy name.

In another verse, Śrīdhara Venkaṭeśa says:

> Taking complete refuge in Śiva and surrendering everything at His care, the *bhakta* prays that whatever the Lord deems beneficial to His devotee He can do as the meek does not know which is ultimately good to himself. (*Śivabhaktikalpalatikā* 16).

A *śiva-bhakta*'s higest state of devotion is one in which he states with a firm conviction: 'All the material pleasures are nothing but producers of misery, while the holy feet of Śiva alone bestow the supreme bliss' (*Śivabhaktikalpalatikā* 20). This conviction shakes all attachment to the worldly enjoyments and prompts the devotee to take refuge in the holy feet of Śiva, just as a person tormented by fire rushes to a water tank (ibid.).

Conclusion

This brief study is only a glimpse of how the emotions, such as love, awe and even disgust, have become richly woven into the Śaiva hymnal literature of the ancient Tamil devotional corpus. In this essay, we have analysed just a few examples from that vast ocean and brought out the contributions of such *bhāvas* in the development and sustenance of *Śiva-bhakti* of the highest order, which is an ever-existent and sustaining theme.

Notes

*All the verse translations in this chapter are by the author unless mentioned otherwise.

1. There is also a reference to the eight-limbed *Śiva-bhakti* in the ancient text called *Śivadharma* 1.27–29.
2. *Mleccha* is generally interpreted as a barbarian who does not conform to the usual Hindu Institutions.
3. Aroor is the name of a Śaiva holy place in Tamil Nadu.
4. Cuntaramūrti's external manifestations of the supreme love towards Śiva are also comparable to the emotional outpourings and external manifestations of the supreme *bhakti* of another great Śaiva saint, Tiruñāṉacampantar, who, upon beholding Śiva enshrined in the temple at the holy place Tiruvārūr, says:

   He bowed low and fell on earth; he trembled;
   He danced, and the hair on his thrilled body
   Stood erect; he beheld before him the True Ens
   Envisioned in his consciousness, and adored;
   With his mind grown calm and with soaring love
   He prostrated on the ground. (*Periyapurāṇam*, 6.511).
5. *vāgarthāviva sampṛktau vāgarthapratipattaye* |
   jagataḥ pitarau vande pārvatīparameśvarau | (*Kumārasambhava*, 1).
   'In order to comprehend the word and its meaning I salute Pārvatī and Parameśvara, the father and mother of this universe who coexist inseparably as the word and its meaning'.
6. The following observation gives the best description of Kāraikkāl Ammaiyār's devotion towards Śiva: 'Jamais croyons-nous, l'amour de Dieu ne s'estexpimé avec autant de tendresse et de poésiequedans les vers de Kāraikkāl Ammaiyār' (Filliozet 1982: Avant-Propos, 1). The translation is as follows: 'Never do we think the love of God (Śiva) has been expressed in such a tender way and poetic beauty than in the poems of Karaikkāl Ammaiyār'.
7. The close similarity between the views expressed by Kāraikkāl Ammaiyār and those found in the *Kumārasambhava* is striking. For instance, Kāraikkāl Ammaiyār's *Aṟputa-t-tiruvantāti* 29 is comparable to *Kumārasambhava* 5.75 (Kale 1917: 36): 'And him she addressed – 'indeed thou dost not know Hara aright, since thou talkest thus to me. The dull witted find fault with the course of life of the magnanimous, which is not in common with that of other people, and the motive of which is difficult to divine'.

8. As an example we may cite the life of Mūrkkanāyaṉār, who used to earn money by gambling in order to regularly feed the devotees of Śiva (see *Periyapurāṇam* 3618–29).
9. See Bhāsarvajña's commentary *Ratnaṭīkā* on *Gaṇakārikā* 1.3.6.
10. Kaṇṇappar's story is comparable to that of Kaṇṇappanāyaṉār as (*Periyapurāṇam* 650–830).

References

Kāraikkāl Ammaiyār's works:

Filliozet, Jean (ed.). 1982. *Chants Dévotionnels tamouls de Kāraikkāl Ammiyār*. Pondicherry: Institut Français d'Indologie.

Pechilis Prentiss, Karen. 2012. *Interpreting Devotion: The Poetry and Legacy of a Female Bhakti Saint of India*. Routledge Hindu Studies Series. New York: Routledge.

Gaṇakārikā:

Dalal, Chimanlal Dahyabhai (ed.). 1920. *Gaṇakārikā of Ācārya Bhāsarvajña,with Four Appendices Including the Kāravaṇa-Māhātmya*. Baroda: Oriental Institute.

Kumārasambhava of Kālidāsa:

Kale, M. R. (ed. and trans.). 1917. *Kālidāsa's Kumārasambhava*, cantos I–VII. Bombay: Standard Publishing Company. 2nd edn.

Nānārthaśabdakośaḥ of Medinīkāra:

Jibanandavidyasagarabhattacharya (ed.). 1897. *Nānārthaśabdakośaḥ by Medinīkāra*. Calcutta: Kalikata Press. 2nd edn.

Periyapurāṇam:

Ramachandran, T. N. (trans.). 1990. *St. Sekkizhar's Periyapuranam*, part 1. Thanjavur: Tamil University.

——. 1995. *St. Sekkizhar's Periyapuranam*, part 2. Thanjavur: Tamil University.

Arumuka Navalar (ed.). 1951. *Periyapurāṇameṉṟuvaḻaṅkukiṟa Tiruttoṇṭarpurāṇam, Cēkkiḻārnāyaṉāraruḷicceytatu*. Chennai: Vidyanupalana Press. 8th edn.

Raghuvaṃśa of Kālidāsa:

Kale, M. R. (ed. and trans.). 1924. *The Raghuvaṃśa of Kālidāsa, with the commentary Saṃjivani of Mallinātha Edited with a Literal English Translation, Copious Notes in Sanskrit and English, and Variant Readings*. Bombay: Standard Publishing Company.

Śivabhaktikalpalatikā and *Śivabhaktilakṣaṇam* of Śrīdhara Venkaṭeśa:

Śāstrī, T. M. Nārāyaṇa (ed.).1919. *Śrīdharastutimaṇimālā*. Kumbakonam: Sarada Vilas Press.

Śivadharma:

Śivadharma. Institut Français de Pondichery Transcript 32 (IFP. T. 32), paper transcript(s) from the Collections of the French Institute, Pondicherry.

Śivamahimnastava:

Brown, William Norman (ed. and trans). 1965. *The Mahimnastava or Praise of Shiva's Greatness*. Poona: American Institute of Indian Studies.

Sūta Saṃhitā:
Panshikar, Vasudeva Laxman Shastri and Vinayak Ganesh Apte (eds). 1924–25. *Sūtasaṃhitā with the Commentary Tātparyadīpīkā of Madhāvacārya*, 3 vols. Pune: Ānandāśrama Press.
Śvetāśvatara Upaniṣad:
Śarmā, Tulasīrāma (ed.). 1985. *Śvetāśvataraupaniṣad*. Delhi: Eastern Book Linkers.
Tēvāram:
Iyer, T. V. Gopal (ed.). 1984–85. *Tēvāram*, 2 vols. Pondicherry: Institute Français d'Indologie.
Shulman, D. David (trans.). 1990. *Songs of the Harsh Devotee: The Tēvāram of Cuntaramūrtināyaṉār*. Philadelphia: University of Pennsylvania.
Tirumurai:
Ramachandran, T. N. (trans.). 1995. *Tirumurai the Sixth: St. Appar's Thaandaka Hymns*. Dharmapuram: Dharmapuram Aadheenam.
Tiruvācakam:
Balasubramaniam, K. M. (ed. and trans.). 1958. *Tiruvācakam Māṇikkavācakar Aruliyatu*. Madras: Chennamalleswarar and Chennakesavaperumal Devasthanam.
Pope, Rev. G. U. (trans.). 1900. *The Tiruvācagam or 'Sacred Utterances' of the Tamil Poet, Saint and Sage Māṇikkavācagar*. Oxford: Clarendon Press.

5

Love Never Tasted Quite Like This Before

Śṛṅgāra-rasa *in the Light of Two Texts from a Sahajiyā Vaiṣṇava Notebook*

Neal Delmonico and Aditi Nath Sarkar*

The focus of this study is the idea of 'erotic love' or *śṛṅgāra*, as expressed in two texts belonging to a late religious tradition in India, referred to as Sahajiyā Vaiṣṇavism. *Śṛṅgāra* is a word used in the ancient text on dramaturgy, *Nāṭyaśāstra* (*The Treatise on Drama*, 4th–5th century CE) to distinguish sublime erotic love, as experienced in art, from ordinary, quotidian erotic love called *rati* (the desire to engage in or the act of engaging in sex). *Śṛṅgāra*, thus, comes to stand for the highest, the most sublime experience of erotic love one can have and, even more than this, the highest or 'peak' experience of human life itself. This is well demonstrated by some of the commonly met folk etymologies of the word *śṛṅgāra*: *śṛṅgam ārate* ('one rises to or reaches the peak')[1] and *yena śṛṅgam ucchrayo rīyate* ('that by which the heights are reached').[2]

Erotic love is embodied in this tradition, in a religious persona or identity called the *mañjarī-svarūpa* which we translate as the 'flowering bud' identity. Though neither of the texts discussed in this chapter actually uses this term, the ways in which the sought-after emotional state is described in them and the fact that the 'flowering bud' identity is found all over the notebook from which the texts were drawn, indicate that we are dealing here with an early form of the identity, not yet fully developed or clearly named when the texts were composed. The 'flowering bud' identity is, as we will demonstrate, a metaphoric representation of participation in a sublime, erotically charged, emotional condition, personified by Rādhikā, Kṛṣṇa's primary lover in the Vaiṣṇava mythology, who is regarded not only as the highest expression of *śṛṅgāra*, but also as the 'mother-bush' from which all of the flowering buds grow. Cultivating the 'flowering bud' identity, therefore, means connecting with Rādhikā and sharing her emotional experience of sublime erotic love for Kṛṣṇa.

The two short texts used in this study come from a practitioner's notebook which belongs to a fascinating blend of religious and intellectual traditions common in the 18th and 19th centuries CE in colonial Bengal. Before examining the specific ideas and practices found in these texts, we need to place this notebook in its proper cultural context, and this means we need to sort out some of the more important streams of the tradition that went into the making and use of this notebook. A quick scan of the contents of the notebook as a whole informs us that one of the major religious traditions embodied in this collection is the Caitanya Vaiṣṇava tradition, the powerful religious and literary movement-turned-tradition in Bengal and in other parts of north and east India, dating back to the lifetime of saint Śrī Caitanya (1486–1533 CE). The tradition that crystallised around Caitanya, quite diverse in itself, was a revival of much older forms of devotional Vaiṣṇavism, but with a number of new twists.[3] The sub-tradition to which these texts belong appears to have diverged from the mainstream of Caitanya Vaiṣṇavism with an important and enigmatic figure named Mukundadāsa Gosvāmī (second half of the 16th century CE and first half of the 17th century CE), who belonged to the third generation of the followers of Caitanya.

The other forms of Vaiṣṇavism, exemplified mostly by traditions still vibrant in south India,[4] focus on Viṣṇu or Nārāyaṇa, regarded as the universal, omnipotent, omniscient god-king, responsible for the periodic creation, maintenance and destruction of the cosmos; or on the regal Rāma, the righteous king whose heroic story is told in the great epic, the *Rāmāyaṇa*. The Caitanya tradition, instead, focuses on Kṛṣṇa, not the Kṛṣṇa who, in the Purāṇic tales, kills numerous demons, nor the Kṛṣṇa who comes to lift the burden of arrogance, exploitation and selfishness from the back of the Mother Earth, nor even the Kṛṣṇa who, as Arjuna's charioteer, guides him in his moment of crisis before the great battle, described in the India's greatest epic, the *Mahābhārata*. The

Caitanya tradition focuses on Kṛṣṇa who is the lover-boy, who steals the clothes of girls in the cowherd settlement called Vraja, and later dances the 'circle-dance' (*rāsa-līlā*) with them. The Caitanya tradition is deeply influenced by, perhaps, the greatest of the Purāṇas, the *Bhāgavata Purāṇa* (5th or 6th century CE), which, unlike the earlier treatments of the life of Hari,[5] devotes 45 poetic chapters (10.1–45) to his boyhood. Kṛṣṇa is Viṣṇu–Nārāyaṇa taken down from his majestic cosmic throne, stripped of his weapons and sceptre of supreme power, armed with a bamboo flute and stick, and thoroughly humanised (*dehaṃ mānuṣam āśritya*, *Bhāgavata Purāṇa*, 10.1.11) as a simple cowherd boy tending cattle, killing demons (well, there is still some divine power there) and, most importantly, flirting with and bedding the cowherd girls.

The humanising and erotic turn, evident in the *Bhāgavata Purāṇa*'s treatment of Kṛṣṇa, further underwent a number of developments between the time of its composition and the time of the appearance of Śrī Caitanya. Most notable among these was a blending with an earlier literary stream that paired Kṛṣṇa with a lover, Rādhā, who is fully his match and whose name means 'success, prosperity' and is derived from the root *rādh* which means 'to thrive or prosper; to satisfy or please'. Rādhā first appears in a Prakrit anthology of poetry called *Gāthāsaptaśatī* or *Gāhāsattaśaī* (*The Seven Hundred Stanzas*), attributed to Sātavāhana king Hāla (2nd century CE):

> By the breath of your mouth, Kṛṣṇa,
> You blew the cow-dust off of Rādhikā
> And stole from these other cowherder girls
> Their conceited self-appraisals (*Gāthāsaptaśatī* 1.89).[6]

Not only is Rādhā represented as the love interest of Kṛṣṇa, she is also distinguished from and raised above all other cowherd girls (*gopīs*). Though the *Bhāgavata Purāṇa* is later than the anthology of Hāla, if our chronology is correct, Rādhā's name does not appear anywhere in the *Purāṇa*. There is possibly, however, an indication that the author(s) of the text was/were aware of Rādhā's special connection with Kṛṣṇa in the literary world of amorous poetry, in a verse from *Skandha* 10 that describes the 'circle-dance'. According to this verse, during one evening, a special cowherd girl is accompanied by Kṛṣṇa to a place of solitude for a while. The other cowherd girls notice her footprints heading off into the surrounding forest, next to his footprints. As the *Bhāgavata Purāṇa* (10.30.28) puts it:

Solicited by her, Hari,
The Lord and controller of all,
Left us aside and being pleased,
Govinda took her to a private place.[7]

The use of the word *ārādhita* ('solicited', 'honoured', 'worshipped') as an adjective of Kṛṣṇa here suggests that this special cowherd girl whom Kṛṣṇa took apart from the others was Rādhā, and the word would certainly have brought her to mind for learned audiences of the text.

Nevertheless, Rādhā's personality does not receive any real development, nor does her love relationship with Kṛṣṇa take on any emotional shape or depth until the composition of the *Gīta-govinda* (*Song of Govinda*) by Jayadeva in the 12th century CE. From then on Rādhā plays a central role as Kṛṣṇa's lover, primarily, it must be said, in the vernacular literature of Bengal and Mithilā, through the charming and rustic poem or collection of poems called *Śrī Kṛṣṇa-kīrtana* (*The Glory of Śrī Kṛṣṇa*, 14th century CE) by Caṇḍīdāsa (Rādhā at this early state is not distinguished from Candrāvalī who later becomes her chief rival for Kṛṣṇa's affections), and through the songs of Vidyāpati (15th century CE). These were Caitanya's sources for his understanding and appreciation of the love of Rādhā and the other cowherd girls for Kṛṣṇa.

Here we encounter important elements of the second major stream of Indic religious thought and practice that blends with the older forms of Vaiṣṇavism to form Caitanya Vaiṣṇavism and its offshoots, referred to collectively as Sahajiyā Vaiṣṇavism.[8] This stream can be connected with the development of Tantrism and the tantric worldview towards the beginning of the common era. Tantrism as a distinct way of viewing the nature of the world and of attempting to control it through ritual has influenced all the major religious traditions of India, transforming even the older, southern versions of Vaiṣṇavism, through the production of a body of texts called the *Āgama*s (lit. 'received' texts), into something other than what they were. That is to say, they became much more dependent on the use of sacred diagrams (*yantra*s and *maṇḍala*s), the power of sacred sounds (*mantra*s), sacred images (*mūrti*s), and a pairing of all the great male gods with consort goddesses (*śakti*s or 'powers').

Though Tantrism is a complex religious and philosophical development and cannot easily be defined, there are certain elements that one expects to be present in varying degrees in most of the religious traditions it has influenced. Among these elements are a worldview that envisions the world of duality as reducible to cosmic male and female aspects; a focus on the body, especially on the engendered human body, as a means to salvation; and a belief in the intimate connection between the microcosmos (the body) and the macrocosmos (the universe) such that the latter is entirely represented in the former and can be manipulated by manipulating it. Behind the duality, however, is recognised a unity or non-duality, which is generally conceived of as or symbolised by the sexual union of the male and female principles of the cosmos. Sexual union symbolises primordial unity, the time before Time when there was no creation, and yet the creation's very source and impulse, the Big Bang, if one may call it so.

Gavin Flood, in his recent book *The Tantric Body* (2006), presents another interesting perspective on Tantrism that is relevant to the texts discussed in this essay. He suggests that the most fundamental aspect of Tantrism is found in the divinisation of the body. In order to worship a deity, one has to become divine, and the tantric tradition is about ways of ritually transforming the body into a divine body. As Flood (2006: 11) says:

> The empowering of the body, which means its divinisation, is arguably the most important quality in tantric traditions, but a quality that is only specified within particular traditions and texts. Becoming divine is an ancient trope in Indian civilisation. The practitioner in ritual contexts becomes divine such that his or her limited subjectivity is transcended or expanded and that subjectivity becomes coterminous with the subjectivity of his or her deity, which is to say that the text is internalised and subjectivity becomes text-specific.

According to Flood, the divinisation of the body is also at the same time and necessarily an entextualisation of the body. That is to say, the text becomes 'inscribed' on the body, and the subjectivity (i.e., the understanding of who one is, that goes along with the body, what the 'I' refers to) is similarly shaped or inscribed by the texts. The texts are not just read; they become lived. Or, to put it another way, reading a text means bringing it to life, embodying it. As we will see, this quite aptly fits in with the understanding of the texts we discuss here, at least for the followers of this tradition. The identity of the practitioner is created by the texts, and the body is understood in terms of how the texts describe the body, such that the body becomes a 'walking text'. The very existence of this 19th-century CE notebook that has collected together, perhaps over a lifetime of religious practice, a variety of texts, suggests that something like 'entextualisation' was going on in the religious life of the owner of this notebook. Moreover, the same is as true for the mainstream, orthodox Caitanya Vaiṣṇavism as it is for its Sahajiyā offshoots. We will see in more detail what the typical subjectivity created by these texts is and how it is achieved and brought to life by the practitioner. Additionally, we will see how the body becomes divinised or entextualised by these texts through initiation and ritual practice. Thus, Tantrism stands at the very core of the blend of traditions that we see represented in these texts.

The *Bhāgavata Purāṇa*, which was a major source of inspiration and entextualisation for the Caitanya tradition, also shows elements of tantric influence, reinforcing in Caitanya Vaiṣṇavism and its offshoots, tantric influences received from other sources.[9] Probably, the clearest reference to a tantric practice comes from the 'circle-dance' of Kṛṣṇa with the cowherd women who, in response to the enchanting sound of Kṛṣṇa's flute, left their homes and families and joined him in the forest for the night. During the dance in which Kṛṣṇa expands himself into as many forms as there are women, such that each woman thinks he is only with her, the following verse occurs:

> In this way, he cherished those nights,
> Which were radiant with moonlight,
> Every desire of his come true,
> With those ladies so fond of him,
> His semen (*saurata*) withheld inside of himself,
> All those nights the very settings
> For the flavour (*rasa*) of autumn poetry (*Bhāgavata Purāṇa* 10.33.26).[10]

This verse caused the Caitanya tradition's authoritative commentators some trouble and forced them to come up with some creative misreadings. Its simplest and most direct meaning is that Kṛṣṇa withheld his semen (*saurata*) inside himself.[11] This implies that coitus took place between Kṛṣṇa and the cowherd women and he used a well-known tantric technique of stopping his ejaculation, thereby demonstrating his control over his sexual urges. The ability to stop the flow of semen during coitus and redirect it into the mystical system of *nāḍī*s and *cakra*s (subtle energy channels and centres mapped on to the body in the Tantras) is considered a *siddhi* or sign of accomplishment in the tantric traditions. Kṛṣṇa, thus, appears here as a tantric adept and the cowherd women as his *sādhikā*s or female practice partners.

Another evidence for the *Bhāgavata Purāṇa*'s tantric leanings comes at the end of the five chapters on Kṛṣṇa's 'circle-dance' with the cowherd women. When asked why such activities of Kṛṣṇa with the cowherd women were recounted in the first place, Śuka[12] responds:

> This Viṣṇu's play with the wives of Vraja
> One should listen to as well as narrate.
> One who does so with faith attains
> The highest *bhakti* to the Lord
> And easily throws off desire,
> The heart's disease, and with dispatch
> Becomes a person self-possessed (*Bhāgavata Purāṇa* 10.33.39).[13]

A final stream needs to be distinguished in the blend of tantric and Vaiṣṇava traditions in order for our analysis to approach completeness. This stream is the philosophical and literary stream of *rasa*-aesthetics which originated in the ancient disciplines of Sanskrit literary criticism or dramaturgy sometime shortly before or towards the beginning of the common era. *Rasa*, however, is a wonderfully multivalent word with a long and diverse history of use and meaning. It not only means flavour, juice or essence, but also operates in the field of medicine, referring to elixirs or liquid medicines, either herbal or fabricated out of mercury. Such *rasa* elixirs are believed to be capable of curing diseases. Then again, in the old Indic pseudoscience of alchemy, *rasa* is synonymous with ambrosia or nectar (*amṛta*), the potent drink which bestows on its drinkers immortality. *Rasa*, in fact, comes to mean mercury itself in the tradition of Indian alchemy. As a term often met in these texts and also in the texts of the orthodox Caitanya tradition, it seems to carry or imply at various places all these different meanings and other new ones as well.[14]

Rasa in aesthetics refers to the pleasurable experience a connoisseur[15] has in relationship to drama and poetry, and all the other arts as well. *Rasa* is the reason people enjoy art. The idea of *rasa* might be compared with eating food. *Rasa* corresponds to the taste or flavour of the food. As taste or flavour, *rasa* makes the eating of food a pleasure. If it has no flavour or a bad flavour, the food is not a pleasure to eat. Thus, the chef strives to create food that is pleasant to eat and also nourishing. So, too, does the artist make art. But what is it that makes art pleasurable? According to Sanskrit literary criticism, it is the emotional content of a work of art that makes it pleasurable. Thus, *rasa* is a kind of essential or generalised emotion created in an audience by the artist's expert representation of life-like events in the work of art. *Rasa* was first discussed in *Nāṭyaśāstra*, an ancient Sanskrit text on dramaturgy attributed to a sage named Bharata. Though this is the earliest surviving discussion of *rasa*, it is clear from the treatment found in the text that it had been discussed and developed before in other texts by other authors (Druhiṇa, for instance) that are no longer available (see *Nāṭyaśāstra* [hereafter *NŚ*] 6.16).

Rasa is a huge and fascinating topic, but one into which we cannot enter very far here in this essay. Suffice to say that of the various emotions experienced in the course of human life, only a few are considered powerful enough or to recur often enough to become foundations for *rasa*. *Nāṭyaśāstra* 6.15 enumerates only eight *rasa*s. They are: the erotic (*śṛṅgāra*), the comic (*hāsya*), the pathetic (*karuṇa*), the furious (*raudra*), the heroic (*vīra*), the terrifying (*bhayānaka*), the disgusting (*bībhatsa*) and the marvellous (*adbhuta*). To these another is added later (*NŚ* 6.83), called the peaceful (*śānta*). These are the relishable forms of ordinary emotions called *bhāva*s, the mental 'states', or in the case of these nine, the *sthāyibhāva*s, the lasting or enduring mental states, which are: love, mirth, sorrow, anger, courage, fear, aversion, and wonder (*NŚ* 6.17). The enduring mental state at the base of the peaceful is tranquility or dispassion (*NŚ* 6.83). These emotions from ordinary life when represented in poetry and drama by creative and skilful artists are experienced by cultured members of the audience as the *rasa*s. To distinguish *rasa*s from the ordinary emotions, they are given different names. So, one could say that according to this understanding of the functioning of art, quotidian emotions are transformed into sublime or otherworldly emotions.

In the course of the history of thought on *rasa*, various writers began to ask themselves which of the nine *rasa*s was the primary *rasa*. The *Nāṭyaśāstra* seems to give this process a start by deriving some of the *rasa*s from other *rasa*s. Thus, according to the text, the comic *rasa* developed out of the erotic *rasa*, and from the furious came the pathetic. From the heroic came the marvellous and from the disgusting came the terrifying (*NŚ* 6.36). But was there one *rasa* from which all the others were derived or produced? Though different writers took different positions, the one *rasa* that emerged most often as the source of all the other *rasa*s was the erotic. One of the greatest literary critics and theoreticians of India, Abhinavagupta of Kashmir (10th–11th century CE), recognised the erotic as the primary or dominant *rasa*, primarily on the basis of the vastly more numerous verses, plays and poetry which evoke it and, of course, its greater aesthetic interest. Abhinavagupta, however, did not claim that all the other *rasas* were produced or derived from the erotic *rasa*. For that, he was in favour of the peaceful, which resembles the kind of repose (*viśrānti*) which he saw as concluding the *rasa* experience. King Bhoja of Dhārā in Marwar (11th century CE) did create a theory of *rasa* in which all the *rasas* — and he recognised more than just the usual eight or nine — derived from the erotic *rasa*, *śṛṅgāra*. In his formulation, the erotic is viewed as the very force that drives aesthetic experience, even when it poses as one of the other *rasas*. In its full experience, it returns to the peak of erotic *rasa*. This line of aesthetic thought with its recognition of the possibility of transforming emotions from quotidian to sublime or divine and its focus on the erotic *rasa* as either the primary *rasa* or as the source of the other *rasas*, fed into the tantric stream and the Vaiṣṇava stream to produce a more powerful influence in shaping the texts studied in this essay and to encourage the proliferation of numerous other texts and movements in late mediaeval India (16th–18th century CE).

Rasa as medicine or as mercury in the traditions of Āyurveda and alchemy, respectively, has already been discussed in great depth by David Gordon White (1996) and others. It is not necessary to do more than sketch them briefly here. *Rasa* as medicine was regarded as a means of curing diseases and regaining health and longevity. While initially these benefits were thought of in physical terms, they soon came to be applied metaphorically to the existential situation of living beings in the world which was viewed as a kind of metaphysical illness. *Rasa*, thus, came to stand for the means of attaining freedom from the cycle of death and rebirth, or, in other words, *mokṣa* or liberation. But what kind of *rasa* might have this effect? The aesthetic *rasas* of Abhinavagupta and Bhoja were considered liberating but only temporarily so. They provided a taste or glimpse of liberation (*mokṣa*) but nothing more.[16] Here, the *rasa* of alchemy steps in. *Rasa* as mercury when treated with mica and sulfur and cooked by heat in the laboratory is transformed into an elixir of immortality. Later, when the practitioner ingests it, he becomes immortal. When this process is internalised, and the *rasa* of alchemy is homologised with the semen of man, its heating in the oven of controlled sexual practice, as described in these texts, and its being mixed with the menstrual blood and other fluids of the female partner, transform it into the elixir of immortality. Raised up the spine to the thousand-petalled lotus at the top of the skull, the *rasa* rains down in a rain of bliss transforming the practitioner's corruptible body into an incorruptible body of bliss and immortality.

These, then, are some of the ideological and practical influences on the texts that are studied here: Vaiṣṇava, tantric and rasic. The complete bilingual edition and translation of the texts studied here, with an extensive introduction and full annotation, will appear shortly under the title *Love in the Land of Heroes: Two Sahajiyā Texts from a Mid-nineteenth Century Bengali Notebook* (Delmonico and Sarkar forthcoming). A cross-section of Sahajiyā texts from earlier centuries, such as the old Buddhist *Caryāpadas* (11th–12th century CE) and the songs of Caṇḍīdāsa (14th century CE), and later centuries, such as some of the short works of Mukundadāsa (17th century CE) and the *Vivarta-vilāsa* (18th century CE), will be included in the appendices of this bilingual edition to provide a sense of the historical growth and transformation of the tradition to which the two texts discussed in the chapter belong.

The Notebook, Texts and Authors

The two texts discussed in the essay are taken from Calcutta University manuscript 3437. One is a short text of 40 lines attributed to an author named Sanātana and the other, a longer text of over 500 lines by an author named Taraṇīramaṇa. Both texts are written in Bengali. We have examined only a microfilm copy of this manuscript,[17] and consequently our remarks on it are limited in scope. Unlike most older Bengali manuscripts, which are long (horizontally) and narrow, MS 3437 is approximately one-and-a-half times longer vertically than it is horizontally. The pages are definitely intended to be turned on the vertical axis, again unlike the bulk of the older Bengali manuscripts. In short, it is very much like a notebook in the style familiar to us. Each left-hand page is numbered on the upper right-hand corner. The numbers go up to 35, followed by three somewhat damaged pages, i.e., there are 73 pages in all. The manuscript is evidently in more than one handwriting. The manuscript appears to have been the property of Śrīmantarāma Dāsa, of the village Mahurā or Mahuṛā, and at least parts of it were copied in *sāl* (Bengali Era) 1259 (1852) and 1260 (1853). The village Mahurā may possibly be one of the two villages, each called 'Mahurapur' and located in the Muraroi and Mayureshwar *thānas* (police jurisdictions) respectively, in Birbhum district (Ray 1966).

In spite of the many clear acknowledgments of Bengali Caitanya Vaiṣṇavism in some parts of the notebook, the two texts are remarkable for the complete absence of any references to Caitanya or of the terminology familiar to the post-Caitanya Sahajiyā movement. As such, they bear evidence of a pre-Caitanya Sahajiyā Vaiṣṇava tradition in Bengal. About the identity of the author of the first text, Sanātana, we at present unfortunately know nothing else. Given the un-commonality of the name, it is likely we are meant to believe that the author was the famous follower of Caitanya, Sanātana Gosvāmī of Vṛndāvana (present-day Uttar Pradesh). The second text has been edited and printed as *Taruṇiramaṇera* [*sic*] *Padāvalī o Sahaja Upāsanā Tattva* in *Bangīya Sāhitya Pariṣad Patrikā* (1355 BE, i.e., 1949, no. 4). Our reading, by and large, agrees with Basanta Roy, the editor of this edition. Roy gives the name of the author of the text, however, as Taruṇīramaṇa. Yet, we notice that the anthology *Vaiṣṇava Padāvalī* of Harekṛṣṇa Mukhopdhyya (1980) adopts 'Taraṇi-' for this author. Referring to the anthology *Aprakāśita Padaratnāvalī* edited by Satīśacandra Rāya, where many poems by a 'Taraṇiramaṇa' [sic] occur, and surveying the growing number of other poems by 'Taruṇīramaṇa', including his own unpublished finds, Roy suggests that there may well have been an excellent and prolific poet by this name, who may also have been known as 'Taraṇīramaṇa Caṇḍīdāsa' (in the style of 'Dvija-', 'Baḍu-' and 'Dīna-' Caṇḍīdāsa whose separate identities were widely accepted). If the 'Taruṇīramaṇa' mentioned in the *Siddhāntacandrodaya* (*Moonrise of Settled Teaching*) of Mukundadāsa, compiled in the early 17th century CE, is the same as the author of our second text, then this text may have been more influential and older than hitherto suspected.

The Flower-bud Nature

The *mañjarī-svarūpa* or the 'flowering bud' identity — or, as Flood (2006: 5, 11–12) refers to it, 'subjectivity' — is an identity deemed by the orthodox and the Sahajiyās alike as suitable for being in close proximity to Rādhā and Kṛṣṇa and for serving them. It is the identity (consciousness-body included) of a young cowherd girl, roughly the eternal age of 12 and a half or 13, which, as we saw, was etched in the notebook at an odd place. *Mañjarī* means 'flowering bud', which, as we will see later in the essay, is significant for its relationship to the plant it is a flowering bud of. The *mañjarī* is a symbol of distinctive non-duality. It is part of the plant, yet it is also distinctive in form, shape and function. It represents that by which the plant grows and reproduces, the plant at the peak of its reproductive powers — the essence of the plant distilled. Similarly, the *mañjarī* is regarded in Caitanya Vaiṣṇavism as intimately connected with Rādhā, as extensions of her that are nevertheless part of her very being, and yet so many distinctive expressions of that being. The classic description of the *mañjarī* as a young cowherd girl is found in a passage of the *Padma Purāṇa*:

> One should think of oneself there among them in the form of an enchanting woman, possessed of youth and beauty, just past puberty, conversant with the many arts and crafts, suitable for Kṛṣṇa's enjoyment, but who, though requested by Kṛṣṇa, is opposed to enjoyment with him, a follower of Rādhā intent upon her service, loving Rādhā even more than Kṛṣṇa, bringing about, out of love and with great care, the meetings of those two each day, and overwhelmed with the joys of their service. Visualising oneself in this way, one should perform service there beginning from the period of Brahman [one and a half hours before sunrise] until late at night.[18]

This passage concerns mental or contemplative service. Thus, it begins with 'one should think of oneself as' (*ātmānaṃ cintayet tatra*). It is, therefore, a practice or ritual, described and enjoined by a text (actually several parallel texts, since this passage also appears verbatim in the tantric *Sanatkumāra Saṃhitā* and is a clear example of what Flood calls 'entextualistion'). The body and subjectivity of the follower are shaped and created by the text. A complex practice of meditation/visualisation called 'Remembering the Sports of Rādhā and Kṛṣṇa in the Eight Periods of the Day' (*Aṣṭakālīya-līlā-smaraṇa*) is constructed around this textually constructed body–subjectivity (Delmonico 1986). The day is traditionally divided into eight periods, and in each period the practitioner is charged with imagining, according to set textual guidelines, what Rādhā and Kṛṣṇa are doing during those times and, placing herself in her 'flowering bud' identity into the activity with them, helping them do it. It seems clear from the contents of the notebook, that Śrīmantarāma practiced this kind of contemplation at some point in his religious career. He not only had copies of the texts that describe this practice, but also had a list of the 'flowering bud' identities of all the members of his *guru*-lineage. Such a list is called a *siddha-praṇālī*, or 'list of the accomplished' (read 'flowering bud') identities of one's preceptors.

One can gain some idea of how the orthodox tradition thought of the 'flowering bud' identity in relationship to the honoured deities, Rādhā and Kṛṣṇa, from some interesting passages found in arguably the most important of the visualisation-texts of the Caitanya tradition, the *Govinda-līlāmṛta* (*Immortal Sports of Govinda*) by Kṛṣṇadāsa Kavirāja (1518–1612 CE). The *Govinda-līlāmṛta* is a major, full-length poem (*mahākāvya*), containing 23 chapters and about 2,500 stanzas. In this text, Kṛṣṇadāsa Kavirāja describes in great detail the activities of Kṛṣṇa and Rādhā over

24 hours, divided into the eight significant periods of the day. It is the narrative upon which many practitioners meditate and into which they insert themselves in their 'flowering bud' identities as observer–participants in those activities. Early in the tenth chapter of the text, which is in the long mid-day period of the eight periods, Kṛṣṇadāsa Kavirāja expresses what must have then been the accepted view on how the 'flowering bud' identities are connected with Rādhā and Kṛṣṇa:

Seeing, in the forest bower,
Rādhā's friends so profoundly pleased,
In fact, overwhelmed by shudders and all,
Their faces blossoming with joy,
Because of their (Rādhā and Kṛṣṇa's) intense embrace
Vṛndā said to Nāndīmukhī,
'Amazing! Hari embraces Rādhā
And her friends though not connected with that
Became thoroughly filled with joy.

When he is not seen, they want to see him;
When he is not touched, they want to touch him;
When he is touched, they pretend to be envious.
Thus their actions are amazing'.

Nāndīmukhī replied to her,
The controller of the forest,
'The lovely ladies of Vraja
Are way beyond this world,
Their minds and their bodies are for
The happiness of Kṛṣṇa, nothing more.
Their acts are not so amazing, therefore'.

The friends of Rādhikā — who is
The pleasure-bestowing power
Of the Moon of Vraja's Lilies
And the vine of the divine love
That is the central core of that power —
Are like her buds, leaves, and flowers,
Are in truth all equal to her.
When she is thrilled and enlivened
By being sprinkled by the juice
Of the ambrosia of Kṛṣṇa's sports,
Their joy is born a hundred times greater
Than their own sprinkling. This is no surprise (*Govinda-līlāmṛta* 10.12–16).[19]

Here, the floral metaphor is quite clear. The 'flowering bud' identity is one of the five types of friends of Rādhā. Thus, they are intimately connected with her. Rādhā is compared with a vine. The vine of divine love, *prema*, and the friends or *sakhi*s of Rādhā are like the vine's buds, leaves and flowers. Whatever happens to Rādhā, the vine, also happens to the friends, the buds, leaves and flowers, of the vine. This metaphor reveals the close relationship between the 'flowering bud' identity and Rādhā. This relationship is primarily a relationship of unity, but unity with a difference or distinction. It is a relationship of difference in identity. The 'flowering bud' identities are regarded in some respects as different expressions of the love Rādhā feels for Kṛṣṇa.

However, there is no mention of the 'flowering bud' (*mañjarī*) identity in either of the Sahajiyā texts discussed here. This is perhaps added evidence that these texts are quite early. The 'flowering bud' identity and its attendant visualisation practices develop only in the second or, perhaps, third generation of the followers of Caitanya. The 'flowering bud' identity is mentioned in the *Amṛtaratnāvalī* (*The Necklace of Immortality*), one of the texts attributed to Mukundadāsa Gosvāmī, a third-generation follower of Caitanya and disciple of Kṛṣṇadāsa Kavirāja. The text has been translated by Glen A. Hayes (2000). It is said there:

> 38. The Female Partner who is imbued with Divine Love is the vessel of shimmering Divine Essence.
> The Inner Body was born in that ocean of Divine Essence.
>
> 39. In the Vraja heaven, the adept acquires an eternal Inner Body.
> That is why it is called the blessed [*mañjarī*] Inner Damsel Body.
>
> 40. Through Divine Essence, the Inner Body is born, becoming a vessel of Divine Love.
> And through that Inner Body one becomes conscious of the true nature of passion (ibid.: 320).

Hayes' translation for *mañjarī* is 'Inner Damsel Body'. Thus, it appears that in the Sahajiyā Vaiṣṇava traditions, the 'flowering bud' body or *mañjarī-svarūpa* is created through the sexual practices performed with a partner of the opposite sex. Though most of the texts are written from the male perspective, women practitioners also acquire 'flowering bud' identities in the same way.

In the texts under consideration here, what one gains through the sexual practice is somewhat differently characterised. In the text attributed to Sanātana, one gains 'both conditions' or 'the condition of both' (*duhābhāva*), which presumably means the combined dispositions of both genders. The male 'completes' the female and vice versa. They recover in themselves a primordial, trans-gendered unity by uniting with each other. Sanātana says:

> Putting penis in vagina
> You should remain joined together.
> The two will attain the both-ness in the two (Song 1, verse 7).[20]

The other text by Taraṇīramaṇa says much the same thing in several places, occasionally in almost the very same words:

> The image of the knower of *rasa*,
> The form of sexual love,
> That is the innate man.
>
> The erotic love of copulation,
> Feeling like a knower of *rasa*,
> If one practices it one becomes it.
>
> The two in the feeling of both,
> . . .
>
> The *rasa* of joined dispositions.
>
> The two in the *rasa* of both,
> Possessed by erotic love,
> The two controlled by both.
>
> The one who will be it
> Is the one who will gain it.
> This is the way of innate man.
>
> A passionate mind
> Contemplating passion
> Always . . . love (241–45).[21]

In other places, Taraṇiramaṇa is more explicit:

> Now I narrate the truths about *mānuṣa-sādhanā* [the human-like practice]. By tasting it, the aches of the heart go away. By placing your own

disposition (*svabhāva*, here, penis)[22] in her place. Take her own disposition (*svabhāva*, here, vagina) carefully. Ceasing sexual intercourse **30(B)** lie on the left; accepting her to be yourself, be of pure mind. Thinking her to be the hero (the *nāyaka* or male partner), the king of *rasa*, put yourself in her place, and become the beautiful one [i.e., the woman] (107–10).[23]

Other goals of such sexual practice are also recognised by Taraṇiramaṇa in his work. One quite in line with the influence of *rasa*-alchemy, is the 'cooking' or ripening of the body, by which he means it becomes less corruptible, more long-living and, eventually, even immortal:

Listen attentively to the practice of sexual love. Advance with one's own wife (*svakīyā*); stir the *rasa* around. First, for six seasons,[24] in the passion of *svakīyā*, making the mind unmoving, with *yantra* (here: penis) in *yantra* (here: vagina). Remembering the guru, perform the recitation of the names. Retain it in the heart, remain in the heart, make the mind still. Silently the immature body will become ripe. Another six seasons (*ṛtu*) perform the recitation of the guru-*mantra*. Forgetting yourself, let the guru take over the body, [and] the sexuality of the living being (*jīva*) will go away at this. Listen, O greatly lucky one! Again for six seasons **31(B)** recite the primary incantation (*mūla-mantra*).[25] Kṛṣṇa will be your guru. You will attain that body, by rendering still the movement of the genitals (Taraṇiramaṇa 121–25).[26]

Another is the raining down of bliss through the body, as the following passage proclaims:

The unbroken sweet *rasa* is called white sugar (*miśri*). Golden hued, it rains down ceaselessly. That eternal *rasa*, the origin of all, sports in eternity. Secretly it rains down on the limbs of both. That *rasa* is named the great non-material (*mahā-aprākṛta*). It sports and rains down constantly, ceaselessly. **29(A)**. In both bodies ceaseless is that shining transformation.[27] The organs of both overflow with that hundred times purified essence. (80) That is the equivalent of the rapturous divine love (*rasa-prema*) of Rādhā and Kṛṣṇa; the eternal is never eternally destroyed, but is constantly manifest. If the *rasa* becomes sweet there is no disease or death. Rādhā and Kṛṣṇa sport constantly in the body. Defeating death one goes to the abode of the eternal. His residence is always near the eternal. If the *rasa* of sweet erotic love is born in the body, at that time the eternal substance, Rādhā and Kṛṣṇa, is also gained. Becoming established (*vartamāna*)[28] in the *rasa* of sweet erotic love, he does not fear even great cataclysms (Taraṇiramaṇa 76–85).[29]

We can see here most clearly the distinction between the orthodox and Sahajiyā Vaiṣṇavism: while sharing the same or similar goals, the divinisation of the body and its emotions, they appeal to different ways of achieving it. The orthodox tradition relies primarily on the power of mind and imagination, and various forms of meditation or visualisation to transform the human bodily identity into a divine bodily identity that is deemed suitable for intimate service to the practitioners' chosen and beloved deities. Sahajiyā Vaiṣṇavism uses the body to bring about that transformation. In both communities, the effort is to overcome lust or *kāma* and transform it into *prema* or love. Both communities share approximately the same understanding of the difference between lust and love. Lust is selfish and concerned only with one's own pleasure or enjoyment. Love is altruistic and concerned primarily with the pleasure and well-being of the one loved. Thus, the process of transforming the one into the other is a process of sacrifice or self-denial. One has to reprogramme oneself in order to respond to stimuli in different ways. Reprogramming either takes place on the imaginative plane of the visualisation practice in the orthodox tradition, or it takes place in the sexual practice of the Sahajiyā, in which arousal is maintained for long periods — the heat of passion being the heat that ripens or 'cooks' the body — but without consummation. The shorter text by Sanātana, however, presents an interesting perspective on this:

> If semen is spilled in erotic play,
> How can one hear of that and yet
> Call it erotic love?
>
> If erotic play is not truncated (*khaṇḍa*),
> They call it full, godly passion (*īśvara-rati*).
>
> (Yet even if) semen is spilled,
> The *rasa* will not be broken.
> The erotic love of *rasa*
> Is itself controlled by *rasa*.
> A well's water is not lost by sprinkling.
> *Rasa* is the same; mark this, Steadfast One (Song 1, verses 2–5).[30]

From this passage, we can see that the goal is for the man not to allow himself to attain orgasm. If that happens and he spills his seed, it is not considered to be true erotic love (*śṛṅgāra*). However, the text tells us that if one does spill one's seed, it is not the end of the world. Here, *rasa*, perhaps meaning 'mood' or 'intention', remains whole. The example is rather charming: a little sprinkling does not dry out the well. In other words, do not be discouraged; continue with the practice trying to control your reactions. What exactly is meant by 'the erotic love of *rasa* is itself controlled by *rasa*' (*rasera śṛṅgāra rasete baśa*) is not clear here. We take it to mean that occasional physiological mishaps do not seriously affect one's overall progress towards transmuting one's baser affections into *rasa*.

There is a third possibility for the cultivation of the 'flowering bud' identity. Both systems might be used together, as appears to have been the case with Śrīmantarāma. Both systems are represented in his notebook and we suspect he practiced both.

As the Caitanya tradition developed and became more settled and established, the idea of the 'flowering bud' identity became more developed and clearly conceived. The second- and third-generation followers of the tradition determined that the 'flowering bud' identity was to have 11 aspects or components. According to Gopālaguru Gosvāmin (16th–17th century CE) in *Gaura-govindārcana-smaraṇa-paddhati* (311–12), the earliest authority on the subject available to us, the 11 details about the 'flowering bud' are: (*a*) name (*nāma*), (*b*) form (*rūpa*), (*c*) age (*vayas*), (*d*) colour of dress (*veśa*), (*e*) relationship (*sambandha*), (*f*) group (*yūtha*), (*g*) order (*ājñā*), (*h*) service (*sevā*), (*i*) highest aspiration (*parākāṣṭhā*), (*j*) dependent female servant (*pālya-dāsī*), and (*k*) residence (*nivāsa*). They are explained in the *Gaura-govindārcana-smaraṇa-paddhati* (312–23) in the following manner:

(*a*) 'Name' refers to a 'flowering bud' in terms of *rūpa-mañjarī* (beautiful flowering bud), *lavaṅga-mañjarī* (clove flowering bud), etc. This is always, of course, a feminine name and ends with the word *mañjarī* or 'flowering bud'. This is a secret name, since the disciple having received this name is not to reveal it to others unless, at some future time, he himself takes disciples. During the visualisation practice, the practitioner is to think of himself under that name.

(*b*) 'Form', of course, is the body of a young cowherd girl which the practitioner must envision as his own and which is beautiful enough to 'mystify the three worlds and arouse the desire of Kṛṣṇa'.

(*c*) 'Age' is usually 13 years and some months. This places the 'flowering bud' just past puberty in the age called *kaiśora*, i.e., between 10 and 15 years, considered to be the period of the greatest blossoming of sweetness and beauty. Rādhā and her friends are slightly older than the 'flowering buds'.

(*d*) 'Dress' consists of various colours of silk *sārīs* with various ornaments and designs.

(*e*) 'Relationship' is the connection between the objects of service (Rādhā and Kṛṣṇa) and the servant, which arises out of the practitioner's own peculiar mental attitude. This relationship should never be exchanged for another relationship even at the risk of life.

(*f*) 'Group' refers to the various groups of *gopīs* (cowherd women). Every 'flowering bud' belongs to a group of 'flowering buds' who are friends and who stay together. Rādhā and her chief friends are the group leaders of the other cowherd girls. The disciple is placed in one of these groups, usually the same as his *guru* belongs to, and must remain loyal and obedient to the leader of that group who, in turn, is loyal to Rādhā.

(*g*) 'Order' is the order or permission given by the leader of the group (for one's *guru*) to the 'flowering bud' who then performs some special kind of service.

(*h*) 'Service' for Rādhā and Kṛṣṇa means fanning them, giving them betel nut, preparing snacks and sweets, etc.

(*i*) 'The Highest Aspiration' is to achieve perpetual friendship with Rādhā and Kṛṣṇa, as did the model 'flowering bud', *rūpa-mañjarī*, who was believed to be the same as Rūpa Gosvāmī in earthly life.

(*j*) 'Dependent Female Servant' is said to be she who in her heart is an eternal servant, sweet-spoken and completely dependent.

(*k*) 'Residence' is the place in the eternal Vraja in which the 'flowering bud' lives.[31]

Conclusion

The Bengali phrase or formula, *duhe duhābhāva*, seems to encapsulate the highest vision of erotic love, *śṛṅgāra-rasa*, in the two Sahajiyā texts discussed in the essay. We translate this phrase as: 'the two (lovers) feel the feelings or emotional conditions (*bhāva*) of each other'. The phrase suggests an extraordinary level of intimacy in which the partners, in a sense, exchange places or reach a level of sensitivity in which each feels the feelings of the other as his/her own. It also suggests an experience of completeness or wholeness in which the two 'halves' of the human person (*puruṣa*), which were split asunder in the primordial moment of distinctive creation and individuation, as imagined in a passage of one of the oldest Upaniṣads (*Bṛhadāraṇyaka Upaniṣad* 1.4.5), are finally re-united into the wholeness of their being. This is the core of the religious identity that we call the 'flowering bud' identity. The term, however, that our texts use for this condition of fullness is *mānuṣa*, 'becoming fully human'. Gone are the divine aspirations and dependencies of the earlier periods of Indian religious history. Everything one needs to gain — wholeness, liberation and immortality — is there with us already in the human body. In fact, it has always been with us; it was born with us (*sahaja*).

Gaining the state of *mānuṣa* is not a given for human beings. One must strive for it and have a good guidance. One has to reprogramme oneself, and learn to think and act differently, especially with respect to the most powerful of human drives, sexuality. Thus, the body becomes a kind of alchemical laboratory, in which the heat generated by human passion is used to 'cook' the human body, make it harder and more indestructible, and reduce its fluids to their shining essences, no longer useful for procreation, but essential now for gaining longevity and eventual immortality. *Rasa* is now no longer just the aesthetic experience; it becomes the elixir of immortality, instantiated in the physical substances of semen and menstrual blood, the powerful bearers of life. One must learn to control those and not let them slip away or be wasted. The result of that would be death.

Finally, there are unmistakable and shocking inversions of the texts. The texts turn everything upside down and downside up. Men strive to become women; and women, men. Low-caste women become *gurus* of the whole world. The physical world outweighs and outshines the spiritual world. The caste system is turned upside down, the low becoming high and the high, low. Gods are regarded as less than fully human. Paramours become the basis of erotic love instead of one's duly wedded husband or wife. Substances considered polluting and unclean become not only pure, but also the means of salvation and ultimate blessedness. It is a brave new world that rises out of the rubble of the tired, powerless, old world, a world in which erotic love envisioned as the opposite of a selfish act of self-gratification is the centerpiece.

Notes

*The transliterations from the University of Colcutta manuscript that follow attempt to present as authentically as possible the peculiar and even idiosyncratic spelling choices of the original. We are after all dealing with a Practitioner's very personal note-book. These texts were given to us for translation by the late Professor Edward C. Dimock, Jr at the University of Chicago. Our major influence in these studies remains his *The Place of the Hidden Moon: Erotic Mysticism in the Vaiṣṇava Sahajiyā Cult of Bengal* (1966).

1. We are not sure of the source of this etymological explanation of *śṛṅgāra. Śṛṅgāra* is clearly derived from the word *śṛṅga* which means 'horn, tusk, peak, pinnacle', and may be related to *śiras* or 'head'.
2. Bhaṭṭa Nṛsiṃha's commentary on Bhoja's *Sarasvatī-kaṇṭhābharaṇa* 5.1–3 (Raghavan 1978: 399).
3. Vaiṣṇavism, or the worship of Viṣṇu, the enterer or pervader, is one of the most ancient religious traditions in India. Viṣṇu, though sparingly praised in the Vedas, appears to represent, even at that early stage in the development of Indic religion, the 'totality' (Kuiper 1962: 137–51).
4. For instance, the Śrī Vaiṣṇava and the Mādhva traditions represent older forms of Vaiṣṇavism.
5. Namely, the *Harivaṃśa* (*c.* 2nd century CE) and the *Viṣṇu Purāṇa* (*c.* 4th century CE), which only briefly mention the 'circle-dance' or *rāsa-līlā.*
6. This particular verse is attributed to poet Poṭṭisa):

   muhamāruenạ taṃ kaṇha goraaṃ rāhiāeṃ avaṇento |
   etāṇaṃ ballavīṇaṃ aṇṇāṇa vi goraaṃ harasi || *poṭṭisassa* |
   [Sk.: *mukhamārutena tvaṃ kṛṣṇa gorajaḥ rādhikāyāḥ apanayat* |
   etāsāṃ ballavīnāṃ anyāsāmapi gauravaṃ harasi || *poṭṭisasya* |]

   The text is from Basak (1971); the translation is Delmonico's.
7. *anayārādhito nūnaṃ bhagavān harirīśvaraḥ* |
   yanno vihāya govindaḥ prīto yāmanayadrahaḥ ||
8. The term *sahajiyā* comes from the Sanskrit word *sahaja* which means 'born with' or 'natural'. It has also come to mean 'easy' in many of the vernacular languages. Here, it means that the tools needed for attaining enlightenment or liberation or divine love (*preman*) are already naturally in one's possession: in one's body and its desires. By using one's body and harnessing or directing one's desires one can, therefore, easily gain the ultimate goal. In this sense, liberation is one's natural state, already within you. There are a number of groups that fit into this collective, many of which developed distinctive identities around the time the British gained control of India from its Mughal rulers in 1757. Some of the names of such groups are Āul, Fakir, Sāin, Sahebdhani, Kartābhajā, etc. In this collective, we would also include the famous Bāuls of Bengal who have become known around the world because of their distinctive style of singing and riddle

competitions in song. Purno Das Baul, who has travelled throughout the West, for instance, belongs to this loose-knit group.

9. Other possible sources for tantric influences found in the Caitanya tradition are the *Gopālatāpanīya Upaniṣad* (which, though identified as an Upaniṣad, is really a Tantra explicating the Gopāla-*mantra*), the *Brahma Saṃhitā* (only Chapter 5, which was supposedly discovered by Caitanya himself and copied during his pilgrimage to south India), the *Sanatkumāra Saṃhitā*, the *Gautamīya Tantra*, etc.
10. *evaṃ śaśāṅkāṃśuvirājitā niśāḥ*
sa satyakāmo 'nuratābalāgaṇaḥ |
siṣeva ātmanyavaruddhasaurataḥ
sarvāḥ śaratkāvyakathārasāśrayāḥ ||
11. *Saurata* means that which is produced from *surata* or sexual intercourse. In males, this would be their semen. To take it as amorous feelings or emotions, as some of the commentators do, is a bit far-fetched, and one has to ask why one would want to withhold those inside oneself. I think it pretty clearly means semen here.
12. Śuka or Śukadeva was the son of Vyāsa, the mythic author of the *Bhāgavata Purāṇa*. Śuka is the primary reciter of the *Purāṇa*, though his recitation begins only in *Skandha* 3 and ends with Chapter 5 of *Skandha* 12.
13. *vikrīḍitaṃ vrajavadhūbhiridaṃ ca viṣṇoḥ*
śraddhānvito 'nuśṛṇuyādatha varṇayedyaḥ |
bhaktiṃ parāṃ bhagavati pratilabhya kāmaṃ
hṛdrogamāśvapahinotyacireṇa dhīraḥ ||
14. David Gordon White (2003: 4, 11, 184–88) gives a more complete history of the use and meanings of the word *rasa*. He (ibid.: 356n14) points to several passages from the *Atharvaveda* wherein *rasa*, he says, is connected with water and the healing arts, but these connections on inspection seem quite tenuous. *Rasa* only occurs there as the juice of plants. The waters and semen are not clearly connected with *rasa* in those texts.
15. The connoisseur is referred to in Sanskrit as the *sahṛdaya*, the one who 'shares heart'.
16. The great *rasa* theorist, Abhinavagupta, in his commentary on the *rasa-sūtra* cites the view of one of his predecessors, Bhaṭṭa Nāyaka, who regarded *rasa* as like the tasting of the supreme Brahman (*brahmāsvāda-savidha*). Abhinavagupta agrees with him on this point. Both, however, recognise that tasting *rasa* (*rasāsvāda*) and tasting the supreme Brahman are different in that the former is temporary and fleeting, while the latter is permanent and deeply transformative. See R. Gnoli's translation and discussion of Abhinavagupta's commentary on the *rasa-sūtra* of the *Nāṭyaśāstra* (1985: 48).
17. We are grateful to the late Professor Edward C. Dimock, University of Chicago, for kindly making this film available to us.

18. *Pātāla-khaṇḍa* 83.7–11, and *Sanatkumāra Saṃhitā* 36.184–88. The latter version, for instance, is as follows:

ātmānaṃ cintayettatra tāsāṃ madhye manoramām |
rūpayauvanasampannāṃ kiśorīṃ pramadākṛtiṃ || 184 ||
nānāśilpakalābhijñāṃ kṛṣṇabhogānurūpiṇīm |
prārthitāmapi kṛṣṇena tato bhogaparāṅmukhīm || 185 ||
rādhikānucarīṃ nityaṃ tatsevanaparāyaṇām|
kṛṣṇādapyadhikaṃ prema rādhikāyāṃ prakurvatīm || 186 ||
prītyānudivasaṃ yatnāttayoḥ saṅgamakāriṇīm |
tatsevanasukhāsvādabhareṇātisunirvṛtām || 187 ||
ityātmānaṃ vicintyaiva tatra sevāṃ samācaret |
brāhmamuhūrtamārabhya yāvatsāntā mahāniśā || 188 ||

19. *tayordṛḍhāliṅganataḥ sutṛptāḥ*
kampādisampannicitāḥ samīkṣya |
sakhīrmudotphullamukhīrnikuñje
nāndīmukhīṃ sā vadati sma vṛndā ||

āścaryaṃ hariṇā rādhā gāḍhāliṅgitā ciram |
tadasaṅgatiyuktāpi nirvṛtāsīt sakhītatiḥ ||

adṛṣṭe darśanotkaṇṭhā dṛṣṭe'smin sparśalālasā |
sparśe'sya serṣyavāmyaṃ taccitramāsāṃ viceṣṭitam ||

nāndīmukhī tāmavadat vaneśvarīṃ
lokottarāṇāṃ vrajasubhruvāṃ sadā |
kṛṣṇaikasaukhyārthaśarīracetasāṃ
tattanna citraṃ kila ceṣṭitaṃ yataḥ ||

sakhyaḥ śrīrādhikāyā vrajakumudavidhorhlādinīnāmaśakteḥ
sārāṃśapremavallyāḥ kiśalayadalapuṣpāditulyāḥ svatulyāḥ |
siktāyāṃ kṛṣṇalīlāmṛtarasanicayairullasantyāmamuṣyāṃ
jātollāsāḥ svasekācchataguṇamadhikaṃ santi yattanna citram ||

20. *liṅge liṅga die joḍita rabe |*
duhe duhābhāba duhete labe ||

21. *rasika mūrati, śṛṅgāra ākṛti,*
sahaja mānuṣa se |
ramaṇaśṛṅgāra, rasika bhāvana,
haile haiba se ||
duhe duhā bhāva, . . .,
sabhāva saṅgati rasa |
duhu duhā rase, śṛṅgāra āveśe,
duhe duhākāra vaśa ||
je jana haibe, se jana pāibe,

sahaja mānuṣa rita |
anurāga mana, rāgera bhāvana,
sadā [e hānilava] prita ||
The ellipses represent places where the manuscript is damaged.

22. The double meaning, disposition and genital, becomes particularly thick in this section.
23. That is, knowing her to be yourself, become the beautiful woman.
ibe kahi mānuṣa sādhana tatta kathā |
tāhāra āśvāde jāẏa hṛdaera vethā ||
āpanāra svabhāva svapibe tāra sthāne |
tāhāra svabhāva nibe karie yatane ||
śṛṅgāra chāḍīẏe tāra **30(B)** *suti rabe bāme* |
tāhāke āpāna māni rabe śuddha mane ||
tāhāre nāeka rasarāja mane kari |
tāhāre āpana sthāne haibe sundarī ||
24. The word for season, *ṛtu*, can also mean one menstrual period, i.e., a month. In this section, the word usually translates as 'seasons'.
25. This is the Gopāla-*mantra* for both orthodox and Sahajiyā traditions: *klīṃ kṛṣṇāya govindāya gopījanavallabhāya svāhā*. This paired with the Kāma-*gāyatrī* (*klīṃ kāmadevāya vidmahe, puṣpabāṇāya dhīmahi, tanno'naṅgaḥ pracodayāt*) are the two main *mantra*s of the Caitanya tradition.
26. *śṛṅgāra sādhana, tāhāra karaṇa,*
śunaha karie mana |
sakiẏāra saha, bāḍāie neha,
kara rasa āvartana || (1)
sakiāra rāge, saḍa ṛtu āge,
susthira karie mana |
jantre jantra puri, guruke smaṅari,
kara nāmera jāpana ||
hṛdae rākhibe, hṛdae thākibe,
sthiratā karie mati |
gumari gumari, pakkatā haibe,
apakka e deharati ||
saḍa ṛtu puna, karibe sādhana,
guru-mantra jāpanete/
āpanā tulibe, gurudeha nibe,
jīva-rati jābe tāthe ||
śuna mahābhāga, puna saḍa rāga,
31(B) *jāpana je mūla-mantra*/
guru kṛṣṇa habe, se deha pāibe,
sthakita cālana jantra//
27. We read *viśrāma* to be a mistake for *aviśrāma*. However, retaining *viśrāma*, the line could be read: In both bodies that pause is that shining transformation.

28. This word has also a technical sense in the later tradition, meaning 'the perfected body'.

29. *tāra para dugdha joge bhiẏāna karaẏe* |
sitāmiśri nāma tāra nirvighne tā haẏa ||
akhaṇḍa madhura rasa sitāmiśri nāma |
hemavarṇa variśaṇa haẏa avirāma ||
sarvādya se nityarasa nityete ramaẏa |
gopanete duhā aṅge variṣaṇa haẏa ||
sei rasa mahā aprākita tāra nāma |
vihāre variṣe rasa sadā aviśrāma ||
29(A) *duhu dehe viśrāma sei ujjvala vikāra* |
dagamaga duhu aṅga sata śuddha sāra ||
rādhākṛṣṇa rasaprema ekui se haẏa |
nitya nitya dhvaṃśa nāi nitya virājaẏa ||
madhura haile rasa jvarāmṛtyu nāi |
rādhākṛṣṇa viharae dehe sarvathāi ||
mṛtyuke kariẏe jāẏa jāẏa nityasthāna |
nitya sampraẏa tāra haẏa avasthāna ||
madhura śṛṅgāra rasa dehe janamile |
rādhākṛṣṇa nitya vastu prāpti sei kāle ||
madhura śṛṅgāra rase vartamāna haẏa |
mahā mahā pralaẏādi nāhi tāra bhaẏa ||

30. *śṛṅgārate śukra skhalita hole* |
śunite śiṅgāra kemane bale ||
yadi bā śiṅgāre khaṇḍa naẏa |
pūrṇa īśvara rati tāre kaẏa ||
vīrya khaṇḍa nahe khaṇḍībe rasa |
rasera śiṅgāra rasete baśa ||
siñcane nā mare kūpera nira |
temati se rasa śunaha dhīra ||

References

Primary Sources

Bhāgavata Purāṇa:
Śāstrī, J. L. 1988. *Bhāgavata Purāṇa of Kṛṣṇa Dvaipāyana Vyāsa, with Sanskrit Commentary Bhāvārthabodhinī of Śrīdhara Svāmin*. Delhi: Motilal Banarsidass.

Gāthāsaptaśatī or *Gāhāsattasai* of Hāla:
Basak, Radhagovinda (ed. and trans.). 1971. *The Prākrit Gāthāsaptaśatī Compiled by Sātavāhana King Hāla*. Bibliotheca Indica 295. Calcutta: The Asiatic Society.

Govinda-līlāmṛta (*Immortal Sports of Govinda*) of Kṛṣṇadāsa Kavirāja:
Śāstrī, Haridāsa (ed. and trans.). 1977–81. *Govindalīlāmṛtam of Kṛṣṇadāsa Kavirāja with the Commentary of Vṛndāvana Cakravartin*, 3 vols. Vṛndāban: Śrī Gadādhara Gaurahari Press.

Nāṭyaśastra:
Nagar, R. S. (ed.). 1981–84. *Nāṭyaśastra of Bharatamuni with the Commentary Abhinavabhāratī by Abhinavaguptācārya*, 4 vols. Parimal Sanskrit Series 4. Delhi and Ahmedabad: Parimal Publications.
Padma Purāṇa:
Śrīmān Maharṣi Kṛṣṇa Dvaipāyana Vyāsa. 1958. *Padma Purāṇa*, 3: *Pātāla-khaṇḍa*. Gurumandal Series 18. Calcutta: Manasukharaya Mora.
Sanatkumāra Saṃhitā
Śāstrī, Haridāsa (ed.).1990. *Sanatkumāra-saṃhitā*. Kālīdaha, Vṛndāvana: Śrī Gadādhara Gaurahari Press.
Sahajiyā Vaiṣṇava Notebooks:
Sanātana. n.d. Songs 1–3, MS 3437, 16A–16B, University of Calcutta.
Taraṇīramaṇa. n.d. MS 3437, 25A–36B, University of Calcutta.
Roy, Basanta (ed.). 1949 (1355 BE). *Taruṇiramaṇera* [*sic*] *Padāvalī O Sahaja Upāsanā Tattva, Bangīya Sahitya Pariṣad Patrikā*, 4.
Śrībhāgavatam:
Purīdāsa (ed.). 1945. *Śrībhāgavatam*, 3 vols. Mayamansiṃha: Śacīnātharāya Caturdhurīṇa.
Śṛṅgāra Prakāśa of Bhoja:
Raghavan, V. (ed.). 1978. *Bhoja's Śṛṅgāra Prakāśa*. Madras: Punarvasu. 3rd rev. enl. edn.

Upaniṣads:
Svāmī Gambhīrānanda (ed.). 1992. *Upaniṣad-granthāvalī*, 3 vols. Calcutta: Udbodhana Kāryālaya.
Vivarta-vilāsa:
Ākiñcanadāsa. n.d. *Vivarta-vilāsa* (*The Sport of Transformation*). Calcutta: Tarachand Das and Sons.

Secondary Works

Brooks, Douglas Renfrew. 1990. *The Secret of the Three Cities: An Introduction to Hindu Śākta Tantrism*. Chicago: University of Chicago.
Dasgupta, Shashibhusan. 1976. *Obscure Religious Cults*. Calcutta: Firma KLM Private Limited. 3rd edn rpt.
De, Sushil Kumar. 1976. *History of Sanskrit Poetics*. Calcutta: Firma KLM Private Limited.
Delmonico, Neal. 1986. 'Time Enough for Play: Time and Will in Bengal Vaiṣṇavism', in *Gifts of Sacred Wonder*, pp. 107–31. Calcutta: Suvarnarekha.
Delmonico, Neal and Aditi Nath Sarkar. Forthcoming. *Love in the Land of Heroes: Two Sahajiyā Texts from a Mid-nineteenth Century Bengali Notebook*. Kirksville, MO: Blazing Sapphire Press.
Dimock, Edward C. 1966. *The Place of the Hidden Moon: Erotic Mysticism in the Vaiṣṇava Sahajiyā Cult of Bengal*. Chicago: University of Chicago Press.

Flood, Gavin. 2006. *The Tantric Body*. London and New York: I. B. Tauris.
Gnoli, Raniero. 1985. *The Aesthetic Experience According to Abhinavagupta*. Varanasi: Chowkhamba Sanskrit Series Office.
Gosvāmī, Gopālaguru. 1949. *Gaura-govindārcana-smaraṇa-paddhati*, in Haridāsa Dāsa (ed.), *Paddhati-trayam*, pp. 9–107. Gaurabad, Navadvīpa: Haribol Kutir.
Hayes, A. Glen. 2000. 'The Necklace of Immortality: A Seventeenth-Century Vaiṣṇava Sahajiyā Text', in David Gordon White (ed.), *Tantra in Practice*, pp. 308–25. Princeton and Oxford: Princeton University Press.
Kuiper, F. B. J. 1962. 'The Three Strides of Viṣṇu', in Ernest Bender (ed.), *Indological Studies in Honor of W. Norman Brown*, pp. 137–51. New Haven, Conn.: The American Oriental Society.
Mukhopdhyya, Harekṛṣṇa. 1980 [1961]. *Vaiṣṇava Padāvalī* (Bengali). Calcutta: Sahitya Samsada. Rev. edn.
Ray, B. 1966. *Census 1961 — West Bengal District Census Handbook: Birbhum Deputy Superintendent of Census Operations, West Bengal.* Delhi: Manager of Publications.
Urban, Hugh B. 2001. *The Economics of Ecstasy: Tantra, Secrecy and Power in Colonial Bengal.* Oxford: Oxford University Press.
White, David Gordon. 1996. *The Alchemical Body: Siddha Traditions of Medieval India.* Chicago and London: University of Chicago Press.
——. 2003. *Kiss of the Yoginī: "Tantric Sex" in Its South Asian Context*. Chicago and London: The University of Chicago Press.

PART III

Buddhism, Pātañjala Yoga and Śaiva Siddhānta

6

The Buddhist Psychology of Emotions

Varun Kumar Tripathi*

Taking the structural similarity of the way of cognising of either 'emotional' or 'rational' dispositions of mind, a radical division between emotional and rational (that Aristotle once proposed) cannot be postulated. On the same basis, no hierarchy between emotional and rational can be established. This lack of hierarchy should not lead to the construal that all that is emotional can (or should) be sublimated into the rational precisely because the Buddha's teaching in this context thoroughly runs on the principle of replacement (annihilation) of the negative emotions and not on the principle of sublimation. This essay examines how far these premises are philosophically tenable. The intended claim that is to be made on these premises is that the 'emotional' and 'rational' contents or traits of mind may acquire equal cognitive value and may have equal moral efficacy too. The emotional and rational energy or force may be transformed so as to give rise to emotional and rational virtues respectively. A negative emotional trait, force or state of mind (such as 'attachment', 'passion', 'aversion', 'delusion', etc.) can be transformed into or replaced with a positive emotional virtue (such as 'right faith', 'politeness', 'helpfulness', 'empathy', 'moral sense', etc.). Similarly, the so-called rational contents or intellectual traits (such as 'thinking', 'reasoning', 'argument', 'opinion', etc.) can be replaced with rational virtues (such as 'conscience', 'discernment', 'analysis', 'contemplation', 'introspection', etc.). The highest culmination of the former force takes place in the form of *karuṇā* and the latter in the form of *prajñā* (Pāli: *paññā*) in ultimate terms. The aforesaid transformation or replacement presumes dissolution of the negative traits.

The Overview of Emotions in the Buddha's Teachings

Buddhism (as understood through the Buddha's teachings and not through Buddhist philosophies) takes emotions as traits of human psychodynamics that impede spiritual or inner blossoming of a person. Emotions are ordinarily understood by philosophers as something non-rational, something that distorts the reasoning and nourishes prejudices. Even though such reading is right in this context, it cannot provide the complete account of the Buddhist treatment of emotions, nor can it be the final approach for addressing emotions. We rather prefer the approach of recent experimental psychology that takes certain aspects of emotions as both organising (making behaviour effective) and disorganising. Further, there is a prerequisite for understanding the Buddha's treatment of emotions, i.e., any mental disposition or trait cannot be seen in a static sense, but rather they should be seen in a function — in its dynamics, i.e., in terms of its causal genesis and the effects it is likely to produce (its causal efficacy). This is called *citta-santati* (or *santati pravāha* or, *santāna*), the progeny of *citta*. This prerequisite is just a dimension of the insight into the momentary-ness that the Buddha profoundly taught. Additionally, this pre-requisite imparts on us an understanding of the distinction between *citta* (mind) and *caitta* or *caitasika* (mental). They are not different, as the former cannot be grasped without the latter,[1] but their distinctness can very well be discerned.

Emotions are basically states of arousal that take place in relation to our feelings (be it popping up from within or on occasion of coming into contact of the senses with their sense-objects). Emotions are not bare sensations, but they are rather mixed with the primordial predispositions of human psyche,[2] such as 'liking', 'disliking' or 'reluctance'. Emotions function by trends of approach and withdrawal. The approach and withdrawal is also determined by the phenotype factors. Thus, emotions are very complex functions of mind. They are mixed with mental precursors and sensations, and, therefore, understanding them warrants a psychoanalytic approach.

The genesis of emotions can be seen in the broader schema of *paṭccasamuppāda* (the principle of dependent origination), wherein the cause of sensation is described as contact of the senses (+ mind) with their sense-objects or stimuli. The cause of functioning of the senses has its own trajectory into unconscious factors, such as *nāma-rūpa*, *viññāṇa*, *samkhāra*, etc. Once the said contact produces sensations, the emotional faculties get activated. One develops 'passion' or 'repulsion' for certain sensations because of the dominant *āsavas* or predispositions that are prevalent at the moment. Accordingly, the types of sensations are also categorised as *sukhā-vedanā*, *dukkhā-vedanā* and *asukhā-adukkhā-vedanā* — 'pleasurable sensations', 'painful sensations' and 'neutral sensations', respectively. The 'passion' for a particular sensation is called *rāga*, 'repugnance' is called *dveṣa* and 'delusion' (that is a state of not taking cognisance or a sensation) is called *moha*.[3] These are not emotion-episodes but rather the generic categories of feeling or expression of emotions. These are also known as *akuśala-mūla* (root of all emotional disorder and miseries). The naturalistic (unexamined or unaware) behaviour of a person can be interpreted as a function of these emotive dispositions. These are broadly covered by the category of *taṇhā/ tṛṣṇā* (craving) that is a part of the principle of dependent origination.

Behavioural patterns can be interpreted as reactions to stimuli governed by the aforementioned predispositions as per the dominance or orientation. To exemplify: 'greed', 'covetousness', 'temptation', 'possession', 'attachment', 'preference of tidiness and hygiene', 'eroticism', 'narcissism', 'identity', 'desire for self-continuation', etc., are *rāga*-function; 'hatred', 'anger', 'irritation', 'harsh speech-act', 'violence', 'jealousy', 'sadism', 'unfriendliness', 'enmity', etc., are *dveṣa*-function; and ' inertia', 'inactivity', 'reluctance', 'slumber', 'pessimism', 'dullness', 'lack of curiosity', etc., can be interpreted as *moha*-function. The Buddha defines these expressions as *upakleśa* or 'secondary afflictions' (*Majjhima Nikāya* 7).[4] However, behavioural patterns are often quite complex as they result from intertwined predispositions. The behavioural dispositions appear or are expressed not because of a deliberate decision but because of the unconscious modes of the said predispositions which are primitive and deeply rooted proclivities. Our active consciousness does not reach that level; rather, the conscious dispositions are shaped up by those unconscious predispositions. These are referred to as *anusaya/ anuśaya* — those which are latent.[5] The term is taken in the Buddhist tradition as synonymous to pain or suffering. That is why, in the Buddha's realisation of human psychology, the fact of suffering is the fundamental one (the first among the Four Noble Truths: 'There is suffering'). The suffering is that 'I am governed by some latent predispositions of my mind which I do not know', or 'I am a victim of my own predispositions'. The apparent 'choice', 'decision' and 'resolve' are also determined by those latent forces. Cognitively, these choices are mental superstructures imposed upon bare sensations.

In the Buddhist schema of understanding, the inquiry does not stop with the discovery of suffering, but goes ahead to explore the way out of this suffering. In the exploration, each mental disposition is examined in causal terms so that one can really experience one's suffering and find out its cause. That is what the Buddha refers to in the second Noble Truth: 'Suffering has its cause'. The thesis of this noble truth is not as simplistic as it appears to be. Non-realisation of the fact that 'suffering has its cause' leads to the so-called 'pursuit of happiness' and to the moulding of the entire behavioural design towards this pursuit without realising that if suffering has its cause, one has to work on the cause and any attempt other than this to overcome suffering would just be an escape. Happiness cannot be brought about by ignoring the cause of suffering. The pursuit of such happiness (i.e., happiness that can be brought about by ignoring the cause of suffering) is ignorance itself. An examination of emotions in a causal sense leads to revelation of the entire fabrication of ignorance and the entire *santati* that it is likely to yield. Since the nature of Buddhist enquiry is a causal enquiry (psychoanalytic), it does not take any mental state or disposition as 'essential' to human nature; rather, all states are cultivated (*samkhata dhamma*) (*Samyutta Nikāya* 5.47.2). So, no emotional trait is essential to human consciousness. Nature, character, personality trait, etc., do not refer to fixed states.

The *Abhidhammic* Analysis of Emotions

In the Buddha's teachings, the inquiry into human psyche is known as *abhidhamma*. It is a project of knowing and causally sequencing the *dhammas* which is called *dhamma-vicaya*. It is not just the *Abhidhamma Pitaka* (a part of the Pāli canon) which is referred to in this context (Sharma and Seshadri 2000, vol. 1: 526–39) but any inquiry into human psyche that attempts to causally analyse and sequence the mental dispositions, keeping in view that they develop from the principles of mental functioning. As Damien Keown (1992: 58) rightly puts it:

> The goal of the *Abhidharma* is to pick away at the subtle threads of the world of *prajñapti* and to uncover the world of real existence of *dharmas* which lies beneath. In this way it is hoped to come face-to-face with reality 'as it really is' (*yathā-bhūta*). It should be pointed out that although these *dharmas* are real they are not in any sense permanent: if they were there could be no scope for change or personal development.[6]

Moreover, there is no way of understanding the emotive functions of human consciousness and of removing the emotional dysfunctions apart from the analysis of *dharmas* — the dispositions which are cognitive atoms that one can experience or know.

The question before a project of analysis of emotions is whether we can cognise the emotive *dharmas* without mixing the emotions in those *dharmas*. Emotion in a narrow sense is a subjective element that one applies to sensations in order to give sensations a meaning. The pure perception, as the Buddhist philosopher Dignāga presents it, is always bereft of intellectual or subjective elements.[7] With such a perception when an emotional state is examined, its causal psychogenesis is revealed. When examined thus, honestly and carefully, we find two different tracks of genesis of emotions, authentic and inauthentic. They can be categorised as:[8]

(*a*) Emotions as pushed forth by *āsavas* as reaction towards unexamined feelings, leading to formation of five types of defilements of consciousness (*pañca-nīvaraṇa*).
(*b*) Emotion as sensitivity towards the suffering of fellow beings that arises only when defilements of one's consciousness are stripped off (*anācchādita citta*).

The two tracks themselves came forth through different tracks. The former, in a naturalistic way of living, engenders and strengthens the defilements of consciousness on account of their causal efficacy. To elaborate: mental dispositions are not static; they are in function, i.e., if they are (or felt) they will give rise to other mental dispositions. What the Buddha discovered is that the naturalistic emotional way of being gives rise to five types of defilements (which are barriers for further understanding): *kāmaccanda* (eros), *vyāpāda* (thanatos), *uddhacca-kukkucca* (restiveness), *thīnimiddha* (inertia) and *vicikicchā* (distrust about virtues) (*Majjhima Nikāya* 10). They can be taken as emotional terminals, wherein all emotions of this type terminate. The Pāli canon wonderfully presents the Buddha's analysis of the development of emotional traits.[9] One receives a variety of sense-data from the environment (especially in terms of one's companionship and interactions therein) which undergo mental processing (*manasikāra*) that results in the formation of concepts, beliefs, opinions, prejudices, complexes, etc., which, in turn, push reactions. These are essentially mental preoccupations. Being preoccupations of mind, they function as factors for concealing awareness about one's own mental functions.[10] These preoccupations act as walls wherefrom any new sensation returns; this is called reaction. The reactions may be just mental, or they can assume the form of speech-act or motor effect, depending on which *saṃkhāra* (predisposition or sedimentation) is at work — *mano-saṃkhāra, vacī-saṃkhāra* or *kāya-saṃkhāra* (predispositions of mind, speech or body). The results of these reactions are experienced as miseries.

The second type of sensitivity is a new quotient that arises only after the removal of defilements and on regaining awareness about one's functions of mind. The removal cannot take place by applying any measure against those defilements; rather, it happens by inculcating suitable virtues. This takes place in a right environment, which, for Buddhism, is the companionship of enlightened people.[11] The difference between these two types of emotions is that the former arises as the opposite of 'reason' and the latter is just a part of awareness or intelligence. In the latter case, in fact, the difference between reason and emotion is dissolved. Both faculties merge into a kind of higher state of 'sensitive intelligence'. This is the state where *prajñā* and *karuṇā* sway in resonance, as will be explained later in the essay. Precisely, an appropriate emotional trait (which is a response and not a reaction) must be in consonance with the right understanding (*sammā-diṭṭhi*).

Another important aspect of the Buddhist analysis of emotions is that it presents a framework of primordial illusions of four types that serve as grounds for the function of emotional predispositions (*Samyutta Nikāya* 3.24). If the earlier analysis presents the psychological dimension of the genesis of emotions, the analysis of primordial illusions presents the said genesis from a cognitive point of view. These illusions are of the nature of naturalistic ignorance in which one lives, betokening an unexamined life. These are unconscious presuppositions about everything that have their source in the utter reliance on sensory knowledge. These illusions are: (*a*) taking 'impermanent as permanent'; (*b*) taking 'impure as pure'; (*c*) taking 'suffering as pleasure'; and (*d*) taking 'non-self as self' (with regard to five aggregates: forms or body, sensations, names or language, sedimentations or impressions, and cognitive or conscious episodes). Assuming these unconsciously, one's 'attachment', 'desire', 'repugnance', 'hatred', 'craving', 'delusion', etc., get functional. 'Awareness' is precisely the opposite of the above, i.e., taking 'impermanent as impermanent' and so on. Once mind is aware of the true nature of sensations, and so on, there arise 'non-attachment', 'non-repugnance', 'non-delusion', 'tolerance', 'patience', 'forgiveness', 'fraternity', 'mental peace' and 'freedom', 'empathy', and, ultimately, 'compassion'. In a sense, the aforesaid illusions and emotional predispositions (*āsavas*) support each other. If one asks why we carry these illusions, the answer is that we have an unconscious craving for deriving pleasure from sensations, and so on; that is why we continue to take the impermanent as permanent and so on.

Now, it is obvious that what is called *āsava* (emotional predisposition) from an emotional point of view is called *avijjā* (ignorance or intellectual disorder) from a cognitive point of view. In fact, these two can be distinguished but not separated. So, if at the level of emotional and intellectual dysfunction the emotional and intellectual dispositions can be seen in a relation, then once they are dissolved, the sprouting of a new consciousness in the form of compassion (*karuṇā*) and intelligence (*paññā*) can also be seen in relation to one another, i.e., as two dimensions of a holistic understanding that an enlightened person discovers.

The Big Question: Sublimation or Dissolution

What is understood as emancipation, salvation or annihilation of *āsavas* in Buddhism is not, in any sense, sublimation of the negative traits (emotional or rational). Given the first logic of *santāna* — the psychological progeny — a negative trait (*āsava*) can engender miseries only. Rather, considering the dominant trait or predisposition in a person, he or she is recommended to practice suitable virtues. For example, a *rāga-carita* person (whose passions are dominant) can begin with the practice of virtues, such as service (*sevana*), right faith (*saddhiyam*), etc; a *dveṣa-carita* person (whose repugnance is dominant) can begin with analysing the *dhammas* and apply reasoning to identify the *kleśas* (ailments of mind, equal to *nīvaraṇa*), and so on. So, the dominant negative trait of a person is pragmatically utilised to develop suitable counter-virtues and to make one develop awareness about his or her traits in order to be free from that negative trait.[12] These prescriptions are used as medicines; once the ailment is cured, there is no need for medicine. When a negative emotional trait is replaced with a positive one, the replaced trait becomes *functionally* non-existent, i.e., it is *dissolved* in true sense of the term. Buddhism prescribes a variety of techniques to make one free from a negative trait (*akuśala dhamma*), but they all work on the principle of replacement and not through sublimation. Fighting with the *akuśala* is no way to do away with them, but inculcating a suitable counter-virtue (*kuśala*) is.

Given the importance of the second logic of *āhāra*, a trait or predisposition exists in mind because it gets suitable nourishment; the way out of any psychological disorder or miserable 'function' (Maha Thera 1956: 185–87) is to stop the nourishment (through conducive thought, will or activity) of those functions. This is possible by nourishing the counter-virtues. A trait survives in the mind because it is maintained by suitable and repeated thinking, willing, craving, speech, and activities. The Buddha explains in an elaborated manner the persistence of all the categories of *paṭiccasamuppāda* and their nourishment (*Majjhima Nikāya* 9). A deep insight into human psychic function is that there is no treatment or psychotherapy possible for a mental ailment or disorder other than the removal of the nourishment, a measure that one consciously or unconsciously chooses to take. An *āhāra* is a psychological support system and needs to be understood carefully so as to realise an emotive function. So, if we want a cure for an emotional disorder, such as anger, we must examine our expectations (or hatred) associated with the stimuli of anger. Similarly, moral virtues are not naturally present in human psyche; they spring forth because of additional sensitivity, or else they are inculcated through suitable nourishment which is required until the mind becomes completely free from defilements.

The third is the logic of *saṃkhāra*, i.e., impression, sedimentation or cultivation. Any trait, negative or positive, is a cultivated one (Sharma and Seshadri 2000, vol. 1: 499). Nothing can be taken as a drive or instinct inbuilt in the human psyche (*citta*). They are cultivated in certain circumstances and can be de-cultivated or deconstructed by alteration of the circumstances or environment. Whatever sense-data one receives or activities one performs (at all the three levels: mental, verbal and bodily) they leave certain impressions (*saṃkhāra*) which keep on accumulating (as sediments) unless one stops and erases them with illuminating awareness. It is these accumulations that form the so-called *unconscious*. That is why the Buddha calls all the *dhammas saṃkhata-dhammas* (cultivated); the *nibbāna* (which is shunning of all the *āsavas*) alone is *asaṃkhata-dhamma* (non-cultivated). Given the aforementioned threefold logic, only the dissolution principle is commensurate with the scheme of the Buddha's interpretation of emotions.

Emotional and Rational: The Case of the *Viśuddhimaggo*

There have been approaches of reading Buddhist psychology that depict human psyche as a battleground of reason and emotion.[13] These approaches are not correct in the context of Buddhism. There is a tension between reason and emotion because we often do not have emotions for reasonable things or intellectual support for right emotions (that are required for well-being and co-existence). Not all emotions are bad. Modern psychologists also recognise afflictive and non-afflictive emotional states and traits (Ekman et al. 2005: 59). There is no such tussle unless there is a division of mind. It is mistakenly believed that the Buddhists aim at a vacuity and there is no involvement of emotions in human good. In fact the Buddhists do acknowledge that emotion or feeling is an important aspect of the human good or human reality. As Keown (1992: 225) notes:

> Human good cannot be complete if it is only participated in by the intellect; to be fully realized it must be seen as good and *felt* as good, and this involves an appropriate emotional response. Aristotle's doctrine of the means is essentially an attempt to establish where an appropriate emotional response lies.

The principle that works behind it is that a human good is not participated in its fullness unless it is intensely experienced as good in the integrity of one's consciousness. This is certainly a project of identification of proper relation between reason and feeling.

In this connection, one may refer to the *Viśuddhimaggo*, a text by Buddhaghoṣa[14] (4th–5th century CE), that schematises all the issues and practices of the Buddha's teaching. The text describes six dominant predispositions[15] which may be consistently found in a person or may even work variedly from time to time. Buddhaghoṣa also acknowledges the somatic conditions that shape the predispositions. He discusses the verity of behavioural expressions and associated emotions based upon the dominant trait and how the expressions and emotions can be changed, re-directed or transformed by transforming the traits through practice of certain virtues. There is no common or fixed prescription for a particular individual and for all the time. Yet, the principle of their working can be laid down on a universal scale as the Buddha did in his exposition of *paṭiccasamuppāda*. Thus, the text clarifies an essential aspect of the Buddhist insight into emotions. Based upon this brief description of the *Viśuddhimaggo* approach, we intend to establish that cognition and emotions are intertwined. They are different points in one common scale and not two radically different faculties. The exposition also precludes the approach of 'faculty psychology'. There is no hierarchy between emotional and rational traits. Once the 'emotional' is transformed into or replaced with compassion (*karuṇā*), that is the ultimate blossoming of the emotional trait, and the 'rational' with holistic intelligence (*prajñā*), the removal of aforesaid illusions and realisation of impermanence and non-self (which is the ultimate blossoming of cognitive trait) takes place, and then there is no difference between emotion and reason. Sensitivity and intelligence[16] are just two dimensions of the authentic being, a being whose *āsavas* (defilements) are completely dissolved.

Conclusion

In recent times, we witness a growing understanding of emotions among psychologists that has come far ahead of Aristotelian distinction between cognition and emotion. The outcome of recent pondering over the distinction between cognition and emotion has provided enough grounds to look into the Buddha's treatment of these mental processes. As a result, a consensus for the time being comes up on the dilution of a fixed distinction between the two. Consequently, modern psychologists prefer to use the term 'affective-cognitive interaction' (Ellis and Newton 2005: 23–55) for these mental episodes — this can very well be called *manasikāra* or *prajñapti* in the Buddha's terms.

We cannot come to the simplistic conclusion that all emotions are good or useful, or even that all emotions are bad and are of the nature of dysfunction. Buddhism maintains that certain affective-cognitive states are afflictive (or disorganising) regardless (of the degree) of their magnitude or the context in which they arise (Ekman et al. 2005: 60). The insight of *santāna* gives us a ground to identify certain affective-cognitive interactions as afflictive for they disrupt the equipoise of mind, trigger anxiety, fill the mind with fear or anger, and thus destroy the source of well-being. The source of well-being is a flow of (not a state of) ailmentless mindfulness that the Buddha called *samāhita-citta*.

Psychologists do not distinguish between beneficial and harmful emotions (ibid.: 61). The goal of therapeutic psychology to improve one's emotional life is not to get rid of or transcend a harmful emotion, but to regulate the experience or reaction trigerred by such an emotion. The Buddha paves a path for complete emancipation from such mental ailments (*cetokhila*) by erasing them totally and forever. Furthermore, the path can be used for modifying affective traits. Modern psychology does not have a clear goal of well-being; that is why it fails to understand what emotions we need and what not.

Notes

* I gratefully acknowledge T. R. S. Sharma's contribution in creating my interest in the subject and imparting valuable insights and thank Aleksandra Wenta for her encouragement.

1. Any detailed discourse on this issue is deliberately avoided here lest one should enter the field of mind sciences.
2. As per the Pāli canon, there are three primordial predispositions called *āsavas*: (*a*) *kāma-āsava* (the desire for what one likes); (*b*) *bhava-āsava* (the instinct of self-continuation); and (*c*) *avijjā-āsava* (the state of non-apprehension of true nature of things).
3. Though *moha* serves as a common factor involved in both *rāga* and *dveṣa* functions, it is basically a state of not being aware of the true nature of the stimuli and their impermanence.
4. It may also be noted how modern psychologists prefer using 'affective realm' for emotions, moods and dispositions (Oatley et al. 2006: 27–31).
5. The so-called 'pleasant sensations' give rise to the 'latent sensuous greed' (*rāgānusaya*). Similarly, the 'painful sensations' give rise to the 'latent hatred' or 'anger' (*patighānusaya*) and so on (*Majjhima Nikāya* 44).
6. Here *abhidharma* is the Sanskrit version of the Pāli term *abhidhamma*, *prajñapti* is 'conceptual reality' (I prefer to put it as 'cognitive episode') and *dharmas* can be taken as 'dispositions'.
7. *pratyakṣam kalpanāpoḍham* (Dignāga's *Nyāya Bindu*, in Stcherbatsky 1999: 150).
8. I take the cue from the following account in *Dīgha Nikāya* 3.11: *Katamo eko dhammo visesabhāgiyo? Yoniso manasikāro — ayam eko dhammo visesabhāgiyo* and *Katamo eko dhammo hānabhāgiyo? Ayoniso manasikāro —ayam eko dhammo hānabhāgiyo.*
9. See, for example, *Samyutta Nikāya* 5.46.4.
10. An initial stimulus (sensation) received in a given environment leads to the formation of wrong beliefs (*assaddhiyam*), concepts, ideas, images, etc. After getting complicated, they result in a complex behaviour. That is to say, a behavioural response is a constitution of multiple psychic facts. If one attends to these improperly, they result in the loss of awareness about the very nature of their content or referent. This 'improper attention' (*ayoniso manasikāro*) results in the concealment of awareness (*asatāsammpajaññam*). It is the inappropriate attention which can be called 'emotional disorder'. The contents of the basic sensory inputs are prone to undergo *ayoniso manasikāro*, insofar as they are received in a chaotic environment (people and interpersonal relations), and also because they have already attracted formation of psychic facts accordingly. The concealment of awareness generates the 'loss of control over senses and motor effects' (*indriya*

asamvaram), which is the behavioural disorder (*tīni duccaritāni*) characterised by three types of misconduct: (*a*) 'association', 'aversion' and 'delusion' at the mental level; (*b*) shortcoming of speech act at the speech level; and (*c*) 'stealing', 'accumulation', 'violence', 'adultery', etc., at the physical level. These behavioural disorders strengthen the five fundamental miseries (*pañca-nīvaraṇa*). A mental state overpowered by these miseries is the state of ignorance (*avijjā*). The Buddha calls the process as the process of nourishment (*āhāro*) of ignorance (*Aṅguttara Nikāya* 10.7.1).

11. The Buddha also exposes a counter-scheme, described as *yoniso manasikāro*, for attaining mental peace and emancipation. That scheme tends to alter the *output variables* by proposing alteration to the *input variables*. If *input variables* are rightly attended to, they are processed to engender positive virtues (*bahukārā dhammā*). An 'appropriate attention' that means being attentive about the nature of *input variables* (considering them as are mere clinging of mind and their contents as momentary, i.e., perishable [*anicca*] and, therefore, regarding them as the non-self [*anattā*]) would not attract inappropriate processing. An 'appropriate attention' (*yoniso manasikāro*) engenders happiness (*pomojjam*); happiness engenders delight (*pīti*); delight removes restiveness (*kāyo pasambhati*), engendering calmness; calmness engenders contentment (*sukham vedeti*); content mind achieves equipoise of mind (*samādhiyati*). It is only in a state of equipoise of mind that one sees or experiences things as per their true nature (*yathābhūtam jānāti passati*), becoming aware of the sensations (*nibbindati*) in which one's awareness does not get ensnared by stimuli. Then springs dissociation (*virajjati*) and the dissociated mind enjoys emancipation (*vimuccati*). The Buddha designates these virtues (*dhamma*) as extremely advantageous (*bahukārā*) (*Dīgha Nikāya* 3.11).
12. For example, if a person has developed a habit of getting attached to whatever situation/relation he/she comes across, i.e., his/her attachment trait is dominant, he/she is prescribed to be in companionship of the right-minded people whom he/she may like (or live at such a place). Suppose, we just start teaching him/her that attachment is wrong, he/she may psychologically reject the whole teaching. In other words, Buddhism prescribes the varied treatments depending upon the need of a person.
13. As Padmasiri de Silva (1976: 1) paraphrases Rune E. A. Johansson (1969: 24), emotions are generally regarded in the mind of the Buddhist as aspects of our personality that interfere with the development of a spiritual life, as unwholesome states ethically undesirable, and as roadblocks to be cleared in the battleground between reason and emotion. In keeping with this perspective, emotions are described as states of 'agitation' or 'imbalance'.
14. *Viśuddhimaggo* is perhaps the last major work composed in Pāli language and regarded as the lexicon of Buddhism.

15. These are 'attachment', 'aversion', 'delusion', 'faith', 'understanding', and 'reason' (Buddhaghoṣa 2009, Cariyākathā, Kammaṭṭhānagahaniddesa section: 141–53).
16. See *Majjhima Nikāya* 9, 62 and 137.

References

Primary sources

Buddhaghoṣa. 2009. *Viśuddhimaggo*, ed. Swami Dwarikadas Shastri, 3 vols. Varanasi: Bauddha Bharati.

Sankrityayana, Pandit Rahula (trans.). 1933 and 1964. *Majjhima Nikāya* (Hindi). Saranath and Varanasi: Mahabodhi Sabha.

Shastri, Swami Dwarikadas (ed.). 2002. *Aṅguttara Nikāya* (Pāli), 4 vols. Varanasi: Bauddha Bharati.

—— (ed.). 2005. *Dīgha Nikāya* (Pāli), ed. Swami Dwarikadas Shastri, 3 vols. Varanasi: Bauddha Bharati.

—— (ed.). 2007. *Majjhima Nikāya* (Pāli), ed. Swami Dwarikadas Shastri, 3 vols. Varanasi: Bauddha Bharati.

—— (ed.). 2008. *Samyutta Nikāya* (Pāli), ed. Swami Dwarikadas Shastri, 4 vols. Varanasi: Bauddha Bharati, 2008.

Secondary works

Ben-Ze'ev, Aaron. 2000. *The Subtlety of Emotions*. Cambridge, MA and London: MIT Press.

Bilimoria, Purushottama, Joseph Prabhu and Renuka Sharma (eds). 2008. *Indian Ethics: Classical Traditions and Contemporary Challenges*. New York: Oxford University Press.

de Silva, Padmasiri. 1976. 'The Psychology of Emotions in Buddhist Perspective, Sir D. B. Jayatilleke Commemoration Lecture, Colombo, 1976', http://accesstoinsight.org/lib/authors/desilva-p/wheel237.html (accessed 25 July 2012).

Ekman, Paul Davidson, J. Richard, Matthieu Richard, and B. Alan Wallace. 2005. 'Buddhist and Psychological Perspectives on Emotions and Well-Being', *Current Directions in Psychological Science*, 14(2), http://alanwallace.org/wellbeing.pdf (accessed 15 December 2012).

Ellis, Ralph D. and Natika Newton (eds). 2005. *Consciousness & Emotion*, vol. 1. Amsterdam and Philadelphia: John Benjamins Publishing Company.

Johansson, Rune E. A. 1969. *The Psychology of Nirvana. London*: George. Allen and Unwin.

Keown, Damien. 1992. *The Nature of Buddhist Ethics*. New York: Macmillan.

King, Winston L. 1964. *In the Hope of Nibbāna*. La Salle: Open Court.

Maha Thera, Narada Ven. 1956. *A Manual of Abhidhamma*. Kuala Lumpur: Buddhist Missionary Society.

Oatley, Keith, Dacher Keltner and Jennifer M. Jenkins. 2006. *Understanding Emotions*. Cambridge, MA: Blackwell Publishing. 2nd edn.

Sharma, T. R. S. and C. K. Seshadri (eds). 2000. *Ancient Indian Literature: An Anthology*, 3 vols. Delhi: Sahitya Academy.

Stcherbatsky, F. Th. 1999. *Buddhist Logic*. Delhi: Low Price Publications.

Wallace, B. Alan. 2000. *The Taboo of Subjectivity: Towards a New Science of Consciousness*. New York and London: Oxford University Press.

7

Between Impetus, Fear and Disgust

'Desire for Emancipation' (Saṃvega) from Early Buddhism to Pātañjala Yoga and Śaiva Siddhānta

ANDREA ACRI

In mainstream Indic philosophical and soteriological traditions, emotions are generally associated with lower instincts and irrationality. Emotions, like passions, are regarded as bondages for the soul (be it conceived as Spirit, Self or subtle body) of the individual, being the untoward responses of the subject's deeply entrenched attachment for the sensory objects. Such emotions are, for instance, craving (*tṛṣṇā*), or the six core emotions of (sensual) desire (*kāma*), anger (*krodha*), cupidity (*lobha*), excitement (*harṣa*), pride (*māna*), and intoxication (*mada*) — collectively called *ṣaḍvarga* ('the six [faulty] aggregates') or *ariṣaḍvarga/ṣaḍripu* ('the six enemies') — against which any spiritual practitioner (*sādhaka*) must fight a heroic battle in order to attain final emancipation.

There are, however, emotions that, even though dominated by a strong psycho-physical element of passion, are considered positive and desirable events in the practitioner's path to enlightenment. Examples of such positive emotions are compassion (*karuṇā*), benevolence (*maitrī*), devotion (*bhakti*), i.e., for one's *guru* or *iṣṭadevatā*, and such like. Among such emotions or states of mind is *saṃvega*. Albeit inherently ambivalent, and perhaps even paradoxical — for it is by no means 'mild' and positive per se — *saṃvega* occurs in philosophic-religious texts to mark a watershed event in the career of the *sādhaka* seeking emancipation from the cycle of *karma* and the worldly bonds. As such, *saṃvega* has been translated in a variety of manners, viz., as 'impetus, excitement', 'fear', 'disgust' or 'desire for emancipation'. It is clear that *saṃvega* denotes a strong feeling, causing an everlasting impression in the mind of the *sādhaka*. Gnoli (1985 [1956]: xlvi), when commenting on *Śiva Sūtra* 1.12 (*vismayo yogabhūmikā*, 'The yogic stages are astonishment'), compares *saṃvega* to *vismaya* 'astonishment', regarding both as constituting a mystical and aesthetic experience.[1] Coomaraswamy (1943: 174) defines *saṃvega* as an instance of 'aesthetic shock',[2] 'the agitation of recognition' or, in popular parlance, an 'aha experience'. Thus, the Sanskrit word implies a violent emotion, a charged emotional state, by means of which the *yogins* realise the pitiful condition of human birth, as well as of the entire world of reincarnated beings. This emotion prompts them to long for higher stations.

While the occurrences of *saṃvega* in the Buddhist and, to a lesser extent, Jaina traditions have already been made the subject of study, this concept has rarely, if ever, been discussed in the context of Brāhmaṇical traditions. In this essay, I attempt at filling this gap by focusing on the theistic traditions of Pātañjala Yoga and early Śaiva Siddhānta. First, I will discuss the general, non-technical meaning that *saṃvega* retains in Sanskrit literature at large. I will then review the usage of the word in the Buddhist and Jaina contexts. On that basis, I will investigate the function of *saṃvega* in the Pātañjala Yoga system, specifically in the *Yoga Sūtra* and the popular commentaries thereof. I will then move to the early Śaiva Siddhānta scriptures where, even if the term *saṃvega* does not generally occur as such, comparable terms and concepts are featured in analogous contexts.

Since the sources taken into account in this chapter display a remarkable similarity of themes, I argue in favour of a 'subtle link' connecting the early Buddhist and Jaina traditions to the Brāhmaṇical system of Pātañjala Yoga and early mediaeval Śaiva Siddhānta. To strengthen my point, I present data from Old Javanese Śaiva texts, which possibly feature an interesting doctrinal blend bridging the Pātañjala and the Śaiva Saiddhāntika traditions.

Etymology of *Saṃvega*

Saṃvega derives from the (un-prefixed) Sanskrit root *vij*, which Monier-Williams relates to the Latin *vigor* and the English 'vigour', 'vigorous'. Various verbal forms from *vij* already occur in the *Ṛgveda* and in the early Brāhmaṇas with the meaning 'to move with a quick darting motion, speed, heave (said of waves)'; 'to start back, recoil, flee from'; to speed, accelerate'; 'to increase'; 'to terrify'.[3] The nominal stem *vega* is glossed by Monier-Williams as, among others, 'violent agitation, shock, jerk'; 'rush, dash, impetus, momentum, onset'; 'impetuosity, vehemence, haste, speed, rapidity, quickness, velocity'; 'outbreak, outburst (of passion), excitement, agitation, emotion'.[4] S.v. *saṃvega*, Monier-Williams (1899: 115) lists three main meanings or semantic areas, viz., (*a*) 'violent agitation, excitement, flurry' (*Mahābhārata*, *Kathāsaritsāgara*, etc.), (*b*) 'vehemence, intensity, high degree' (*Uttararāmacarita*, *Rājataraṅgiṇī*), and (*c*) 'desire of emancipation' (Hemacandra's *Pariśiṣṭaparvan*). In so doing, Monier-Williams slightly improves upon Böhtlingk and Roth's *Sanskrit-Wörterbuch* (1990[1885–75], vol. 7: 473), which only gives (*a*) *eine heftige Gemüthsaufregung* ('a violent mind excitement') (*Yoga Sūtra* 1.21), and (*b*) *Heftigkeit, Gewalt, hoher Grad* ('violence, force, higher degree'), therefore omitting the third meaning 'desire of emancipation'[5] recorded by Monier-Williams. Similarly, Apte (1956: 1592) records (*a*) 'agitation', (*b*) 'violent', (*c*) 'haste', and (*d*) 'agonising pain, poignancy'.

Apart from a reference to a single occurrence of *saṃvega* in the *Pariśiṣṭaparvan* by the Jaina polymath Hemacandra, recorded by Monier-Williams as meaning 'desire of emancipation', major Sanskrit dictionaries do not acknowledge the word as a specific technical term in the context of philosophy and soteriology. Rather, they gloss *saṃvega* on the basis of its occurrence in the Vedic texts, in the Epics, and in *kāvya* literature, where (as a substantive) it generally denotes an emotional state of excitement, fright or intense pain, or (as an adjective) a high degree of intensity of any action, process or state. Now, it is somewhat difficult to justify by way of etymology the former meaning on the basis of the latter two. In what way excitement, fear, haste or intensity would relate to 'desire of emancipation'? Some light on this matter is thrown by some early attestations of *saṃvega* in non-Sanskrit Buddhist literature, viz., the Pāli canon, which would appear to pave the way for the usages of the word found in later Sanskrit Buddhist and Jaina sources, as well as Brāhmaṇical Sanskrit philosophical texts.

Saṃvega in Buddhist Sources

The import and significance of *saṃvega* in the Buddhist sources through centuries, from the Pāli canonical scriptures to mediaeval Sanskrit biographies of the Buddha, has been investigated by Coomaraswamy (1943), Giustarini (2012), and especially Brekke (2002).[6]

In his short contribution,[7] Coomaraswamy notes that *saṃvega* is associated with 'trembling' in both the Vedic corpus and the Pāli canonical scriptures, wherein it stands for 'a state of shock, agitation, fear, awe, wonder or delight, induced by some physically or mentally poignant experience' (Coomaraswamy 1943: 176). In the *Sutta Nipāta*, it denotes 'dismay', whereas in the *Visuddhimāgga* it rather means 'to stir up' (a sluggish mind); in the *Saṃyutta Nikāya*, it means a 'great thrill' or *mahā saṃvega* (ibid.: 174–76). On the basis of canonical occurrences, Giustarini (2012: 513) defines *saṃvega* as an important stimulus to undertake the journey to liberation, being 'an uncomfortable stirring factor' that often goes together with *nibbidā* (Sanskrit *nirveda*), 'the healthy disenchantment towards the lures of *saṃsāra*'. *Saṃvega* often implies a sense of urgency (akin to Pāli *ubbega* and Sanskrit *udvega*), which is at the base of 'a conversion from indulgence in defilements to endeavour in the path', being 'both a result of applying attention to the intrinsic suffering of the conditioned realm, and a dramatic switch of pursuit'; in either cases, urgency appears to be connected with the perception of danger (*bhaya*) and plays an important role in triggering the dispassion that ultimately results in liberating knowledge (ibid.: 522–23).

According to Brekke, *saṃvega* and the ideas it conveyed played an important role in the Buddhist soteriology from an early period, as can be guessed by the copious references to the term in the Buddhist textual corpus. In *Mahāvagga* 1.20.17, the verbal form *samvejeyyan* — 'I should stir up', i.e., 'trigger an emotional disturbance that leads to religious motivation' — occurs in the context of the Buddha's attempt to proselytise the stubborn, hair-matted ascetic Kassapa (see Brekke 2002: 30). In the *Saṃyutta Nikāya* (Freer 1884: 197), *saṃvega* denotes an agitation instilled in the mind, but for a noble aim, for 'when the monks are properly agitated, when they experience a sufficient amount of *saṃvega*, their religious discipline will improve' (Brekke 2002: 82). Here, *saṃvega* has the function to 'wake up' negligent monks to their prescribed practice. Elsewhere in the *Saṃyutta Nikāya* (Freer 1898: 130), the state of *saṃvega* is to be achieved by means of meditation on the image of a skeleton or corpse, this being intended to generate fear and disgust in the practitioner.[8] In the *Itivuttaka* (Windisch 1898: 29–30), which devotes a whole *sutta* to it, *saṃvega* is regarded, along with exertion (*padhāna*), as a disposition towards the destruction of the intoxications of mind (*āsavas*), which leads one closer to the path to *arhant*-ship. By comparing these visualisation techniques with other similar techniques described in the passages of the Pāli canon, it becomes apparent that they are used as 'stratagems' to favour the growth of dispassion and detachment in the practitioner, who thereby experiences a desire for deliverance (Brekke 2002: 83–84).

Saṃvega's connection with both fear and agitation is illustrated through the simile of the lion in passages of the *Saṃyutta Nikāya* (Freer 1890: 84–86) and *Aṅguttara Nikāya* (Morris 1955: 33–34). On this simile, Brekke comments:

> Here the role of the Buddha in the world of gods and men is compared to the role of the lion in the world of animals. When the lion roars all other animals experience fear, agitation and trembling (*bhayaṃ saṃvegaṃ santā saṃāpajjanti*). They creep into their holes, jump back into the water, run off into the forest or fly up in the air. The king's elephants break their bonds, void their excrements and run to and fro. In the same way, when a Buddha arises in the world and teaches the Dhamma the gods experience fear, agitation and trembling (2002: 83).

The image of the animals fleeing in agitation from the source of danger calls to mind the original meaning of the root *vij*, i.e., 'to move with a quick darting motion, speed, heave . . . to start back, recoil, flee from'. According to Śāntideva's *Bodhicaryāvatāra* and *Śikṣāsamuccaya*, the reason to undertake religious life in the forest is fear (*bhayabhūta*) (ibid.: 85–86).[9]

The use of *saṃvega* in the sense of 'emotional disturbance that leads to religious motivation' is attested in the biographies of the Buddha written in the early centuries of the Common Era. For instance, according to *Buddhacarita* 3.37 and 3.40, it is precisely the experience of *saṃvega* that leads prince Siddhārtha to abandon his princely life and start his ascetic career (ibid.: 53, 61). Here too, *saṃvega* appears to be a positive perturbation becoming a motivating factor, which precedes, and is propaedeutic to, the experience of conversion. As E. H. Johnston, the editor and translator of the *Buddhacarita*, argued: '[S]*aṃvega* as a religious term denotes the first step towards conversion, when the perturbation of mind is produced by something and leads to consideration of the inherent rottenness of the world and so to the adoption of the religious life' (1935–36: 32n4).

An analogous usage of *saṃvega* is attested in Buddhaghoṣa's *Viśuddhimāgga*. In Buddhaghoṣa's exposition of fear and its connection with religious motivation, dispassion presupposes fear, and is a state in between the latter and the desire for emancipation (Brekke 2002: 84). In this particular instance of the *Viśuddhimāgga* (Rhys Davids 1920: 135), *saṃvega* denotes a type of fear triggered by the sights of birth (*jāti*), ageing (*jarā*), sickness (*vyādhi*), and death (*maraṇa*). A similarly 'negative' connotation of *saṃvega* occurs in the Pāli *Mahāvaṃsa* 1.1 and 23.62,[10] wherein it is translated by W. Geiger (1912: 2, 160) as 'emotion' and 'moved', implying a feeling of horror at and recoil from the world and its misery. As such, it is apparently contrasted in the text to *pasāda* 'serene joy', a feeling of satisfaction and peacefulness that follows upon the reception of the Buddha's doctrine.

Saṃvega also plays a role in the Sanskrit Buddhist literature of the Sarvāstivādins,[11] as well as in the *Abhidharmakośabhāṣya*, mostly with the meaning of 'an emotional perturbation motivating the religious life' (Brekke 2002: 83). Louis de la Vallée Poussin (1991: 1208n273), referring to a passage on the three *abhijñās* ('special knowledges', or supernatural faculties)[12] in Saṅghabhadra's commentary on Vasubandhu, renders *saṃvega* as 'disgust': 'By the first, one sees the suffering of self and others; by the second, the suffering of others, and one experiences *saṃvega* or disgust; thus disgusted, one produces the third, and one sees the happiness of Nirvāṇa'.

Saṃvega in Jaina Sources

Saṃvega features as a prominent doctrinal item in the early Jaina texts and mediaeval commentaries thereof. An early characterisation of *saṃvega* as both spiritual craving and fear of worldly bondage is found in the *Uttarajjhāyā* in Ardha-Māgadhī (*Uttarādhyayana Sūtra* in Sanskrit).[13] In Chapter 29 of the text, 73 stages are distinguished in the process leading to the destruction of *kamma/karma* and final liberation. *Saṃvega* or 'longing for liberation' constitutes the very first stage, followed by *nivveda/nirveda* or 'disgust':

> [*saṃvega*] Sir, what does the soul obtain by the longing for liberation? By the longing for liberation the soul obtains an intense desire of the Law; by an intense desire of the Law he quickly arrives at an (increased) longing for liberation; he destroys anger, pride, deceit, and greed, which reproduce themselves infinitely; he acquires no (bad) Karman, and ridding himself of wrong belief which is the consequence of the latter, he becomes possessed of right faith; by the purity of faith some will reach perfection after one birth; nobody, however, who has got this purity, will be born more than thrice before he reaches perfection.
>
> [*nirveda*] Sir, what does the soul obtain by disregard of worldly objects?[14] By disregard of worldly objects the soul quickly feels disgust for pleasures enjoyed by gods, men, and animals; he becomes indifferent to all objects; thereby he ceases to engage in any undertakings, in consequence of which he leaves the road of Samsâra and enters the road to perfection[15] (Jacobi 1973 [1895]: 161–62).

Mediaeval Jaina authors and commentators categorise *saṃvega* as part of *samyaktva* or *samyagdṛṣṭi* ('right belief'), under the sub-category *guṇa* (e.g., Pūjyapāda, 5th century CE, on the *Tattvārtha Sūtra*; and Āśādhara, 13th century CE) or *liṅga* (e.g., Hemacandra, 11th–12th century CE). In either case, *saṃvega* apparently denotes a sort of 'spiritual craving' (Williams 1991 [1963]: 42). Pūjyapāda describes it as an ever-present fear of the cycle of transmigration; similarly, to Āśādhara, it embodies fear of the unstable *saṃsāra*, which brings sickness, sorrow and sudden calamity. According to Amitagati, *saṃvega* denotes an unwavering attachment to *deva*, *guru* and *dharma*.

Hemacandra, who in his *Yoga Śāstra* provided Monier-Williams with the basis for translating *saṃvega* as 'desire for emancipation', regards it as 'the desire for *mokṣa* arising from the realisation that the pleasures of gods and men are, in the last resort, unsatisfying' (Williams 1991 [1963]: 42). The general Jaina view holds that the first *guṇa* of the category *samyaktva* is *saṃvega* or 'desire for release', and the third, *nirveda* or 'disgust'.[16] Hemacandra call these 'characteristics' (*lakṣaṇa*).[17] According to him, *saṃvega* springs from a 'peaceful passion' or emotion (*śama*), which seems to be at odds with its original meaning of 'agitation, impetus'.[18]

Saṃvega in Pātañjala Yoga

As we have seen in the preceding sections, both Buddhist and Jaina sources provide ample justification for the use of *saṃvega* as a religious kind of perturbation or 'longing for the unseen', which arises as a result of either fear, disgust or dispassion, caused by the realisation of the miseries and painfulness inherent in the *saṃsāric* condition. As this particular meaning is not attested in the earliest Sanskrit sources, which constantly use the form *saṃ-vij* in the sense of 'violent agitation, excitement', it might be suggested that Sanskrit borrowed such meaning from either the Buddhist or Jaina vernacular texts. As has been amply demonstrated, several important features of the Sanskrit Brāhmaṇical philosophical texts were, in fact, borrowed from Buddhist sources. Some of the best-documented examples of this doctrinal and terminological borrowing may be found in the *Yoga Sūtra*, wherein technical terms and lists of psychological or meditative states have been shown to have earlier counterparts in early Buddhist — and even earlier Jaina — texts.[19] In fact, the *sūtra* where *saṃvega* occurs belongs to a cluster of *sūtras* that display terminology similar to and lists of doctrinal items parallel to those of the early canonical Buddhist literature. One may, therefore, argue that *saṃvega*, too, is likely to be one among the several technical terms lent by Buddhism to Pātañjala Yoga.

Brekke comments on the occurrence of *saṃvega* in *Yoga Sūtra* 1.21:

> [*S*]*aṃvega* is a feeling that puts extra energy and commitment into the meditation practice. *Saṃvega* is here a quality that makes *samādhi* easier to attain. However, neither Patañjali nor the commentators discuss the nature of *saṃvega* and it is therefore difficult to judge how close it is to the concept in Buddhism or Jainism (2002: 82).

Brekke is right in noting that absence of a positive definition[20] makes it arduous to understand the nature of *saṃvega* in the classical Yoga system, as well as its link with the Buddhist and Jaina counterparts. Yet, a close investigation of the context of the *Yoga Śāstra*[21] in which the term is used, as well as a comparison with the sources of related philosophic-religious systems, shows a clear affinity of the Pātañjala *saṃvega* with the (earlier) Buddhist and Jaina counterparts.

That *saṃvega* must have played an important role in the classical Yoga system is beyond doubt, considering that it is seemingly characterised as either a method in yogic practice or a characteristic of the *yogins*, and, therefore, a prerequisite for success in achieving the state of contentless absorption (*asaṃprajñātasamādhi*) — the most perfected psychic state leading to isolation (*kaivalya*), the highest goal recognised by Pātañjala Yoga. *Sūtra* 1.21, featuring the only occurrence of *saṃvega* in the *Yoga Sūtra*, is to be read together with the adjacent *sūtras* 1.20 and 1.22–23 as forming a thematic block that outlines the means of the *yogins*, and the latter's categorisation, along the path towards contentless absorption. *Sūtra* 1.20 declares that contentless absorption follows upon faith, energy, mindfulness, absorption, and insight (*śraddhāvīryasmṛtisamādhiprajñāpūrvaka itareṣām*); these, as the *Yogasūtrabhāṣya* explains, have to be regarded as the *yogins*' means or methods (*upāya*).[22] *Sūtras* 1.21–22, if read together with the *Bhāṣya*, become a sort of *locus classicus* for the categorisation of yogic practitioners according to the quality or gradation of their *saṃvega*, which in this context is generally rendered by some English translators as 'intense' (e.g., Woods 1914: 47) — this being an adjective referring to the quality or degree of the *yogins*' *upāya*, i.e., '(spiritual) means', 'method' or 'practice'— or as 'intensity' or 'fervour' (e.g., Pines and Gelblum 1966: 319). In fact, the *sūtras* themselves merely hint at the existence of different types of *yogins*, some of who are nearer than others to the goal of contentless absorption mentioned in *sūtra* 1.18. Bronkhorst's translation[23] of *Yoga Śāstra* 1.21–22 runs:

> For the [yogins] with sharp intensity [mental absorption without object-consciousness (*asaṃprajñātasamādhi*)] is near.[24]
>
> Those yogins, indeed, are [of] nine [kinds], being of gentle, moderate and vehement method; that is to say: of gentle method, of moderate method, of vehement method. Among them, the [yogin] of gentle method is of three kinds: with gentle intensity, with moderate intensity, with sharp intensity. Likewise the [yogin] of moderate method [and] likewise the [yogin] of vehement method.[25]
>
> There is a superiority (*viśeṣa*) even to that, on account of [the method] being gentle, moderate or vehement.[26]
>
> Because [the method is] gently sharp, moderately sharp, vehemently sharp, [there is] 'superiority even to that': even to that special [mental absorption which is due to being with sharp intensity]; the attainment of mental absorption and the fruit of mental absorption is near to him who is of gently sharp intensity and also of vehement method, nearer than that to him who is of [vehement method and] moderately sharp intensity, nearest compared to that to him who is of [vehement method and] vehemently sharp intensity[27] (Bronkhorst 1985: 191–92).

Having noted that the introduction to *sūtra* 1.21 found in the *Bhāṣya* describes a ninefold classification of the *yogins*, Bronkhorst (1985: 191–94) argues that such a classification is nowhere implied in the *sūtra* itself, which at best presupposes a threefold classification of the *yogins*, whose intensity in practice is gentle, moderate and sharp. The *sūtra* that follows (1.22) does not define the categories of gentle (*mṛdu*), moderate (*madhya*) or vehement (*adhimātra*) either, but seems to consider them as attributes of the method (*upāya*). The question as to whether the two *sūtras* 1.21 and 1.22, if read together, may indeed provide a basis for the *Bhāṣya*'s understanding of a ninefold classification of the *yogins*, need not detain us further here.[28] What seems more relevant to our discussion is to point out that the *Bhāṣya* subdivides each of the three main categories of the *yogins* following gentle, moderate or keen methods into three sub-categories, depending on the intensity (*saṃvega*) of their practice being gentle, moderate or keen. However, no explanation of what these terms exactly stand for is given in either the *sūtras* or the *Bhāṣya*, which only positively identify a category of the *yogins* defined as *tīvrasaṃvega* 'whose practice is keenly intense (?)'.

As noted earlier, previous translators of the *Yoga Śāstra* have tended to ignore the usage of *saṃvega* as 'desire for emancipation' in the Buddhist and Jaina contexts, rendering it as 'intense'/'intensity' (referring to the *yogins*' practice or religious observance). In fact, the meaning 'desire for emancipation' may be regarded as encompassing, and in any event implying, all the other attested meanings of *saṃvega*, viz., 'impetus' (for religious practice), 'disgust' (for human birth), 'fear' (of *saṃsāra*), and 'dispassion' (towards worldly pleasures). Each one of these equally possible translations may be applied to the context of *Yoga Śāstra* 1.21–22. Whatever the intended meaning of *saṃvega* may have been, it is precisely according to their *saṃvega* that the *yogins* are arranged in a hierarchy, understood as degrees of nearness to the attainment of the highest type of *samādhi*. What exactly this nearness consists of is left unexplained in both the *sūtras* and the *Bhāṣya*. However, if we compare the terse account of the *Yoga Śāstra* to other sources of the classical Yoga tradition, it appears that 'nearness' is to be understood in terms of future reincarnations occurring before the attainment of final emancipation. This is hinted at by Vācaspati Miśra (9th century CE) in a fragment of his commentary (*Tattvavaiśāradī*) to *Yoga Śāstra* 1.21, where he refers to 'belief and the other qualities' (*śraddhādayaś . . . yogopāyās*), as per *sūtra* 1.20, in connection to the ninefold categorisation of the *yogins*, described in the *Bhāṣya*:

> Someone raises the objection that if belief and the other qualities are means for [attaining] yoga, then all [the yogins] without distinction would possess concentration and its results. Whereas it is observed that in some cases there is perfection (*siddhi*); in other cases the absence of perfection; in some cases perfection after a delay; in other cases perfection after still more delay; [and] in other cases quickly. In reply to this objection he says: 'Now these yogins are of nine kinds'. Those are called [followers of gentle or moderate or vehement methods], in whose case . . . the methods, that is, belief and the other [means], become gentle or moderate or vehement. 'Intensity' is passionlessness[29] (trans. Woods 1914: 47).

Vācaspati Miśra's reading of the *sūtra* implies that *saṃvega*, glossed as 'passionlessness' (*vairāgya*), is precisely the element thanks to which some *yogins* attain perfection quicker than others, even though they are all putting into practice the spiritual methods described in *sūtra* 1.20. This interpretation seems to suggest that *saṃvega* is a quality rather than a means (*upāya*).[30]

Vācaspati Miśra's gloss of *saṃvega* as *vairāgya* may give us a clue as to what the former exactly consisted of for the author of the *Yoga Śāstra*, where neither a positive definition of *saṃvega* nor a gloss is provided. What 'emotion' did this quality trigger in the *yogin*? Following the lead of *vairāgya*, let us turn to *Yoga Śāstra* 3.50–51. There we find a characterisation of the *yogin* who, having realised that his Self is undefiled (*śuddha*) by the three qualities or *guṇas* (*sattva, rajas, tamas*), attains discrimination and isolation, thereby gaining supernatural powers (*sūtra* 3.50); however, as we are told, he should exercise passionlessness (*vairāgya*) even towards those 'worldly' manifestations of his newly attained state of perfection. If he is invited by supernatural entities to partake of heavenly pleasures, he should refuse and consider in his mind the following:

> 'Baked upon the terrifying coals of the cycle of existence and wandering in the darkness of birth and death, in a difficult way I have found the lamp of yoga that dissipates the darkness of the hindrances. And these winds of pleasures born from lust are enemies of that [lamp]. Now that I have attained this light, how could I be led astray by the mirage that are the pleasures, and make myself fuel for that fire of the cycle of existence as it flares up once again? Fare thee well, pleasures similar to dreams and to be craved for by vile folk!' Thus resolved in his mind, he should then practice absorption (*Yogasūtrabhāṣya* 3.51, trans. Woods 1914: 286).[31]

This description of the *yogin*'s attitude conforms seamlessly to the characterisation of *saṃvega* given in Pāli and Sanskrit texts as fear of the terrifying *saṃsāra* and disgust for the bonding pleasures, as well as 'impetus' and determination to continue on his ascetic path.

An analogous account is found in the *Dharma Pātañjala*, an Old Javanese Śaiva text that contains a commentary to the *Yoga Sūtra* related — albeit by no means identical — to the *Bhāṣya* (see Acri 2011a). In the section of the text based on *Yoga Śāstra* 3.51 (i.e., p. 332.5–14), the *yogin*, thinking aloud, renews his commitment to continue on his path to release without being lured by the invitation of celestial beings and the temptation of taking advantage of his newly acquired supernatural powers, for this will inexorably lead him back to the suffering of the cycle of existence (Acri 2011a: 540–41). Another passage of the *Dharma Pātañjala* is illuminating with respect to both *saṃvega* and the categorisation of the *yogins* according to a progression in time. The Old Javanese text (p. 298.1–4), following the natural order of the topics outlined in the *Yoga Sūtra*, speaks about the concentration (*samādhi*) that the *yogins* obtain when they achieve identity (*sātmya*) with the Lord, thereby sharing with Him His state of supernatural prowess (*kasiddhyan*). In the *Dharma Pātañjala*, this state of identity is evidently intended as the Śaiva equivalent of the supreme state of isolation (*kaivalya*), brought about by non-cognitive absorption according to the *Yoga Śāstra*. The topic of *sūtra*s 1.21 and 22 is treated in the following passage of the Old Javanese text (p. 298.5–12):

> The categories of the state of supernatural prowess are: low, middle and superior. The reason why the condition of supernatural prowess is threefold is that the characteristics of the yogins are three: there is the one [practising] *with gentle intensity*; there is the one [practising] *with moderate intensity*; there is the one [practising] *with keen intensity*. [Practising] *with gentle intensity* means: his practice of yoga and its means is little. He meets the state of supernatural prowess, but it is met after a long time. The one [practising] *with moderate intensity* is as follows: he meets the state of supernatural prowess, but the obtainment is in his next birth. The one [practising] *with keen intensity* is as follows: his way of performing yoga, as well as the correct understanding of it, is intense; that is the reason why he meets the supernatural powers deriving from yoga in his present human birth.[32]

The *Dharma Pātañjala* is at variance with the *Yoga Śāstra* in that it refers to three kinds of supernatural prowess as being the achievement of three categories of *yogin*s, and also because it provides a definition of each category. The Old Javanese text does not recognise the gradation 'vehement' (*adhimātra*) with respect to the method (*upāya*), but rather mentions the gradations of low (*kaniṣṭha*), middle (*madhya*) and superior (*uttama*) as characterising the three categories of supernatural prowess (*kasiddhyan*). These three gradations are, in turn, associated with three categories of *yogin*s on their path to *samādhi* and identity with the Lord, namely those who practice respectively with gentle intensity (*mṛdusambega*), with moderate intensity (*madhyasambega*) and with keen intensity (*tībrasambega*), thereby obtaining their goal with lower or higher speed. This can be summarised in the following scheme:

kaniṣṭha-kasiddhyan	*madhya-kasiddhyan*	*uttama-kasiddhyan*
mṛdusambega	*madhyasambega*	*tībrasambega*
The *yogin* obtains the state of supernatural prowess in a long time (i.e., not before many births).	The *yogin* obtains the state of supernatural prowess in another birth (i.e., in his next birth).	The *yogin* obtains the supernatural powers deriving from his intense practice in his present human birth.

Both the *Dharma Pātañjala* and the *Tattvavaiśāradī* identify different categories of *yogins* according to their state of 'perfection', or even 'supernatural prowess' (respectively *siddhi* and *kasiddhyan* — the latter being an Old Javanese abstract noun from the Sanskrit base-word *siddhi*), obtained respectively after a delay/several human births, after still more delay/one more human birth, or quickly/during the *yogin*'s present life. It now becomes apparent that the 'nearness' (*āsannaḥ*) referred to in *Yoga Sūtra* 1.21 is to be understood in terms of subsequent reincarnations.

If we compare *Yoga Śāstra* 1.20–22 and the *Tattvavaiśāradī* thereon with the passage on *saṃvega* from the Jaina *Uttarajjhāyā* quoted previously, we clearly see the presence of analogous themes, as well as comparable lists of items. In both texts, these items or stages are understood not simply as a series but as one arising from the other. The Jaina source describes longing for liberation as triggering an intense desire of the Law, which itself triggers an (increased) longing for liberation, resulting in right faith; in the purity of faith, causing some to reach perfection after one, two or three births; and in the attainment of disregard for worldly objects, disgust for pleasures and of indifference. Similarly, *Yoga Śāstra* 1.20 describes faith (*śraddhā*, itself connected to purity, as per the *Bhāṣya*: *śraddhā cetasaḥ samprasādaḥ*) as triggering fervour (*vīrya*), mindfulness (*smṛti*), absorption (*samādhi*), and insight (*prajñā*), which ultimately lead to contentless absorption. Furthermore, as noted by Woods (1914: 45–46), these five items were already taught by the Buddha in the *Majjhima Nikāya*, and the simile of the mother related by the *Bhāṣya* to illuminate the *sūtra* is found in the *Metta Sutta* of the *Sutta Nipāta*. This leaves little doubt as to the originally Buddhist derivation of these doctrinal themes.

Let me conclude by discussing the last of the *upāyas* listed in the relevant section of the *Yoga Śāstra*, i.e., devotion to God. As is evident from its introduction, *sūtra* 1.23 is understood by the *Bhāṣya* as being connected to the preceding two:

> Is mental absorption nearer only as a result of this, or is there some other method too for its attainment, or not? [The *sūtra* says:] 'Or as a result of devotion to God'.[33]

The *Bhāṣya* seems to put on the same level the *yogins* who practise devotion to God and the *yogins* who are characterised by keen intensity of practice (*tīvrasaṃvega*), as they are all regarded as becoming 'most near' (*āsannatamaḥ*) to the goal of *samādhi*. More explicitly, and in a pronounced Śaiva theistic fashion, the *Dharma Pātañjala* (p. 298.14–19) declares that the *yogin* who performs *yoga* with keen intensity is superior to the others, and obtains the state of supernatural prowess already in his present life by virtue of devotion to God. This, in Śaiva jargon, amounts to saying that the *yogin* recognises his divine nature, obtaining the Lord's divine powers and becoming a visible counterpart of Śiva.

The perception of devotion to God as the peak of the *yogin*'s career, and its connection with *saṃvega*, is noteworthy. As we will see in the next sections, the theistic element forms a distinctive feature of Sanskrit and Old Javanese Śaiva recasts of the theme of *saṃvega*.

Saṃvega in Old Javanese Śaiva Texts

As we have seen, the *Dharma Pātañjala* incorporates elements from the Pātañjala Yoga system into a thoroughly theistic (i.e., Śaiva) doctrinal and soteriological framework. Whereas this text is unique in the Javano-Balinese tradition in that it closely follows a version of the *Yoga Śāstra*, and goes as far as substituting the Śaiva *ṣaḍaṅgayoga* with the Pātañjala *aṣṭāṅgayoga*,[34] other Old Javanese Śaiva texts may be regarded as representing positions that stand midway between the Pātañjala and the Saiddhāntika systems. As such, they may either constitute a potpourri of Śaiva and Pātañjala yoga elements, or document an early historical strand of Śaivism that emerged from a scriptural tradition that has not — or only scantily — survived in the Indian subcontinent.

An echo of the accounts of the *Dharma Pātañjala* and *Tattvavaiśāradī* presented earlier is detectable in the *Vṛhaspatitattva.* In 52.58–69, an experience akin to the *saṃvega* encountered by the *yogin* at the beginning of his career seems to be represented, recast in a Śaiva garb so as to fit in the context of the doctrine of *karma*.[35] The Old Javanese text states that it is because of the neutrality of good and bad actions in his subtle body that a human being is prompted to embark upon the career of man of religion (Old Javanese *viku* = Sanskrit *bhikṣu*) that eventually will lead him to the position of leader among *yogins* (*yogīśvara*), and thus liberation — not in his present life, but in the next one:

> If his former actions, as a human being, were neither bad nor good, that is the reason why he again takes birth as a human being. Free from his good and bad actions in former human lives, he obtains the state of a man of religion, and he is able to perform the observances dedicated to the Lord. But that [man of religion] does not know of his state as leader

> among yogins during his lifetime. He dies and again becomes a human being. In that [birth] he will obtain the state of a leader among yogins (*Vṛhaspatitattva* 52.58–69).[36]

Even though *saṃvega* is nowhere mentioned in the passage, the indication as to when the *yogin* will attain perfection (here intended as *yogīśvara*-hood), namely in his next life, hints at a similarity of context between this passage and the aforecited accounts of the *Dharma Pātañjala* and *Tattvavaiśāradī*. The type of *yogin* described in the *Vṛhaspatitattva* would correspond to the middle category of *yogin*s according to the classical Pātañjala classification, namely those characterised by *madhyasaṃvega*.

That the aforecited passage is related to the concept of *saṃvega* may also be inferred from another passage of the *Vṛhaspatitattva*, which also deals with *karma* and his effects on determining the course of life of a person who commences the religious career. In 3.23–25, the Lord explains that the career of a man of religion begins when a soul has reincarnated as a human being after having spent his good *karma* in heaven. The Lord continues (3.25–31):

> Then the state of desire for emancipation (*ka-sambega-n*) comes into being, as well as love, meritorious acts and devotion. He brings all of them into being. That is the cause of the love of the Lord towards him. The Lord loves him. [Therefore,] he is able to see the latent impressions connected with his human birth, as well as hunger, hot and cold, the sinfulness and dirtiness of being incarnated. As soon as he sees them, he says: 'Ah! Extreme is the pain connected with the human state, and whenever one has a body it is inevitably experienced. Ah! What is the true course of my existence?' He then goes to a master, in order to enquire about the meaning of existence. He is instructed by the sage.[37]

Here, we come across a cliché encountered in the Buddhist literature, namely the *yogin*'s initial experience of the misery and painfulness of his human state is caused precisely by *saṃvega*. The meaning of *saṃvega* that best fits the context of this passage is 'desire for emancipation',[38] i.e., the religious feeling that awakens the spiritual seeker up to the experience of latent impressions, and prompts him to start the ascetic career by looking for a suitable *guru*. The reference to the 'Lord's love' (*sih bhaṭāra*) towards the *yogin* who is invested with *saṃvega* adumbrates the concept of the Lord's grace — a concept that, as we will see later, plays an important role in Śaiva Siddhānta.

The aforecited passage of the *Vṛhaspatitattva*, insofar as it regards the arising of *saṃvega* in the *yogin* as a result of the Lord's love towards him, echoes the definition of *īśvarapraṇidhāna* given in both the *Yogasūtrabhāṣya* and the *Dharma Pātañjala*. According to the *Bhāṣya* (1.23.4–5):

> Because of the excellence of his devotion [the Lord] is inclined to him (i.e. the yogin) and favours him simply on account of his longing for [the Lord]. It is also by virtue of his longing that the attainment of absorption and the fruits of absorption are very close within the yogin's reach.[39]

In the *Dharma Pātañjala* (286.19–21), it is only through the love of the Lord towards the *yogin* who incessantly practises *samādhi* (thus apparently belonging to the category of *tīvrasaṃvega*) that he can attain the state of *yogīśvara* and become the visible manifestation of the Lord's powers. To the question of Kumāra as to what is the reason for the Lord's supernatural powers being finally made manifest in the *yogin*, Śiva replies:

> [T]he Lord has affection for the yogin. For what reason would He have affection? Because of his exertion in performing absorption at all times during day and night. That is the reason of the affection of the Lord toward the yogin. The impurities in his body and his suffering will be annihilated by Him (*Dharma Pātañjala* 286.19–21).[40]

The aforecited Old Javanese passages illuminate the context of the terse references to *saṃvega* in the *Yoga Śāstra* and related Sanskrit texts, which appear to be applied to different categories of *yogins* ordered according to their practice and closeness (in terms of reincarnations) to the desired goal of emancipation. The higher categories of *yogins* are linked to an experience (*saṃvega*) — itself resulting from an act of love or 'grace' by the Lord — that prompts them to take the first step along the path towards liberation.

Saṃvega in Early Śaiva Saiddhāntika Scriptures

Having analysed *saṃvega* in the Pātañjala Yoga tradition, as well in the Śaiva sources belonging to the pre-modern Javano-Balinese tradition, I now turn to early seminal scriptures of the Śaiva Siddhānta. These belong to the pan-Indian corpus of Sanskrit scriptures referred to as (Siddhānta) Āgamas or (Siddhānta) Tantras, the earliest of which were compiled from *c*. 6th to 9th century CE.

Interestingly, either the word *saṃvega* or terms expressing analogous concepts occur in the passages of Siddhānta Tantras that share the same context, namely the discussion of neutral or perfectly balanced *karma*. This state is linked to the descent of the Lord's power (*śakti*) into the *yogin*, which prompts him to seek Śaiva initiation that ultimately leads to liberation. This situation of karmic impasse is elaborated in the early Saiddhāntika formulations of the doctrine of *karmasāmya* or 'balance of *karma*'. The balance of *karma*, caused by the equiponderance of two actions of different polarity, has the power of blocking the soul's capacity to experience and necessarily precedes the descent of the Lord's salvific power before initiation. Some of these themes we have already encountered in the passages of the Old Javanese texts discussed earlier, where we are told that *yogins* in the early stages of their ascetic careers, following an equiponderance of *karma*, experience *saṃvega* — intended as either disgust, fear or religious élan — and, benefiting from the Lord's love at the same time, seek for a *guru* who can instruct them. Let us now take a closer look at the Saiddhāntika passages.

The *Kiraṇa Tantra* refers to the doctrine of *karmasāmya* in Vidyāpāda (hereafter VP) 1.20cd–21:

> Then it (i.e. the soul) experiences its entire experience, being either happy or otherwise, according to his karman. When [good and bad] actions have become equal, by virtue of the power of an interval of time, at that time, through an intense descent of power, the soul is initiated by his guru and becomes omniscient like Śiva, devoid of any limitation of knowledge[41] (translation mine).

The basic idea conveyed by the passage is that the condition of equivalence of *karma*, which is attributed to the salvific descent of the Lord's grace, instills in the human being a feeling of dispassion towards worldly experiences. He then seeks initiation from a *guru*, following which he obtains the state of Śiva-hood.[42] According to *Kiraṇa Tantra* (VP 5.5–6b),[43] the descent of the Lord's power prompts fear of worldly existence (*bhavabhayaprada*) and causes one to seek a teacher:

> Just as the sudden falling of a thing instills fear, so too the descent of power is said to instill fear of worldly existence. [Just as] one gets out of the way of that [falling object], so too the soul [goes] towards a teacher [in order to receive initiation][44] (trans. Goodall 1998: 330–31).

Rāmakaṇṭha's commentary paraphrases the verses, explaining that the union with the Lord's power, although beginningless, is intended as a 'fall' because it instills fear of worldly existence, and adding that this power has to be regarded as the triad of Vāmā, Raudrī and Jyeṣṭhā (*vāmādi*). The *Kiraṇa* (VP 5.6c–8b) continues:

> Just as a teacher awakens pupils that have fallen asleep in front of him with a stick, so too Śiva awakens those asleep in the slumber of delusion with His power. When [a soul attains] realisation of his own nature, then it is said that [Śiva's power has] fallen. Therefore it is a fall of power. The [expression] 'fall' [is used because it] expresses the signs [characteristic of a fall][45] (trans. Goodall 1998: 331).

Both the *Kiraṇa* and Rāmakaṇṭha's commentary thereof call to mind the function attributed to *saṃvega* in the canonical Buddhist sources, such as the *Saṃyutta Nikāya*, where it 'awakens' to their duty the lazy monks who have fallen asleep. The final portion of the commentary on these verses clarifies the process of purification undergone by the soul:

> Thus when this same [power] has, in accordance with [a soul's] fitness because of the ripening of his impurity, generated that particular knowledge that is a means of destroying that [impurity], in a sequence starting with distaste for worldly existence, then it is said, figuratively, that Jyeṣṭhā , the cause of this effect, has 'fallen' as power. This has been taught [in *Kiraṇa* VP 2.29cd with] 'After the blocking of the power [of *mala*] he [viz., the soul] is made without desire for existence'. And in the venerable *Mataṅga* [VP 10.25cd]: 'His impurity shaken off for ever, he becomes dispassionate towards rebirth in this world'. And also in the venerable *Svāyaṃbhuva* [1.17]: From the fall of that [power], his impurity, the cause of the birth in this world, wastes away. When this [*mala*] is worn away, there is a desire to go to the supreme state, than which there is nothing higher[46] (ibid.: 332).

The aforecited passage, discussing mainstream Śaiva ideas on the descent of salvific power, presents several themes found in many descriptions of *saṃvega* that we have come across so far. According to Rāmakaṇṭha, this process of destruction of the innate impurity represents 'a sequence starting with distaste for worldly existence' (*saṃsāravaitṛṣṇyādikrama*). To illustrate this point, Rāmakaṇṭha quotes from three authoritative Siddhānta Tantras,[47] according to which the soul experiences a lack of desire for existence (*bhavaniḥspṛha*, as per *Kiraṇa* VP 2.29d),[48] a feeling of dispassion towards the world (*saṃsārāt sa virajyeta*, as per *Mataṅgapārameśvarāgama* VP 10.25c),[49] and a desire for emancipation, i.e., to reach the highest state (*yiyāsā syāt paraṃ niḥśreyasaṃ prati*, as per *Svāyaṃbhuvaūtrasaṅgraha* VP 1.17cd).[50] All the aforementioned characterisations encompass the manifold aspects and nuances of *saṃvega*, viz., fear, disgust, dispassion, and religious élan. These emotional states are propaedeutic to the realisation of the human being's true condition or potential, which is a far cry from the pitiful state of *saṃsāric* existence in which he is entangled.

Through the aforecited passages, it is possible to trace a history of the development and transformation of *saṃvega*, which appears to have been 'borrowed', as it were, by the Siddhānta Tantras from the earlier Buddhist and Pātañjala texts and recast in a Śaiva fashion. This was done by tying *saṃvega* to such fundamental Śaiva tenets as the depletion of *mala* by means of the descent of the Lord's power, which may immediately precede initiation or coincide with it — the *guru* representing Śiva's counterpart. To this end, it is worth pointing out that the Śaiva texts often speak about a 'violent descent of power' or *tīvraśakti(ni)pāta*, the *tīvra-* corresponding to the *tīvra-* used in *Yoga Śāstra* 1.21–22 to refer to the highest form of *saṃvega*, itself tied to the highest category — among nine — of the *yogins*. The 10th–11th-century CE Śaiva theoretician Abhinavagupta in *Tantrāloka* 13.129–132 formulates a subdivision of the *yogins* into nine categories, according to the degree of *śaktipāta* experienced by them, viz., violent (*tīvra*), moderate (*madhya*) and gentle (*manda*), each of which are further subdivided into three degrees (e.g., *mandatīvra, madhyatīvra, tīvratīvra*, etc.), yielding a total of nine types of *śaktipāta*.[51] The *yogins* experiencing *tīvratīvraśaktipāta* belong to the highest category. Abhinavagupta, thus, appears to have reformulated the categorisation of the *Yoga Śāstra* in Śaiva terms, substituting *saṃvega* with *śaktipāta*, and polarising the theistic element already present *in nuce* in the Pātañjala account towards a markedly Śaiva direction.

Conclusion

From our survey, it appears that the concept of *saṃvega*, and the emotions evoked by it, played an important and productive role in several non-Brāhmaṇical and Brāhmaṇical schools of thought during a period of more than a thousand years. Although a process of direct filiation is difficult to establish with any certainty, it seems likely that ideas around *saṃvega* first developed in the early Buddhist, or possibly Jaina, milieux, and were then passed on to the Brāhmaṇical circles, specifically the

Pātañjala Yoga system as canonised in the *Yoga Śāstra*, as well as the early Śaiva Saiddhāntika scriptures. In the Brāhmaṇical scriptures, *saṃvega* (or any comparable term/concept standing for it) underwent a progressive shift of emphasis towards a theistic dimension, spanning from its linkage to devotion towards the Lord (*īśvarapraṇidhāna*) in the *Yoga Śāstra* to the Śaiva doctrine of impurity-destroying Lord's grace (*śaktipāta*) descending on the initiand who had experienced a karmic impasse.

What all these systems appear to agree on is the conceptualisation *saṃvega* as a watershed event in human life, i.e., an emotionally charged experience of fear, disgust and/or dispassion, all of which are conducive to the desire for emancipation. This 'paradoxical' side of *saṃvega* perfectly exemplifies the doubleness and the ambivalent nature of emotions in Indic thought: negative and fearsome entanglements to be abandoned when raw and uncontrolled, but means to salvation when 'purified' and occurring in the controlled minds of the *yogin*s.

Notes

1. According to Gnoli (1985 [1956]: xlvi):

   'The general idea underlying these words (compare, in this connection, also the Pāli and Buddhist term *saṃvega*) is that both the mystical and the aesthetic experience imply the cessation of a world — the ordinary, historical world, the *saṃsāra* — and its sudden replacement by a new dimension of reality. In this sense the two are wonder or surprise. A parallel of this idea of a kind of wonder which fills the soul in front of the beautiful or of the sacred, exists in the western thought also'.
2. Namely, 'the shock or wonder that may be felt when the perception of a work of art becomes a serious experience'.
3. Coomaraswamy (1943: 174) reports the meaning of 'trembling' as well.
4. Compare the verbal stem *saṃvij*, rendered as 'to tremble or start with fear, start up, run away'; 'to fall to pieces, burst asunder'; 'to frighten, terrify' (in the causative).
5. Indeed, in the appendix to the Petersburger's dictionary (Böhtlingk and Roth 1990 [1855–75], vol. 7: 1815), *saṃvega* does feature, but is simply glossed with an interrogative mark and a reference to Hemacandra's *Yoga Śāstra* 2.15.
6. Brekke (2002: 63) maintains that the concept of *saṃvega* is akin to the concept of 'cognitive dissonance', formulated by Western psychology.
7. Apparently, unacknowledged by both Brekke (2002) and Giustarini (2012).
8. A discussion of the motif of the 'cremation ground' as a *locus* conducive to experiencing *saṃvega* in post-Aśokan hagiographies may be found in Wilson (1996: 15). Mrozik (2007: 90) notes that shocking statements on the foulness

of female bodies, such as those made in Śāntideva's *Śikṣāsamuccaya* (*c.* 7th century CE), 'were intended to evoke strong feelings of shock, agitation, and fear, known in Sanskrit as *saṃvega*. *Saṃvega* arises when the truth of Buddhist teachings finally hits home and becomes personally relevant. In the context of an ascetic discourse on bodies, it is the moment when a person realizes, perhaps for the first time, the truly unsatisfactory nature of bodied being. Wilson thus aptly characterizes *saṃvega* as an "aha experience" which enables a person to see the world "through the eyes of a renouncer"'.

9. On the 'paradox of fear', i.e., the fundamental doubleness to it in Indian religious thought, Brekke (2002: 75) pertinently observes: 'On the one hand, fear is the natural state of saṃsāric existence . . . Conversely, freedom from fear is an important aspect of complete religious realization. On the other hand, fear is a necessary state of mind in the striving to escape saṃsāric existence and achieve freedom. Fear should be cultivated as the basic motivating factor in the religious life. Thus, fear is both a negative thing from which beings should try to escape through religious exertion and a positive thing without which the very same exertion is impossible'. See also Giustarini (2012: 513). On the similar understanding of fear in the non-dualistic Kashmir Śaivism, see Aleksandra Wenta's essay (Chapter 3, this volume).
10. This is a Buddhist chronicle of Sri Lanka dating back to *c.* 6th century CE.
11. For example, the *Prātimokṣasūtra* (p. 2).
12. These *abhijñā*s are: remembrance of former existences, which puts an end to error relative to the past; consciousness of death and rebirth, which puts an end to error relative to the future; and consciousness of the destruction of the *āsava*s, which puts an end to error relative to the present.
13. According to the text's editor J. Charpentier (1922: 40), this source is a collection of materials differing in age, part of which may date back to the beginning of the Common Era, or even earlier.
14. Jacobi (1973 [1895]: 161n1) adds that another possible translation of *nirveda* would be 'aversion to the Cycle of Births'.
15. Original text as in the edition by Charpentier (1922: 198–99).
16. The other three *guṇa*s are tranquility (*śama*, *upaśama*), devotion (*bhakti*) and compassion (*anukampā*).
17. See, for instance, *Yoga Śāstra* 2.15 (Qvarnström 2002: 182) and *Ādīśvaracaritra* of the *Triṣaṣṭiśalākāpuruṣacaritra* 1.891 (Johnson 1931: 81).
18. 'Equanimity (*śama*) is the non-rising of the worst degree of passions, either by nature or from the sight of the results of passions. It is of *saṃ* called desire of emancipation (*saṃvega*) when there is disgust with the objects of the senses on the part of one meditating on the results of karma and the worthlessness of *saṃsāra*. This thought of the one desiring emancipation, "Dwelling in *saṃsāra* is like a prison; relatives are like bonds", is called disgust with existence (*nirveda*)' (*Ādīśvaracaritra* 608–617, in Johnson 1931: 205).

19. There are, for example, the series of four *brahmavihāras*, viz., *maitrī*, *karuṇā*, *upekṣā*, and *muditā*; the series of *vīrya*, *smṛti* and *samādhi* (these three qualities seem to be attributed by the Buddha to his former Śramaṇa-teachers, and, therefore, might have been developed in a pre-existing Brāhmaṇical milieu); such terms as *sarvajñatā*, *citta*, *dharmamegha*, *kleśa*, *karma*, and *bhūmi*; and the various lists of supernatural powers (*siddhi* or *ṛddhi*). A useful survey of the existing literature on this matter may be found in Sarbacker (2005: 75–110).
20. I wonder whether it is not purely coincidental that the commentator in the *Yogasūtrabhāṣya* does not elaborate on the term, with which he might have been unfamiliar (or which, conversely, might have been perceived by him as too Buddhist-tinted).
21. Hereafter, I will refer to *Yoga Śāstra* as a textual unit comprising the *Yoga Sūtra* along with the *Yogasūtrabhāṣya*. The 'original' denomination of the treatise as *Pātañjala Yoga Śāstra* has become amply clear thanks to the philological work by Maas (2006). I concur with Bronkhorst (1985) and Maas (2006, 2009) that the *Bhāṣya* was written by the same author who brought the *sūtra*s together. Bronkhorst attributes its authorship to Vindhyavāsin (who defines himself as a 'Pātañjala') or to different hands from his same school, whereas Maas attributes it to Patañjali himself.
22. *Upāyapratyayo yogināṃ bhavati*, '[Contentless absorption] caused by [spiritual] means is that to which the yogins attain' (Woods 1914: 46).
23. Bronkhorst's translation is itself influenced by that of Woods (1914: 47–48).
24. *Tīvrasaṃvegānām āsannaḥ.*
25. *Te khalu nava yogino bhavanti mṛdumadhyādhimātropāyāḥ / tad yathā: mṛdūpāyo madhyopāyo 'dhimātropāya iti / tatra mṛdūpāyas trividhaḥ / mṛdusaṃvego madhyasaṃvegas tīvrasaṃvega iti / tathā madhyopāyas tathādhimātropāya iti / tīvrasaṃvegānām āsannaḥ.*
26. *Mṛdumadhyādhimātratvāt tato 'pi viśeṣaḥ.*
27. *Mṛdutīvro madhyatīvro 'adhimātratīvra iti / tato 'pi viśeṣaḥ tadviśeṣād api, mṛdutīvrasaṃvegasyāsannaḥ, tato madhyatīvrasaṃvegasyāsannataraḥ, tasmād adhimātratīvrasaṃvegasyādhimātropāyasyāpy āsannatamaḥ samādhilābhaḥ samādhiphalaṃ ceti.*
28. In commenting upon *sūtra* 1.22, the *Bhāṣya* imposes a further threefold subdivision on the category of *yogins* whose intensity is sharp (*tīvrasaṃvega*) and whose method is vehement (*adhimātropāya*): of mildly sharp intensity, of moderately sharp intensity, and of vehemently sharp intensity. Bronkhorst (1985) regards these *sūtras* as exemplifying the discrepancy between the contents of the *sūtra*s and the interpretation thereof advanced by the author of the *Bhāṣya*, which he detects in several instances of the *Yoga Śāstra*. On the basis of such discrepancies, Bronkhorst (1985: 194) comes to the important conclusion: 'The author of the *Yogabhāṣya* himself collected the *sūtra*s on which he was to write his commentary, perhaps from different quarters,

and that he sometimes gave them an interpretation which suited his purposes, even while knowing the original interpretation of those *sūtras*'. For a discussion of *Yoga Śāstra* 1.21–23 in the light of the Old Javanese *Dharma Pātañjala*, see Acri (2012).

29. *Nanu śraddhādayaś ced yogopāyās tarhi sarveṣām aviśeṣeṇa samādhitatphale syātām / dṛśyate tu kasyacit siddhiḥ kasyacid asiddhiḥ kasyacic cireṇa siddhiḥ kasyacic ciratareṇa kasyacit kṣipram ity ata āha — te khalu nava yogina iti / upāyāḥ śraddhādayo mṛdumadhyādhimātrāḥ prāgbhavīyasaṃskārādṛṣṭavaśād yeṣāṃ te tathoktāḥ / saṃvego vairāgyam.*

30. As argued by Bhattacharya (1979), who holds that *saṃvega* can only be a quality and not a means (*upāya*) — the means being *vairāgya, abhyāsa* and *īśvarapraṇidhāna*, mentioned in *Yoga Sūtra* 1.12 and 1.23.

31. *Ghoreṣu saṃsārāṅgāreṣu pacyamānena mayā jananamaraṇāndhakāre viparivartamānena kathaṃcid āsāditaḥ kleśatimiravināśī yogapradīpas / tasya caite tṛṣṇāyonayo viṣayavāyavaḥ pratipakṣāḥ / sa khalv ahaṃ labdhalokaḥ, katham anayā viṣayamṛgatṛṣṇāyā vañcitas tasyaiva punaḥ pradīptasya saṃsārāgner ātmānam indhanī kuryām iti / svasti vaḥ svapnopamebhyaḥ kṛpaṇajanaprārthanīyebhyo viṣayebhya ity evaṃ niścitamatiḥ samādhiṃ bhāvayet.*

32. *Lvirnya kasiddhyan kaniṣṭha, madhya, mottama, mataṅnyan tǝlu ikaṅ kasiddhyan, apan tǝlu lakṣaṇa saṅ yogi, hana mṛdusambega, hana madhyasambega, hana tībrasambega, mṛdusambega ṅaranya, akǝdik denyāṅabhyāsa yoga, lāvan sādhananya, amaṅguh ta sira kasiddhyan ndān malavas ya kapaṅguh, maṅkana ta saṅ madhyasambega, amaṅguh sira kasiddhyan, ndān ri janmanira sovah ikān pamaṅguh, kunaṅ saṅ tībrasambega, tībra tǝkapnira gave yoga, lāvan pramāṇanya, ya mataṅnyan paṅguh, ikaṅ yogasiddhi i janmanira maṅke.* A discussion of this passage and related Sanskrit sources may be found in Acri (2012).

33. *Athāsya lābhaḥ bhavaty anyo 'pi kaścid upāyo na veti / īśvarapraṇidhānād vā.*

34. On this aspect of the text, see in particular Acri (2013).

35. A view that strikingly echoes the doctrine of equiponderance of *karma* found in the Śaiva Tantras, and that is, therefore, relevant to our discussion of *saṃvega* is found in the *Kitāb Pātañjala*, al-Biruni's Arabic rendering of the *Yoga Sūtra* with a Sanskrit commentary that is probably based on, although not identical with, the *Yogasūtrabhāṣya*, and which is influenced by a mediaeval Indic theistic milieu. The relevant passage of the Arabic text reads: 'Thus if both (i.e. merit and demerit) are not simultaneously annulled detachment does not come about and the cycle (of birth and death) is not cut off. However, the ascetic referred to above has annulled the effects of the two as far as the future is concerned, both of them being annihilated or nearly (annihilated)' (Pines and Gelblum 1989: 269). Here, 'detachment', marked by the translators as a textual problem, might be a translation of *saṃvega*.

36. *Tan ahala tan ahayu pagavenya ñuni riṅ mānuṣa / ya ta mataṅyan pañjanma mānuṣa muvah / luput sakeṅ halahayu pagavenya ñuni riṅ mānuṣa / kapaṅgih*

taṅ kavikun denya / vənaṅ gumavayakən brata bhaṭāra / nda tar vruh ta ya riṅ kayogīśvaran ri kāla niṅ huripnya / pəjah ta ya / maṅjanma ta ya muvah / irika ta yan pamaṅgihakən kayogīśvaran denya.

37. *Kadadi pvekaṅ kasambegan lavan sih puṇya bhakti / kadadi pvekaṅ kabeh denya / ya ta sambandhanya sih bhaṭāra iriya / masih bhaṭāra iriya / katon taṅ janmavāsanā denya / lavan lapa panas tis / pāpa kleśa niṅ maṅdadi / yāvat tinonya liṅnya / i harah atyanta lara niṅ janma karih / sabarinyan pāvak juga hana bhinuktinya / apa ta lari hambana ri dadiṅku harah / mara ta ya ri saṅ paṇḍita / tumakvanakna kaliṅan iṅ dadi / vinarah ta ya de saṅ ṛṣi.*
38. This is how the term translated by Sudarshana Devi, who refers to Hemacandra's *Yoga Śāstra* in support of her translation. The term *saṃvega* (constantly spelled *sambega*) in the sense of either 'desire for emancipation/ religious perturbation', 'violent agitation/excitement' or 'kind disposition' (evidently a case of semantic shift from the original Sanskrit) is attested elsewhere in Old Javanese literature, i.e., in the *Rāmāyaṇa Kakavin* (*c.* 9th century CE), a vernacular poem largely inspired by the Sanskrit *Bhaṭṭikāvya*. *Sarga* 24 presents an allegory between birds and ascetics for satirical purposes (Acri 2011b). In stanzas 24.112, the *kuvoṅ*-bird (probably black coucal, or in any event a bird akin to the cuckoo) is represented as a sham ascetic practicing some kind of Pāśupata observance; a starling warns the other birds that the alleged 'kind disposition' (*sambega*) of the *kuvoṅ* is not to be trusted, and he is accused of using his call inviting to perform asceticism in holes in the ground as a way to conceal his secret intention to kill. Given the presence of puns in almost every stanza of this *Sarga*, it is likely that the meaning of 'desire for emancipation' or 'intensity' (in religious practice) is also implied, as the bird is apparently trying to lure the birds by giving a false impression of holiness. This is a common theme in Sanskrit fables, where sham ascetics often exploit their call to fulfil their profane purposes.
39. *Bhaktiviśeṣād āvarjitas tam abhidhyānamātreṇānugṛhṇāti / tadabhidhyānād api yogina āsannataraḥ samādhilābhaḥ samādhiphalaṃ ceti.*
40. *Hasih sira bhaṭāra ri saṅ yogi . . . / apa dumeh sirāsiha ri saṅ yogi / saṅka ri pamrihnira gave samādhi / satatā riṅ rahine vəṅi / ya mataṅnyan asih bhaṭāra ri saṅ yogi / hinilaṅakənira ta kleśa ri śarīra lāvan lāranira.*
41. *Tataḥ sukhādikaṃ kṛtsnaṃ bhogaṃ bhuṅkte svakarmataḥ / same karmaṇi sañjāte kālāntaravaśāt tataḥ / tīvraśaktinipātena guruṇā dīkṣito yadā / sarvajñaḥ sa śivo yadvat kiñcijjñatvavivarjitaḥ.*
42. The same idea is conveyed by the *Dharma Pātañjala* (p. 286.19–23) in a slightly different language: 'The Lord has affection for the *yogin* . . . The impurities in his body and his suffering will be annihilated by Him. At last, the suffering of the yogin will be made visible, for the maculation obstructs the former powers of the Soul' (*hasih sira bhaṭāra ri saṅ yogi / . . . hinilaṅakənira ta kleśa ri śarīra lāvan lāranira / kābhibyaktā kalāra saṅ yogi vəkasan / apan ikaṅ mala tumutupi śakti niṅ ātmā ṅūni*).

43. Being entirely devoted to the doctrine of *śaktipāta* and *karmasāmya*, Chapter 5 of the *Kiraṇa Tantra* came to represent a sort of *locus classicus* for it. A most concise definition of these two terms is found in verse 5.8cd–9ab (Goodall 1998: 333–35), 'the time of the descent of this [power] is also [that of] the equal balance of [simultaneously maturing] actions. The time is [that of] a balance of past action. [The two blocking actions are] either destroyed or [rendered] unequal' (*tannipātasya saḥ kālaḥ karmaṇāṃ tulyataiva ca // tulyatvaṃ karmaṇaḥ kālaḥ kṣīṇaṃ vā yadi vāsamam//*).
44. *Nipāto bhayado yadvad vastunaḥ sahasā bhavet / tadvacchaktinipāto 'pi prokto bhavabhayapradaḥ // tasmād anyatra yāti eva tathātmā deśikaṃ prati.*
45. *Gurur yathāgrataḥ śiṣyān suptān daṇḍena bodhayet // śivo 'pi mohanidrāyāṃ suptāñ chaktyā prabodhayet / yadā svarūpavijñānaṃ patiteti tadocyate // tasmāc chaktinipātaḥ syān nipātaś cihnavācakaḥ.*
46. *Evaṃ saiva malaparipākayogyatānusāreṇa yadā viśiṣṭaṃ tannivṛttyupāyavijñānaṃ saṃsāravaitṛṣṇyādikrameṇa janayati tadā jyeṣṭhā śaktitvena kāryahetuḥ patitety upacārād ucyate / yad uktaṃ kṛtvā tacchaktisaṃrodhaṃ kriyate bhavaniḥspṛhaḥ / iti srīmanmataṅge 'pi saṃsārāt sa virajyeta pradhvastakaluṣaḥ sadā / iti / śrīmad svāyambhuve 'pi tannipātāt kṣaraty asya malaṃ saṃsārakāraṇam / kṣīṇe tasmin yiyāsā syāt paraṃ niḥśreyasaṃ prati / iti.*
47. The authoritativeness and normativity of the Siddhānta Tantras quoted by Rāmakaṇṭha clearly results from the fact that these very passages are again quoted, in the same order, by Rāmakaṇṭha in his commentary on *Kiraṇa* VP 5.9e–10b; the *Kiraṇa* and *Svāyaṃbhuva* only are quoted again in VP 5.13cd. *Svāyaṃbhuva* VP 1.17cd is quoted by Rāmakaṇṭha in his commentary on the *Mataṅga* (VP 10.25).
48. 'After blocking the power of that [*mala*], [Śiva] makes [the soul] devoid of all the desires of [this-worldly] existence'. Rāmakaṇṭha glosses *bhavaniḥspṛha* as 'devoid of anger, attachment, and other such passions' (*krodharāgādirahitaḥ*; see Goodall 1998: 256).
49. Elsewhere, the *Mataṅga* proclaims that the power of the Lord renders him who has experienced a karmic impasse 'dispassionate towards [all worldly] experience, towards this terrible ocean of worldly existence with its manifold troubles' (*bhogaparāṅmukham / nānāyāsān mahāghorād asmat saṃsārasāgarāt*, VP 13.19bcd; verses 15–19 are quoted and tentatively translated in Goodall 1998: 339n325). Among the meanings of *parāṅmukha* are 'averse from, hostile to, regardless of, shunning, avoiding'.
50. *Svāyambhuva* VP 1.18 adds: 'This soul, having approached a preceptor, having its bonds cut by *dīkṣā*, obtains equality with Śiva; it is without *mala*, without the ailing behind [objects]' (*sa deśikam anuprāpya dīkṣāvicchinnabandhanaḥ / prayāti śivasāyujyaṃ nirmalo 'niranuplavaḥ*) (Filliozat 1994: 29).
51. See, for comparison, the table drafted by Bronkhorst (1985: 191) on the basis of *Yogasūtrabhāṣya* 1.21, where the gradations are *mṛdu, madhya, tīvra* (for *saṃvega*) and *mṛdu, madhya, adhimātra* (for *upāya*).

References

Primary Sources

Abhidharmakośabhāṣya of Vasubandhu:

De la Vallée Poussin, Louis (trans.). 1991. *Abhidharmakośabhāṣyam of Vasubandhu*, vol. 4. Berkeley: Asian Humanities Press.

Ādīśvaracaritra in *Triṣaṣṭiśalākāpuruṣacaritra* of Hemacandra:

Johnson, H. M. (trans.). 1931. *Triṣaṣṭiśalākāpuruṣacaritra or the Lives of Sixty-three Illustrious Persons: Ādīśvaracaritra*, vol. 1. Baroda: Oriental Institute.

Aṅguttara Nikāya:

R. Morris (ed.). 1955. *Aṅguttara Nikāya: Catukka Nipāta*, part 2. London: Published for the Pali Text Society by Luzac.

Buddhacarita of Aśvaghoṣa:

Johnston, E. H. (ed. and trans.). 1935–36. *The Buddhacarita or the Acts of the Buddha.* Calcutta: Baptist Mission Press.

Dharma Pātañjala:

Acri, A. 2011a. *Dharma Pātañjala; A Śaiva Scripture from Ancient Java Studied in the Light of Related Old Javanese and Sanskrit Texts.* Groningen: Egbert Forsten Publishing.

Itivuttaka:

Windisch, E. (ed). 1898. *Iti-Vuttaka.* London: Henry Frowde for Pali Text Society.

Kiraṇāgama:

Goodall, D. (ed. and trans.). 1998. *Bhaṭṭarāmakaṇṭhaviracitā kiraṇavṛttiḥ: Bhaṭṭa Rāmakaṇṭha's Commentary on the Kiraṇatantra*, vol. 1, chapters 1–6. Pondicherry: Institut Français de Pondichéry and École française d'Extrême-Orient.

Mahāvagga:

Oldenberg, H. (ed.). 1879. *Vinaya Piṭakaṁ: The Mahāvagga*, vol. 1. London: Pali Text Society.

Mahāvaṃsa:

Geiger, W. (trans.). 1912. *The Mahāvaṃsa or the Great Chronicle of Ceylon*. London: Henry Frowde.

Mataṅgapārameśvarāgama:

Bhatt, N. R. (ed.). 1977. *Mataṅgapārameśvarāgama (Vidyāpāda) avec le commentaire de Bhaṭṭa Rāmakaṇṭha.* Publications de l'Institut Français d'Indologie 56. Pondicherry: Institut Français d'Indologie.

Prātimokṣa Sūtra:

von Simson, G. (ed.). 1986. *Prātimokṣasūtra der Sarvāstivādins.* Gottingen: Vandenhoek and Ruprecht.

Saṃyutta Nikāya:

Freer, L. (ed.). 1884. *Saṃyutta-Nikāya of the Sutta-Piṭaka*, part 1. London: Henry Frowde for Pali Text Society.

Freer, L. 1890. *Saṃyutta-Nikāya of the Sutta-Piṭaka*, part 3. London: Henry Frowde for Pali Text Society.
——. 1898. *Saṃyutta-Nikāya of the Sutta-Piṭaka*, part 5. London: Henry Frowde for Pali Text Society.
Śiva Sūtra of Vasugupta with Commentary *Śivasūtravimarśinī* of Kṣemarāja:
Chatterji, J. C. (ed.). 1911. *The Shiva Sūtra Vimarshinī; Being the Sūtras of Vasu Gupta with the Commentary Called Vimarshinī by Kṣhemarāja*. Kashmir Series of Texts and Studies (KSTS) 1. Srinagar: Archeological and Research Department.
Svāyambhuvasūtrasaṅgraha:
Filliozat, P.-S. (ed. and trans.). 1994. *Svāyambhuvasūtrasaṅgrahaḥ: Vidyāpādaḥ Sadyojyotiṣkṛtaṭīkāsahitaḥ* (*The Tantra of Svayaṃbhū: Vidyāpāda with the Commentary of Sadyojyoti*). Delhi: Indira Gandhi National Centre for the Arts (IGNCA) and Motilal Banarsidass.
Tantrāloka of Abhinavagupta:
Śāstrī, Mukunda Rāma and Madhusūdana Kaula Śāstrī, (eds). 1918–38. *The Tantrāloka of Abhinava Gupta with Commentary by Rājānaka Jayaratha*, 12 vols. Allahabad: India Press; Bombay: Shri Venkateshvar Press; Srinagar: Research Department, Jammu and Kashmir State.
Tattvavaiśāradī of Vācaspati Miśra:
Āgāśe, Kāśīnātha Śāstrī (ed.). 2004. *Vācaspatimiśraviracitaṭīkāsaṃvalitavyāsabhāṣyasametāni Pātañjalayogasūtrāṇi* (*The Yogasūtras of Patañjali Accompanied by the Bhāṣya of Vyāsa and the Tattvavaiśāradī, Commentary of Vācaspati Miśra*). Pune: Ānandāśramamudraṇālaya.
Uttarajjhāyā or *Uttarādhyayana Sūtra*:
Charpentier, J. (ed.). 1922. *The Uttarādhyayanasūtra, Being the First Mūlasūtra of the Śvetāmbara Jains*. Uppsala: Appelbergs Boktr.
Jacobi, H. (trans.). 1973 [1895]. *Jaina Sūtras: The Uttarādhyayana Sūtra, the Sūtrakritāṅga Sūtra*, part 2. New Delhi: Motilal Banarsidass.
Viśuddhimāgga of Buddhaghoṣa:
Rhys Davids, C. A. F. (ed.). 1920. *The Visuddhimagga of Buddhaghosa*, part 1. London: Pali Text Society.
Vṛhaspatitattva:
Sudarshana Devi (ed. and trans.). 1957. *Wṛhaspati-tattwa: An Old Javanese Philosophical Text*. Nagpur: International Academy of Indian Culture.
Yoga Śāstra of Hemacandra:
Qvarnström, Olle (ed.). 2002. *The Yogaśāstra of Hemacandra: A Twelfth Century Handbook on Śvetāmbara Jainism*. Cambridge, MA: Harvard University Press.
Yoga Śāstra or *Yoga Sūtra* and *Yogasūtrabhāṣya* of Patañjali:
Āgāśe, Kāśīnātha Śāstrī (ed.). 1904. *Pātañjalayogadarśaṇa, with the Vyāsa-Bhāṣya of Vyāsa, the Tattva-Vaiśāradī of Vācaspati Miśra, and the Rāja-Mārtaṇḍa of Bhoja Rāja*. Poona: Ānandāśrama.

Woods, J. H. (trans.). 1914. *The Yoga-system of Patañjali*. Cambridge, MA: Harvard University Press.

Secondary Works

Acri, A. 2011b. 'More on Birds, Ascetics, and Kings in Central Java: Kakawin *Rāmāyaṇa*, 24.111–115 and 25.19–22', in A. Acri, H. Creese and A. Griffiths (eds), *From Laṅkā Eastwards: The Rāmāyaṇa in the Literature and Visual Arts of Indonesia*, pp. 53–91. Leiden: KITLV Press.

——. 2012. '*Yogasūtra* 1.10, 1.21–23, and 2.9 in the Light of the Indo-Javanese *Dharma Pātañjala*', *Journal of Indian Philosophy*, 40(3): 259–76.

——. 2013. 'Modern Hindu Intellectuals and Ancient Texts: Reforming Śaiva Yoga in Bali', *Bijdragen tot de Taal-, Land- en Volkenkunde*, 169: 68–103.

Apte, V. S. 1956. *The Practical Sanskrit-English Dictionary*. Poona: Prasad Prakashan. Rev. enl. edn.

Bhattacharya, R. S. 1979. 'What is the Means Other than the Īśvara-Praṇidhāna', in J. P. Sinha (ed.), *Ludwik Sternbach Felicitation Volume*, part 1, pp. 485–89. Lucknow: Akhila Bharatiya Sanskrit Parishad.

Böhtlingk, O. and R. Roth. 1990 [1855–75]. *Sanskrit-Wörterbuch*, 7 vols. St. Petersburg. Delhi: Motilal Banarsidass.

Brekke, T. 2002. *Religious Motivation and the Origins of Buddhism: A Social-psychological Exploration of the Origins of a World Religion*. London and New York: Routledge Curzon.

Bronkhorst, J. 1985. 'Patañjali and the Yoga Sūtras', *Studien zur Indologie und Iranistik*, 10: 191–212.

Coomaraswamy, A. 1943. 'Saṃvega, "Aesthetic Shock"', *Harvard Journal of Asiatic Studies*, 7(3): 174–79.

Giustarini, G. 2012. 'The Role of Fear (*Bhaya*) in the *Nikāyas* and in the *Abhidhamma*', *Journal of Indian Philosophy*, 40: 511–31.

Gnoli, R. 1985 [1956]. *The Aesthetic Experience According to Abhinavagupta*. Varanasi: Chowkhamba Sanskrit Series Office. 3rd edn.

Maas, P. A. 2006. *Samādhipāda; Das erste Kapitel des Pātañjalayogaśāstra zum ersten Mal kritisch ediert / The First Chapter of the Pātañjalayogaśāstra for the First Time Critically Edited*. Aachen: Shaker Verlag.

——. 2009. 'The So-called Yoga of Suppression in the *Pātañjala Yogaśāstra*', in E. Franco (ed., in collaboration with D. Eigner), *Yogic Perception, Meditation, and Altered States of Consciousness*, pp. 263–82. Vienna: Verlag der Österreichischen Akademie der Wissenschaften.

Monier-Williams, M. 1899. *Sanskrit-English Dictionary*. Oxford: Clarendon Press.

Mrozik, S. 2007. *Virtuous Bodies: The Physical Dimensions of Morality in Buddhist Ethics*. Oxford: Oxford University Press.

Pines, S. and T. Gelblum. 1966. 'Al-Bīrūnī's Arabic Version of Patañjali's Yogasūtra: A Translation of His First Chapter and a Comparison with Related Sanskrit Texts', *Bulletin of the School of Oriental and African Studies*, 29: 302–25.

Pines, S. and T. Gelblum. 1989. 'Al-Bīrūnī's Arabic Version of Patañjali's Yogasūtra: A Translation of the Fourth Chapter and a Comparison with Related Sanskrit Texts', *Bulletin of the School of Oriental and African Studies*, 52: 265–305.
Sarbacker, S. R. 2005. *Samādhi: The Numinous and Cessative in Indo-Tibetan Yoga*. Albany, NY: State University of New York Press.
Williams, R. 1991 [1963]. *Jaina Yoga: A Survey of the Mediaeval Śrāvakācāras*. Delhi: Motilal Banarsidass.
Wilson, L. 1996. *Charming Cadavers: Horrific Figurations of the Feminine in Indian Buddhist Hagiographic Literature*. Chicago: University of Chicago Press.

PART IV

Aesthetics

8

Moha Kāla

Aporias of Emotion in Indian Reflective Traditions

D. Venkat Rao

The Singular–Plural Path

There are at least two interwoven paths to explore the ends of emotions in Indian (Sanskrit) reflective traditions. These paths can be configured as *śāstra-* and *kāvya-mārgas*. Ālaṃkārikas (poet–thinkers) like Ānandavardhana, Rājaśekhara and Abhinavagupta among others, configure the ends of the emotions on these critical circuits. These paths, however, despite their seeming parallelism, cannot be conflated with the deeply sedimented hierarchic division between poetry (art) and philosophy (truth) that is ingrained in European thought from Plato to contemporary times.[1] It is such a division and opposition of art and philosophy that undermines and subordinates emotions, and privileges and valorises the discourse of truth. Such a hierarchy is alien to Sanskrit reflective traditions of thought. Consequently, reflections on emotions will have a different orientation among these traditions. This essay is an attempt to explore the double binds of emotions in the Indian reflective traditions.

The Greeks viewed emotions to be feminine and dangerous. As it is well known, Plato banished poets because they were believed to stir emotions. Aristotle endorsed emotions, but only in a moderated form; he recommended emotional therapy (by means of art, i.e., tragedy) by first stirring up and then purging them away. Stoics thought that emotions must be eradicated as irrational forces. Christianity drawing on Stoics framed emotions as repressible 'bad thoughts' (Origen) or reprehensible temptations or sins (Sorabji 2000: 5–13). Curiously, the entire debate on emotions in the Western heritage appears to be caught in the division between the two poles of rationality and irrationality. The Indian position seems significantly different from this heritage. You cannot choose to escape emotions, for you, as a living being, are the effect of emotions. Nor can you simply celebrate them, for they will abandon you to the repetitive cycle of existence. You need to learn to live with them, with a cultivated distance from them, as a mere carrier of the effects of emotions.

Given that the question of emotions in the West is anchored in the relationship between the discourse of art and truth, it is worthwhile sketching the way in which the double path of *śāstra* and *kāvya* is conceived and the modes in which their filiation with emotions gets articulated in the Indian thought. In his inquiry into the *Kāvyamīmāṃsā*, Rājaśekhara devotes a short section to what he calls *śāstranirdeśa* (*Indications of Scripture*). In a delicate but profound account, Rājaśekhara identifies two prominent modes in which the *vāṅmaya* (the pervasive utterance) has proliferated namely, *śāstra* and *kāvya*. While sketching the relation between *śāstra* and *kāvya*, this section goes on to describe most economically the modes of composing *śāstra* and the styles of their *saṃvāda*s (dialogues). Since without the knowledge of *śāstra* one cannot acquire any knowledge of *kāvya*, one has to cultivate *śāstra* intimately first, Rājaśekhara proclaims:

> *śāstra pūrvakatvāt kāvyānāṃ, pūrvaṃ śāstreṣvabhiniviśeta/*[2]
>
> As *kāvya*s precede *śāstra*s, one must first attend to the *śāstra*s (*Kāvyamīmāṃsā* 2, in Sreeramachandrudu 2003: 4).

Rājaśekhara's reflective configuration of the *vāṅmaya* disallows rigorous differences between *śāstra* and *kāvya*. Although he maintains definable differences between these two domains, the peculiar placement of *kāvya* or *sāhitya-vidyā* ('learning about literary composition') in the internally differentiated domain of *śāstra* he clearly denies any rigid separation of these two modes of reflection. Let us look at what he does in this regard, a little closely. First, he divides the *vāṅmaya* into *śāstra* and *kāvya* and, then, *śāstra* into an-agentive (*pauruṣeya*) and agentive compositions. Among the an-agentive compositions, he places the four Vedas along with their six *aṅgas* (he mentions the five Upavedas as well). Here, Rājaśekhara proposes that, given its work of elucidating the meaning of the Veda (the task of *śāstra*), *alaṃkāra-śāstra* occupies the place of the seventh *aṅga* among the *śāstras*. If these 10 domains form the an-agentive field of *śāstra*, another set of four (Purāṇa, Ānvīkṣiki, Mīmāṃsā, and Smṛtikalpa) are reckoned as agentive *śāstras*. Here again, Rājaśekhara denies any oppositional relationship between *śāstra* and *kāvya*. For he places *kāvya* in the cumulative list of an-agentive *and* agentive *śāstras* (along with their internal ramifications: 18 Purāṇas, 18 Smṛtis). If the combined domains run into 14 fields, *kāvya* is designated as the 15th (*pañcadaśaṃ kāvyaṃ vidyāsthānam*) and as the pivot of all these 14 domains of learning (Sreeramachandrudu 2003: 9). Therefore, it moves with/after all the *śāstras* (ibid.: 10).

Perhaps, in order to incorporate other crucial domains among the list of *śāstras*, Rājaśekhara designates yet another set of fields as domains of learning (*vidyās*). He includes two from the earlier list but brings in two new ones. Thus, we get Ānvīkṣiki (which is further expanded into six logical–disputational modes), *trayī* (the three Vedas), *varta* (trade, business, cultivation), and *daṇḍanīti* (punitive strategies). In this new set, he positions the literary composition in the fifth place: *pañcamī sāhityavidyā*. If *śāstra* consists of learnable sets — an-agentive and agentive — then *vidyā* is configured as the faculty that enables the discernment of *dharma* and *adharma*. In other words, *kāvya*, too, occupies the position that *śāstra* is accorded in the *vāṅmaya*. Thus, though differentiable, *śāstra* and *kāvya* are intimately affiliated. They mutually sustain each other. The *śāstra* trait can brighten *kāvya* and the *kāvya* trait can supplement the texture of the verbal flavour of *śāstra* (ibid.: 45).

As can be noted from the foregoing discussion, Rājaśekhara neither unifies *kāvya* with *śāstra* nor conflates even *alaṃkāra-śāstra* with either an-agentive or agentive *śāstras*. He accords distinctive places to *kāvya* and *kāvyaśāstra* in the *vāṅmaya*. Although Rājaśekhara's account does not gain any undisputed universal or normative status, his conception of distinctions between *śāstra* and *kāvya* finds currency in the Sanskrit literary inquiries. While no one denies the critical constitutive role of the internally differentiated *śāstra* in conceiving *kāvya*, or formulating *kāvya-śāstra*, none of them surrenders or reduces either *sāhitya-vidyā* or *sāhitya-śāstra* to an existing type of *śāstra*. Rājaśekhara sees the mode or impulse of *kāvya* as an integral force of *śāstra* which can be composed and elicited by a deeper exposure to the *śāstra* domains (domains never segregated from each other). Rājaśekhara goes on to elaborate the sources for composing *kāvya* (*kāvya-yonis*) comprehensively. Yet, a true and distinguished poet for him is the one who emerges from none of these existing *yonis*: her/his coming is unprecedented. In other words, the irresistible generative impulse (that which is the distinct force of *kāvya*) bursts forth from the already available generated elements, forms and substances. But the impulse erupts in such a way that it remains unique and unforeseen. Therefore, although the *kāvya* impulse can be seen among an-agentive compositions, the latter cannot be confused with the *kāvya* composition; the latter comes forth outside the womb but draws its elements from multiple wombs. Same is the case with *sāhityaśāstra*. It draws on the twin domains of *śāstra*, but comes forth as a distinct reflective–creative form. Hence the unique position for these two modes: *kāvya/śāstra* in the *vāṅmaya*, Rājaśekhara affirms.

For Rājaśekhara, the most distinguishing feature of *sāhitya-vidyā* is the ability to compose 'sound' and 'sense' in a mutually conducive and effective form. It is not mere learning and practice alone that, though necessary, can provide such ability. What is essential for *kāvya* is the articulated force:

> *sā (śakti) kevalaṃ kāvye hetuḥ/*
>
> That articulated force (*śakti*) alone is the source of *kāvya* (*Kāvyamīmāṃsā* 4, in Sreeramachandrudu 2003: 30–31).

Rājaśekhara goes on to add that the acts of focused attention and learning, all that must be learnt, can only help the blossoming of the articulated force (ibid.: 30–31). It is such an un-derivable and incalculable force that sets the poet apart from the 'masters of sound and sense', i.e., grammarians and logicians, Rājaśekhara contends. He asks: Why are these masters of *śāstra* not able to compose poetry? Their enormous learning brightens their utterance-pervaded sense of sight (*vāṅmaya-netra*); but only the one who can bring forth a novel or unprecedented entity into existence in his utterance excels among great poets; only his utterances will be pure and venerable, says Rājaśekhara (ibid.: 212). Rājaśekhara's conception of the articulated force (*śakti*) that brings forth the 'unprecedented' can be said to have a more general validity that cannot be confined to the domain of literary composition. That which can bring forth the 'unprecedented' is the (almost) irresistible and inescapable generative impulse; it is precisely this force that has not only released the immeasurable generic diversity of the *vāṅmaya*, but has also ceaselessly proliferated divergent *genos/jāti*s of Indian cultural formations over millennia. No one has had or will have the capability to measure the effects of this generative articulated force. No one, says Rājaśekhara, even if he lives for a thousand years will be able to fathom the ends of the spaces of learning (ibid.: 9). Every generic form he refers to can be composed uniquely by *śāstra* and *kāvya* composers and, therefore, they are countless:

> *kṛtibhiḥ svatantratayā praṇītā itya saṅkhyeyā anākhyeyāśca* / (*Kāvyamīmāṃsā* 2, ibid. 2003: 13).
>
> *Śāstra* compositions are done in singular independent forms. Therefore, these are countless and impossible to recount.

Rājaśekhara goes on to say that the sense or orientation of the learned ones toward various compositions will be multi-faceted and infinite (*ity-ananto 'bhi yuktānāmatra saṃrambha vistaraḥ*, *Kāvyamīmāṃsā* 2.6, ibid: 14). It cannot be elaborately recounted; the sensible-learned men (*bhāvaka/paṇḍita*) should discern it (ibid.).

Similarly, the *Śukranītisāra* declares the infinite cross-hatching and proliferation of *jāti*s on the one hand, and the genres of *vidyā*s and *kalā*s on the other. Neither of these can be counted exhaustively:

> Infinite *genos* result and it is impossible to tell them.
>
> Subjects of learning and gestural forms (arts) are endless, and it is impossible to count them (*Śukranītisāra* 4.3.11, 23, in Singaracharyulu 2002: 284, 286).[3]

In other words, the text points out that through corruption or miscegenation *jāti*s come forth endlessly (infinitely), and no one can recount or name them. Recitations and gestural handiworks are infinite, and counting or reckoning them is impossible. The generative impulse that disseminates genres and *genos* defies any form of totalisation. Although Rājaśekhara and the *Śukranītisāra* are surely aware of the proliferation of *jāti*s and genres — we must point out in passing that they largely confine themselves to the Sanskrit *vāṅmaya* in their accounts — Rājaśekhara displays with certainty his competence in different languages. They both acknowledge the 64 *kalā*s associated with divergent *jāti*s.

Performative Response

The *vāṅmaya* differentiates itself internally and proliferates in multiple genres across heterogeneous *jāti*s, and this disallows any normative hierarchy. We come across yet another significant aspect of the *vāṅmaya* which differentiates it radically from the European heritage. This aspect is deeply related to the question of reception of the emotions and results from the very same reflective–creative impulse that disallows any rigorous *śāstra–kāvya* hierarchy. As this *vāṅmaya* does not designate or accord a distinctive space of privilege to any discourse called philosophy (considered entirely unique to the European heritage), it does not erect any celebrated space for the discourse of the so-called literary critic too (a creation of German Romantic thought). It may seem totally counter-intuitive to contend that a tradition with such highly developed abstract thought and rigorous *saṃvāda* traditions over millennia, on the one hand, and the robust and lively literary inquiries over a millennium, on the other, should eschew space for philosophy and literary criticism. The absence of such meta-discursive spaces, however, is in order within a heritage that articulates the relationship between *śāstra* and *kāvya* in such non-hierarchical and interanimating modes. Let us turn to the literary inquiry of Rājaśekhara once again to gather reflections on this matter.

Taking into account their innate articulated force combined with extensive learning, Rājaśekhara differentiates between three kinds of poets: *śāstra-kavi*, *kāvya-kavi* and *ubhaya-kavi*:

(*a*) The *śāstra-kavi* is the learned–reflective poet who composes *śāstra*s in poetic form: *yacchāstrakaviḥ kāvye rasasampadaṃ vicchinatti* ('the *śāstra-kavi* beautifies the wealth of flavours in the *kāvya*', *Kāvyamīmāṃsā* 5, in Sreeramachandrudu 2003: 44).

(*b*) The *kāvya-kavi* is the creative–innovative poet who composes unprecedented reflective expressions. The *kāvya-kavi* dissolves the rebarbative mode of *śāstra* with his articulated force.

(*c*) The *ubhaya-kavi* is the one who excels in both the forms of *vāṅmaya*, that of *śāstra* and *kāvya*.

Rājaśekhara goes on further to classify the *śāstra-kavi*s into three and the *kāvya-kavi*s into eight different types and cites examples of their modes of composition. Cultivated in the enumerative–reflective tradition — a tradition that endeavours to reflect and articulate across the range of sub-particulate elemental entities to the most gigantic individuated phenomena — Rājaśekhara excels in attending to the minutiae of difference. Without getting drawn into these differentiae, one can point to the permeable relation between the poet and *śāstrakāra*. If the *śāstra-kavi* can clarify the encrypted, elucidate the ambiguous, elaborate the condensed, and condense the elaborate, the poet, too, can excel in such creative–reflective compositions, for the latter has mastery in the composition of 'sound' and 'sense' in unforeseen modes. In other words, *kāvya* and *śāstra* can be similar but significantly different — the articulated force permeates them and sets them apart. Therefore, it is not that *śāstra* can have a meta-position with regard to *kāvya* and turn the latter into its object for explication. If at all the literary inquiries[4] reiterated anything, time and again, it is this: *kāvya-tattva* — the essence of *kāvya* — is not the province of the existing ancillaries of Vedic learning (Vedāṅgas and Ānvīkṣiki).

The profound enigma or secrecy of the literary composition, says Rājaśekhara, can be discerned only by the learned ones and serve only the competent person. The only exceptional stratagem for gaining the essence of the literary composition is, after learning all that needs to be learnt, to achieve the most singular concentration of the 'mind' (*manas*) (Sreeramachandrudu 2003: 30). What kind of learned and competent person can discern such an enigma? To answer this question, Rājaśekhara classifies the generative gift of the articulated force into two different kinds in the same way he distinguishes between *kāvya* and *śāstra*. As noted earlier, these 'kinds' or 'types' are not impermeable asymptotes or chiasmic antinomies as such. Rājaśekhara specifies these as *kārayitrī* and *bhāvayitrī* forces. Although these are typically further refined and differentiated, let us focus for now on these generic rubrics. *Kārayitrī* is the generative impulse that induces the poet to compose poetry. Such an impulse or force is a transgenerational gift or endowment, but this endowment can be enhanced through learning or through rituals. Yet, all these cultivations of the sources of heritage must be achieved only in the temporal finite existence in the world (ibid.: 33–34).

If *kārayitrī* impels the poet to compose *kāvya*, *bhāvayitrī* is the force that enables the *bhāvaka* to respond. As Rājaśekhara says, the great tree called the poet's work will bear fruit only when the *bhāvaka* exists, otherwise such a tree will be devoid of flowers and fruits. The organic trope here makes the *bhāvaka*'s function internal to the poetic work. Rājaśekhara provides two opposed views about the status of the *bhāvaka*. One received position contends that any poet can reflect and respond, and anyone who can reflectively conceive can be a poet. Then, what is the difference between the poet and the reflective being or the forces of *kārayitrī* and *bhāvayitrī*? Those teachers who wish to differentiate between them do not consider the *bhāvaka*-poet as occupying a lowly reputation:

> *bhāvakastu kaviḥ prāyo na bhajatyadhamāṃ daśām/* (*Kāvyamīmāṃsā* 4.11, Sreeramachandrudu 2003: 36).
>
> The poet who is a *bhāvaka* does not generally receive an inferior position.

Kālidāsa, for instance, differentiates between these two articulated forces on the basis of the forms that they emerge in and the matter they deal with. Therefore, as Kālidāsa opines (*iti Kālidāsaḥ*), reflective responsiveness is different from poetry (ibid.: 36). Thus, one may be competent, points out Rājaśekhara in support of Kālidāsa's view, only in composing poetry; and another one only in listening to and commending it. It is possible that both competencies could reside in the same person. Yet, these two virtues need not be conflated and unified. Is not the stone that yields gold different from the touchstone that can be used to test gold? Just as *śāstra* and *kāvya* are not identical so too are the articulated forces of *kavi* and *bhāvaka* (*Kāvyamīmāṃsā* 4.12, ibid.: 36–37).

Yet, there appears to be neither hierarchy nor opposition between these generative forces. They are interanimating faculties. Rājaśekhara gives the example of a poet who is ashamed to read his poetry, for he laments that he does not find a *bhāvaka* who is himself a poet and is capable of grasping the virtues and lapses of poetry. The one who inquires deeply into the essence of poetry can be rarely found in a thousand. Rājaśekhara points out that such an inquirer (*tattvābhiniveśin*) is the one who reflects effectively on the sonic verbal textures, who delights in listening to pithy wise counsels, who savours the dense elixir and flavours of poetry, who searches for and grasps the sealed core of the poem, and who discerns the labour of composing poetry. Very few poets with the fruits of intractable virtuous acts alone are lucky to get such a reflective and responsive person. Others are agonised over failing to get such a *bhāvaka*. Such a reflective and responsive figure is everything for the poet — master, friend, minister, pupil, and teacher. Anthologies of poetry may abound in every house, but those that remain engraved on the mental plaques of *bhāvaka*s can only be either two or three, says Rājaśekhara (ibid.: 38–39).

Cordial Receptions

In Rājaśekhara's account, *bhāvaka* is perhaps another term for *sahṛdaya*. Despite such singularly critical space that *bhāvaka/sahṛdaya* occupies in the literary inquiries of Rājaśekhara and others, interestingly, we do not get to learn any specific discourse that is peculiar to *bhāvaka* in these inquiries. In other words, nowhere does Rājaśekhara and other literary inquiries describe, analyse or specify any systematic articulation of the discourse or response of the *bhāvaka*. On the contrary, the *bhāvaka*'s response appears to be essentially non-verbal in the main:

> *satkāvyevikriyāḥ kāścidbhāvakasyollasantitāḥ/*
> *sarvābhinayanirṇītau dṛṣṭā nāṭyasṛjā na yāḥ//* (*Kāvyamīmāṃsā* 4.18, in Sreeramachandrudu 2003: 39–40).
>
> Even the creator of *Nāṭyaśāstra* who specified various kinds of enacted gestures could not imagine the kinds of mental dis-figurations that a *bhāvaka* goes through while listening to a good work.

Some *bhāvaka*s express their response in (onomatopoeic) exclamations, such as 'Oh!' or 'Aah!'; others carry their responsive reflections silently in their hearts; still others react through spontaneous physical or bodily response (*sāttvikabhāva*) — such as sweating, shaking, trembling, trepidation, shudder, palpitation, etc., what Seneca calls 'first movements' — and gestures of the limbs (Sorabji 2000: 5–6, 75–92). Yet others through embodied enactments generate their reflective response (Sreeramachandrudu 2003: 40).[5] It must be clear from Rājaśekhara's account that the *bhāvaka* is not someone with any systematised verbal discourse that one can find in a literary critic. He is the articulate experiencer of the poetic effect and his modes of articulations are essentially embodied, enacted and performative ones. The *bhāvaka* is not a hermeneutically programmed wordsmith appropriating the work of a lithic meta-position. In other words, behind the figure of the literary critic (of the West) there is the whole of Christian hermeneutics (Sznondi 1995).

*Bhāvaka*s may differ in their approach on the basis of their own ability or endowment. Some look only for the virtues in a *kāvya*, others for the failures. But *bhāvaka*s do not appear to be discursive figures; they are more like singer–poets and dancers, performative in their responsiveness. One can, perhaps, argue that one must look for such verbalised response in unrecorded instantial or spontaneous reaction in the very context after the poetic performance.[6] One can, perhaps, see such a possibility in the scenes of *kāvya-parīkṣā* ('test of poetry') that Rājaśekhara refers to. But in the *kavi-samāja* ('the poet's contest') that Rājaśekhara details, there is no distinct figure called *bhāvaka* or *sahṛdaya*. This separate category is redundant, as the poets and the learned *śāstra-kavi*s all can be *bhāvaka*s. The space contains Sanskrit poets, learned of all the Vedas and *aṅga*s, *dārśanika*s, *paurāṇika*s, *paṇḍita*s of *smṛti*s, doctors, astrologers, dancers, actors, singers, and a whole range of others (well versed in the 64 *kalā*s). All the *kāvya* and *śāstra* tests Rājaśekhara refers to are not conducted by any separate category of people called *bhāvaka*s or *sahṛdaya*s (Sreeramachandrudu 2003: 152). Therefore, one could, perhaps, argue that the non-discoursing *bhāvaka-sahṛdaya* is either a praxial or a potential poet himself. In other words, the performative response of the *bhāvaka* can, in all likelihood, manifest more in his/her poetic compositions. That is, a *sahṛdaya-bhāvaka* would, almost instinctively, enact and perform his response in the *kavi-samāja*, on the one hand, and silently weave his verbal response in a new composition, on the other. We have no direct access to the *sahṛdaya-bhāvaka*'s response in *kavi-samāja,* but it is possible to track the responsive and endearing reception of earlier poets by later poets in the tradition. This mode of responsive reception can be seen in most of the *bhāṣā* literary traditions of the second millennium CE. Thus, for instance, Nannaya, the celebrated Telugu poet of the 11th century CE, in his *Teluguizing* of the *Mahābhārata* (Subramaniam 2000–07), not only receives Vyāsa into Telugu (and thus inaugurates a continuous Telugu literary tradition) but also offers a sustained and insightful commentary in a poetic form on the former. Such a responsive reception is possible only in the case of a *sahṛdaya-bhāvaka*. Such a mode of responsiveness can be seen in the entire *vāṅmaya*; the Sanskrit *vāṅmaya* (along with its cross-hatching double track of *śāstra-kāvya*), it can be contended, renewed itself in its dissemination precisely through such responsive reception across millennia. It must, however, be mentioned that the nomenclature *sahṛdaya-bhāvaka* is a peculiar formulation not only in the case of literary inquiries, but it could also be at work even in the case of the dissimilar twin — the domain of *śāstra* too. Every new *śāstric* genre — *mantra, sūtra, śloka, kārikā, vṛtti, vyākhyāna*, and other such forms — is the decisive consequence of a cultivated responsiveness to what one receives or is endowed with.

The Chiasmic Body

Now that we have been able to configure the relationship between the two interrelated paths of the Sanskrit *vāṅmaya* which form the media of emotions and identify the mode of responsive reception that fecundates and disperses the *vāṅmaya*, we should attend to the epistemic status of emotions in these interanimating orbits. Just in order to retain the comparative line that we sketched earlier, we may point out that in the hierarchically divided European intellectual history emotions became casualties of the reigning logos. In contrast to the cognitively effective and rational logos, emotions are considered to be devoid of knowledge and patently the pulls of the irrational and wildly unpredictable forces. By Plato's time, emotions were bracketed with the orgiastic Dionysiac passions and were regarded as imminent threats to aristocratic logos, logos being already sanctified from the mnemocultural nuthos. Plato was profoundly aware of the emotional affect of music and, therefore, insisted on the strict regulation of music: he condemned the Dionysiac musical performative cultures as 'theatrocracy' and repulsed them in his *Laws* (1952: 675–76; Weber 2004: 33–39). Deeply bifurcated from the rational discourse of philosophy, the emotions were pushed into the matrix of the arts or literature. Almost 2,000 years later, Nietzsche rebelled against this violent hierarchy, reversed this Platonism and celebrated art against truth — the discourse of logos (see Nietzsche 2003; Heidegger 1991: 142–50, 216).

In the absence of such a divided hierarchy in the Sanskrit *vāṅmaya*, Nietzsche (or Heidegger) would have become useless. Significantly, newer modes of reflection and being could come forth without any explicit declarations of rupture or subversion; the integral mode of responsive reception runs together with continuities and innovative transfigurations without avowed ruptures (or 'revolutions'). This could perhaps be due to the absolutely irreducible context that served as the ground for the articulation of the entire praxial learning of the Sanskrit *vāṅmaya*. This *vāṅmaya* comes forth and spreads across as an immeasurable mnemocultural formation.

Mnemocultures are cultures of cultivated memory. What is central to these formations is that they articulate their memories through embodied and enacted modes, through performative modes of speech (song) and gesture. They evince a kind of cultivated indifference toward lithic (inscriptional) representations and prosthetic repositories to disseminate and replenish their mnemocultural heritages. As it is well known, the lithic and pictorial (plastic and visual) turns occurred in the Sanskrit reflective traditions rather belatedly — nearly two millennia after the spread of mnemocultural formations — in the post-Aśokan era. Pāṇini had no use for a script or stylus (though these scribal surrogates of memory were already available in his context). All that must be learnt and articulated must remain praxial and performative in mnemocultures. Moreover, and more crucially, the Sanskrit *vāṅmaya* not only cultivated vibrant performative media but preoccupied itself actively with the most primordial and absolutely irreducible material medium called the 'body' or the 'body complex' in articulating the ends of being. Sanskrit mnemocultural learning is fundamentally a learning *of* the body complex; it is indifferent to surrogate material substitutes — but it remains inconceivable outside the experiential body complex. All learning is *about* the body as a precisely graded, discrete but related senses and the beyond of the senses; all learning about this subtle relation of the sensible complex and the non-sensible or untouchable other or *para*, therefore, belongs to and takes place in the spatio-temporal complex (*kṣetra*) of the body. *Śāstra-vāṅmaya* is essentially a relentless praxial inquiry into that untouchable *para* that inhabits the body like a guest, a silent witness in the finite abode of the senses which plays the host; it is an inquiry into the relation between *śarīra* and *para* — indeed, a *śārīraka-mīṃāṃsā*. The central concern of this inquiry focuses precisely on praxial–affective complex and orients it. The most singular praxial end of this inquiry is to discern a mode of being that releases it (the being) from the deeply determining binds and bonds of living within the finite instance of embodied existence. Life, in other words, is decisively caught in the aporia of praxial–affective motifs in existence, for they are these material emotive–cognitive faculties that rivet the body that they bring forth in the double binds. The double path of the Sanskrit *vāṅmaya* worked through these binds in multiple ways and disseminated genres and *genos* across millennia. Let us explore the aporia of the body complex a little more.

Double Binds of the Apparatus

The *śāstra-vāṅmaya* broadly separates the senses into two sets — interior and exterior. The exterior set consists of a cluster of five perceptual faculties and another cluster of five actional faculties. These clusters of exterior sets, in their turn, yield distinct effects for each of the elements of the clusters. The exterior set, with its perceptible and actional clusters, operates mainly or only in the specific moments of temporal present. They respond to a vanishing or given present — with their ephemeral effects. In contrast to the evanescing exterior set is the interior set, which consists of a subtly graded cluster of three (or five) faculties. Unlike the exterior cluster, the interior one receives and relays temporal effects across intractable pasts and indeterminable futures.

All the discrete elements in different clusters and across clusters are graded in accord with their subtlety, and the latter implies the passageway across the material physical gross forms to the un-formable, untouchable and non-configurable force of *para* within the embodied existence of life. Another commonality that cuts across these two sets is that all the elements, irrespective of their location and effect, are little more than a transfigurement of three absolutely fundamental clinamen of elements. Those drifting elements with neither origin nor end, neither in themselves substantial nor subtle, yield to interminable origination and dissolution of forms ranging from the subtlest to the grossest. Nothing can master or control these elements and their clinamenal drift terminally.

The vicissitudinal elemental set is also a quality-effecting vector in the formation of the bodies in the world. Amplified expression of a specific quality transfigures the orientation of a particular body. Thus, when all the three elements are in an equipoise and in serenity of stasis, nothing can come forth. But once a disturbance or distortion of the elements occurs, then begins the emergence of entities: crisis generates creativity. Why does such a disturbance occur at all? When an equally powerful force — a force without a beginning or an end, without any attributes of creative elements, and as unreachable and untouchable as the force that contains the potentially clinamenal elements — when such inarticulable forces cross and commingle as in a cosmic erotic act, radically heterogeneous entities, body complexes shoot up and proliferate. The disturbance itself can be noted as the effect of the exemplification of the impulsive–actional element (*rajas*). Alternatively, the very same force, without form or substance, internally divides itself in a playful mood and releases the palpable sets and clusters of the body complexes.

> It is said that when the drifting quality-elements are in poise there is silence of stasis (*laya*) but distortion among them engenders creation (*Vāyu Mahāpurāṇa* 5.9, in Chandrasekharasarma 2003: 30–31).

The first born of such a cosmic upheaval is the graded but non-substantial and subtle 'interior set of faculties'. The first interior (and exterior) faculties — called the 'heightened one', 'lofty' or *mahat* — emerge when the quiet-calm element (*sattva*) receives emphasis and from this faculty comes forth ipseity that seeks attention toward itself; this ipse factor is the effect of the amplification of the impulsive–actional element. Impacted by ipseity in varying gradations, two critical faculties, viz., discerning (*buddhi*) and desiring-determining (*manas*), emerge in the interior set. Similarly, through the operation of the quality-effecting elements (with the impulsive–actional) the 'external set', too, emerges, and prior to that comes forth (with the amplification of the lethargic–dark *tamas* element) the set of massive entities called the *bhūtas* (sky, air, water, fire, and the earth). The exterior and interior sets, with their precisely differentiated clusters, however, do not stand as some rigidly barricaded faculties. The perceptual set reaches into and the actional set receives from the interior cluster essentially through the dynamic desiring–determining faculty (*manas*). The *manas* receives the vanishing currents of perceptual set and filters them through the discerning faculty — which, in turn, filters what it received further to the higher and subtler faculties, until the verge of the untouchable forces. The *manas* is not simply a transparent medium vehiculating the messages from the perceptual cluster. It is a lively, anamnestic and meditative faculty; as such, it carries on intimations for intractable duration from immemorial resources. As such, it is also affected by the transgenerational pulls of desire (*vāsanā*). Impelled to recall durationally and exposed to the onslaught of ephemeral, instantial perceptions, the *manas* is pulled and pushed by the undecidable and indeterminable intimations. The *manas* pulses to determine its orientation and offers itself to the discerning faculty, on the one hand, and induces the actional set to plunge into activity, on the other. The body complex is the decisive medium and effect of the relentless churning of the variegated elements, faculties and temporalities. The emotions induce and intensify this churning.

The entire machinery of the senses, with its intractable relays and qualities across unfathomable duration, composes and puts to work the body complex. But, as pointed out earlier, the ephemeral and instantial body comes forth along with an alterity — *para*, which inhabits it by remaining outside the range of the machinery. An excess (or even lack — for *para* is an-agentive, 'passive' and unsubstantial) inheres the work of the apparatus which the latter cannot grasp, let alone generate. But gathering from across intractable duration, immeasurable formations and discontinuous relays, this apparatus shelters in each finite being a set of antinomous cognitive–conative motifs. The antinomy in the set is the effect of the amplification of the serene–quiescent element (*sattva*) or the dark–indolent element (*tamas*). To be sure, the actual set consists of only four affective–cognitive motifs and their distortion results in the opposite set. These emotive-edifying motifs are: (*a*) morality (*dharma*), (*b*) knowledge (*jñāna*); (*c*) non-attachment (*vairāgya*), and (*d*) lordship (*aiśvarya*). Perversion of these very motifs will result in: (*a*) wickedness (*adharma*), (*b*) nescience (*ajñāna*), (*c*) 'terminable indulgence' or cycle of birth and death (*saṃsāra*), and (*d*) absence of power (*anaiśvarya*). The apparatus of the senses with its subtle and delicate modulations inherits and generates the body complex.[7]

Now, the desiring and determining faculty of the *manas* and the discerning faculty of the *buddhi* through their appropriate filtering mechanisms can become gratificatory sources for *para*, for the yearning and discerning faculties continuously refine what they receive from the apparatus of the senses and transmit the intimations of the sensuous to the gratificatory verge of the unreachable and the untouchable. Yet, by realising and discerning the irreducible distance and difference between *para* and the gratificatory apparatus, this faculty can also make the releasement of the inhering witness guest from the cloying binds and bonds of the apparatus, even as it inhabits the body. Without such a releasement, the *śarīra*-apparatus would reduce the alterity to the apparatus and succumb to the amplification of the dark indulgences of the indolent element. The ineluctable consequence of such deleterious indulgence and ignorance is that the sensory apparatus condemns itself to a machinic reproduction of the body complexes which disavows the discernible any chance of releasement in each embodied existence; such a disavowal embraces the perverted cognitive–conative motifs and engulfs one in relentless sorrow:

> Wherever there is indulgent longing there is sorrow (*Bṛhadāraṇyaka Upaniṣad* 1.4, in Ramakotishastri 1989: 93).

The transgenerational elements of the apparatus and the interior faculties that track and relay them across immemorial but discontinuous duration render *mohakāla* — the temporality of longing — indeterminable; yet, we can only sense *moha* in the articulations of the apparatus in its very specific temporal manifestations in the embodied existences.

Mohakāla is temporal and timeless; it throbs with the generative impulse which brings forth the machinic and the unprogrammable (chance of releasement) in the singularity of the body complex. Given the heterogeneity of relays and articulations of the apparatus, and the intricate articulations and modulations of the faculties, no sovereign ipse can master and regulate the work of the apparatus. The chance of existence cannot guarantee its effects in advance. The affective–cognitive pulls and pushes that occupy the apparatus can swerve the being in unpredictable drifts.

The *śāstra-vāṅmaya* intimates us of the heterogeneous articulations of the generative–affective apparatus. Brought forth as the effect of such an apparatus, but serving as its ineluctable medium, everybody is exposed to the play of the chiasmic antinomies. What one does with such vicissitudinal endowment in one's existence is forever open to determination — a determination, however, with no guarantees. Configuring such an aporetic weave of existence, the *śāstra-vāṅmaya* is more inclined to induce a praxial response rather than to erect a demonstrable theoretical edifice. Aporias, perhaps, require path-breaking action rather than a logical resolution to the double binds of existence. If the 'indulgent longing' or 'passion' binds one in phenomenal creations, the cultivation of 'non-attachment' sustains meditative concentration. Such an attention without objectal world releases one from longing and passion. All this must be quiescently experienced in praxial existence (*Sāṃkhya Sūtra* 2.9, 3.30, in Agrawal 2001: 167, 178). Any amount of discursive reckoning of these aporetic intimations will remain asymptotic to the praxial response that the *vāṅmaya* invites from its addressees.[8] The *vāṅmaya* at one moment radically declares itself to be a suspendable apparatus from within.

Muṇḍaka Upaniṣad 1.4, 1.5 (Sreeramachandrudu 1984: 187–88) includes the entire Vedic *vāṅmaya* and differentiates and distances it from the praxial learning of *para*. Experiential discernment of the radical 'alien inside', the bonding and binding apparatus of passions is analogous to the learning *of* the other (*paravidyā*), beyond the indulgent rigmarole of ceremonies, rituals and recitations (*aparavidyā*). In such an intimation, the *śāstra-vāṅmaya* itself performs and puts to work the double bind of existence: *It is a medium that intimates a learning but suspends itself in experiencing it.* The medium takes one to the verge where even that medium itself must be suspended while putting it to work.

Paths of the Literary Inquiries

If the *śāstra-vāṅmaya* invites us to learn to live in the double bind of existence, then the *kāvya-vāṅmaya* induces precisely the varied experiential flavours of living in the chiasmatic antimonies of existence. *Śāstra* intimates the learning in the labyrinth, and *kāvya* induces the taste of the affective–conative and cognitive relays of the apparatus that binds and bonds every being. Although the entire *vāṅmaya* is deeply concerned with the fundamental question of being in the world — about the irreducible material and physical entity, and the temporal and timeless pulls and pushes of living that buffet it transgenerationally — the *kāvya-vāṅmaya* instantiates very specific finite beings, their response to the challenge and their chance of living in the world. Thus, *kāvya* can instantiate any life or learning from across any domain and any period. There is nothing in the world, declares Bharata (*Nāṭyaśāstra* 1.116, in Rao n.d.: 15) while composing his response to what all he had received, that the embodied and performative articulations of dance cannot show:

na taj jñānaṃ na tac chilpaṃ na sā vidyā na sā kala/
nāsau yogo na tat karma nāṭye 'smin yan na dṛśyate//

No knowledge, craft, wisdom, art, yoga, ritual-act exists which cannot be shown in the dance-drama/theatre.

Bhāmaha adopts Bharata's view and accords *kāvya* the same capacious responsive ability.[9] Literary inquiries across centuries have received and responded actively to Bharata's own responsive compositions. Thus, Bharata configures the performative of dance as drawing on the resources of the Vedas: verbal imports from the *Ṛgveda*, gestural idiom from the *Yajurveda*, musical notes from the *Sāmaveda*, and the delighting flavour from the *Atharvaveda*. Therefore, he calls his unprecedented composition 'the fifth Veda'; the performative form of dance is, indeed, the composition of a delighting enacting medium that receives from the entire heritage.[10] But unlike the *śāstra-vāṅmaya*, this practical and reflective composition (*Nāṭyaśāstra*) focuses on the contrary pulls of sorrows and delights of the worldly existence, and composes the enactments of dance through the embodied gestures of the limbs. A strikingly singular feature of Sanskrit reflective traditions is that sustained and well-developed praxial and insightful thoughts on performative, musical, image, and verbal creations have emerged from *within* these specific domains. Drawing on the *śāstra-vāṅmaya*, one of the inaugural compositions on the plastic visual forms, the *Citra Sūtra*, begins with the most fundamental aporetic question:

> How can one give form to *para* which is said to be devoid of form, smell, taste, and who is said to lack sound and touch? (*Viṣṇudharmottara Purāṇa*, 44.1, in Seetaramanjaneyulu 1988: 153).

As in the case of the *kāvya-vāṅmaya*, here too the path of individuated conceptions and formations of the apparatus — a sort of simulacra of embodied existence — are seen as passageways to the praxial reach of the untouchable other. The apperceptional icon (*mūrti*) is seen only as a facilitating medium for groping toward the unreachable proximity of inhering alterity. In other words, the material, physical body complex is the only inescapable medium for sensing the imperceptible. Similarly, the *saṃgīta-śāstra* comes forth through the entire apparatus of the interior and exterior faculties, the indestructible set of elements, and their relays and formations. For Śārṅgadeva, it is the intimations of the inhering *para* in the body complex that fire the perceptual apparatus to generate music (Lath 1995; Sharma 1995). Such reflective compositions are woven largely by the practitioners of these creative forms or by those who are intimately involved in these traditions. In other words, each of the visual, verbal, musical and performative domains has sustained a vigorous praxial reflective tradition of its own. These compositions cannot be treated as domain-specific critical works — works that offer analyses of any specific empirical creation.

'Critical appreciation' of empirical works is alien to the Sanskrit *vāṅmaya*. The *vāṅmaya* induces a mode of praxial reflection or 'action knowledge' which can be put to work, i.e., practised in any specific contexture of life. Here, it must be emphasised that what the *vāṅmaya* offers is not any monological normative code of practice as such, but a mode of being that is reflexively praxial in its interminable improvisation of the modes of being in the world. Such a praxial reflexive generative mode has no use for the figure of the philosopher, who is accorded a position of privilege in the heritage of the West, as he can offer theoretical explanations about the objects of the world. The philosopher figure occupies a meta-position with regard to the objects and claims mastery over them. As pointed out earlier, praxial learning and philosophical theorisation are heterogeneous in their orientation. Aesthetic theory and critical commentaries on specific works in verbal and visual domains remain the bi-products of philosophical theorisation in the West (de Man 1986: 3–26).[12] Given that the praxial learning has no use for meta-positions — for such a learning must be put to work in each singular endowed existence — we cannot label the domain-specific reflective practical compositions of *nāṭya*, *sārasvata*, *saṃgīta*, and *śilpa* as philosophical–aesthetic discourses. Each domain drew on the common śāstric heritage in its singular way and brought forth a distinct *śāstra* as a medium and effect of praxial learning. The compositions of *nāṭya*, *śilpa*, *alaṃkāra*, and *saṃgīta* are all deeply concerned with the worldly existence where the sensory apparatus exposes every being to the upheavals of life. Thus, Bharata (*Nāṭyaśāstra* 1.114, in Rao n.d.: 15) intimates, without ambiguity, that *nāṭya* is aimed at reaching out to all kinds of distraught hearts:

> *duḥkhārtānāṃ śramārtānāṃ śokārtānāṃ tapasvinām/*
> *viśrāntijananaṃ kāle nāṭyam etad bhaviṣyati//*
>
> For all those who are in distress, exhausted, sorrowful, and pitiable, dance will generate restfulness in them.

Disseminative Detours

As is well-known the *śāstra-vāṅmaya* of *śruti*, *smṛti* and the *darśana*s severely delimit the set of its implied addressees. Even if some of them have consequences for the other demarcated set (*śūdra*s, for instance), the sound/letter of the (Veda) *śāstra* is addressed only to the specific set of the twice-born (*dvijā*). Yet, through an extraordinary detour, the *vāṅmaya* disperses itself across an immeasurable range of *genos* over millennia. The living on of the *vāṅmaya* is deeply dependent on this disseminative detour. The generative impulse of the *vāṅmaya* breached the detour with unprecedented genres and reached out to the unforeseen — beyond the boundaries of the twice-born. This decisive breach paves the detour with massive mnemocultures of *itihāsa*, *purāṇa*, *saṃgīta*, and *kāvya*, on the one hand, and the performative, visual and plastic domains, on the other. The detour transfigures the heritage of praxial learning by re-articulating it with worldly instantiations of singular lived experiences buffeted by the binds and bonds of life. The epic compositions, the *Rāmāyaṇa* and the *Mahābhārata*, for instance, annotate and reiterate such reflective praxial modes of being in the world. But across all these transfigurations and proliferations, the critical affirmation of praxial learning — the essential import of the *vāṅmaya* — is unmistakably palpable.

Thus Bharata (*Nāṭyaśāstra* 1.113, in Rao n.d.: 15) announces his new composition to be for all:

> *etad raseṣu bhāveṣu sarvakarmakriyāsvatha/*
> *sarvopadeśajananaṃ nāṭyaṃ loke bhaviṣyati//*

> Composed of motifs and flavours of all certified acts, the composition will be a source of learning for all.

It should be noted, however, that while dispersing the heritage of the *vāṅmaya*, Bharata subtly but definitively improvises and transfigures the imports of the *vāṅmaya*. He infuses a significantly novel notion of flavour (*rasa*) in the conception of cognitive–affective motifs of the *śāstra-vāṅmaya*, discussed earlier (although he claims to receive it from the *Atharvaveda*, his way of putting to work of this notion of flavour — *rasa* — remains unprecedented). With this seminal experiential figure, Bharata does not just inaugurate his new reflective praxial composition, but opens up radical generative possibilities across unforeseen domains. It is this very figure of jouissance — delighting *rasa*— that animated literary inquiries of the Sanskrit *vāṅmaya* over a millennium. His being enriched by varied motifs deriving from diverse moments of stress and strain and following the episodes of the worldly existence is the reason why he has composed *nāṭya*, says Bharata (*Nāṭyaśāstra* 1.112, in Rao n.d.: 15). It is through a peculiar and complex commingling of the worldly events and responses they elicit, that *nāṭya* evokes the experiential flavour called *rasa*. Precisely because it is something to be tasted, the experience induced or evoked by means of the bodily enacted worldly experiences and feelings — the resulting effect is termed *rasa* — that which appeals to the faculty of taste. With this gastronomical (and medicinal) trope of *rasa*, Bharata has not only conserved the imports of the *śāstra-vāṅmaya* but extended them in order to impregnate the conceptions of unprecedented reflective–creative forms.

Following Rājaśekhara, we can broadly define these forms as literary learning (*sāhitya-vidyā*) and supplementary learning (*upa-vidyā*). The latter are specifically counted as the 64 arts. The supplementary status of these arts, however, does not suggest any inferiority of these arts. In fact, for Rājaśekhara, these arts are the life-sustaining sources for the literary learning (*Kāvyamīmāṃsā*, in Sreeramachandrudu 2003: 13–14). This is eloquently borne out by the fact that what Bharata conceives in the context of a patently supplementary performative mode (*nāṭya*) becomes the seminal source for sustaining the literary inquiries across centuries. It may appear completely counter-intuitive to claim that the experience of this gastronomical effect is a counter-aesthetic (in the literal Greek sense) experience. The *rasa* experience cannot be equated with the feelings generated by the perceptual–cognitive–conative–actional apparatus of the senses; it is not identical to the taste of a juice as such. The apparatus carries only what the senses channel; it delimits the range and reach of the cognitive–conative even when they are transgenerational and timeless in their relays. Now, Bharata does not deal with these very machinic worldly occurrences of embodied existence directly; he presupposes them. But in the presupposition and reception of what preceded him, Bharata focuses entirely on one specific node of the antinomous cognitive–conative set of motifs. Given the concentrated attention that the literary learning and the arts pay to individuated being's existence in the worldly binds, Bharata preoccupies himself with the node of the *rāga* motif — that of the 'affect' or 'passion'. But in his responsive reception of this motif, Bharata minutely individuates significantly different divisions and shades of the *rāga* motif and specifies distinct modes and means of inducing them imaginatively. In other words, what the *śāstra-vāṅmaya* condenses into a singular motif, the *kāvya-kalā-vāṅmaya* elaborates and improvises extensively. Thus, Bharata differentiates 49 cognitive–conative motifs and divides them into three different groups. The first set consists of eight stable patterned cognitive conations (*sthāyibhāvas*); the second one has a set of eight passive–responsive affects (*sāttvikabhāvas*); and the third is composed of 33 volatile or shifting emotive feelings (*sañcāri/vyabhicāribhāvas*). Given that the indolent and dark (*tamas*) element has a determining effect on the antinomous motifs, they need awakening and activation. The *kāvya-kalā-vāṅmaya* with the faculty of imagination[12] (*ūha*) induces palpable conditions by three distinct means of gesture, speech and somatic modes of enactment. These conditions activate the motifs in different degrees.

The work of the *kāvya-kalā* aims at evoking any of the stable structures of feeling with the performative resources of the body. But given the fact that the stable set of motifs referred to here is not the one that is literally experienced in the worldly living of the sensory apparatus, the imaginative faculty brings forth a simulacral, virtual motif that can be most experientially savoured. *Rasa* is an effect of such an imaginative invocation of affective–cognitive motif that one is exposed to in the worldly existence. Therefore, *rasa* will always be an unverifiable, immeasurable and irreducible experiential flavour. It cannot be conflated or reduced to the motifs of worldly learning, though the latter are precisely what get invoked by the generative lever of the imagination. As the virtual offers the *jouissance* of the real, without the verifiable or objectifiable real and evidentiary appurtenances, the experience of the virtual is often confused with the worldly physical experience. What needs notice here is not the imaginative sleight of hand that can conjure up an experience but the actuality of an embodied experience that does not derive from the empirical being (actor, character, the audience), invoked by the chiasmic antinomies of the apparatus.

The Literary Alterity

Bharata's extraordinary (de)tour de force has generated vigorous responses over millennia. He specifies and names (probably inherited ones) the three sets of structural motifs and feelings that were actively received and transfigured in the later millennia, i.e., from the early first millennium CE till the end of second millennium CE.[13] Praxial reflections across the *kāvya-kalā* traditions enhanced the flavours, designated them for all the 49 motifs and some went on to declare the infinity of flavours. A significant portion of these responsive reflections concentrated on the etiology of the experience of flavour. Can *rasa* be reduced to the characters — the singular individual beings caught in the double binds of existence in the remote past? Or, given their remoteness to the moment of the *kāvya-kalā* composition of their experience, can it be located in the actors on a stage? Or, given the ultimate likely destinations of these *kāvya-kalā* transfigurements of life can *rasa* be found in the experience of the audience or the listener (*bhāvaka*)? Despite apparent difference in responses, all the literary–reflective figures (largely from Kashmir) receive and put to work the resources of the heritage transfigured by Bharata. The debate, indeed, re-invigorates the *kāvya-kalā-vāṅmaya*'s relation to the *śāstra-vāṅmaya*, for none involved ever deviated from the basic praxial–reflective conceptions of the body complex and its chance and predicament in the antinomous apparatus of existence. None undermined the experiential savouring of the taste and its radical asymptotic relation with the empirically definable psychobiographical and evidentially verifiable instantial being caught in the churn of existence.

Given the critical significance of experience or taste (experiencing of either gustatory or erotic flavours) what experience does to the receiver or the experiencing being is an important question. But as discussed earlier, it must be noted that the ultimate addressee, the experiencing receiver of the poetic or theatrical composition, is not empirically determined. Consequently, we do not see any specific discourse of the *sāmājika* or *sahṛdaya* with regard to any specific work, unless — and this is of critical significance here — the implied addressee is also the poet or playwright, i.e., the implied addressee of the *kāvya* or *kalā* is a poet himself, whether the poet is empirically identified or not. The *sahṛdaya* is the real or potential poet. Therefore, the only mode in which the *bhāvaka-sahṛdaya*'s response can be formed is *kāvya-nāṭaka* form itself. Consequently, as argued earlier, an autonomous discourse or response of *sahṛdaya* in a discursive form becomes redundant in the reflective traditions here.[14] Experience here has only praxial consequences — either the mode of being is transformed and/or it can transform the modes of performative compositions. Unlike in the *śāstra-vāṅmaya*, almost all the practitioners in the *kāvya-mārga* (path of poetic utterance) explicitly analogise *kāvya* with the body or body complex. Although the focus of attention of the *śāstrakāra*s remains the enigmatic body complex, they do not reckon their own compositions in terms of heteronomously constituted body. The *kāvya-vāṅmaya* (especially in the literary inquiries) receives precisely this conception of the body and names *kāvya* as a body with the apparatus of cognitive-perceptual-actional limbs inhabited by an unverifiable, untouchable alterity. Therefore, any attempts to reduce the *kāvya*-body to its perceptual set of limbs or mere 'sound' and 'sense' of the words or forms are strongly contested. Although these limbs are of critical necessity for a *śarīra* or body to exist, *kāvya*'s distinction (from other reflective-praxial compositions) can only be sensed as a non-sensible secret that lurks outside but *within* the sensorium of the apparatus. As the *śarīra* comes forth with its *para*, so does *kāvya* with its *ātman* — a *that-its-own-in-me* — which cannot be grasped only by the discrete limbs of the body (*Dhvanyāloka* 1.2, in Sreeramachandrudu 1998: 56, 533). For Ānandavardhana, this inhering alterity of *kāvya* is *dhvani* (resonance): *kāvyasyātmā dhvaniriti budhairyaḥ* ('the learned ones enounce that *dhvani* is *kāvya*'s *ātman*') (*Dhvanyāloka,* 1.1, ibid.: 10). According to Abhinavagupta's commentary on *Dhvanyāloka* 1.1, *rasadhvani* is the *ātman* of *kāvya*, which can only be tasted by the un-fragmented faculty of discernment (Sreeramachandrudu 1998: 28).

The imports of the *śāstra-vāṅmaya* are ubiquitous in the conception of *kāvya* by Ānandavardhana and Abhinavagupta. Ānandavardhana's concentrated critique of the skeptics of *dhvani*'s essential distinction and space terms them as *abhāvavādin*s. In Abhinavagupta's commentary, these skeptics are clearly named as the Buddhists, Jainas and Cārvākas — precisely those who denied any epistemic status to *ātman* in the Indian reflective traditions. Thus, Ānandavardhana and Abhinavagupta can be said to have actively participated in the extended contestations of the *śāstra-vāṅmaya* — but now in a transfigured domain of the literary inquiries of the *kāvya-mārga*.

Aporetic Longings

The generative impulse of the Sanskrit *vāṅmaya* expresses itself in the inextricably braided double strand of the *śāstra-* and *kāvya-vāṅmaya*, but their modes of approaching the inhering alterity are distinct and distinguished. The *śāstra* strand propounds the constitutive relation between transgenerational cognitive–conative apparatus and the formation of the body complex; this strand regards the work of the 'interior set' — especially the discerning faculty — to filter the contrapuntal or chiasmic communications from the double binds of existence and enables the embodied being to see the absolute distinction between the apperceptual apparatus and the alien guest (*para*). Such a task would involve a cultivated turning away of concentrated attention from the desiring–determining faculties, vicissitudinal pulls and volitional pushes for ephemeral gratifications of the ipse, for the gratificatory motifs will forever bind and bond the body to the machinic gyrations of existence. Only an unattached involvement in the apparatus can provide a chance of experiencing the delight that results from sensing the non-sensible, the untouchable alien in the host of the body — intimates the *śāstra*. Whereas in the literary inquiries *rasa* can be seen as an experiential flavour, there is no consensus on which of the *rasa*s can be seen as the ultimate in endowing the delight. Or, in other words, the literary inquiries pluralise the paths of experiencing the non-derivable and unattached delight. Perhaps the most explicit parallel to the *śāstra* path of experience in the *kāvya-mārga* emerges in the *kāvya-kalā* inquiries of Ānandavardhana and Abhinavagupta. Even here, it must be pointed out that there is a significant difference in the approaches of these two inquiries. For Ānandavardhana, the *rasa* experience is a virtual enjoyment of a simulacrally generated, reflective creations of worldly living, i.e., the *kāvya-kalā* experience cannot be reduced to or derived directly from the vagaries of ephemeral existence in the world. On the other hand, for Abhinavagupta, the delighting experience can be evoked from both the worldly life and the virtual world of *kāvya-kalā*s.

In other words, both the affective–cognitive motifs of the *rāga* node of existence and the structures of reflective feelings evoked by means of enacted lives entail identifiable delight; moreover, they can also be causally related. Abhinavagupta contends that it is the real-life experience of sorrow in witnessing the death of one of the Krauñca birds that Vālmīki's compassionate verse emerged. Some modern commentators consider this argument as untenable, for they claim that it lacks the support of the tradition and treats Abhinavagupta as a stubborn argumentator (Sreeramachandrudu 1998: 128).[15] But given Abhinavagupta's grounding in the *śāstra-* and *kāvya-vāṅmaya*, it is difficult to reduce his position to such confusion. Nowhere in the *Locana* does Abhinavagupta claim that everyday experiences *as they are* evoke the non-phenomenal experiential flavours as such. He only mentions that the daily events may provoke the stable affective–cognitive motifs. But from this he does not directly or causally draw the conclusion that either the daily events or the effects they provoke *as such* yield the *rasa* experience. On the contrary, confirming the relationship between *śāstra* and *kāvya* learnings, he supplements the stable motifs with a critical inflection. He claims that the non-phenomenal delighting experience can be possible even in the case of the stable cognitive–conative motifs provided one achieves *bhāva-śānta* — serene quiescence with regard to the invasive motifs of passion. He further claims that such cultivated calming can also yield delighting experience. Here, he seems to draw his intimations directly from Yoga. He contends that disarticulating or unbinding oneself from the indulgent actions would yield calmness. Without such a persistent cultivation, he argues citing a *kāvya*, the body as the abode of passions would destroy itself:

> The body is the ground for the *rāga* (passion) and I don't believe that this does not erase or destroy itself (Abhinavagupta's commentary on *Dhvanyāloka* 3.26, in Sreeramachandrudu 1998: 720–21).[16]

Both Ānandavardhana and Abhinavagupta echo Śaṅkara, who, drawing on the *śruti*, sees the seed of sorrow inhering in desire: *tṛṣṇā ca duḥkha bījam* (*Chāndogya Upaniṣad* 7.23.1, in Veereswarasarma 2002: 247). Abhinavagupta's recourse to the *Yoga Sūtra* 3.10[17] in his commentary on *Dhvanyāloka* 3.101 (Sreeramachandrudu 1998: 723–24) appears more directly when he addresses a trickier question in the context of literary inquiry: If the state of delighting experience of serene calmness was to be accessed only after overcoming or detaching oneself from worldly binds and bonds, can such a state ever be articulated at all? (Sreeramachandrudu 1998: 727) Here, citing the *Yoga Sūtra* 3.10, Abhinavagupta's answer is both a No and a Yes! He explains that those who have been able to turn away from the tangle of worldly motifs are able to attain the state of serenity, but such a final stage, like the comparable orgasmic consummational stage, is indescribable (*śṛṅgārāderapi phalabhūmau avarṇanīyataiva*);[18] it can only be savoured in experience (ibid.). But even among such accomplished figures who have experienced such a state — such as king Janaka — may not be able to maintain themselves in such a state permanently. The lapses and gaps of such a state in a serene figure too are amenable for expression, contends Abhinavagupta. These lapses could be sensed in the declarations of the ipse, such as 'I am this', 'this is mine', 'I am . . .'. For Abhinavagupta, the supreme experiential flavour of serenity is like the profound state of equanimity and stasis before the crisis of phenomenal emergence. In other words, 'before' the reiterated beginning, there is serene equanimity (of the elements). From such a state emerge the clinamen of transgenerational motifs — but once they are exhausted they return to the state of serenity. Abhinavagupta, while commenting on *Dhvanyāloka* 3.26, gains this insight from Bharata himself:

> *svaṃ svaṃ nimittamāsādya śāntādbhāvaḥ pravartate//*
> *punarnimittāpāye tu śānta eva pralīyate//* (ibid.: 725–26).[19]

> Every motif during its function emerges from serenity; once the function reaches its end the motif submerges back into the serene stasis.

Serenity, Abhinavagupta asserts, results from the liquidation of the indulgent motifs. The end of passion or emotions is, in the ultimate reckoning, the dissolution or disarticulation of all emotions and cognitions in the delighting 'emotion' which is a non-emotion only to be experientially savoured. There appears to be only a breath of difference between the two experiences of emotion and non-emotion but that breath appears to make infinite difference between the two. This is the terminus, which is the state before the beginning, where the double strands of the *vāṅmaya* co-articulate. The convergence of the *śāstra* and *kāvya-kalā* strands is clearly articulated by both Ānandavardhana and Abhinavagupta. More than Ānandavardhana it is Abhinavagupta who, while commenting on *Dhvanyāloka* 3.25, offers an extended articulation of *śāstra-kāvya* strands in configuring the ultimate flavour of experience:

> The non-emotional flavour of calm-serenity is the fruit of the ultimate releasement and as it is related to the ends of man it is supreme among the flavours (ibid.: 730–31).[20]

In contrast, most of Āṇandavardhana's discussion of the flavour of serenity until the last chapter of the *Dhvanyāloka* pertains to the appropriateness of combining different flavours in a *kāvya* (ibid.: 698–742). As in the case of the body, the various limbs of the poetic body too must contribute collectively to generating a singular entity; in such an entity all the disparate flavours must flow together to intensify the ultimate flavour from the confluence. Such an ultimate flavour for Ānandavardhana remains the *śānta* (calm-serenity) *rasa*. *Śānta* results from the *tṛṣṇā kṣaya sukha* — the delight resulting from the depletion of desire (*Dhvanyāloka* 3.25, ibid.: 723). In Ānandavardhana's reckoning, Vyāsa reaches the pinnacle of his poetic achievement in the *Mahābhārata* when he evokes, after the decimation of Pāṇḍava and Yādava/Vṛśṇi clans, the ultimate emotion of *nirveda* — quiescence of *manas* (the desiring–determining impulse) beyond pain and pleasure:

> Wishing to elevate the world totally drowned in overwhelming passion (*moha*), [Ānandavardhana says,] Vyāsa offered the most luminous and translucent light of learning (*Dhvanyāloka* 4.136, ibid.: 961).[21]

But several times Vyāsa himself observed, says Ānandavardhana:

> As this worldly system grows sterile, the worldly affairs or the entirety of worldly matter becomes aberrant, one shows terminal indifference toward the worldly existence: there is little doubt in this matter (*Dhvanyāloka* 4.137, ibid.: 961–62).[22]

The *Mahābhārata* evokes such an ultimately terminal indifference, observes Ānandavardhana. If such a *vairāgya* (the motif of indifference) paves way for the releasement as the ultimate end of man, the flavour of *śānta*, too, is the most appropriate corresponding (non-conative) flavour that *kāvya* can evoke, argues Ānandavardhana. These two ultimate non-worldly relations to the worldly existence are experienced as non-ipsocratic savouring of embodied existence in the world. The *śāstra* and *kāvya* strands weave the *Mahābhārata* exquisitely and succeed in evoking the experience of the inarticulable. Ānandavardhana instantiates both the great compositions — the *Rāmāyaṇa* and the *Mahābhārata* — as exemplifications of the *kāvya-mārga*.[23]

Breaching Paths

The *kāvya-vāṅmaya* composes its path by orienting all the distinct part-flavours to flow into and intensify a specific flavour among them in the entire composition. Thus, for Ānandavardhana, the *Rāmāyaṇa* sustains and consummates the experiential flavour of compassion, and the *Mahābhārata* with all its unbearable devastations nurtures and intensifies the experiential flavour of calm-serenity. These two flavours, however, are not necessarily the only ones to be privileged as the sources of ultimate experience. Other contenders are the erotic, wonderment and the devotional. In other words, any experiential flavour (any *aṅga* or limb of the poetic body), in principle, can be the source of consummate experience (*aṅgī* or the total effect) for the entirety of the *kāvya-śarīra*. Ānandavardhana parallels the interanimating *kāvya-* and *śāstra-mārgas*. If the serenity of sense, gained by the nurturing of uninvolved involvement, non-indulgent participation in the binds and bonds of existence, is the destinal experience of *kāvya*, it is a responsible reception of what the *śāstra-mārga* offers as the ultimate experience of releasement from the indulgences of the worldly existence. In other words, the ends of man are perennially and intensely entangled with the pulls and pushes of the intransigent forces with which the cognitive–conative apparatus composes the body complexes. If the *śāstra-mārga* cultivates releasement in order to experience the inarticulable (the alien inside and outside), the *kāvya-mārga* communicates that the praxial mode of tending the depletion of desire or waning of *mohakāla* can release the experience of delight.

The *śāstra* and *kāvya* have shared ends, but their praxial *mārgas* are different (Sreeramachandrudu 1998: 970–72). Nowhere does any *kāvya-kalā* inquiry imply the secondarity or redundancy of its *mārga*. On the contrary, the distinctions are actively practised. The *śāstra-mārga* yearns for the ultimate end of man – the terminal releasement in existence, whereas the *kāvya-mārga* invokes a non-sensible sense of experiencing a flavour. For Abhinavagupta, commenting on *Dhvanyāloka* 1.18 (Sreeramachandrudu 1998: 247) this savouring of delighting flavour itself, as it is internally experienced by singular beings (but without necessarily being personal), is a kind of cognition (*jñāna-viśeṣa*). This would be a kind of cognition, however, that is heterogeneous to the perceptual–cognitive faculties of the exterior or interior set that make the apparatus (ibid.: 257). In other words, each of these paths fundamentally plays out only through the medium and effect of the body complex — the ultimate aporetic abode of the affective apparatus and the untouchable *para*. The double path needs to be explored praxially and reflexively; no amount of talking about the path can approximate the experience of walking the path.

Given the constitutive significance of the reasonable passions in the formation of the body complex, the double strand of *vāṅmaya* can neither erase nor ignore their durational work in the instance of existence. They must always be negotiated with and praxially tapered off (*kṣaya*) in the embodied lives. The *vāṅmaya* — especially the *kāvya-kalā* strand — configures such a sense from the deepest involvement with the worldly existence, with all sorts of inextricable filiations with objects, relations, yearnings, and haunting. As no political or ethical system can match the force of the transgenerational *rāga*, none can guarantee any certitudes of defense against it. All claims to such systems themselves will become the secure abodes of passions. This does not, however, imply that instantial existence is at the mercy of uncontrollable irrational forces (the Stoic premise). What the praxial–reflective mode of the *vāṅmaya* in its conception of the body complex as a medium and effect of contrary forces — machinic and unprogrammable, sensible and untouchable — intimates is the aporia of existence as an endowment (gift *and* curse) and a chance at once. The task at hand, then, is putting to work these contrapuntal or chiasmatic forces in the instant of living — without guarantees. Any coercive programmatic way out of this aporia can yield paralysing repetitions. Therefore, the praxial–reflective *vāṅmaya* responds to the aporetic forces that constitute the body complex as *reasonable* passions. For the *rāga* as well as the vicissitudinal elements and the volatile faculty of *manas* are all open to or amenable to the discerning faculty (*buddhi*). How the faculty responds to the chance and endowment of what it receives remains forever open — at least as long as the generative impulse brings forth the bodies and worlds the existence— that is, as long as passions are at work.

Aporias of existence require breaking of paths, otherwise they paralyse life in the machinic apparatus of existence. Caught in the aporias of existence, everybody is confronted by the interminable quandary: *what do you do with what you have*?

Notes

1. Among the major continental thinkers, Nietzsche thematises this division and discordance between art and truth (Heidegger 1991: 142). From the numerous works, one can cite that of Philippe Lacoue-Labarthe and

Jean-Luc Nancy (1988) as a crucial account of the German Romantic tradition's attempt to grapple with the inherited discordance. Contemporary literary theory can be seen as yet another attempt to deal with this discordance (especially in Derrida's work).

2. All translations from Telugu into English in this essay are mine.
3. *Jāti*s proliferate, contends the *Śukranītisāra*, through corruption or miscegenation, and no one can recount or name them. *Vidyā*s are rendered through face and voice and *kalā*s are those that the dumb and deaf can also render (Singaracharyulu 2002: 284, 286).
4. By literary inquiries, I refer to the traditions of inquiry into the literary (*kāvya*, *sārasvata*) that emerged and proliferated over a millennium from the 8th century CE onwards, drawing on the already extended forms of inquiry into language, utterance, ritual, astral science, and logic. These inquiries were initiated by a group of poet–thinkers called Lākṣaṇikās or Ālaṃkārikas (from Bhāmaha to Jagannātha Paṇḍita and beyond).
5. Curiously, this performative aspect of *bhāvaka* is conspicuous by its absence in the recent reading of Rājaśekhara's account of *pratibhā* by David D. Shulman (2012: 83–89).
6. Mukund Lath (1998: 101–14) provides an impressive instance of such a possibility in the context of musical traditions.
7. The account concerning the complex body apparatus in this section is largely drawn from Īśvarakṛṣṇa's *Sāṃkhyakārikā* (21–49, in Koteswarasarma 1996: 21–43). Also, the entire Sāṃkhya-Yoga chapter of the *Bhagavadgītā* (2.45–72, in *Śrīmadbhagavadgītā* 2003: 112–49) eloquently articulates what is being offered here.
8. There can also be an inversion of the relation between reflection and praxis. One can ritualise one's day-to-day activities and doggedly but mechanically perform the ordained rituals without letting the embodied existence to work through reflective learning. Sorabji (2000: 4), in a related context, in his discussion on the Stoic philosophy and therapeutic exercises argues that separating these two would be like the Western practice of Yoga without grasping the 'theory': '[I]t would be wrong to think that the exercises or the philosophical analysis stand on their own'.
9. Bhāmaha's transformative reception of Bharata is as follows:

   There is no sound, no meaning, no law, and no art that has not been made use in poetry. What a burden the poet has to carry! (*Kāvyālaṃkāra* 5.4, in Sreeramachandrudu n.d.: 22–23).

10. By 'heritage', I refer to the creative–reflective 'thought' formed by Vedas, Brāhmaṇas, Upaniṣads and Sūtras, in other words, the *śruti* and *smṛti* compositions.
11. Concerning a decisive filiation between literary criticism and philosophy, Jacques Derrida (1992: 53) writes: 'In general literary criticism is very

philosophical in its form . . . Literary criticism is perhaps structurally philosophical. What I am saying here is not necessarily a compliment'.

12. Imagination (*ūha*) is a part of the interior set of faculties, which enables movement across temporal and transgenerational communications of traits and traces.
13. Bharata's categories of stable motifs are:

    ratir hāsaś ca śokaś ca krodhotsāhau bhayaṃ tathā
    jugupsā vismayaś ceti sthāyibhāvāḥ prakīrtitāḥ

    The erotic, comical, sorrowful, rage, euphoric-enthusiasm, fright, as well as disgust and awe are the constitutive of the stable motifs (*Nāṭyaśāstra* 6.17, in Rao n.d.: 193).

    Corresponding precisely these motifs are the virtually experienced set of eight flavours:

    śṛṅgāra hāsya karuṇā raudra vīra bhayānakāḥ
    bībhatsādbhutasaṃjñyau cety aṣṭau nāmye rasāḥ smṛtāḥ

    Evocative desire, laughter, endearing compassion, terror, heroic valour, fear, mayhem, wonderment are the eight constitutive flavours (*Nāṭyaśāstra*, 6.15, ibid: 192).

    Bharata goes on to list the volatile set of 33 motifs as well. Later praxial reflections add yet another stable motif that suspends the entirety of the condensed node of passion (*rāga*) and all its extended ramifications; this is called the desire-free stable motif. The corresponding flavour in the virtual experiential domain would be serene calmness. We will return to this theme in the essay.
14. This affective response contrasts fundamentally with the one concerning the relation between art and emotion that Martha Nussbaum, for instance, elaborates in her *Upheavals of Thought* (2001). It should be noted that Nussbaum's entire approach to that relation is spectator-oriented. This is bound to be so due to her basic assumption about emotional response — what she calls 'eudaimonistic judgment' which is centred on privileging the receiver and her discourse. Any art object or any other's life is of concern to me only if it is 'important to my well-being'. 'Eudaimonia' here simply means 'what is it to live for me well?' (ibid.: 49). Consequently, the receiver–spectator and her extended commentary on what is relevant for her well-being occupy the central place in her discourse on emotions. This overpowering discourse of personal well-being leaves one wonder: are not others and what happens to others and lives of others in life and art always instruments for my sense/obsession of my well-being? Do I leave myself at all in such a reckoning? Am I not all the time seeking to remain in my secure position – where my 'own safety is not immediately threatened'? (Nussbaum 2001: 244). Isn't it from such a position that I seek to manipulate

anything that can serve as a 'transitional object' for my flourishing? Doesn't such self-indulgence reinforce an ipsocratic position? Nussbaum's spectatorial discourses weave seductive narratives of such self-flourishing (ibid., especially Chapter 5).

15. See also Pullela Sreeramachandrudu's (1995: 43) preface to Mammaṭā's *Kāvyaprakāśa*.
16. The same verse appears in the English translation of *Locana* as: 'I know youth to be the house of passion, nor am I unaware that it is transient' (Ingalls et al. 1990: 519). As can be seen, the Telugu rendering is closer to the quoted passage.
17. *Yoga Sūtra* 3.10 and 4.27 state that *saṃskāra* accrues when intense attention to the binds and bonds is resisted (Sreeramachandrudu 1992: 112, 169). The two *sūtras*, as cited by Abhinavagupta in his commentary (*Locana*), are: *tasya praśāntavāhitā saṃskārāt* ('such a resistant attention can remain serenely'); and *tacchidreśu pratyayāntarāni samskārebhyaḥ* ('The mind's pure flow of peace comes from one's [repeated] will [to suppress thoughts of sense objects]') (Sreeramachandrudu 1998: 727–28). Ingalls et al. (1990: 521–22) thus translate the second *sūtra*: 'In the intervals [of trance] various worldly cognitions arise because of old predispositions'.
18. It must be noted here that what strikes anyone who confronts the Sanskrit literary inquires is that the operations of figural language is most of the time exemplified by evoking *śṛṅgāra*-erotic allusions. The consistency of such an exemplification across a millennium reinforces emphasis laid on experiential learning/knowing/longing.
19. The translation of the same by Ingalls et al. (1990: 521) is as follows:

    'The emotions arise from peace, each from its
    Peculiar cause,
    And when the cause has ceased, they melt
    Back into peace'.

20. The translation of the same by Ingalls et al. (1990: 525) is: 'Suffice it to say that as the *rasa* of peace leads to *mokṣa*, which is the highest aim of man, it is the most important of all the *rasas*'.
21. The translation of the same by Ingalls et al. (1990: 693–94) is: 'The most compassionate of sages [Bhīṣma] himself asserts the same when he seeks, by imparting the light of his pure knowledge to rescue the world from the cruel illusion in which it is plunged'. Curiously, Ingalls contends: '*Lokanātha* must here be used as an epithet of Bhīṣma'. Bhīṣma does not come across in the *Mahābhārata* as a sage. The Telugu translation clearly shows Vyāsa as the *lokanātha* ('the one who created the world of the *itihāsa*').
22. The translation of the same by Ingalls et al. (1990: 691) is:

    'The more the world's affairs
    go wrong for us and lose their substance,

the more will disenchantment with them
grow, there is no doubt'.

23. We must remember that these compositions break open (before Bharata) the path beyond the delimited constituency of the *śāstra-vāṅmaya* addressee (the *trivarṇikās*) and are brought forth for reflective individuated existences to limitless *jatīs*.

References

Primary Sources

Bhagavadgītā:

Śrīmadbhagavadgītā. 2003. Gorakhpur: Gita Press.

Bṛhadāraṇyaka Upaniṣad:

Ramakotishastri, Brahmashri Suri (ed. and trans.). 1989. *Bṛhadāraṇyaka Upaniṣad* (Telugu). Hyderabad: Surabharati Publications.

Chāndogya Upaniṣad with the *Bhāṣya* of Śaṅkara:

Veereswarasarma, Rayasam (ed. and trans.). 2002. *Chāndogya Upaniṣad with Śankara Bhāṣya* (Telugu). Hyderabad: Sri Sitarama Adi Sankara Trust.

Dhvanyāloka of Ānandavardhana with Commentary *Locana* of Abhinavagupta:

Ingalls, Daniel H. H., Jeffrey Masson Moussaieff and M. V. Patwardhan (trans.). 1990. The *Dhvanyāloka of Ānandavardhana with the Locana of Abhinavagupta*. Cambridge, MA: Harvard University Press.

Sreeramachandrudu, Pullela (ed. and trans.). 1998. *Dhvanyālokamu — Locana Sahitamu* (Telugu). Hyderabad: Shri Jayalakshmi Publications.

Kāvyālaṃkāra of Bhāmaha:

Sreeramachandrudu, Pullela (ed. and trans.). n.d. *Sāṃskrita Vyākhyāna-Vimarśa Sāmpradāyamu: Critical and Commentatorial Tradition in Sanskrit*. Hyderabad: Sanskruta Bhasha Prachara Samiti.

Kāvyamīmāṃsā of Rājaśekhara:

Sreeramachandrudu, Pullela (ed. and trans.). 2003. *Rājaśekhara's Kāvyamīmāṃsā* (Telugu). Hyderabad: Shri Jayalakshmi Publications.

Kāvyaprakāśa of Mammaṭa:

Sreeramachandrudu, Pullela (ed. and trans.). 1995. *Mammaṭa's Kāvyaprakāśa* (Telugu). Hyderabad: Samskruta Bhasha Prachara Samiti.

Mahābhārata (Telugu) of Nannaya, Yerrapragada and Tikkana Somayaji:

Subramaniam, G. V. et al. 2000–07. *Kavitraya Viracita Śrīmadāndhra Mahābhāratamu*. Tirupati: Tirumala Tirupati Devastanamulu.

Muṇḍaka Upaniṣad:

Sreeramachandrudu, Pullela (ed. and trans.). 1984. *Muṇḍakopaniṣad* (Telugu). Hyderabad: Surabharati Publications.

Nāṭyaśāstra of Bharata:

Rao, P. S. R. Appa (ed. and trans.). n.d. *Nāṭya Śāstramu* (Telugu). Hyderabad: Natyamala Prachuranamu.

Sāṃkhyakārikā of Īśvarakṛṣṇa:
Koteswarasarma, Sri Ramachandrula (ed. and trans.). 1996. *Īśvarakṛṣṇa's Sāṃkhyakārikā* (Telugu). Hyderabad: Arsha Vijnana Trust.
Sāṃkhya Sūtra of Kapila:
Agrawal, Madan, Mohan (ed. and trans.). 2001. *Six Systems of Indian Philosophy: The Sutreas [sic] of Six Systems of Indian Philosophy with Original English Translation, Transliteration, and Indices.* Delhi: Chowkhambha Sanskrit Pratishthan.
Śukranītisāra:
Singaracharyulu, K. Alaha (ed. and trans.). 2002. *Śukranītisāramu* (Telegu). Nalgonda: Sahitya Sanmana Samithi.
Vāyu Mahāpurāṇa:
Chandrasekharasarma, Mulampalli (ed. and trans.). 2003. *Śrī Vāyumahāpurāṇamu*, vol. 1 (Telugu). Hyderabad: Sri Venkateswara Arshabharati Trust.
Viṣṇudharmottara Purāṇa:
Seetaramanjaneyulu, Sri Poturi (ed.), Sri Kalluri Venkata Subvrahmanya Deekshitulu and Sri Devarakonda Seshagiri Rao (trans.). 1988. *Śrī Viṣṇudharmottara Mahāpurāṇamu: Andhrānuvāda Sahitamu*, 3 Khaṇḍas (Telugu). Hyderabad: Sri Venkateshwara Arshabharati Trust.
Yoga Sūtra of Patañjali:
Sreeramachandrudu, Pullela (trans.). 1992. *Yogadarśanam* (Telegu). Hyderabad: Ārṣa Vijñāna Trust.

Secondary Works

De Man, Paul. 1986. *The Resistance to Theory*. Minneapolis: University of Minnesota Press.
Derrida, Jacques. 1992. 'This Strange Institution Called Literature', in Derek Attridge (ed.), *Acts of Literature by Jacques Derrida*, pp. 33–75. New York: Routledge.
Heidegger, Martin. 1991. *Nietzsche*, vols 1 and 2, trans. David Farrell Krell. New York: HarperSan Francisco.
Lacoue-Labarthe, Philippe and Nancy Jean-Luc. 1988. *The Literary Absolute: The Theory of Literature in German Romanticism.* New York: State University of New York Press.
Lath, Mukund. 1995. 'The Body as an Instrument: A Theoretical Choice Made by Śārṅgadeva', in Bettina Bäumer (ed.), *Prakṛti: The Integral Vision*, vol. 3: *The Āgamic Tradition and the Arts*, pp. 101–14. Delhi: Indira Gandhi National Centre for the Arts (IGNCA).
——. 1998. *Transformation as Creation: Essays in the History, Theory and Aesthetics of Indian Music, Dance and Theatre*, vol. 1. Delhi: Aditya Prakashan.
Nietzsche, Friedrich. 2003. *The Birth of Tragedy*, trans. Shaun Whiteside. London: Penguin.

Plato. 1952. *Laws*, trans. Benjamin Jowett. Chicago: Encyclopedia Britannica Inc.
Nussbaum, Martha. 2001. *Upheavals of Thought: The Intelligence of Emotions*. Cambridge: Cambridge University Press.
Sharma, Premlata. 1995. 'Mahabhutas in Sangita-Shastra: With Special Reference to Yoga and Ayurveda', in Bettina Bäumer (ed.), *Prakṛti: The Integral Vision: The Āgamic Tradition and the Arts*, vol. 3, pp. 87–100. Delhi: IGNCA. http://ignca.nic.in/eBooks/prakriti_series_03.pdf (accessed 18 September 2014).
Shulman, David D. 2012. *More than Real: A History of the Imagination in South India*. Cambridge, MA: Harvard University Press.
Sorabji, Richard. 2000. *Emotions and Peace of Mind: From Stoic Agitation to Christian Temptation*. New York and Oxford: Oxford University Press.
Sznondi, Peter. 1995. *Introduction to Literary Hermeneutics*, trans. Martha Woodmansee. Cambridge: Cambridge University Press.
Weber, Samuel. 2004. *Theatricality as Medium*. New York: Fordham University Press.

9

Aesthetics of Despair

SHARAD DESHPANDE

Contrary to the assumed invariance of human nature, one may ask: are emotions culturally determined and, therefore, relative to historical periods and civilisational differences that make the emotion-based aesthetic theories to be cultural variants? A plea for discerning 'a new primary emotion . . . that was not recognised by traditional Indian aesthetic doctrines' (Dehejia 2000a: 3) seems to imply this, if one wants to appreciate modern Indian painting in particular, and perhaps modern Indian literature too. This sort of plea highlights the bewilderment of those who are caught in between tradition and modernity, between indigenous and alien, between availability and non-availability of appropriate *śāstra*, a theory, to appreciate anything that is modern, including the modern art. Rather than finding the 'tranquil smile of the Buddha, the majesty of Durgā, the loving tenderness of Pārvatī, the radiance of Naṭarāja' (ibid.: 4), what one now finds is the fragmented human image in place of the 'celestial and semi-divine beings' placed in the 'sensuous and lyrical surroundings' that used to define the traditional Indian art. What one now finds in modern Indian painting is 'the unmistakable stigmata of despair, not just a state of psychological depression but of an utter and hopeless sense of darkness and hopelessness' (ibid.).

How do we engage with this new mode of representation? One's subjective likes and dislikes should hardly matter. The issue involved here cuts deep into the very structuring of aesthetic experience, transcending subjective likes and dislikes, and elevating superficial enjoyment which is nothing else but amusement, to the one which is truly aesthetic.

This, in turn, presupposes one's conception of a work of art. Kant (1952), for example, distinguishes between fine arts, the industrial arts and the arts of the 'agreeable'. Arts of the agreeable, in contrast to the fine arts, are meant for entertainment of the *moment*. They are not expected to last for a significant duration so that they can become objects of *reflection*. The banquet orchestra produces agreeable noise. But we agree to it without paying any specific attention. The arts of the agreeable give pleasure from mere sensations, while in fine arts pleasure accompanies the presentation of aesthetic ideas. For Kant, entertainment, i.e., the art of the agreeable, is that form of art which is 'attended with no further interest than that of making the time pass by unheeded'. The Kantian idea of entertainment allows time to pass without our noticing its passage, i.e., without its *affecting* us (Sanil 2004), i.e., without producing any emotion. But a work of art becomes meaningful in terms of the dominant emotion it expresses; therefore, what is required is a unifying emotion, or a set of such emotions that make a work of art truly aesthetic. Do our indigenous theoretical resources, especially the *rasa*-theory, equip us with the required unifying emotion to appreciate modern Indian paintings that depict the day-to-day, secular and isolated worlds of individuals as opposed to the unfailing presence of the mythical, the religious, and the coherent world in the traditional Indian paintings? Prem Shankar Jha (2000: 17–25) and Ashis Nandy (2000: iii–vii) tell us that the classical Indian aesthetic theory, namely, the *rasa*-theory, is inadequate to structure contemporary aesthetic sensibilities, since it does not recognise what is peculiarly modern, namely, the emotions of despair, banality and absurdity. These are the unifying emotions that structure our contemporary states of consciousness which find their expression in contemporary art and literature. It is possible that despair, or something like that, might have been experienced or might have been known to the humans of the pre-modern societies. But it could not have been a regular and a formal feature of their psyche. Despair, banality and absurdity, as *we* experience them, are the products of modernity; these are typically felt by *us* living in the modern or the postmodern world. They have become almost a regular and formal feature of *our* psyche. And therefore it is only in the modern times that these emotions have received formal recognition in the existentialist philosophies of Kierkegaard, Nietzsche and Sartre, as well as in several works of art of the modern period. The narrative of despair and modernity is not without quirks that invite philosophers' unravelling.

Sociology of Despair

Is aesthetic creation and appreciation necessarily theory-laden? If it is so, then what happens to the hermeneutic freedom of creation and appreciation? These are the perennial questions in aesthetics, but they assume special significance when someone equipped with normative aesthetic theories like Bharata's *rasa*-theory or Kant's aesthetic theory tries to make sense of contemporary art forms, of modern paintings, novels, cinema, or even autobiographies. We find that the canonical theories do not offer interpretative categories to comprehend the expression of despair, absurdity and banality that we find in some contemporary works of art. For Dehejia, Jha and Nandy, this situation arises because these emotions were simply not available for theorising at the time when those theories were formulated. As per Jha's (2000: 9) sociology of despair:

> Despair is sorrow unredeemed by hope. It is powerful emotion born of irreparable loss that modern man is familiar with. It is therefore all the more surprising that it finds no place in the ten *rasas* that are the building blocks of the Indian system of aesthetics.[1]

Nandy (2000: vii) supplements Jha's observations:

> The classical Indian forms of creativity and philosophy of arts in India do not have any recognized place for three states of consciousness: despair, banality, and absurdity. Indian classicism, however does have a place for sorrow, cynicism, pessimism and even self-alienation . . . the trivial, the low brow, and the comic...but it has shown no sign of formally registering a state of despair, an emotion that afflicts, for instance, some works of Van Gogh or Franz Kafka, involving a sense of futility of it all, melancholia or total hopelessness. Nor have they created a place for the cultivated pop that celebrates the banal the way Andy Wharhol does or for the unashamedly surreal.

The exclusion of despair, Jha and Nandy tell us, is due to the very nature of despair and the socio-politico-economic realities in which it acquires existential status. Despair is non-sharable and 'highly personal' emotion whose ontology is grounded in industrial capitalism. It marks the 'rise of individualism and the slow dissolution of the bonds of society' (Jha 2000:10). It subverts reciprocity by competition as the organising principle of social relations, and establishes the primacy of machine over man's needs, thereby depriving the humans of 'their social identities and their social protection' (ibid.: 10). Despair was thus born along with the 'fragmented self' — the 'individual'. But as a representative of the human condition, despair achieved its existential status when it was realised that 'God had failed mankind' (ibid.: 15), giving rise to total hopelessness. The Christian theologians attribute the sense of total hopelessness to the modern secular culture which does not permit any sense of the sacred or the transcendental. This attribution comes succinctly in the declaration that for the modern mind 'God is dead'. Jha and Nandy's sociology of despair is a critique of this modern mind and the resultant modernity.

Historicising Emotions?

What does it mean to historicise emotions? Does sociology of despair suggest that the emotions of despair, banality and absurdity were not felt, or were felt differently by the humans of the pre-modern societies? If that were so, what exactly would be the difference in experiencing a certain emotion under different descriptions? How would one *know* that he/she is experiencing now an emotion *E* under description *m* which is different from experiencing the same *E* under description *n*? Is there a categorial difference between the way despair, banality and absurdity were available to the modern and the pre-modern man? Were these emotions not — in a significantly existential sense — available to the humans of the pre-modern age? These issues collapse into the deep metaphysics of how our worldviews shape our psychology, and how they determine the kind of aesthetic theories that we have. This and related issues extend over the classical aesthetic theories which are based on substantive human psychology and the invariance thesis of human nature. But are emotions vulnerable to the variance of human nature when it is said that they are anchored in the socio-political environment? If that were so, such theories cannot claim universality which is traditionally taken to be the hallmark of a genuine theory.

Too Many Questions

It is often said that works of art express emotions or the states of consciousness which human beings have or are capable of having. The classical Indian aesthetic theory, viz., the *rasa*-theory, makes this point in terms of *sthāyi* (stable) and *vyabhicārī* (transitory) *bhāvas* (i.e., states of consciousness, particularly emotions and feelings). It is another matter, whether certain emotions or states of consciousness have actually been expressed in the works of art belonging to the various periods in history. Except for the art historians, it will be hardly interesting to find out which state/s of consciousness a given work of art expresses and at which point of time. One may perhaps leave this matter to the artists, saying that, after all, they create works of art and it is for them to choose and express any one *bhāva* or a combination of several *bhāvas*. But the matter is not all that simple. One might as well say that the expression of emotions cannot be privileged as an artist's autonomy, but it has more to do with the nature of human beings and, more importantly, with the historical conditions in which the humans live. Affirming its hegemonic status, countless expositions of *rasa*-theory emphasise its psychological foundations, suggesting that the exhaustive list of permanent and transitory emotions given by the *rasa* theorists offer the most comprehensive picture of human nature which will be more or less true under all possible conditions of human existence. But, does not the very idea of 'the most comprehensive picture of human nature' sound dubious, since it is self-evident that changes in the historical conditions, even the geo-physical conditions in which the humans live, are bound to affect the so-called 'comprehensive' picture of human nature? Such a comprehensive picture cannot be ensured, for instance, if we are talking about various skills that the human beings have acquired under different historical conditions. Was, for instance, the human nature less comprehensive before and more comprehensive after the humans have mastered the skill for cycling? Unlike skills, no one learns and masters techniques to feel or experience emotions, though one can acquire and subsequently even master the skill to *exhibit* a certain emotion on a particular occasion. But again, whereas acquiring and mastering skills involve activities, experiencing an emotion is not an activity. But despite being different in this sense, it is not implausible that what is true of skills could also be true of emotions, and in that case the so-called 'comprehensive' picture of human nature in terms of its psychological make-up may still be a myth.

What sorts of things can we say about emotions? Can we say that given the normal circumstances and by virtue of being a human, certain emotions are experienced by everyone while some are not? For instance, can we say that given the kind of human beings that we are, the emotions of love, fear or sorrow are so primal that they are experienced by every human being, while despair, banality and absurdity are not so primal and hence are not experienced by everyone? Are despair, banality and absurdity — as opposed to love, fear or sorrow — personal in the sense that no one can share the feeling of hopelessness, a sense of irrecoverable loss that 'I' experience? Could we also say that feeling certain emotions, such as love or fear, are not linked up with, while the feeling of the emotions of despair or banality are necessarily linked up with such civilisational markers as 'pre-modern' and 'modern' or the 'postmodern'? To complicate the matter further, can we map this on the Western and the non-Western civilisations? Can we say for instance, that as philosophical categories the modern despair and the ancient *duḥkha* belong to different worldviews altogether?

The [In]adequacy of *Rasa*-theory in the Modern Context

Jha and Nandy's extensive sociological observations on despair, banality and absurdity vis-à-vis the *rasa*-theory problematise not only the alleged comprehensiveness of the *rasa*-theory's psychological foundation, but also its adequacy to appreciate various art forms that go under the rubric of 'modern art'. This raises a crucial issue of the connection between theorising in aesthetics and the socio-economic and political conditions in which man lives, stressing 'despair' as a typical modern phenomenon. Drawing a parallel from the practice of science, we can see that the issue that Jha and Nandy raise is that of the adequacy of a theory. In science, the adequacy of a theory is measured in terms of its capacity to accommodate and explain the occurrence of a new phenomenon. Hence, the adequacy of a theory is one of the criteria for a scientific theory to be satisfactory. The history of science is replete with instances of received scientific theories being suitably modified or drastically revised by modifying their presuppositions, or even being discarded if they fail to accommodate new phenomena in their explanatory frame. But can this happen in the aesthetic theories propounded by Bharata, Kant or Croce, which claim universality of a kind? Can aesthetic theories be ostensibly modelled on scientific theories? What criterion of adequacy do scientific theories adopt?

One could give two quick responses to Jha and Nandy's gloss on the *rasa*-theory, but without necessarily defending the *rasa*-theory. The *first* response would be that Bharata's *rasa*-theory is restricted primarily to the craft of theatre. Though it uses many psychological terms, it is not a theory in substantive psychology. Therefore, the discussion on the nature of emotions in Bharata's *Nāṭyaśāstra* has to be contextualised to the requirements of theatre, and specifically to the *expression* of human emotions on the stage. The *second* response would be that Bharata's

Nāṭyaśāstra, which is taken to be the main text of the classical Indian *rasa*-theory, does recognise and has, in fact, listed among the *vyabhicārī bhāvas* (states of consciousness) what is (now) meant by 'despair'. The term *viṣāda* is sometimes translated as 'despair' or 'dejection', and we are familiar with its cognate *nairāsya* in Marathi or *hatāśā* in Hindi. Surely, the issue here is not that of translation of terms, but rather that of knowing what exactly constitutes the content of despair and what range of meanings the term 'despair' covers. This would partly be a philological exercise. But in philosophical parlance, especially in the philosophy of language, this is the issue that Wittgenstein wants us to realise, namely that concepts form a *family*, sharing with one another similarities and differences in terms of various aspects. This, as we know, expels the myth of 'the' meaning of a word or a concept. This insight also applies to the concept of despair. In fact, to historicise an emotion is to hold that it has no ancestry in the functioning of human mind, or that there are no cognate terms forming a family.

The second response to Jha and Nandy's critique would consist in arguing that the *rasa*-theorists do not exclude despair or its analogues altogether from their understanding of human nature; on the contrary, what they do is to treat it as 'transitory' rather than 'permanent' state of consciousness. But then this raises a criteriological question: why the *rasa*-theory does not include despair/dejection in the list of eight *sthāyibhāvas*? It is well known that the *rasa*-theory lists *rati* (love), *hāsa* (laughter), *śoka* (sorrow), *krodha* (anger), *utsāha* (enthusiasm), *bhaya* (fear), *jugupsā* (disgust), and *vismaya* (astonishment) as more or less permanent emotions or states of consciousness; and 34 transient (*vyabhicārī*) emotions or states of consciousness, such as *cintā* (anxiety), *smṛti* (recollection), *vrīḍa* (shame), *harṣa* (joy), *supta* (dreaming), *asūya* (envy), *nirveda* (weariness), *dainya* (depression), *dhṛti* (contentment), *āvega* (agitation), etc. But what does it mean to say that amongst the states of consciousness that human beings have, some are more or less permanent, while some are transient? The difficulty becomes acute in the light of the fact that Bharata does not give any clear definition of *sthāyibhāva*. It is also possible that he must have defined it and the original text contained it. But in the text that has come down to us, the definition in question might have been lost. As has been conjectured by Barlingay (2007: 130–31):

> Bharata in the seventh chapter begins by defining the concepts. First, he defines the *bhāvas*, then he defines *vibhāvas*, *anūbhāvas*, etc . . . After

> this comes a passage where it is said that the *lakṣaṇas* of the *sthāyibhāvas* are already told; i.e. they are already defined and that now the particular *sthāyibhāvas* would be discussed.

In the absence of an explicit definition of what is *sthāyi* in Bharata's text, there is a lot of speculation as to what did Bharata really mean by *rasa*, and accordingly the scholars are divided on the issue of the locus of *rasas* and also on how to interpret the process of creation of *rasas*. As regards the *vyabhicārībhāvas*, it is intuitive that these transient states of consciousness are episodic. But the fact that there is more than one state of consciousness which is supposed to be more or less permanent shows that they, too, are intermittent in certain sense. One cannot have a certain state of consciousness, say the emotion of *śoka* (sorrow) or *rati* (love), non-intermittently. So the alleged permanent and transient nature of emotions or states of consciousness is not to be understood in terms of their alleged temporality.

One way out of this difficulty, i.e., retaining the distinction between the *sthāyi* and *vyabhicārī* emotions without making it dependent on temporal considerations, is to read the difference between *sthāyi* and *vyabhicārī* along the lines of Kantian distinction between the constitutive and regulative principles, by taking the *sthāyi* to be the constitutive and the *vyabhicārī* to be the regulative emotions of human nature. The constitutive emotions of human beings, analogous to Kant's constitutive judgments, would be those whose meaning, truth or legitimacy is not dependent on any further assumptions, hypothetical conditions or suppositions.

One might say that taking into account the kind of human beings that we are, it is impossible to imagine ourselves without the emotions of love, sorrow, anger, fear, etc. In this sense, the eight *sthāyi* emotions or states of consciousness are the constitutive features of human nature. We *are* what we are in terms of the *sthāyi* emotions. The permanence of the *sthāyi* emotions is not dependent on any further assumption. In this sense, they can be said to be the constitutive emotions of human nature. But in the same vein, can we say that the *vyabhicārī* emotions are the regulative features of human nature? What does it mean to say that the 34 transient (*vyabhicārī*) emotions or states of consciousness, such as *cintā* (anxiety), *smṛti* (recollection), *vrīḍa* (shame), *harṣa* (joy), etc., are the regulative features of human nature? In the Kantian framework the regulative principles or judgments are those whose meaning, truth, legitimacy is dependent on further assumptions, hypothetical conditions or suppositions. Likewise, it may be argued that the very transience of the *vyabhicārī* emotions makes them dependent on some further suppositions or assumptions. However, the reading of the *vyabhicārī* emotions on the analogy of the regulative principles in the Kantian theory needs further elaboration.

As has been argued earlier, the classification of all the conceivable emotions or states of consciousness into *sthāyi* and *vyabhicārī* is not to be taken in their literal sense, i.e., in terms of their alleged temporality or duration because, then, it raises the methodological question of the basis or principle of treating one emotion as *sthāyi* (stable) and the other as *vyabhicārī* (transient). In order to make sense of this classification, we need to have a *prior* conception of what it is to be like a human being. For Bharata, the kind of human beings that we are cannot be conceived in the absence of the *sthāyibhāvas*. In this sense, the *sthāyibhāvas* are more or less permanent features of human psyche under all possible conditions of human existence. But this is not so with reference to the *vyabhicārībhāvas*, with reference to which one can always ask a '*why*-question'. For instance, one can ask why Śakuntalā is bashful, i.e., why Śakuntalā feels the emotion of shame or *lajjā* and answer that she feels so because of the emotion of love or *rati*. In this case, the former is dependent on the latter. The important thing to be noted here is that the *expression* of the *sthāyi* emotion is also an emotion that regulates a certain aspect of behaviour. The emotion of *lajjā* in the sense of 'being dependent on' or 'being caused by' the emotion of love (*rati*) is thus the standard explanation that one comes across which can be read in terms Kant's idea of regulative principles.

For the *rasa*-theory, which primarily addresses the making of *nāṭya* (the staged drama), the key terms are the *character* to be enacted, the *actor* who enacts the character, and the *spectator* who witnesses the stage performance. The states of consciousness called *sthāyi* and *vyabhicārī* are to be understood with reference to these three elements. But Jha (2000: 9) rightly notes that the emotion or feeling of despair is supposed to be uniquely personal. No one can share the feeling of hopelessness, a sense of irrecoverable loss that 'I' experience. Hence, the feeling/emotion of despair is not included in the list of *sthāyibhāvas*. But then the question would be: what is the criterion used by the *rasa*-theorists to distinguish between *sthāyibhāvas* and *vyabhicārībhāvas*? The criterion is constructed in terms of the universalisability of a given emotion or a feeling. The emotion or feeling must be capable of being shared between the artist (i.e., an actor) and the spectator. The aim of the *rasa*-theory is to create a *base*, a common ground for the shared emotions that unites not only the artist with his/her audience but also the members of the audience itself. That there are feelings or emotions which are sharable is a *priori* condition because a work of art is essentially communicative. It communicates the artist's emotions or feelings to the spectator. This presupposes that emotions or feelings are sharable, at least *in principle*. But a solipsist, who doubts the existence of 'other' minds, believes that one's experiences are so private, so unique to oneself that they cannot be shared with anyone else. In fact, there is no one else with whom one's experiences can be shared. A solipsist of this sort would argue that despite the best efforts on the part of the artist there remains an unbridgeable gap between what the artist wants to communicate and what the alleged spectator receives. A solipsist, thus, doubts the sharability thesis, namely, that emotions and feelings are sharable even *in principle*. In response to this claim of a solipsist, an analogical argument is often made to argue for the existence of other minds which are equipped with emotions and feelings of the sort that one has. But an argument from analogy cannot offer a full-fledged refutation of the solipsist's claim of the privacy and non-sharable character of one's experiences. The solipsists and those who argue for an unbridgeable gap between 'me' and my experiences and the alleged 'other' in the domain of the philosophy of mind can extend their argument to the stage performance and argue that there is an unbridgeable gap between the actor and the spectator. But following Wittgenstein, we may approach this issue by critiquing the notion of doubt that is at work in the solipsist's position.

Nandy (2000: vii) observes that the feeling of despair is alien not only to the Indian but to many ancient cultures, including the pre-modern Europe. Why this is so is to be understood in a wider sociological perspective rather than taking it to be a mere art-historical fact. Individual and isolated instances representing despair in artistic creations apart,[2] it is claimed that it is only in the modern times that despair as a full blown existential state has 'acquired a serious moral, philosophical and aesthetic status' (ibid.). In other words, 'despair' as an autonomous philosophical category has its origin in modernity. This line of argument suggests that the emotions or states of consciousness that human beings have are historically determined, that rather than being rooted in the human *psyche* they are *caused* by the socio-politico-economic conditions in which humans live. What, then, is the difference between the modern and the pre-modern traditional cultures? And how does that affect the phenomenon of despair and its expression in art?

Sociologists and the historians of cultures have described the difference between the modern and the pre-modern traditional cultures in terms of 'holistic vision' that enabled the traditional cultures view not only the human beings but also the entire natural world as one 'indivisible' whole. The culture that views the nature and the man–nature relationship in its wholeness also views man's relation with others as forming a web of social relations. In such cultures, 'emotions' are essentially shared or are sharable. Emotions that are not so sharable and are utterly individualistic are considered to be 'disruptive' and are often discouraged. On this account, the feeling of grief and the sense of loss, which appears to be utterly private, too are shared. In the words of Jha (2000: 9–10):

> It is religion, philosophy and the bonds of community that between them lift the burden of sorrow and create space for resignation, ultimately acceptance. Each powerful experience of this kind only reinforces the bonds of the individual with the society to which he belongs. In such societies despair may be born but it is not allowed to live.

This kind of harmony is typical of the non-European pre-modern cultures. Europe from the Middle Ages to the end of the 18th century has had this holistic vision of life and it did reflect itself in the European arts of that period. But the emergence of despair is typically a modern phenomenon and is associated with the emergence of individualism of the Renaissance period. The rise of individualism is itself a complex phenomenon that is due to several factors, such as the rise of the new, i.e., Galilean science; the revolt against the authority of the Church; the rise of capitalism; the rise of a powerful philosophical category of individual, as in the domain of politics and morality; and the rise of trade and commerce resulting in new townships and urban life. It is in this complex background that the 'individual', i.e., an *autonomous* agent in the spheres of political, moral, economic, and social aspects, was born. This 'individual' was a Cartesian *cogito*. It was independent of everything else. It was both certain (of its existence) and solitary (in its existence). His emotions, his feelings of happiness as well as of despair, of banality, of absurdity were, in principle, un-sharable. These feelings were not a matter of psychological possession, but they were, so to say, the transcendental conditions of his existence. Certainty and solitude was the hallmark of Cartesian *cogito*.

It is argued that in the South Asian traditions, 'the total existential hopelessness, in a world imbued with sacredness and alive with transcendental possibilities . . . does not easily translate into the hopelessness of the soul . . . In these ancient civilizations despair remains psychophysical response rather than a philosophical position' (Nandy 2000: viii). This is because the ancient and pre-modern cultures had such worldviews that were able to transcend the individual despair into the cosmic understanding of one's own existence. Karṇa, after knowing the secret of his birth, 'has every reason to give in for despair. But he does not. Both life and death continue to make sense to him as the difference between them' (ibid.). The other example that readily comes to mind is that of Sītā of *Rāmāyaṇa*. Portrayed as the most ideal wife of the most ideal husband, viz., king Rāma, Sītā does not give in to despair, though deeply hurt, insulted, made vulnerable, after Rāma abandons her for the sake of *lokāpavāda* ('public censure'). The issue is not that of *our* reading or *our* interpreting the feeling of despair and its expression in the Epics through such historical or imaginary figures. The issue is: how to account for the existential phenomenon of despair in our aesthetic cognition and philosophical theories that are built around it.

The discussion of this issue goes beyond the bounds of textual and philological exercise and becomes an issue that embraces the historical, sociological and cultural dimensions of human existence. Sociologists do agree that despair, being typically a modern phenomenon, has an immediate appeal to and relevance for the 'urbanized and secularized societies where the individual has been atomized and cut off from most community ties and where impersonal, contractual relationships have come to dominate social life' (ibid.). In this context, Dehejia (2000a: 2–3) offers three arguments. First, in contradistinction to the classical Indian art forms, the contemporary Indian art forms, especially painting, pose itself as isolated from other art forms such as folk, performing and literary arts. But one finds a certain interrelatedness amongst the classical art forms. For example, sculpture is related to dance and dance to music. Second, classical Indian art forms are mythical: they are based on religion and literature. But this is not so with modern Indian art, especially painting. It is largely secular, free-standing and individualistic. It is not related to any given literature, i.e., *kāvya*, religion and myth. Third, classical Indian art forms are figurative: they give less importance to landscape than to human figure, and treat tantric art as *yantras*, i.e., sacred diagrams and not a 'high art'. Modern Indian art is exactly opposite of this. In the light of such features that distinguish the classical from the modern Indian art forms, a re-questioning of the classical aesthetic theories is to be undertaken. What characterises the works of some of the modern Indian painters, such as Husain, Ara and Souza, is the deliberate fragmentation and distortion of the human image. Instead of treating this as rupture, one can interpret these works as expressing a new emotion and, therefore, a new worldview. This new representation of human image is markedly different from the mythic *puruṣas* that we are conditioned to 'adore and worship, celebrate, and venerate' (Dehejia 2000a: 4). The usual themes of classical Indian paintings, such as nature, animals, birds, rivers, mountains, and celestial and semi-divine beings, are missing and what occupies now is 'disorder and disarray, banality and starkness' (ibid.). The world of celestial myths, of the *yakṣas* and *gandharvas*, of the Jātakas, of the characters in the *Rāmāyaṇa* and *Mahābhārata*, the world of the royalty, and of the ordinary that used to motivate the artistic impulse of generations of painters, including the legendary Raja Ravi Varma, has vanished into oblivion to pave way for the artistic imagination of modern Indian painters.

Conclusion

Although despair is described as a typical modern phenomenon, for the sake of illustrating its distinctive features it could be distinguished from *duḥkha*, sorrow or suffering. These are the traditional terms that are used not only in the Indian tradition, but in all the religious traditions all over the world. In the Indian context, *duḥkha* is generally taken to be central to all the major Indian traditions, viz., the Hindu, Jaina and Buddhist, barring the Cārvāka. As Dehejia (2000b: 27) observes:

> So integral is the concept of *duḥkha* in the Indian tradition that it is situated within the ambit of the discourse on the human condition and predicament and takes the form of intense questioning of what it is to be a human.[3]

Despite major differences in their metaphysical presuppositions about the nature of the ultimate reality, one thing that is common to them all is that they are all concerned with the liberation of the self from *duḥkha*, arising out of or inherent in the life that one lives. Life, here, is not to be understood as restricted only to the *prapañca* or *saṃsāra*, i.e., worldly affairs and *duḥkha* as *saṃsāric* or *prapañcik*, i.e., suffering or sorrow arising out of the worldly affairs affecting the human body and mind. The *duḥkha* arising out of *saṃsāra* or *prapañca* is psychological in nature. Such a *duḥkha* arising out of the *saṃsāric* or *prapañcik* affairs does not invite serious philosophical considerations. But what is meant by *duḥkha* as a philosophical category is much deeper than this surface understanding. When the Buddha formulates the first *Ārya-satya* as *sarvaṃ duḥkham*, he expressly makes a statement on the human condition. There is an urge, an inner impulse to get rid of *duḥkha*, and the Hindu, Buddhist and Jaina ideals of *mokṣa*, *nirvāṇa*, and *kevala* do presuppose *duḥkha*, i.e., human suffering, and relate it to the quest for ultimate self-realisation. *Duḥkha*, therefore, is a limitation, a constraint, a stricture on the self. Very often, the concept of *duḥkha* is expressed by translating it as 'suffering', 'pain', 'misery', 'misfortune', 'torment' or 'travail'. But these are negative connotations. As Dehejia (2000b: 29) says: '[*D*]*uḥkha* in the Indian philosophic tradition is an exalted state of being that arises from a sense of limitation in the upward and onward reach of the radiant consciousness'. It is a temporary state in the process of realisation of the true nature of the self. Usually, pleasure and pain, *sukha* and *duḥkha*, are seen as antagonistic to each other. But they are not. The Indian tradition takes them to be the 'two states of human mind, *mithuna*' (ibid.), and as such treats them equally. The inability to transcend these two states is what is meant as *duḥkha* in the Indian tradition. *Duḥkha*, as understood in the ancient Indian tradition, and despair, as understood in the background of modernity, stand, therefore, on altogether different philosophical grounds of essence and existence.

Despite their radical difference, can the modern despair negotiate with the ancient *duḥkha*, and if so, on what grounds? This is a philosophical issue. Its resolution implies the coming together of two 'histories': that of the modern Indian art and that of the pre-modern Indian art.

It has been stated earlier that the feeling of despair is essentially unique to the individual concerned. This is the modernist understanding of despair. But in its contemporary appearance, despair is communitarian, i.e., pertaining to the community as such. In the present-day context of East–West divide, globalisation, modernisation, trade, and commercialism, the phenomenon of despair is to be located in 'obsolescence', 'dispensability', 'exile' and 'invisibility' of 'sizable parts of the Indian population' (Nandy 2000: xii), and also of several South Asian communities which are progressively rendered as redundant. The feeling of despair, in this perspective, is thus a common feeling that individual members of community share with one another. This itself should be a ground for providing it a space in the aesthetic cognition and a *śāstra* of the day concerning this cognition.

Notes

1. While Bharata's *Nāṭyaśāstra* mentions eight *rasas*, later theoreticians added two more *rasas*, viz., *śānta* and *vātsalya.*
2. Nandy (2000: vii) cites such instances as Judas's betrayal of Christ and Nietzsche's madman.
3. Dehejia (2000b: 27) gives an excellent account of how the theme of *duḥkha* engulfs the entire Indian metaphysical tradition, comprising the Vedas, the Upaniṣads, the Purāṇas, and even the Epics, i.e., *Rāmāyaṇa* and *Mahābhārata.*

References

Primary Source

Nāṭyaśāstra of Bharata:
Manomohan Ghosh (trans.). 1951. *Nāṭyaśāstra*. Calcutta: Asiatic Society of Bengal.

Secondary Works

Barlingay, S. S. 2007. *A Modern Introduction to Indian Aesthetic Theory*. Delhi: D. K. Printworld (P) Ltd.

Dehejia, Harsha. 2000a. 'Introduction', in Harsha Dehejia, Prem Shankar Jha and Ranjit Hoskote (eds), *Despair and Modernity: Reflections from Modern Indian Painting*, pp. 1–7. Delhi: Motilal Banarsidass.

——. 2000b. 'From Ancient Duhkha to Modern Despair', in Harsha Dehejia, Prem Shankar Jha and Ranjit Hoskote (eds), *Despair and Modernity: Reflections from Modern Indian Painting*, pp. 27–48. Delhi: Motilal Banarsidass.

Jha, Prem Shankar. 2000. 'Sociology of Despair', in Harsha Dehejia, Prem Shankar Jha and Ranjit Hoskote (eds), *Despair and Modernity: Reflections from Modern Indian Painting*, pp. 9–25. Delhi: Motilal Banarsidass.

Kant, Immanuel. 1952. *Critique of Judgment*, trans. J. C. Meredith. Oxford: Clarendon Press.

Nandy, Ashis. 2000. 'Foreword', in Harsha Dehejia, Prem Shankar Jha and Ranjit Hoskote (eds), *Despair and Modernity: Reflections from Modern Indian Painting*, pp. vii–xv. Delhi: Motilal Banarsidass.

Sanil, V. 2004. 'Passing Time: Immanuel Kant Goes to Cinema', *200 Years of Kant: Indian Philosophical Quarterly Special Number*, 3(1–4): 253–77.

About the Editors

Purushottama Bilimoria is Visiting Professor at the University of California, Berkeley and the Center for Dharma Studies, Graduate Theological Union, Berkeley, United States. He is concurrently a visiting scholar at the Institute of International Studies and South Asian Studies in Berkeley as well as a research fellow with the University of Melbourne and Deakin University, Australia. He is an Editor-in-Chief of *International Journal of Philosophy and Traditions* and *International Journal of Dharma Studies*, and of the series *Sophia Studies in Cross-Cultural Philosophy of Traditions and Culture*. His work has focused on verbal testimony (*śabdapramāṇa*) in Indian philosophy, Indian ethics and justice, *Mīmāṃsā-Nyāya* metaphysics and epistemology. He is currently working on volumes on Indian Ethics and the History of Indian Philosophy.

Aleksandra Wenta is currently pursuing a degree in Tibetan and Himalayan Studies at Wolfson College, University of Oxford, United Kingdom, and holds a PhD/Vidyāvāridhi in Āgama Tantra from the Faculty of Sanskrit Vidyā Dharma Vijñāna, Banaras Hindu University, India. She has been a fellow at the Indian Institute of Advanced Study, Shimla, India (2012–14). Her current research is on Kashmir Śaivism, cultural history of Chidambaram and Tantric Buddhism. She is the author of *The Twelve Kālīs: The Secret Doctrine of the Kālīkrama* (2014) and is on the editorial board of the *International Journal of Dharma Studies*.

Notes on Contributors

Andrea Acri is Visiting Research Fellow at the Nalanda-Sriwijaya Centre, Institute of Southeast Asian Studies (ISEAS), Singapore. He has held postdoctoral fellowships in the International Institute for Asian Studies (IIAS), Leiden, the Netherlands; Australian National University (ANU), Canberra, Australia; Oxford Centre for Hindu Studies, Oxford, the United Kingdom; and Asia Research Institute (ARI), National University of Singapore, Singapore. Besides Sanskrit and Old Javanese, his main interests are Śaivism and Tantric Buddhism, and their transfer/transformation along the Maritime Silk Road(s). He has authored *Dharma Pâtañjala: A Śaiva Scripture from Ancient Java Studied in the Light of Related Old Javanese and Sanskrit Texts* (2011) and co-edited *From Laṅkā Eastwards: The Rāmāyaṇa in the Literature and Visual Arts of Indonesia* (with Helen Creese and Arlo Griffiths, 2011).

Bettina Sharada Bäumer is an Austrian Indologist and Visiting Professor of Religious Studies at the universities of Vienna and Salzburg, Austria. She has been living and working in Varanasi, India, since 1967. Her main fields of research are non-dualistic Kashmiri Śaivism, Indian aesthetics, temple architecture and religious traditions of Orissa, and comparative mysticism. She has also been Coordinator of the Indira Gandhi National Centre for the Arts (IGNCA), Varanasi, and Fellow at the Indian Institute of Advanced Study (IIAS), Shimla, India. She has authored and edited a number of books and over 50 research articles, as also translated important Sanskrit texts into German and English. Among her most recent publications is *Abhinavagupta's Hermeneutics of the Absolute: Anuttaraprakriyā* (2011).

Neal Delmonico has taught at Iowa State University and Truman State University, United States, and currently operates a small academic press called Blazing Sapphire Press which specializes in bilingual translations and studies of South Asian religious, philosophical and literary texts and traditions. He is currently working on a three-volume, bilingual translation of Rūpa Gosvāmin's *Ujjvala-nīlamaṇi* ('The Blazing Sapphire') and a bilingual translation and study of Sahajiyā Vaiṣṇava traditions in Bengal called *Love in the Land of Heroes.*

Sharad Deshpande is currently Tagore Fellow at IIAS, Shimla, India, and was formerly Professor and Chair, Department of Philosophy, University of Pune, India. As British Council Visiting Fellow, he lectured at the universities of Oxford, Liverpool, and Aberdeen, United Kingdom, in 1990. As Resident Fellow of Indian Council of Philosophical Research (ICPR), New Delhi, India, he researched on the nature of Negative Action in 1987, and as Visiting Fellow he visited Maison De Sciences de l'aHomme, Paris, France, in 2008. He has also been a Visiting Fellow at various Universities in India, including Central University, Hyderabad; M. G. University, Kottayam; North Bengal University, Siliguri; Utkal University, Bhubaneswar; Rabindra Bharati University, Kolkata; and Mumbai University, India. Besides research articles in professional journals, his publications include *Philosophy of G. R. Malkani: 200 Years of Kant* (1997) and *Aesthetic Theories and Forms in Indian Aesthetic Tradition* (co-*edited, 2008*).

T. Ganesan has been *Directeur de Recherche* at the French Institute, Pondicherry (IFP), India, since 1985. He is currently working on the project, 'A Comprehensive History of Śaivasiddhānta in Tamilnadu', surveying the contents of the entire gamut of Śaivasiddhānta literature that spans more than a millennium. He has authored a book titled *Two Śaiva Teachers of the Sixteenth Century: Nigamajñāna I and His Disciple Nigamajñāna II* (2009), as also edited and translated into Tamil and English the *Śivajñānabodha Sūtra* with the commentary (*Laghumīkā*) of Śivāgrayogī; the *Siddhāntaprakāśikā* of Sarvātmaśambhu; and the *Śivajñānabodha Sūtra* with the hitherto unpublished commentary *Nigamajñānadeśika.*

D. Venkat Rao teaches at the English and Foreign Languages University, Hyderabad, India. His areas of interest include literary and cultural studies, image studies, comparative thought, translation, and mnemocultures. He has published books in English and Telugu.

Aditi Nath Sarkar is currently Visiting Professor at the Dhirubhai Ambani Institute of Information and Communication Technology (DA-IICT), Gandhinagar, Gujarat, India. He has taught at the University of Chicago, Chicago; University of California, Berkeley; and University of Minnesota, Minneapolis, United States. He was also Fellow at IIAS, Shimla, India.

Raffaele Torella is Professor of Sanskrit at University of Rome 'Sapienza', Italy, where he has also taught Indian philosophy and religion and Indology for long. He is the coordinator of the South Asia Section in the Sapienza Doctoral Course in 'Civilisations and Cultures of Asia and Africa', and Director of *Rivista degli Studi Orientali* and *Rivista di Studi Sudasiatici.* Among his main publications are the *Īśvarapratyabhijñā-kārikā of Utpaladeva's with the Author's Vṛtti: Critical Edition and Annotated Translation* (1994); *Eros and Emotions in India and Tibet* (co-authored with G. Boccali in Italian, 2007); *The Philosophical Traditions of India: An Appraisal* (2011); and Sìvasutra with Kṣemaraja's *Vimarśinī* (in Italian, 2013). He has also been the scientific responsible and co-author of the section 'Science in India' in the multivolume work *History of Science* (in Italian, 2002).

Varun Kumar Tripathi is Assistant Professor and Director, School of Philosophy and Culture, Shri Mata Vaishno Devi University, Jammu and Kashmir, India. He was Junior Research Fellow (2001–03) and General Fellow (2004–05) of ICPR, New Delhi, India. His area of interest is Indian philosophy, especially Indian ethics, Indian logic and Pāli Buddhism. He is working on a project on Indian ethics as Associate of the University Grants Commission (UGC) Inter-University Center at IIAS, Shimla, India. He has also edited a volume titled *Kashmir Śaivism and Neo-Tantrism* (forthcoming).

Index

Abhinavagupta, 25, 30, 35, 41, 43, 44, 45, 49n22, 64, 65, 78, 79, 81–83, 84, 85, 90n3, 91n15, 93n26, 94n29, 94n37, 95n41, 102, 106–10, 111, 116, 119, 127, 128n1, 129n5, 163, 164, 177n16, 217, 231, 253, 254, 255, 256, 258, 262n17
Advaita Vedānta, 11, 17, 48n9
aesthetics, 35, 41–45; of *bhakti*, 33, 35, 36, 48n17, 140; critique of, 45, 267–78, emotionalism, 41, 43; passion (*śṛṅgāra rasa*), 36, 42, 140, 163, 164, 170, 171, 172, 173, 174; *rasa*, 41, 42, 43, 45, 138, 162–65, 177n14, 250–52, 253, 254–55; *śānta rasa*, 43–45, 257, 256n20; sensibility, 42; theoreticians, 35, 41, 164, 177n16
Āgamas, 24–25, 111, 159, 214
affect, 5, 6, 12, 16, 46, 47n1, 49n26, 241, 251
affection, 65, 78, 159, 173, 214, 222n42
agitation, 29, 46, 106, 107, 109, 110, 111, 112, 117, 118, 124, 196n13, 200, 201, 202, 203, 205, 218n8, 222n38, 272
Ammaiyār, Kāraikkāl, 33, 146, 147–48, 153n6, 153n7
Ānandavardhana, 41, 42, 44, 45, 231, 253–54, 255–58
anger, 4, 15, 19, 26, 28, 33, 58, 61, 62, 73, 87, 90n4, 103, 107, 108, 145, 163, 187, 192, 194, 195n5, 199, 204, 223n48, 272, 273
anxiety, 19, 46, 49n22, 128n1, 194, 272, 273
Aristotle, 3, 193, 231
Arthaśāstra, 15
asamprajñāta-samādhi, 28
astonishment, 29, 105, 106, 200, 272
attachment, 12, 26, 38, 39, 44, 61, 65, 78, 79, 88, 152, 185, 187, 190, 196n12, 197n15, 199, 205, 223n48
awe, 33, 115, 137, 144, 146, 147, 148, 152, 201, 261
aversion, 5, 46, 60, 88, 163, 185, 195n10, 197n15, 219n14

Bengali manuscripts, 165
Bhagavadgītā, 9, 26, 49, 82, 90n4, 93n23, 93n26, 260n7; Abhinavagupta's commentary on, 82, 84, 93n26; contribution of, 27; desireless action (*niṣkāma-karma*), 27, 61–68; spiritual ideal of a *karmayogin*, 27
Bhāgavata Purāṇa, 158; activities of Kṛṣṇa, 162; Hari, treatment of, 158; Rādhā's personality, 158–59; tantric influences, 161–62
Bhairava, 30, 84, 85, 87, 96n49, 106, 108, 109, 111, 115–17, 119, 121
Bhakti movement, 31–36, 137; aestheticisation of *bhakti*, 35; awe, sense of, 144–45, 146–48; Bhakti protagonists, 31; defining *Bhakti* and *Bhaktas*, 137–40; as the critique of ascetic traditions, 32; ecstatic type of *bhakti* worship,

32; emotionalism of *bhakti*, 32–33; 'flowering bud' identity, 166–74; love, 140–44, 146–48, 151–52; as renunciation, 152; slave, love of a, 149–51; Tamil Śiva-*bhakti* tradition, 32–34, 138–40
Bharati, Swami Veda, 46
body–mind–emotions complex, 12, 21–23, 26, 27, 36–37, 38, 45, 59, 60, 61, 89, 137, 166, 167, 169, 241–59
Brāhmaṇical: emotionlessness, 10–14, 23, 31, 45; fear, 30; forms of ritualism, 35–36; legacy of emotionlessness, 23–24; norms of purity and control, 29–30; orthodoxy and ethics, 118; philosophy, 14–24, 59; purity-bound mentality, 24, 26; orthopraxy of sacrifice, 38, society, 13, 47n7
Bṛhadāraṇyaka Upaniṣad, 26, 175, 245
Buddhism, 31, 32, 36–41; delusions in Buddha's teachings, 39; emancipation, salvation or annihilation of *āsavas*, 191–92, 196n11; emotions in Buddha's teachings, 186–88; Four Noble Truths, 37–38; *Viśuddhimaggo*, 192–94

Caitanya: tradition, 156–61, 173; Vaiṣṇavism, 159, 165–66
Campbell, Joseph, 114, 120
Chāndogya Upaniṣad, 11–12, 13, 255
Cidgaganacandrikā, 118
cognitivist theory of emotion, 6–7, 8, 9, 21
compassion, 31, 39, 40, 48n20, 66, 191, 194, 199, 219n16, 261n13
conative-affective theory of emotions, 6–10
craving, 38, 66, 78, 79, 83, 187, 190, 191, 192, 199, 204, 205
Cuntaramūrti, 33, 34, 140, 143, 145–46, 153n4

Darwin, Charles, 9
Delusion or blindness (*moha*), 15, 19, 28, 38, 39, 47n6, 103, 108, 185, 187, 190, 195n3, 195n10, 197n15, 216
depression, 19, 46, 266, 272
desire (Kāma), 25, 26, 29, 41–42, 46, 168–75, 89–90; in *Atharvaveda*, 71–72; Brāhmaṇical thought on, 26, 27, 72; in *Kaṭha Upaniṣad*, 73; in *Manusmṛti*, 26, 72; syllables, 68
desire for emancipation. *See saṃvega*
desire-motivated actions (*sakāma karma*), 27
despair, 2, 45, 49n26, 110, 266–79; sociology of, 268–69
Devīpañcaśatikā (*Kālīkulapañcaśatikā*), 121, 126
Dharma Pātañjala, 209–14
Dharmaśāstra, 15
Dhvanyāloka, 41, 42, 253, 255–57
disgust, 2, 33, 40, 41, 44, 74, 146, 147, 152, 163, 200, 202, 204, 205, 208, 209, 211, 216
disinterested witness, 17, 48n9
dispassion, 3, 5, 22, 163, 202, 203, 205, 208, 215, 216, 217, 218
duḥkha. *See* sorrow; suffering
Dumont, Louis, 58

emotionalism of *bhakti*, 32–33
emotions: *Abhidhammic* analysis of, 188–91; affective–cognitive motifs of *rāga*, 254–57; Buddhist thought, 1, 186–88; cognitivist theories of, 6–7; of despair, 266–79; in the *kāvya-kalā* traditions, 252–54; as mere 'feelings', 7; mode of responsive reception, 241–42; models of, 1; negative, 49n26; non-cognitive features of, 8; paths of literary inquiries, 247–49; positive, 199; Rājaśekhara's views, 232–40;

rasa-theory, 269–78; *saṃvega*, 199–217; in Sanskritic and Pāli tradition, 2–3; in the *śāstra-mārga*, 258–59; social and moral context, 117–19; in the *vāṅmaya*, 249–52, 259; Western thoughts on, 2–10, 231–32, 241–42
emotive: states, 3, 251; power, 128; theme, 140; dispositions 187; functions, 188, 192; motifs, 245
ethics, 117–18
evaluative judgment, 6

fear, 14, 19, 25, 28, 46, 49n22, 104, 105, 114–15; construction of, 118; cultivation of, 202, 203, 219n9; eliciting questions, 119–20; of contamination, 30; of transmigration, 116–17, 128n1; of death, 123, 204, 205, 208, 209, 215, 216; ordinary, 116; sacralisation of, 115–17; sacred, 116; stirring places and substances, 120–25
frustration, 7, 26, 33, 145–46

Gaura-govindārcana-smaraṇa-paddhati, 173–74
Gombrich, Richard F., 38–39
Govinda-līlāmṛta, 167–68
grief, 5, 7, 8, 12, 15, 19, 42, 49n23, 49n26, 110, 276

hatred, 5, 19, 38, 39, 187, 190, 192, 195n5
heroism: 30, 33, 69; as the spiritual path, 115, 122, 123; as steadfastness (*dhairya*), 115, 126
hopelessness, 266, 268, 269, 271, 274, 277
Hume, David, 2, 4, 5, 47n1
Hybrid Cognitive Theory, 8

ideal of: Brāhmaṇa, 23, 43, 72, 118; spectator, 41, 42, 49n22
Indian Psychology, 1
Indian thought-systems, emotions in, 1–2, 10–14; Brāhmaṇical ideal of emotionlessness, 10–11; control of emotional fluctuations, 14–15; dichotomy between mind, body, and soul, 10; experience of 'pleasure' and 'pain', 15; removal of pains of agency, 15–24; Self–body dualism, 12; theoretical evaluation of, 2; witness-consciousness, 16–17
intensity of emotional experience, 102; agitation, 106–12; disharmony (*vaiṣamya*), 108; divine consciousness, 108; grief, 110; joyful emotions, 104; pleasure from eating and drinking, 105; surprise (*camatkāra*), 105, 109
intoxication, 19, 28, 103, 199, 202

Jainism, 31, 37, 40–41
joy, 12, 19, 28, 33, 49n23, 68, 77, 87, 90n4, 104, 105, 106, 107, 110, 129n3, 139, 143, 145, 149, 167, 168, 272, 273

kalā, 76–77
Kāmagītā, 69
kañcukas, 76–82
Kashmiri Śaiva traditions, 103, 106, 114–17, 124, 127
Kaṭha Upaniṣad, 3, 72, 73, 93n26
kāvya, 41–44, 49n24, 49n25, 140, 201, 231, 232–35
Kiraṇa Tantra, 68, 215
Kramasadbhāva, 119, 126
kṣobha, 29, 48n14, 106–12. *See also* agitation
Kumārasambhava, 148

longing, 26, 33, 46, 78, 88, 140, 151, 204, 205, 211, 214, 245, 246, 254–58
love, 4, 5, 7, 14, 15, 16, 31, 32, 34, 35, 41, 43, 47n7, 49n24, 61, 64, 69, 70, 89, 140–44, 146–48, 151–52, 156–58

Mahābhārata, 8, 157, 257–58; Kāma of, 71
Mahānayaprakāśa, 75
Mahārthamañjarī, 123–24
Mālinīvijaya-vārttika, 64, 74
Mālinīvijayottara Tantra, 65, 83
mañjarī-svarūpa, 156–57, 166–74
mantric potency, 127
Manusmṛti, 15, 26
Mohakāla. *See* longing
Muktika Upaniṣad, 13, 15
Muṇḍaka Upaniṣad, 246

Nāradaparivrājaka Upaniṣad, 13, 14, 15, 16, 47n4, 47n7, 49n23
naturalized spirituality, 5
Nāṭyaśāstra, 35, 41, 42, 156, 163, 177n16, 239, 247, 249, 250, 261n13
negative emotions, 2, 13, 49n26, 103, 108, 185
Niṣkarma-kāma, 61–68; in the *Bhagavadgītā*; 61–62, 66; in the *Mālinīvijaya-vārttika*, 64; in the*Yoga Śāstra*, 63

pain, 8, 19, 20, 26, 46, 60, 74, 129n3, 187, 201, 213, 257, 279; removal of, 15–17,
Pātañjala Yoga, 20–23, 27–29, 40–41, 205–12
passion, 2, 4, 5, 6, 15, 27, 38, 39, 42, 43, 44, 47n1, 60–61, 65, 69, 75–82, 91n16, 93n24, 171, 172, 175, 187, 191, 246, 251, 255, 256, 257, 259
passionate spectator, 42
paṭccasamuppāda (dependent origination), 38, 39, 186, 192, 193
Plato, 3, 231, 241
Platonic love, 4
pleasure, 3, 8, 15, 16, 19, 26, 39, 43, 44, 46, 60, 63, 65, 70, 74, 78, 79, 82, 88, 95, 105, 109, 110, 124, 152, 162, 168, 172, 190, 191, 204, 205, 208, 209, 211, 257, 267, 279
post-Freudian psychoanalytical thinking, 10
prakṛti, 11, 16, 17, 18–20, 22, 48n14, 59, 79

rāga, 26, 48n21, 65–66, 78–82, 187, 191, 195n4, 195, 195n5, 251, 255, 259. *See also* desire (Kāma); passion
Rāmakaṇṭha, 76, 216, 223n47, 223n48
Rāmāyaṇa, 157, 249, 257–58, 277
Repulsion or repugnance (*dveṣa*), 19, 26, 38, 39, 186, 187, 190, 191

Sahajiyā Vaiṣṇava tradition, 35–36, 159, 169–72
Śaiva Siddhānta tradition, 40–41, 77, 200, 214–17
Sāṃkhyakārikā, 11, 17, 18, 19, 20, 59
Sāṃkhya-Yoga doctrines, 17–18, 20, 22–23; body-emotions-mind complex, 22–23
Saṃnyāsa Upaniṣads, 12–13
samprajñāta-samādhi, 28
saṃskāras, 14, 20, 48n12, 120–25, 262n17
saṃvega, 40, 199–217; in Buddhist sources, 201–04; in early Śaiva Saiddhāntika scriptures, 214–17; etymology of, 200–01; in Jaina sources, 204–05; in old Javanese Śaiva texts, 212–14; in *Pātañjala Yoga*, 205–12
Sanatkumāra Saṃhitā, 167
Sanderson, Alexis, 30, 102
Sanskrit *vāṅmaya*, 241
Sarvasāra Upaniṣad, 15
Self, concept of (*ātman*), 10–12; nonduality of, 122–23; for Śaṅkara, 17
sensation, 8, 9, 18, 21, 37, 47n1, 85, 87, 88, 120, 186, 187, 189, 190, 191, 195n5, 195n10, 196n11
senses, 3, 14, 24, 25, 27, 28, 31, 32, 33, 36, 37, 46, 50, 58, 59, 69, 71, 72, 73,

74, 75, 77, 82–89, 92–98, 103–05, 112, 118, 119, 120, 140, 153, 159, 196, 205, 229, 252, 254, 255
shame, 15, 125, 272, 273, 274
shock, 105, 200, 201, 218n2, 218n8
Sinha, Jadunath, 1; Indian psychology of, 45–47
Śiva Sūtra, 83, 86, 125
Śiva, mythology of, 69–70
Śivamahimnastava, 144
Śivopādhyāya, 103, 104, 105, 107
slave, in bhakti, 34–35, 149–51
Solomon, Robert C., 2, 4, 5, 6, 7, 9
sorrow, 12, 19, 33, 49n23, 49n26, 60, 63, 104, 105, 129n3, 145, 163, 205, 245, 247, 249, 255, 261n13, 268, 270, 271, 272, 273, 276, 278
spanda, 29, 107, 110, 117, 129n3
Spandakārikā, 28, 87, 106, 107, 112, 117
Spinoza, Baruch, 4
Śrāmaṇic concept of emotions, 4, 36
Śrī Caitanya Mahāprabhu, 35, 157
Śṛṅgāra-rasa (erotic love), 156–57, 166–74
suffering (*duḥkha*), 8, 18, 19, 20, 22, 34, 37, 38, 39, 46, 48, 49, 59, 60, 129, 187, 188, 189, 190, 202, 204, 209, 214, 223, 228, 278, 279
Sūta Saṃhitā, 151
Svabodhodayamañjarī, 87–89
Śvetāśvatara Upaniṣad, 138

Tamil Śiva-bhakti poems, 32–34
Tantrāloka, 25, 30, 65, 67, 77, 79, 90n3, 91n7, 94n29, 116
tantric Hero, 126–28
Tantrism, 24–30, 64; *camatkāra*, 29; *citta* in, 29; desire (Kāma), 68–75, 89–90; divinisation of the body, 160–61; features of, 115; *kṣobha*, 29; *Niṣkāma-karma* and *Niṣkarma-kāma*, 61–68; passion (*rāga*), 75–89; Pātañjala Yoga, tantric critique of, 29; psychological dimension of, 114; significance of *kāma*, 25–26; tantric revelation, 24–25; tantric *yoga*, 28; as transgressive movement, 29–30
Taraṇiramaṇa, 170–71
Tēvāram hymns, 33, 140, 143–44
thirst (*tṛṣṇā*), 15, 21, 26, 38, 44, 47n6, 48n21, 187, 199, 255, 257
Tirumurai, 33

universal hero myth, 120–25
Upaniṣads, 3, 11, 12, 13, 14, 15, 21, 23, 47n3, 47n5, 68, 72, 86

Vaiṣṇavism: Bengali, 35, 36, 157, 159, 165–66
Veṅkaṭeśa, Śrīdhara, 152,
Vijñānabhairava Tantra, 28, 87, 103, 104, 105, 106
virility (*vīrya*), 109, 126, 127
virtue ethics, 38, 39
Viśuddhimaggo, 192–94
Vyāsabhaṣya, 18, 20, 28

Western thoughts on emotions, 2–10; asceticism, 3–4; bondage, 3; cognitive theory *vs* conative-affective theory, 6–10; distinction between 'reason' and 'emotions', 3; during Enlightenment period, 4; higher passions, 4; Kant's original view, 4; philosophical thinking on emotions, 5; Solomon's account of 'naturalized spirituality', 5; Stoics' view, 4
wretchedness of man, 60–61

Yoga Śāstra, 63, 205, 206, 207, 208, 209, 210, 211, 212, 214, 217, 218, 218n5, 218n17, 220n21, 220n28, 222n38
Yogaś-citta-vṛtti-nirodhaḥ, 22, 28